# Fruits Basket

## Volume 5

### By
### Natsuki Takaya

**WITHDRAWN**

HAMBURG // LONDON // LOS ANGELES // TOKYO

# Fruits Basket

## Table of Contents

# STORY SO FAR...

**Hello, I'm Tohru Honda and I have come to know a terrible secret. After the death of my mother, I was living by myself in a tent when the Sohma family took me in. I soon learned that the Sohma family lives with a curse! Each family member is possessed by the vengeful spirit of an animal from the Chinese Zodiac. Whenever one of them becomes weak or is hugged by a member of the opposite sex, they change into their Zodiac animal!**

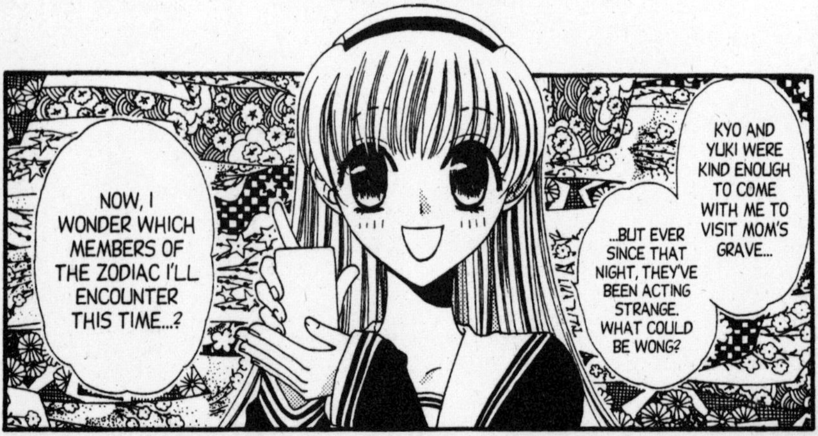

KYO AND YUKI WERE KIND ENOUGH TO COME WITH ME TO VISIT MOM'S GRAVE...
...BUT EVER SINCE THAT NIGHT, THEY'VE BEEN ACTING STRANGE. WHAT COULD BE WONG?
NOW, I WONDER WHICH MEMBERS OF THE ZODIAC I'LL ENCOUNTER THIS TIME...?

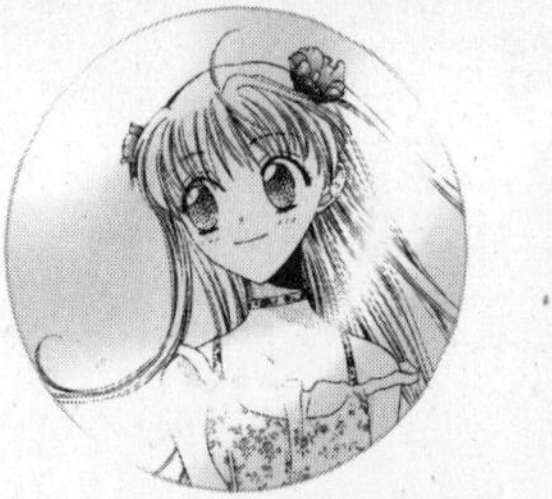

## Tohru Honda

The ever-optimistic hero of our story. An orphan, she now lives in Shigure's house, along with Yuki and Kyo, and is the only person outside of the family who knows the Sohma family's curse.

## Yuki Sohma, the Rat

Soft-spoken. Self-esteem issues. At school he's called "Prince Yuki."

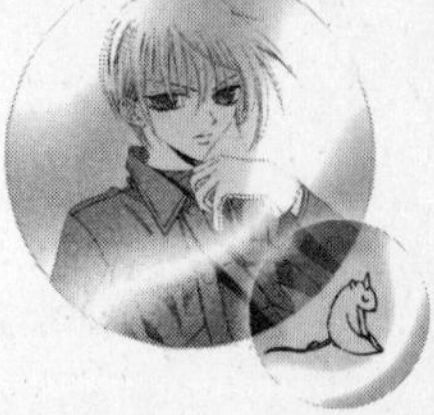

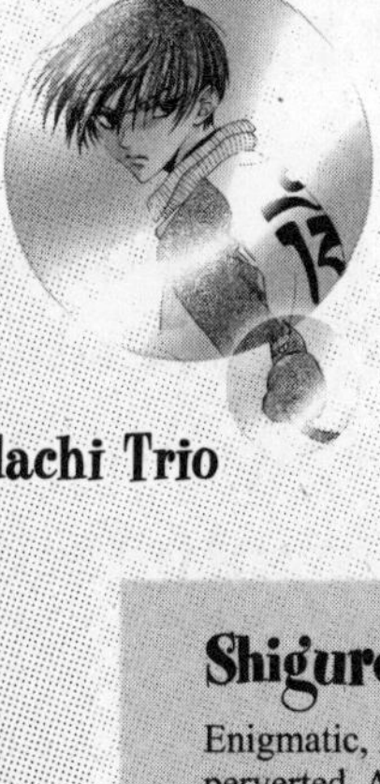

## Kyo Sohma, the Cat

The Cat who was left out of the Zodiac. Hates Yuki, leeks and Miso. But mostly Yuki.

Mabudachi Trio

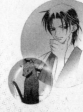

## Shigure Sohma, the Dog

Enigmatic, mischievous and a little perverted. A popular novelist.

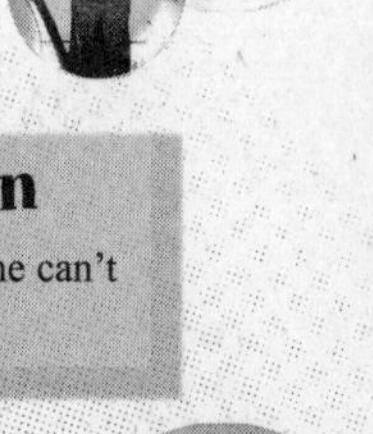

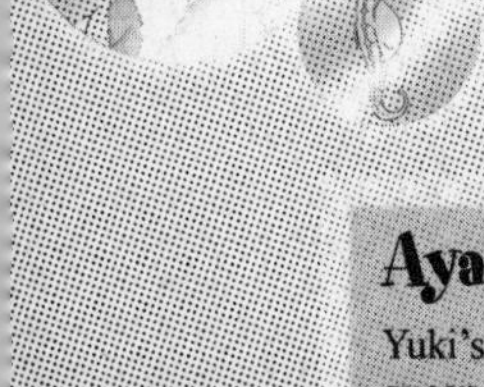

## Hatori Sohma, the Dragon

Family doctor to the Sohmas. Only thing he can't cure is his broken heart.

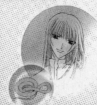

## Ayame Sohma, the Snake

Yuki's older brother. A proud and playful drama queen…er, king. Runs a costume shop.

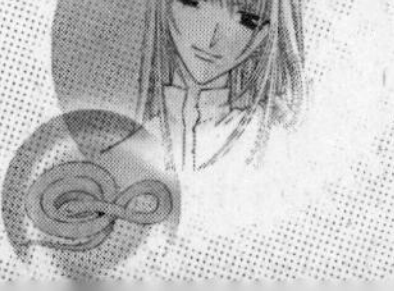

# Fruits Basket Characters

## Kagura Sohma, the Boar

Bashful, yet headstrong. Determined to marry Kyo, even if it kills him.

## Momiji Sohma, the Rabbit

Half-German. He's older than he looks. Mother rejected him because of the Sohma curse.

## Hatsuharu Sohma, the Ox

The nicest of guys, except when he goes "Black." Then you'd better watch out.

## Akito Sohma

The head of the Sohma clan. A dark man of many secrets. Treated with fear and reverence.

## Saki Hanajima

"Hana-chan." Can sense people's "waves." Goth demeanor scares her classmates.

## Arisa Uotani

"Uo-chan." A tough-talking "Yankee" who looks out for her friends.

**Tohru's Best Friends**

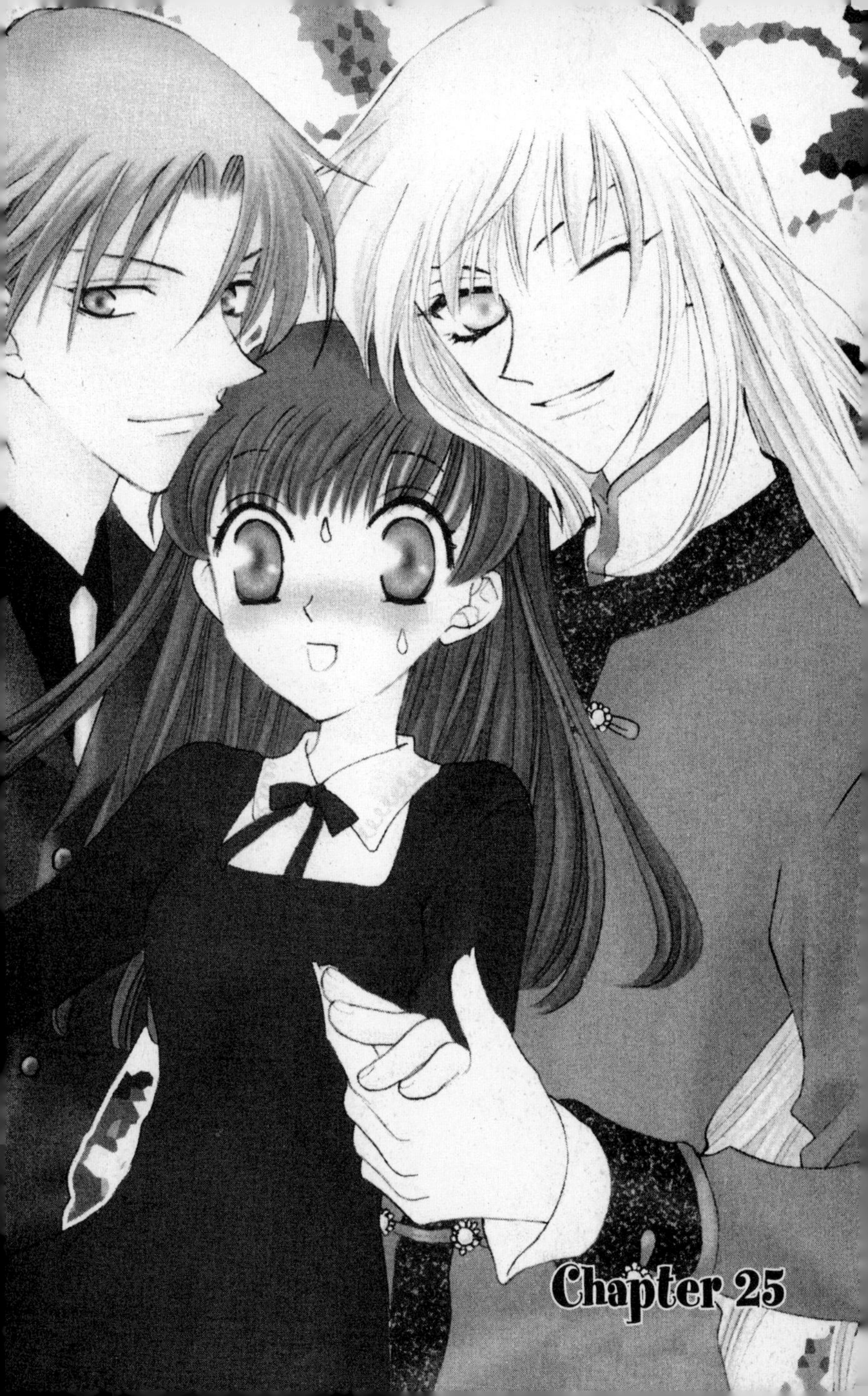
Chapter 25

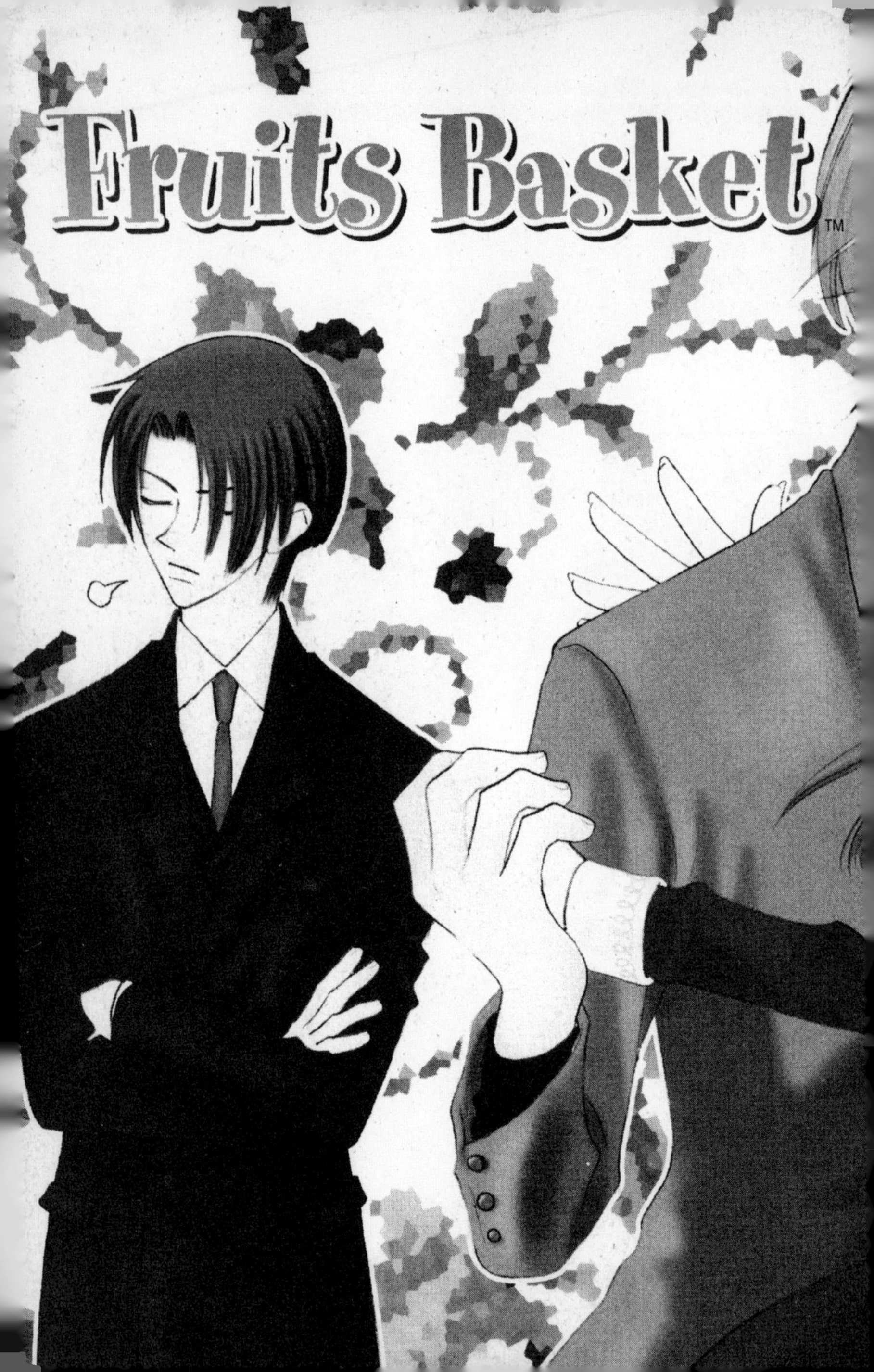
Fruits Basket™

Sometimes, when I can't take the tension, I push the pause button.

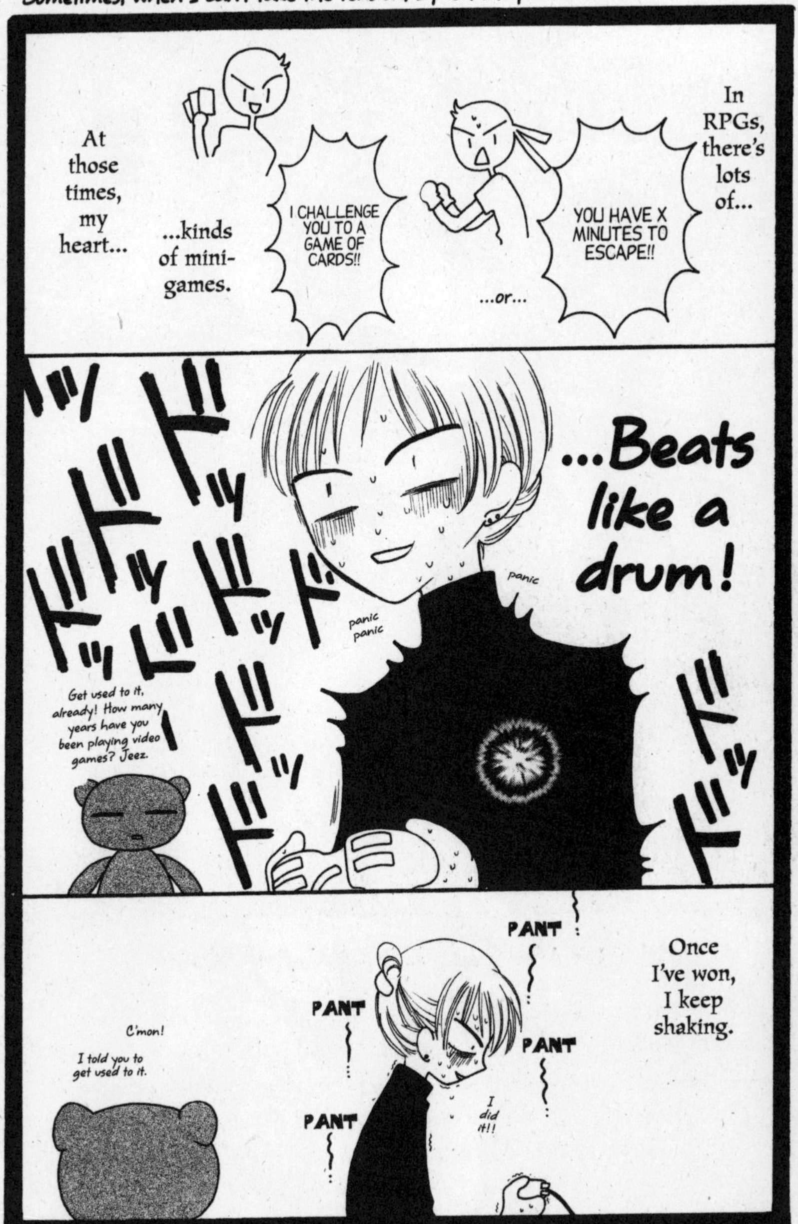

In RPGs, there's lots of...
YOU HAVE X MINUTES TO ESCAPE!!
...or...
I CHALLENGE YOU TO A GAME OF CARDS!!
...kinds of mini-games.
At those times, my heart...
...Beats like a drum!
panic
panic panic
Get used to it, already! How many years have you been playing video games? Jeez.
Once I've won, I keep shaking.
PANT
PANT
PANT
PANT
I did it!!
C'mon!
I told you to get used to it.

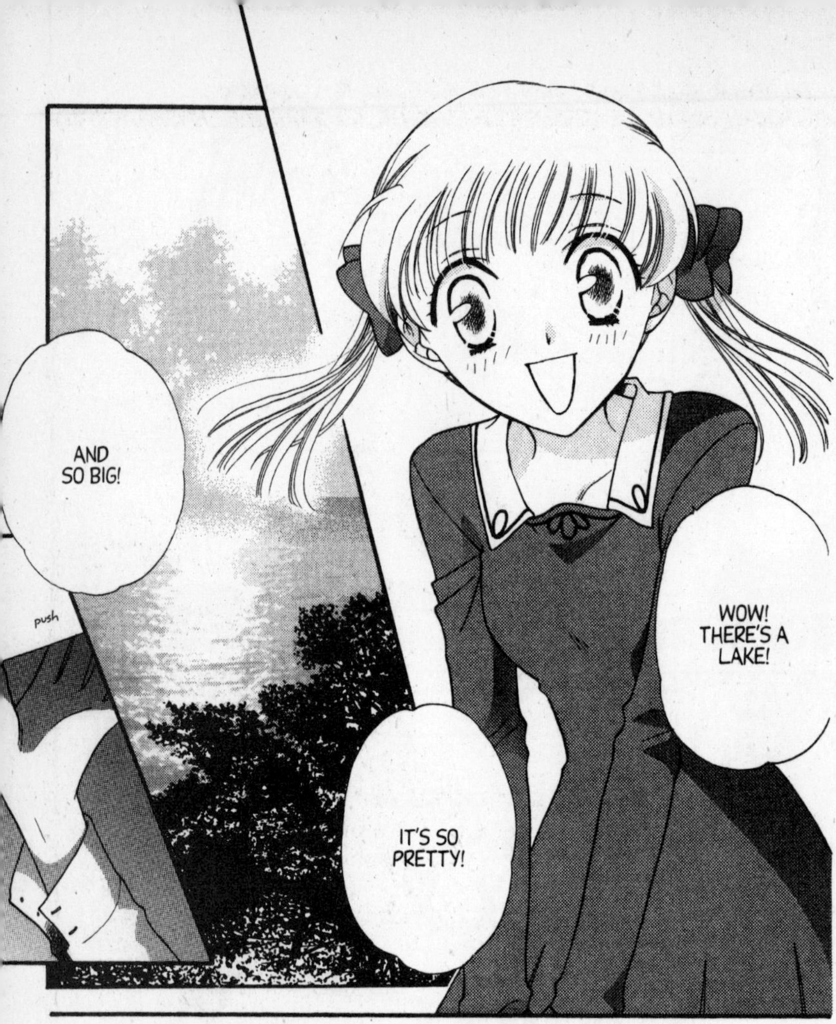
WOW! THERE'S A LAKE!
IT'S SO PRETTY!
AND SO BIG!
push

## ULTRA SPECIAL BLAH BLAH BLAH 1

You know how whenever Kyo and Yuki meet, they say "I really hate this guy"? Basically, what they mean is "I hate him more and more every day." It's hard to convey the nuance... (I get a lot of questions about it.) But I think the rhythm works better that way, so I didn't change it.

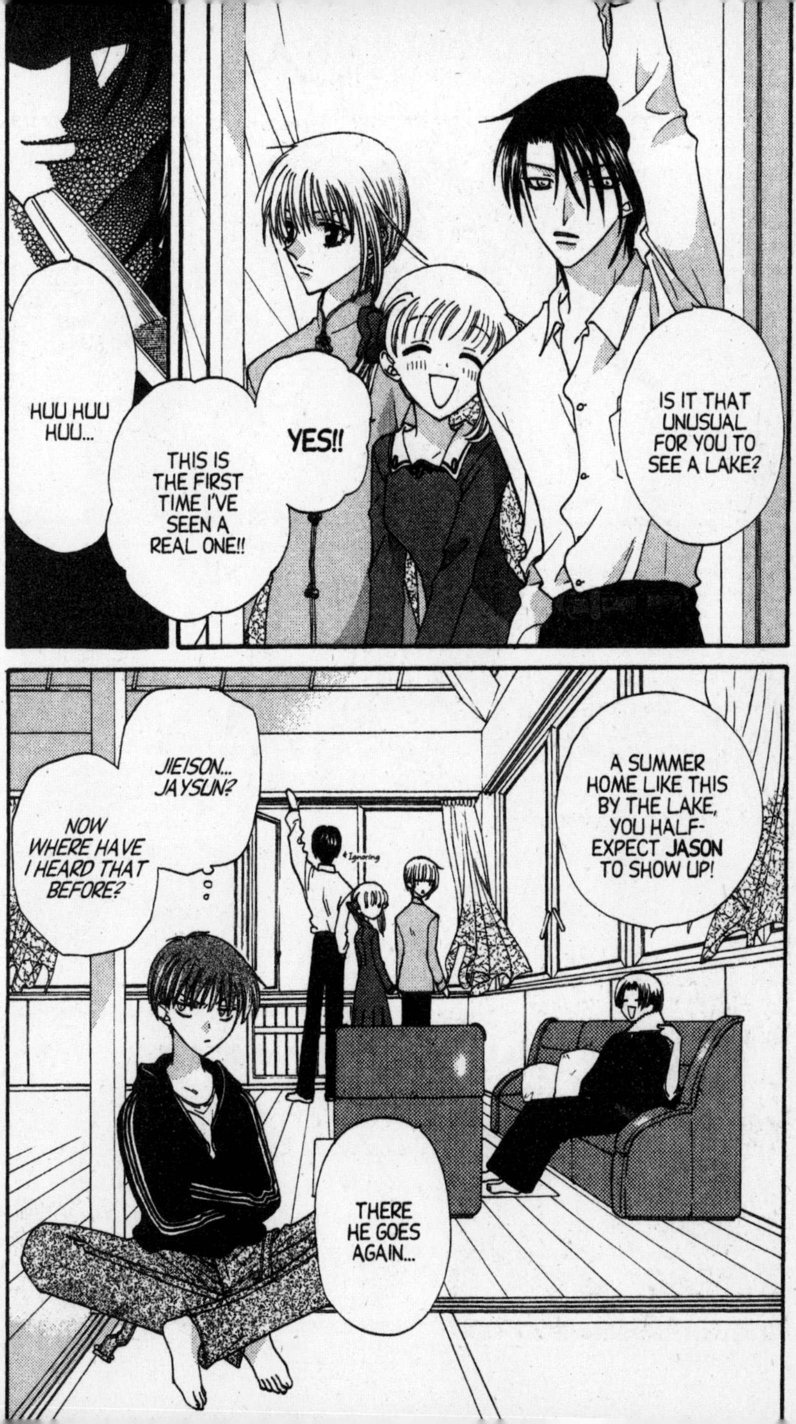
IS IT THAT UNUSUAL FOR YOU TO SEE A LAKE?
YES!!
THIS IS THE FIRST TIME I'VE SEEN A REAL ONE!!
HUU HUU HUU...
A SUMMER HOME LIKE THIS BY THE LAKE, YOU HALF-EXPECT JASON TO SHOW UP!
*Ignoring
JIEISON... JAYSUN?
NOW WHERE HAVE I HEARD THAT BEFORE?
THERE HE GOES AGAIN...

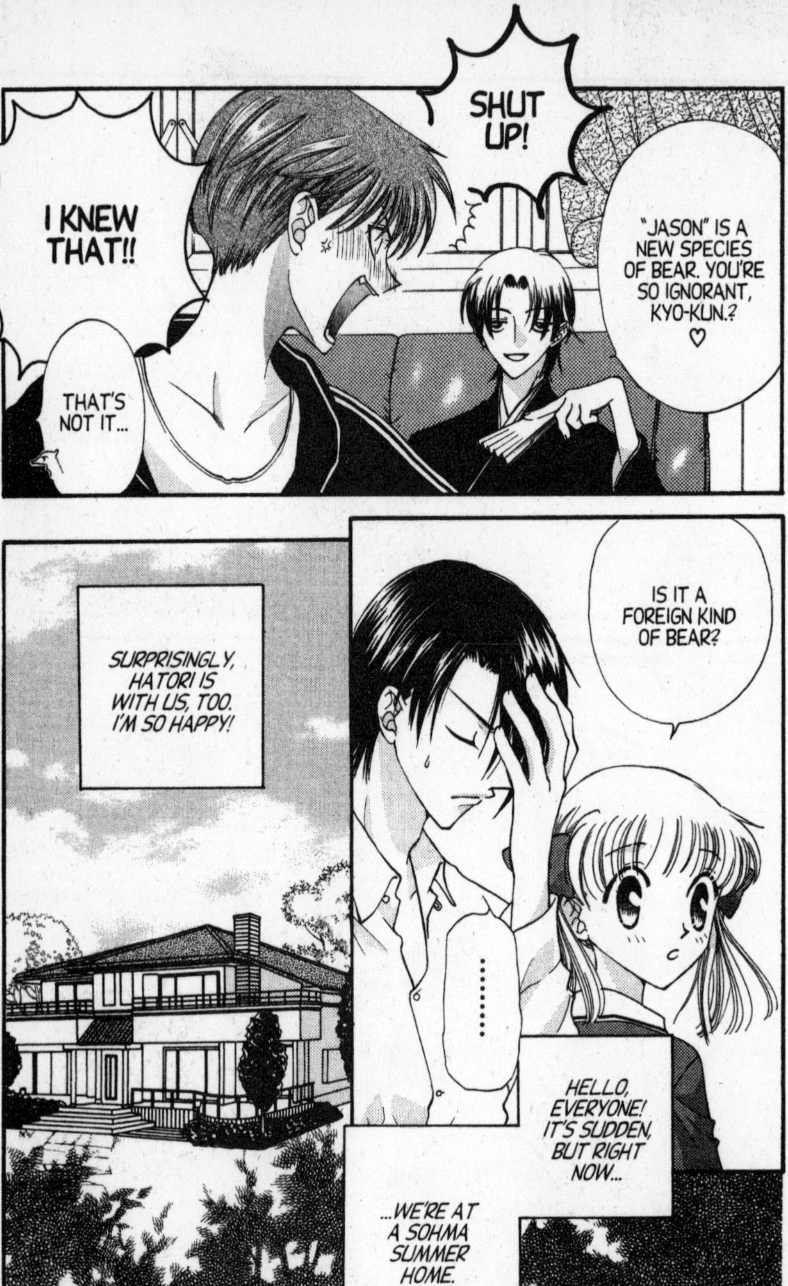
"JASON" IS A NEW SPECIES OF BEAR. YOU'RE SO IGNORANT, KYO-KUN.? ♡
SHUT UP!
I KNEW THAT!!
THAT'S NOT IT...
IS IT A FOREIGN KIND OF BEAR?
........
HELLO, EVERYONE! IT'S SUDDEN, BUT RIGHT NOW...
...WE'RE AT A SOHMA SUMMER HOME.
SURPRISINGLY, HATORI IS WITH US, TOO. I'M SO HAPPY!

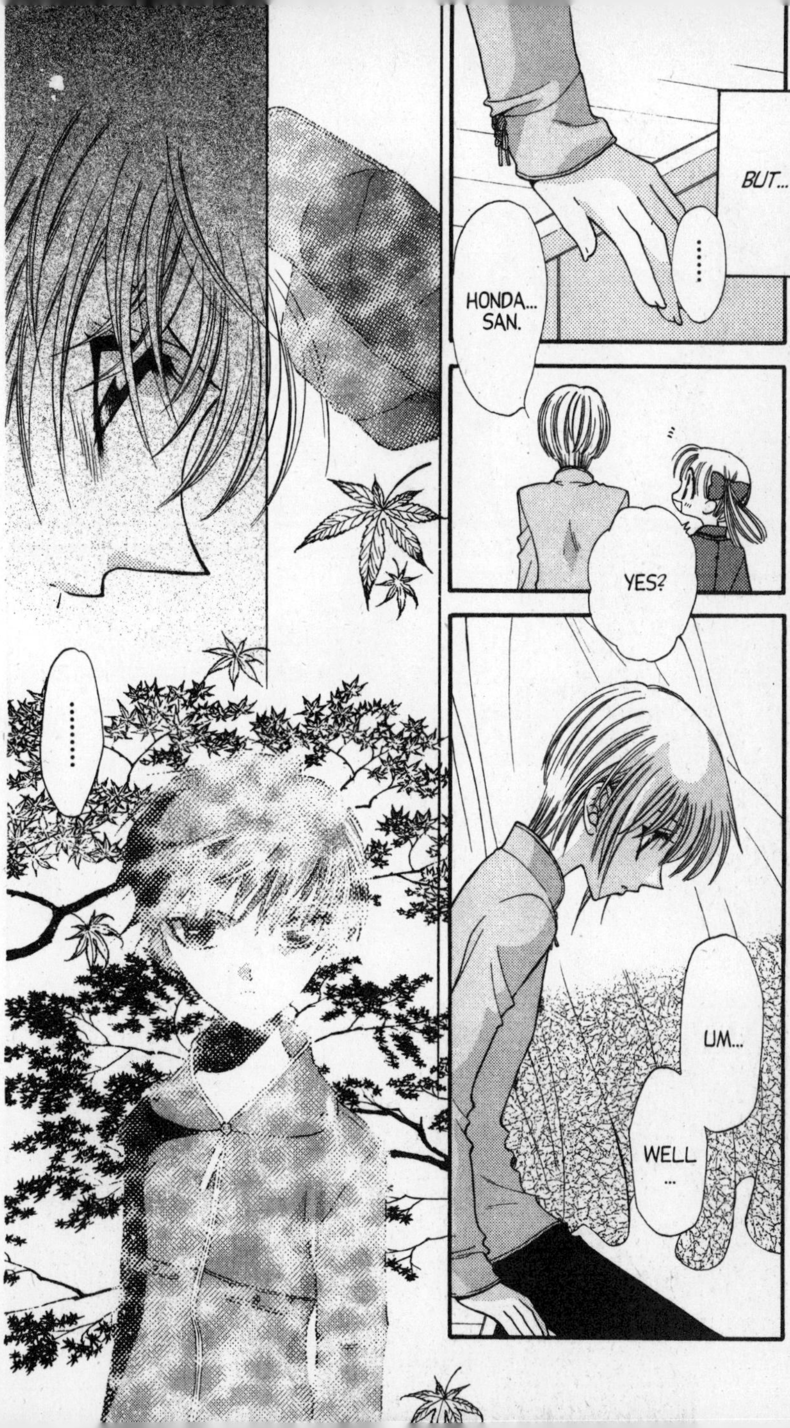
BUT...
......
HONDA... SAN.
YES?
UM...
WELL ...
......

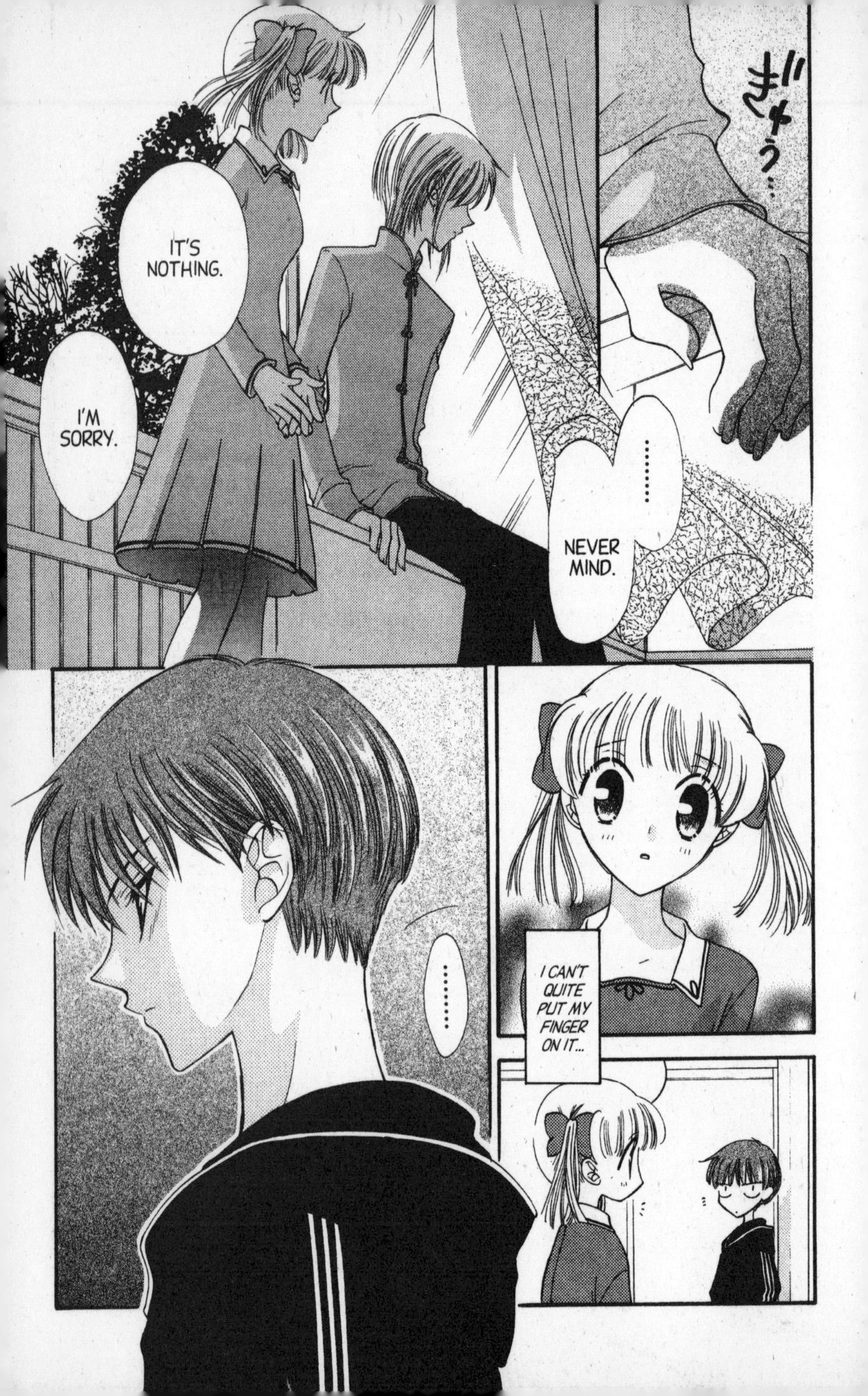
ぎゅう…
……
NEVER MIND.
IT'S NOTHING.
I'M SORRY.
I CAN'T QUITE PUT MY FINGER ON IT...
……

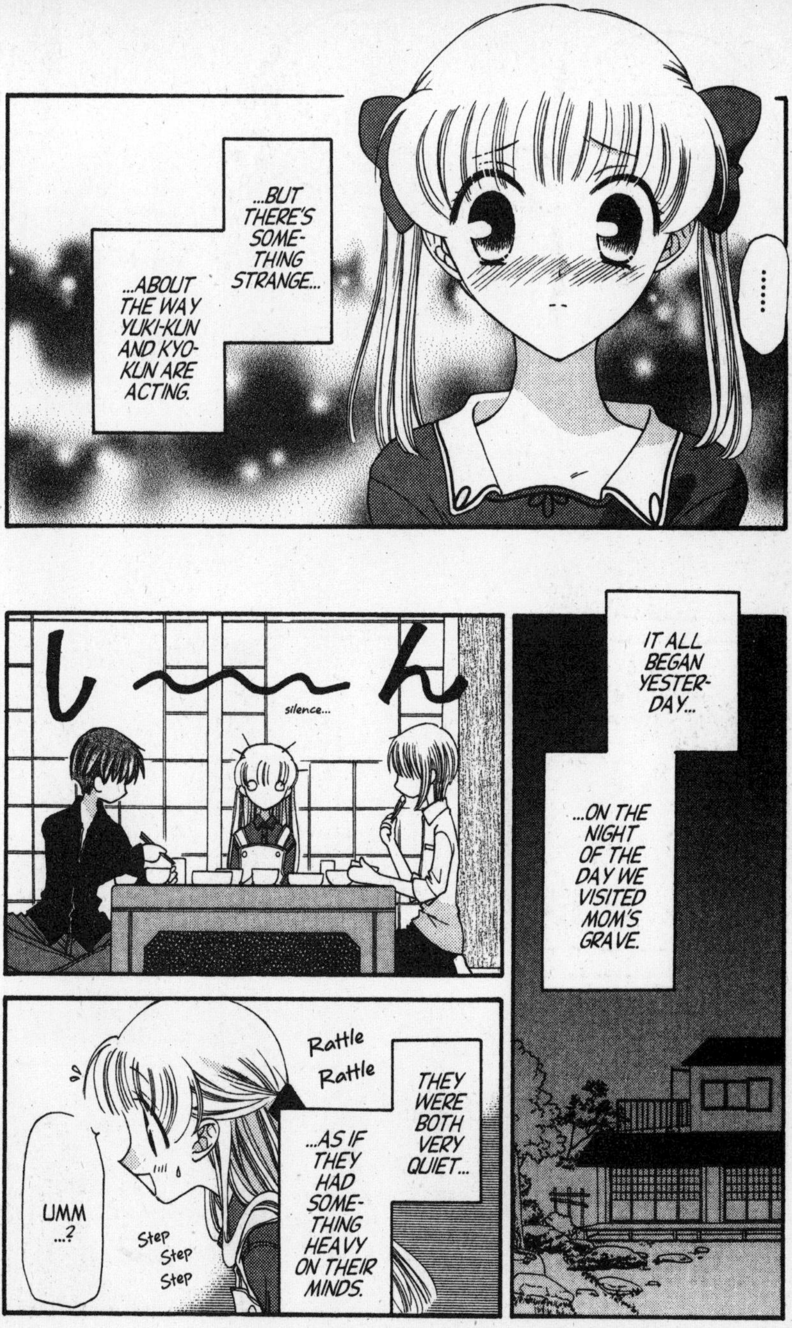
......
...BUT THERE'S SOME-THING STRANGE...
...ABOUT THE WAY YUKI-KUN AND KYO-KUN ARE ACTING.
IT ALL BEGAN YESTER-DAY...
...ON THE NIGHT OF THE DAY WE VISITED MOM'S GRAVE.
し〜〜ん
silence...
THEY WERE BOTH VERY QUIET...
...AS IF THEY HAD SOME-THING HEAVY ON THEIR MINDS.
Rattle
Rattle
UMM ...?
Step
Step
Step

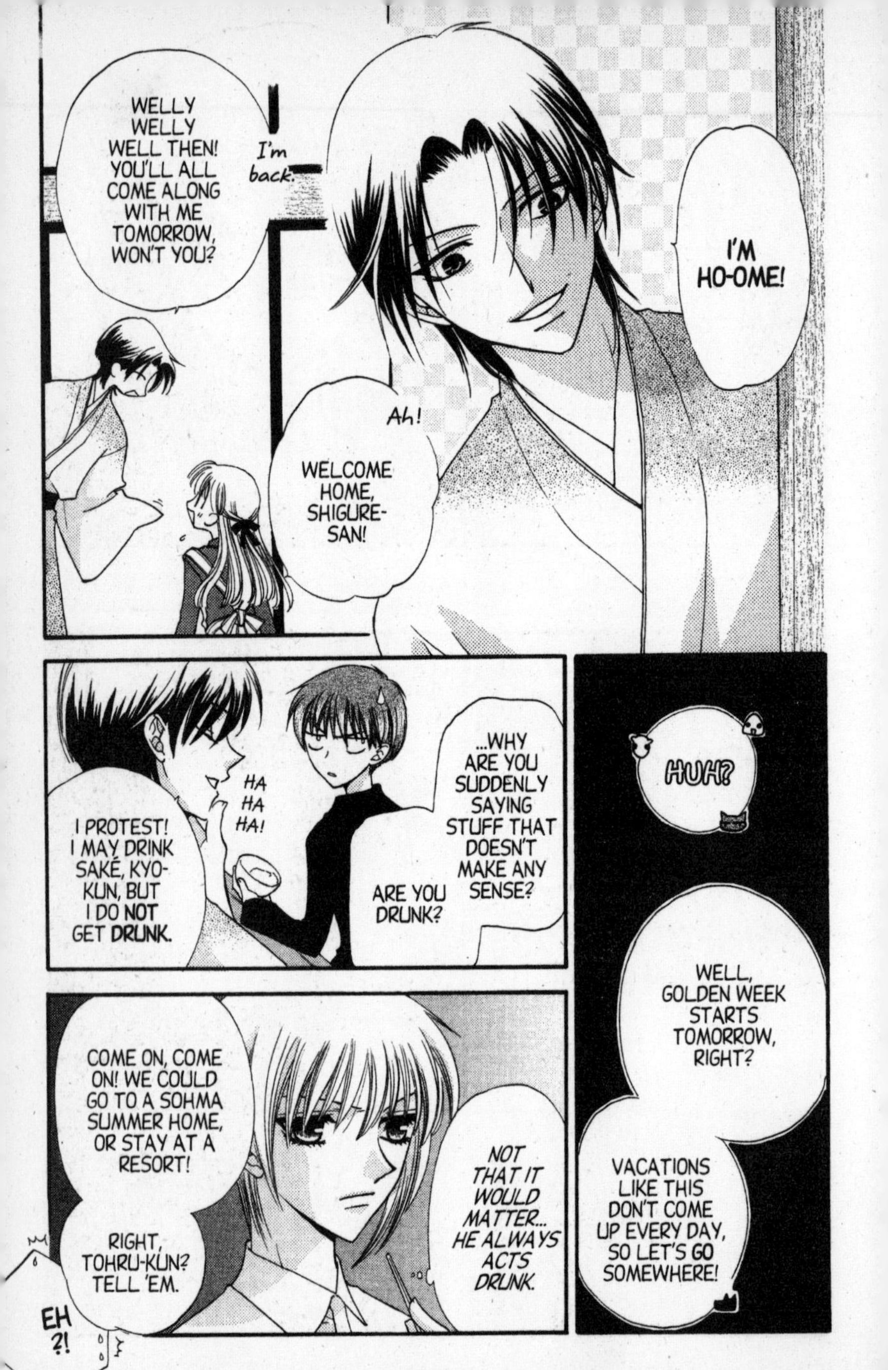
I'M HO-OME!
Ah!
WELCOME HOME, SHIGURE-SAN!
I'm back.
WELLY WELLY WELL THEN! YOU'LL ALL COME ALONG WITH ME TOMORROW, WON'T YOU?
HUH?
WELL, GOLDEN WEEK STARTS TOMORROW, RIGHT?
VACATIONS LIKE THIS DON'T COME UP EVERY DAY, SO LET'S GO SOMEWHERE!
...WHY ARE YOU SUDDENLY SAYING STUFF THAT DOESN'T MAKE ANY SENSE?
ARE YOU DRUNK?
HA HA HA!
I PROTEST! I MAY DRINK SAKÉ, KYO-KUN, BUT I DO NOT GET DRUNK.
NOT THAT IT WOULD MATTER... HE ALWAYS ACTS DRUNK.
COME ON, COME ON! WE COULD GO TO A SOHMA SUMMER HOME, OR STAY AT A RESORT!
RIGHT, TOHRU-KUN? TELL 'EM.
EH ?!

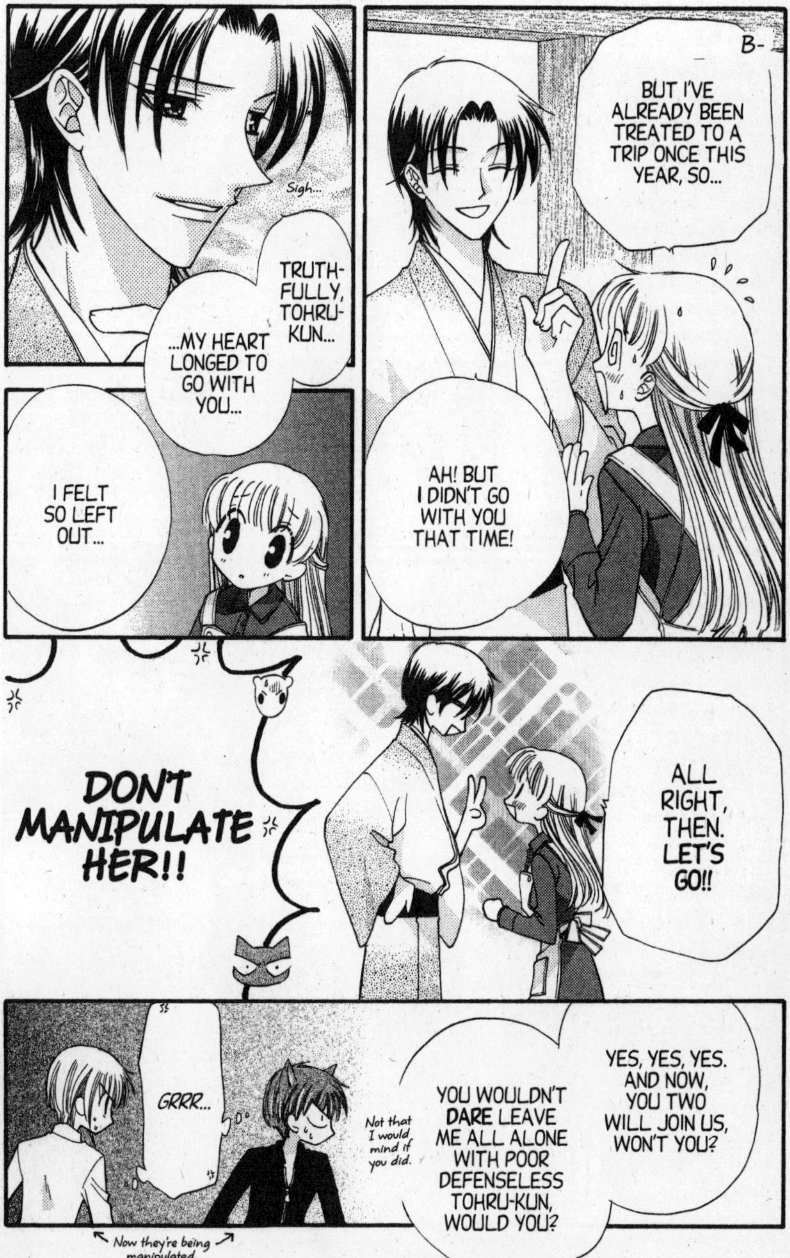
B-
BUT I'VE ALREADY BEEN TREATED TO A TRIP ONCE THIS YEAR, SO...
AH! BUT I DIDN'T GO WITH YOU THAT TIME!
Sigh...
TRUTH-FULLY, TOHRU-KUN...
...MY HEART LONGED TO GO WITH YOU...
I FELT SO LEFT OUT...
ALL RIGHT, THEN. LET'S GO!!
DON'T MANIPULATE HER!!
YES, YES, YES. AND NOW, YOU TWO WILL JOIN US, WON'T YOU?
YOU WOULDN'T DARE LEAVE ME ALL ALONE WITH POOR DEFENSELESS TOHRU-KUN, WOULD YOU?
Not that I would mind if you did.
GRRR...
Now they're being manipulated.

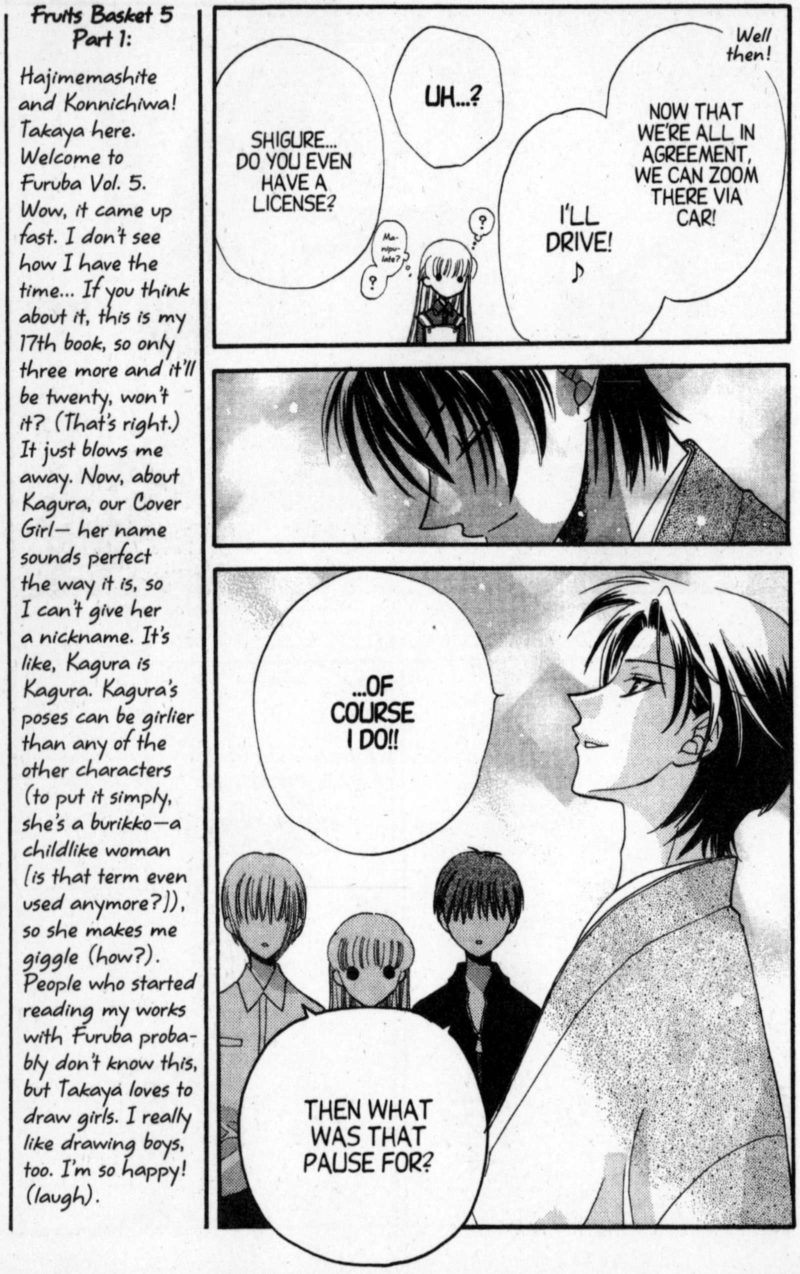
Well then!
NOW THAT WE'RE ALL IN AGREEMENT, WE CAN ZOOM THERE VIA CAR!
I'LL DRIVE! ♪
UH...?
?
SHIGURE... DO YOU EVEN HAVE A LICENSE?
Ma-nipu-late?
?
...OF COURSE I DO!!
THEN WHAT WAS THAT PAUSE FOR?

**Fruits Basket 5 Part 1:**

Hajimemashite and Konnichiwa! Takaya here. Welcome to Furuba Vol. 5. Wow, it came up fast. I don't see how I have the time... If you think about it, this is my 17th book, so only three more and it'll be twenty, won't it? (That's right.) It just blows me away. Now, about Kagura, our Cover Girl— her name sounds perfect the way it is, so I can't give her a nickname. It's like, Kagura is Kagura. Kagura's poses can be girlier than any of the other characters (to put it simply, she's a burikko—a childlike woman [is that term even used anymore?]), so she makes me giggle (how?). People who started reading my works with Furuba probably don't know this, but Takaya loves to draw girls. I really like drawing boys, too. I'm so happy! (laugh).

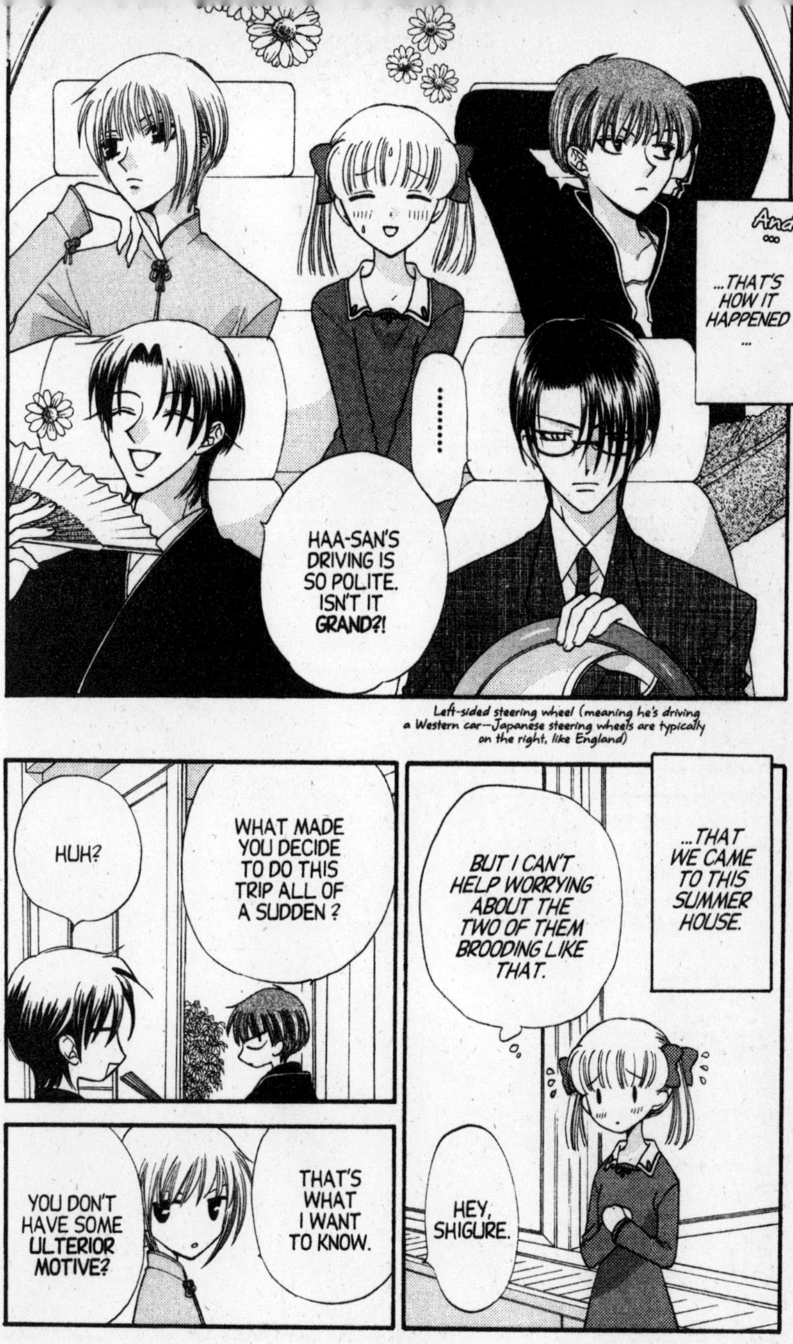
And ...
...THAT'S HOW IT HAPPENED ...
.........
HAA-SAN'S DRIVING IS SO POLITE. ISN'T IT GRAND?!
Left-sided steering wheel (meaning he's driving a Western car—Japanese steering wheels are typically on the right, like England)
...THAT WE CAME TO THIS SUMMER HOUSE.
BUT I CAN'T HELP WORRYING ABOUT THE TWO OF THEM BROODING LIKE THAT.
HEY, SHIGURE.
WHAT MADE YOU DECIDE TO DO THIS TRIP ALL OF A SUDDEN?
HUH?
THAT'S WHAT I WANT TO KNOW.
YOU DON'T HAVE SOME ULTERIOR MOTIVE?

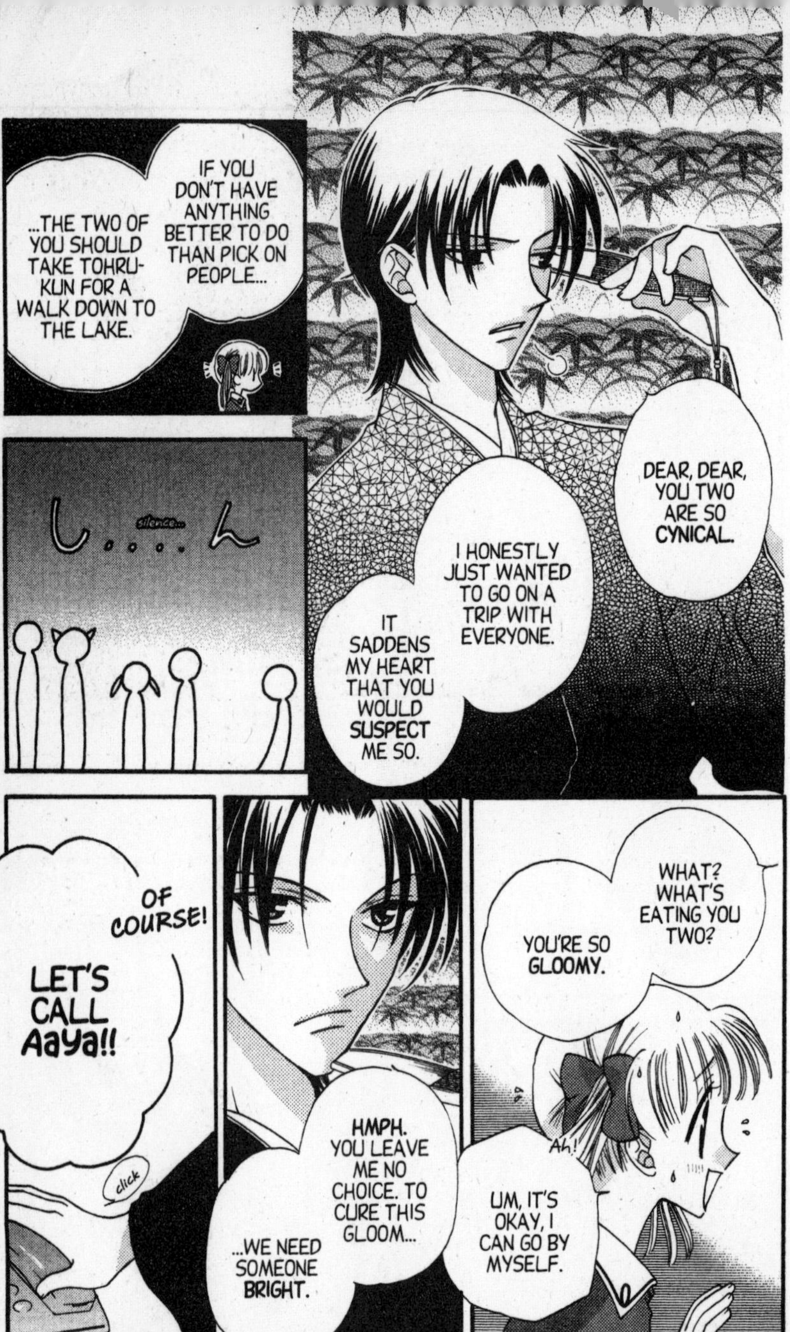
DEAR, DEAR, YOU TWO ARE SO CYNICAL.
I HONESTLY JUST WANTED TO GO ON A TRIP WITH EVERYONE.
IT SADDENS MY HEART THAT YOU WOULD SUSPECT ME SO.
IF YOU DON'T HAVE ANYTHING BETTER TO DO THAN PICK ON PEOPLE...
...THE TWO OF YOU SHOULD TAKE TOHRU-KUN FOR A WALK DOWN TO THE LAKE.
silence...
WHAT? WHAT'S EATING YOU TWO?
YOU'RE SO GLOOMY.
Ah!
UM, IT'S OKAY, I CAN GO BY MYSELF.
HMPH. YOU LEAVE ME NO CHOICE. TO CURE THIS GLOOM...
...WE NEED SOMEONE BRIGHT.
OF COURSE!
LET'S CALL Aaya!!
click

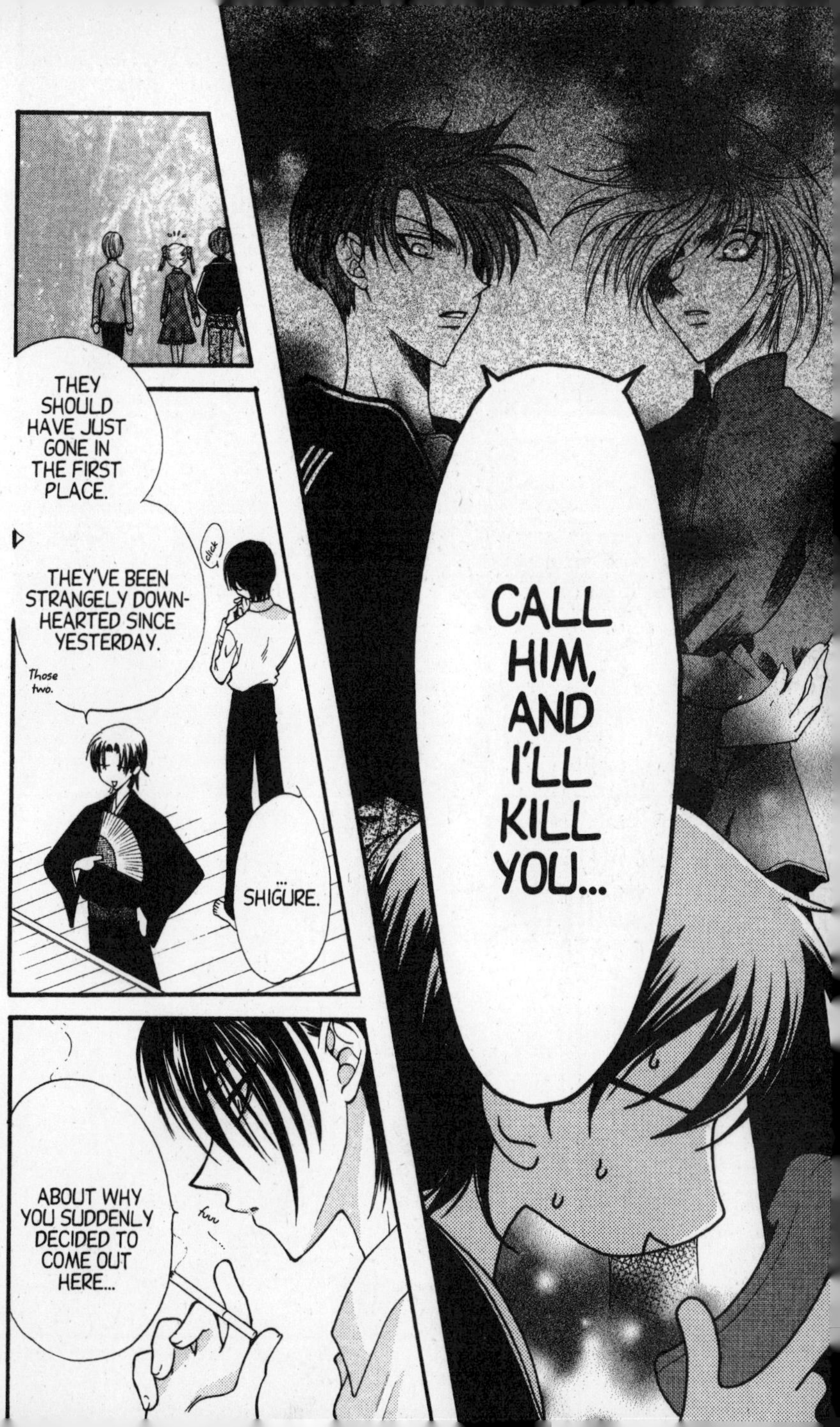
CALL HIM, AND I'LL KILL YOU...
THEY SHOULD HAVE JUST GONE IN THE FIRST PLACE.
click
THEY'VE BEEN STRANGELY DOWN-HEARTED SINCE YESTERDAY.
Those two.
...SHIGURE.
ABOUT WHY YOU SUDDENLY DECIDED TO COME OUT HERE...
fuuu
...

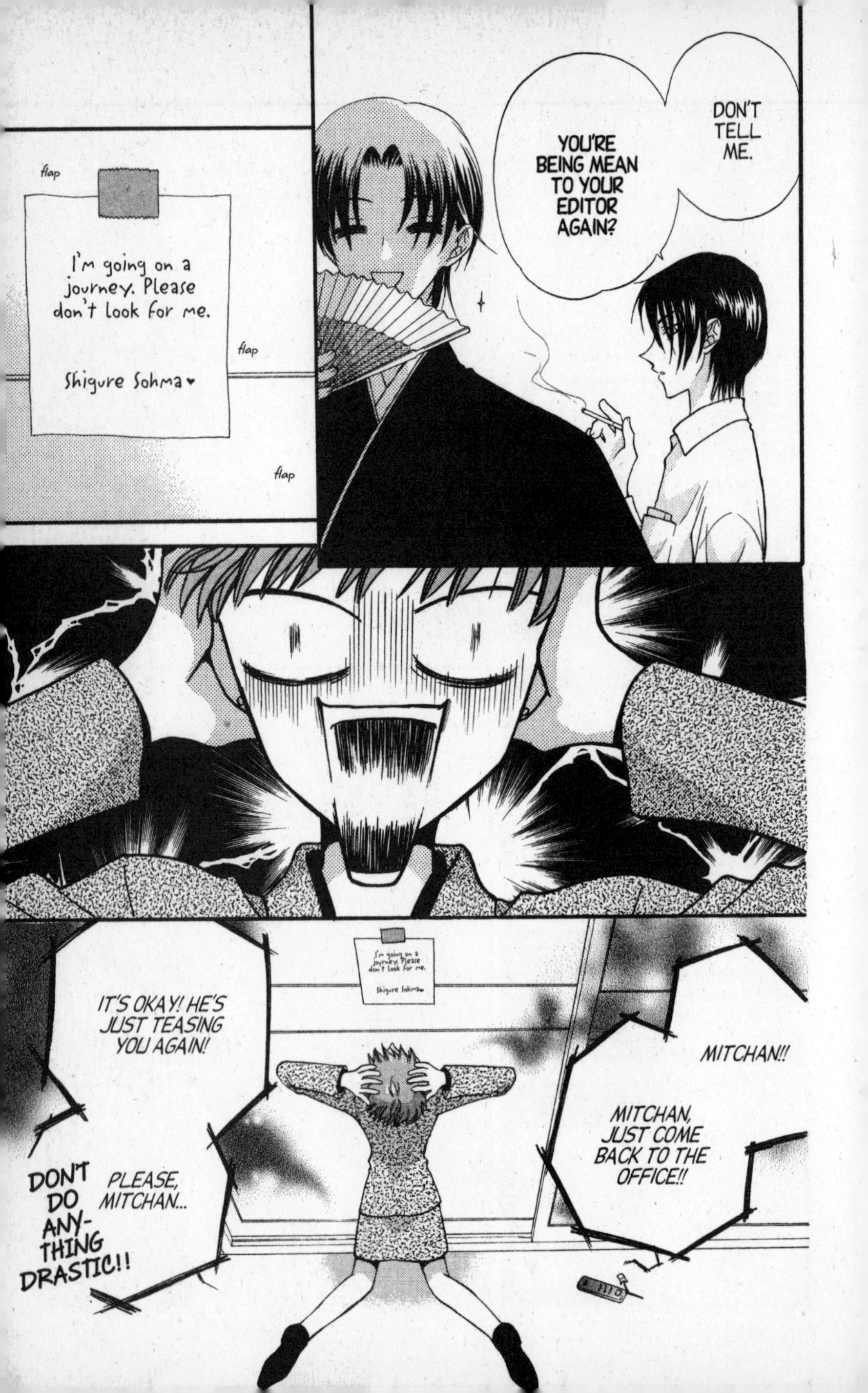
DON'T TELL ME.
YOU'RE BEING MEAN TO YOUR EDITOR AGAIN?
flap
I'm going on a journey. Please don't look for me.
Shigure Sohma♥
flap
flap
MITCHAN!!
MITCHAN, JUST COME BACK TO THE OFFICE!!
I'm going on a journey. Please don't look for me.
Shigure Sohma
IT'S OKAY! HE'S JUST TEASING YOU AGAIN!
PLEASE, MITCHAN...
DON'T DO ANYTHING DRASTIC!!

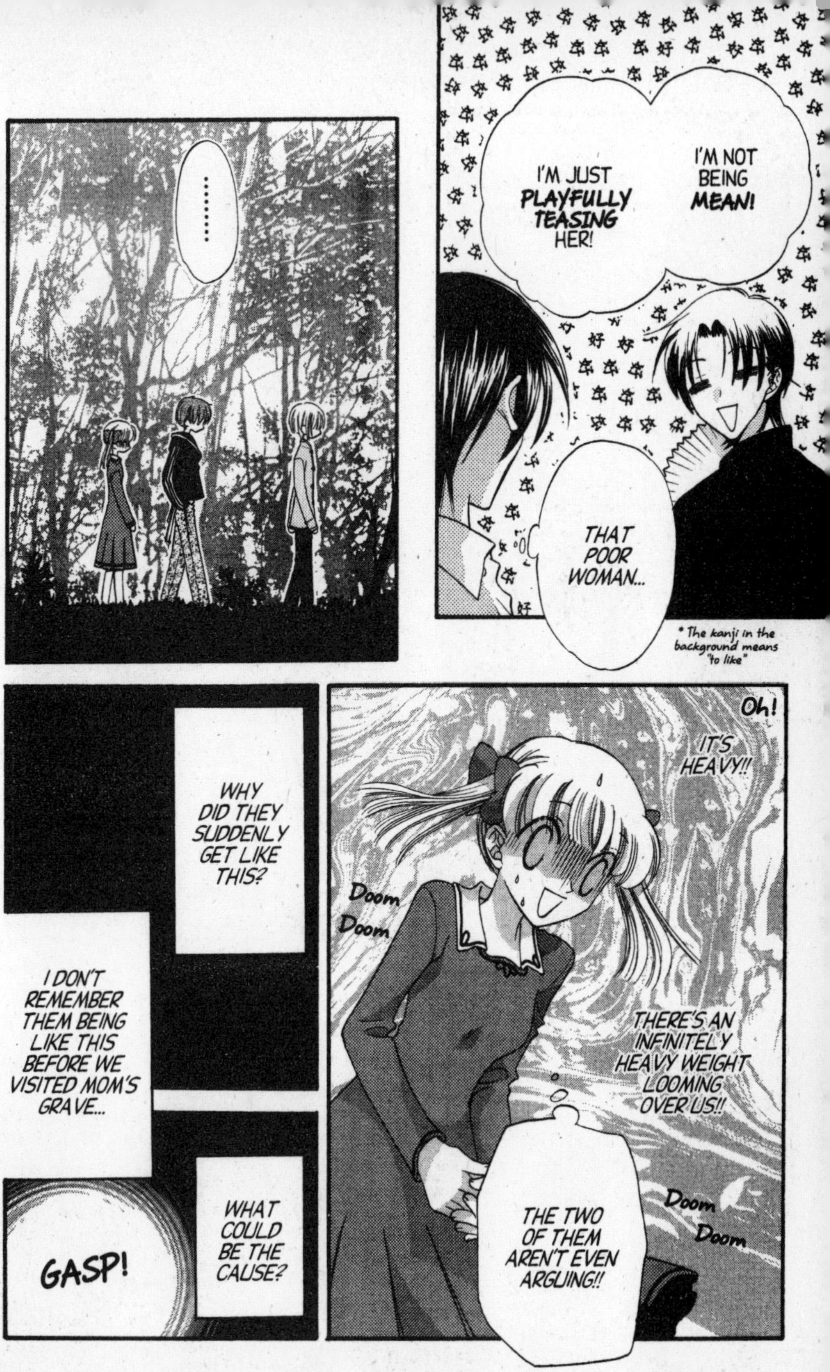
I'M NOT BEING MEAN!
I'M JUST PLAYFULLY TEASING HER!
THAT POOR WOMAN...
* The kanji in the background means "to like"
......
Oh!
IT'S HEAVY!!
THERE'S AN INFINITELY HEAVY WEIGHT LOOMING OVER US!!
Doom Doom
THE TWO OF THEM AREN'T EVEN ARGUING!!
Doom Doom
WHY DID THEY SUDDENLY GET LIKE THIS?
I DON'T REMEMBER THEM BEING LIKE THIS BEFORE WE VISITED MOM'S GRAVE...
WHAT COULD BE THE CAUSE?
GASP!

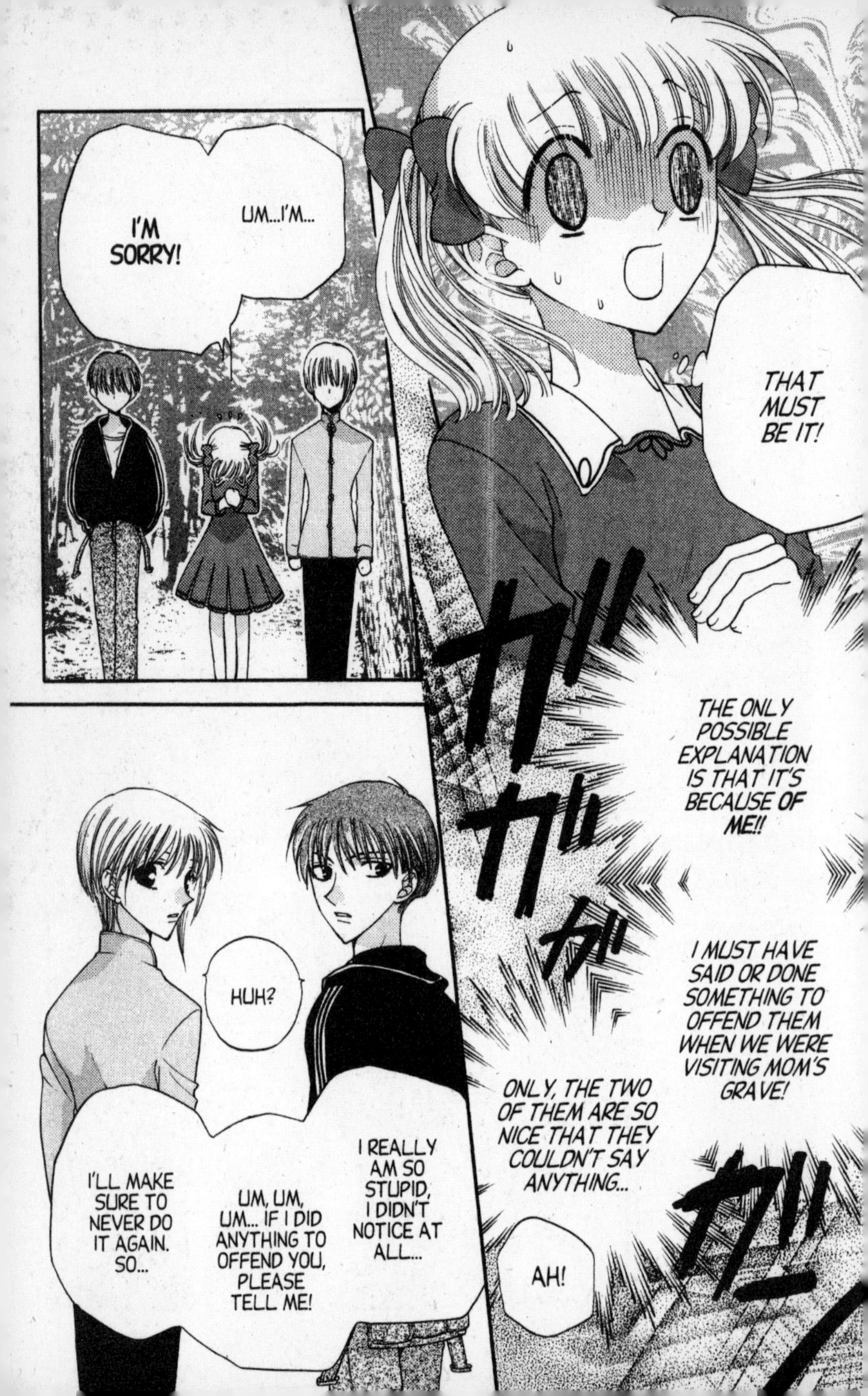
THAT MUST BE IT!
THE ONLY POSSIBLE EXPLANATION IS THAT IT'S BECAUSE OF ME!!
I MUST HAVE SAID OR DONE SOMETHING TO OFFEND THEM WHEN WE WERE VISITING MOM'S GRAVE!
ONLY, THE TWO OF THEM ARE SO NICE THAT THEY COULDN'T SAY ANYTHING...
AH!
UM...I'M...
I'M SORRY!
HUH?
I REALLY AM SO STUPID, I DIDN'T NOTICE AT ALL...
UM, UM, UM... IF I DID ANYTHING TO OFFEND YOU, PLEASE TELL ME!
I'LL MAKE SURE TO NEVER DO IT AGAIN. SO...

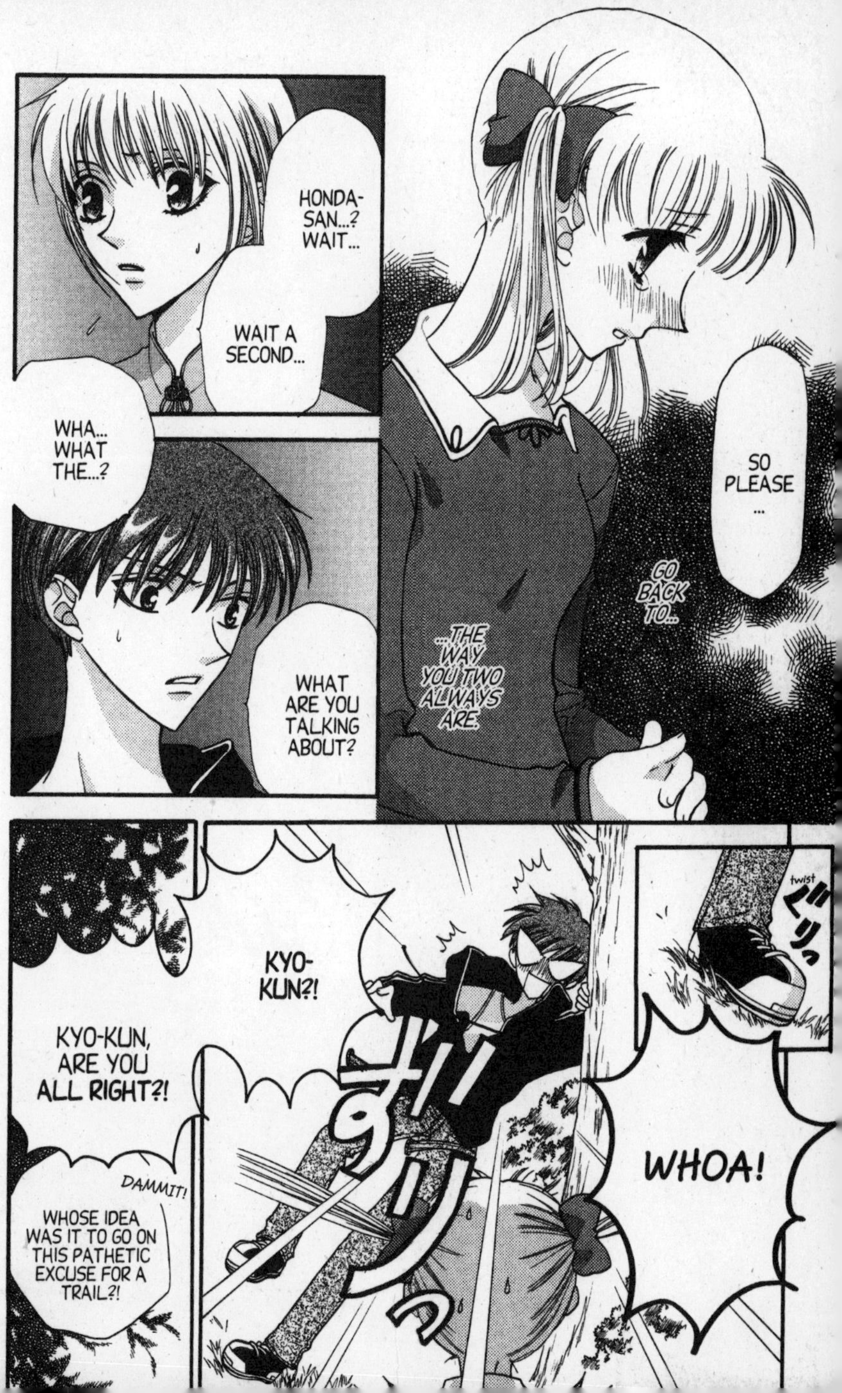
SO PLEASE ...
GO BACK TO...
...THE WAY YOU TWO ALWAYS ARE.
HONDA-SAN...? WAIT...
WAIT A SECOND...
WHA... WHAT THE...?
WHAT ARE YOU TALKING ABOUT?
twist
ぐりっ
WHOA!
ずりっ
KYO-KUN?!
KYO-KUN, ARE YOU ALL RIGHT?!
DAMMIT!
WHOSE IDEA WAS IT TO GO ON THIS PATHETIC EXCUSE FOR A TRAIL?!

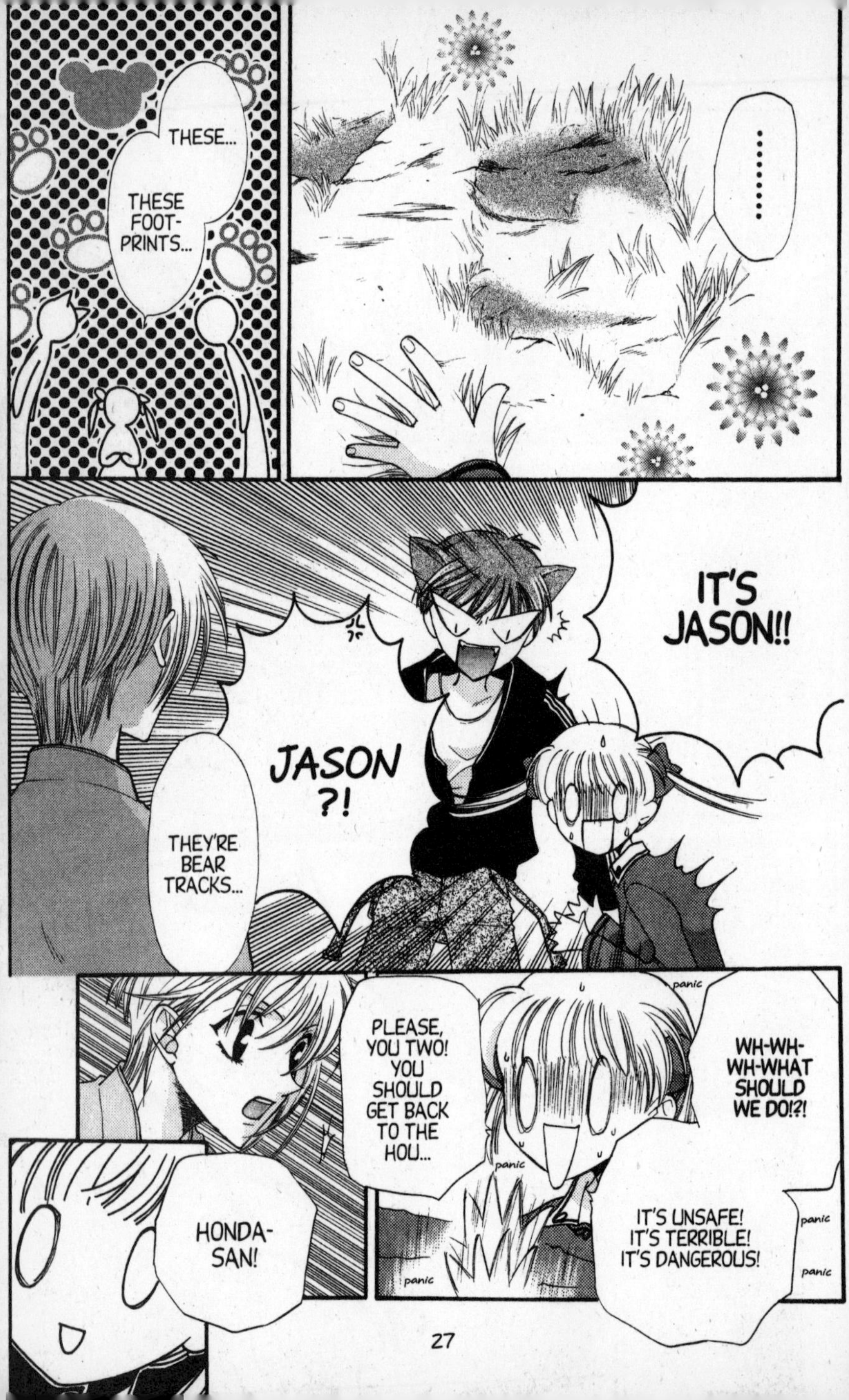
……
THESE...
THESE FOOT-PRINTS...
THEY'RE BEAR TRACKS...
IT'S JASON!!
JASON ?!
panic
WH-WH-WH-WHAT SHOULD WE DO!?!
panic
IT'S UNSAFE! IT'S TERRIBLE! IT'S DANGEROUS!
panic
panic
panic
PLEASE, YOU TWO! YOU SHOULD GET BACK TO THE HOU...
HONDA-SAN!

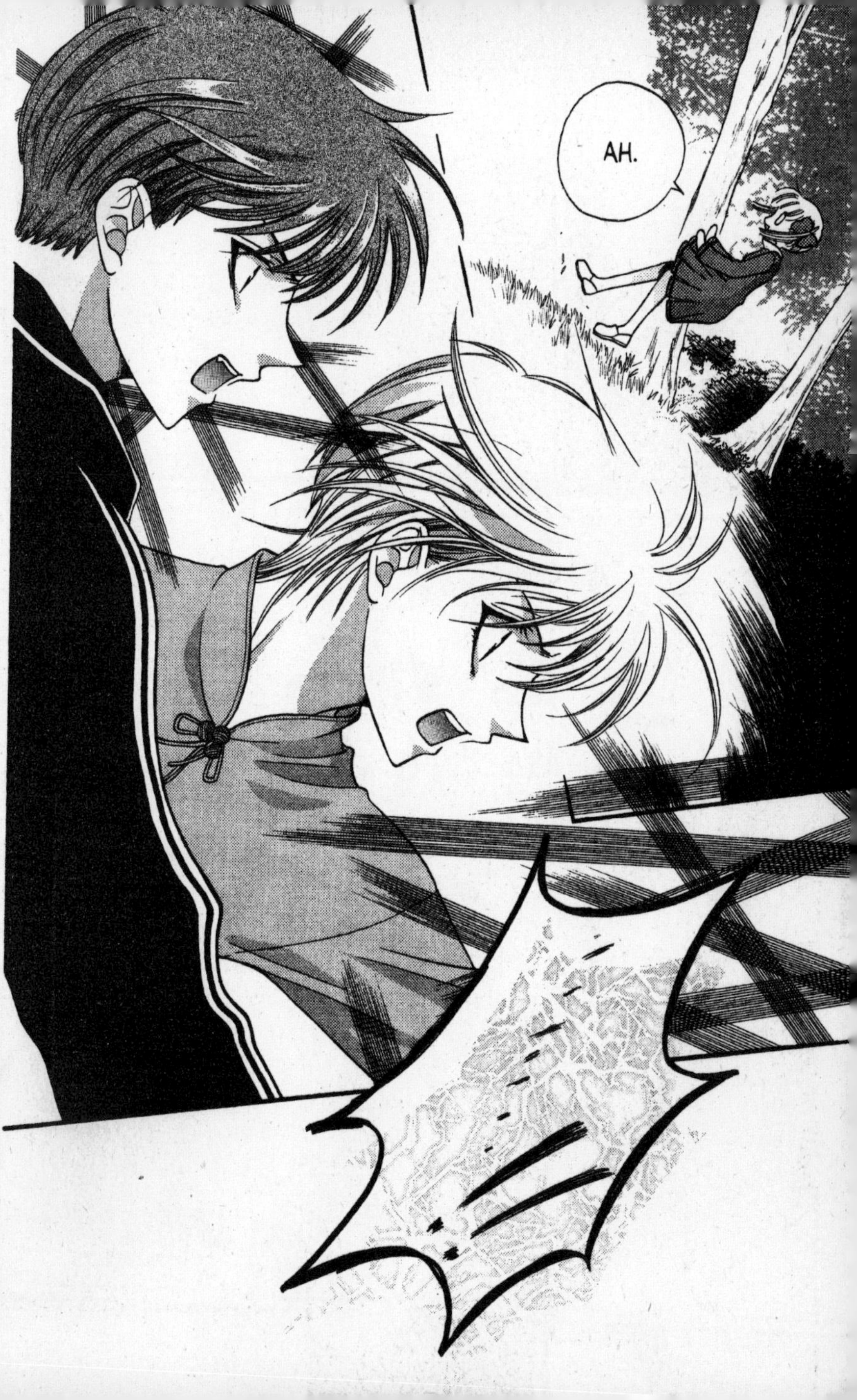
AH.

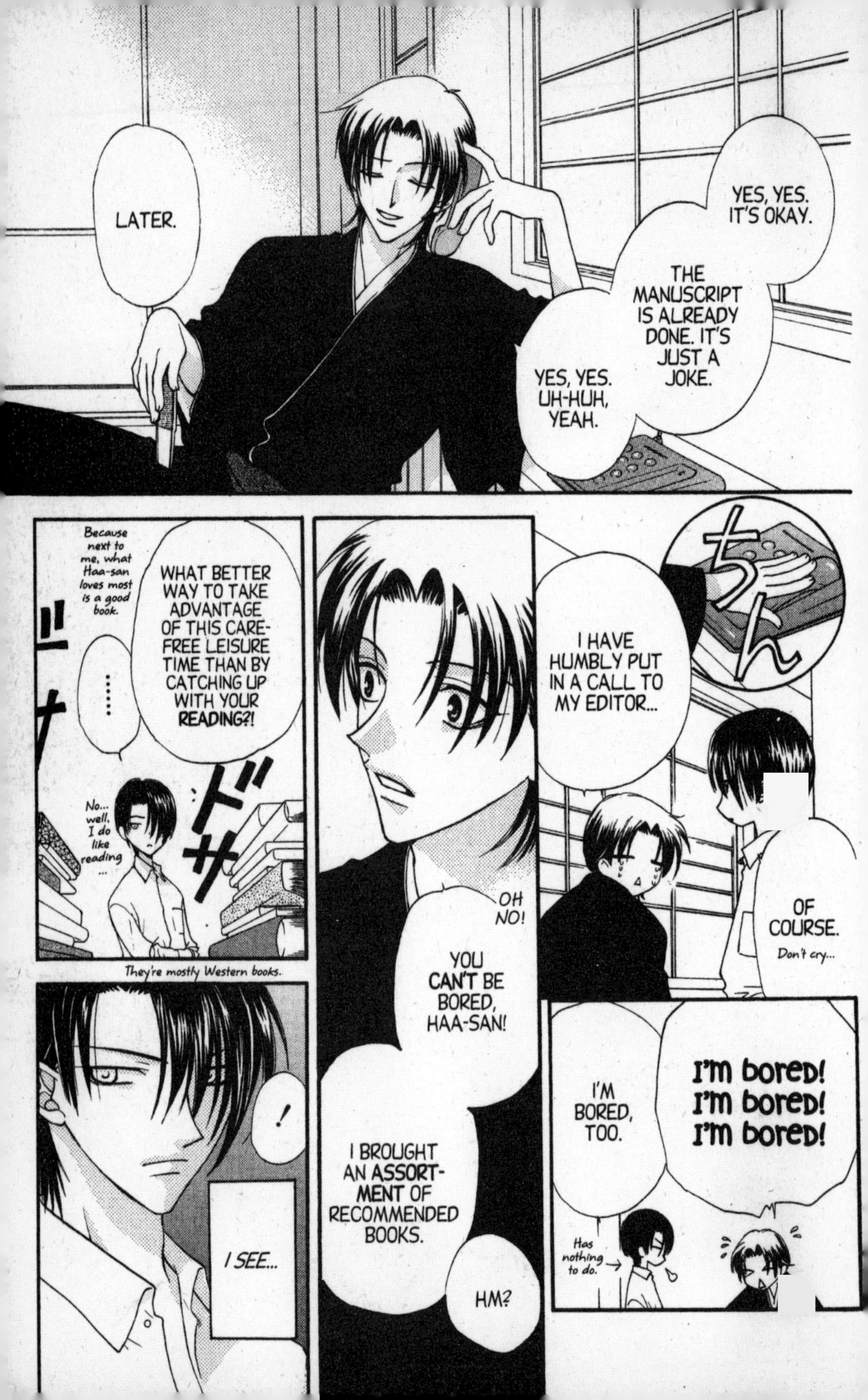

YES, YES. IT'S OKAY.
THE MANUSCRIPT IS ALREADY DONE. IT'S JUST A JOKE.
YES, YES. UH-HUH, YEAH.
LATER.
ちん
I HAVE HUMBLY PUT IN A CALL TO MY EDITOR...
OF COURSE.
Don't cry...
I'M BORED! I'M BORED! I'M BORED!
I'M BORED, TOO.
Has nothing to do.
OH NO!
YOU CAN'T BE BORED, HAA-SAN!
I BROUGHT AN ASSORTMENT OF RECOMMENDED BOOKS.
HM?
WHAT BETTER WAY TO TAKE ADVANTAGE OF THIS CAREFREE LEISURE TIME THAN BY CATCHING UP WITH YOUR READING?!
Because next to me, what Haa-san loves most is a good book.
......
ドサ
No... well, I do like reading...
They're mostly Western books.
!
I SEE...

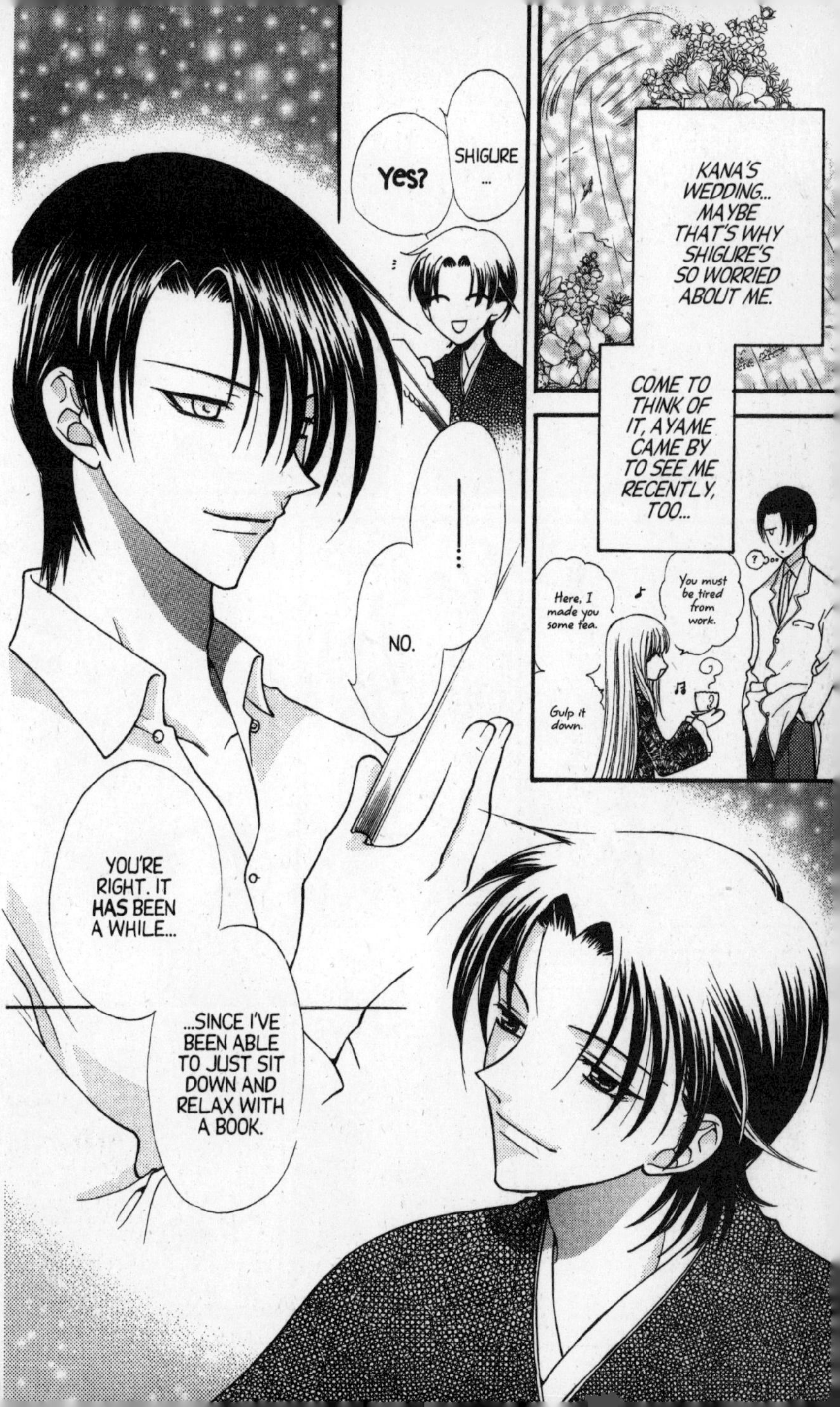
KANA'S WEDDING... MAYBE THAT'S WHY SHIGURE'S SO WORRIED ABOUT ME.
SHIGURE ...
Yes?
COME TO THINK OF IT, AYAME CAME BY TO SEE ME RECENTLY, TOO...
You must be tired from work.
Here, I made you some tea.
Gulp it down.
......
NO.
YOU'RE RIGHT. IT HAS BEEN A WHILE...
...SINCE I'VE BEEN ABLE TO JUST SIT DOWN AND RELAX WITH A BOOK.

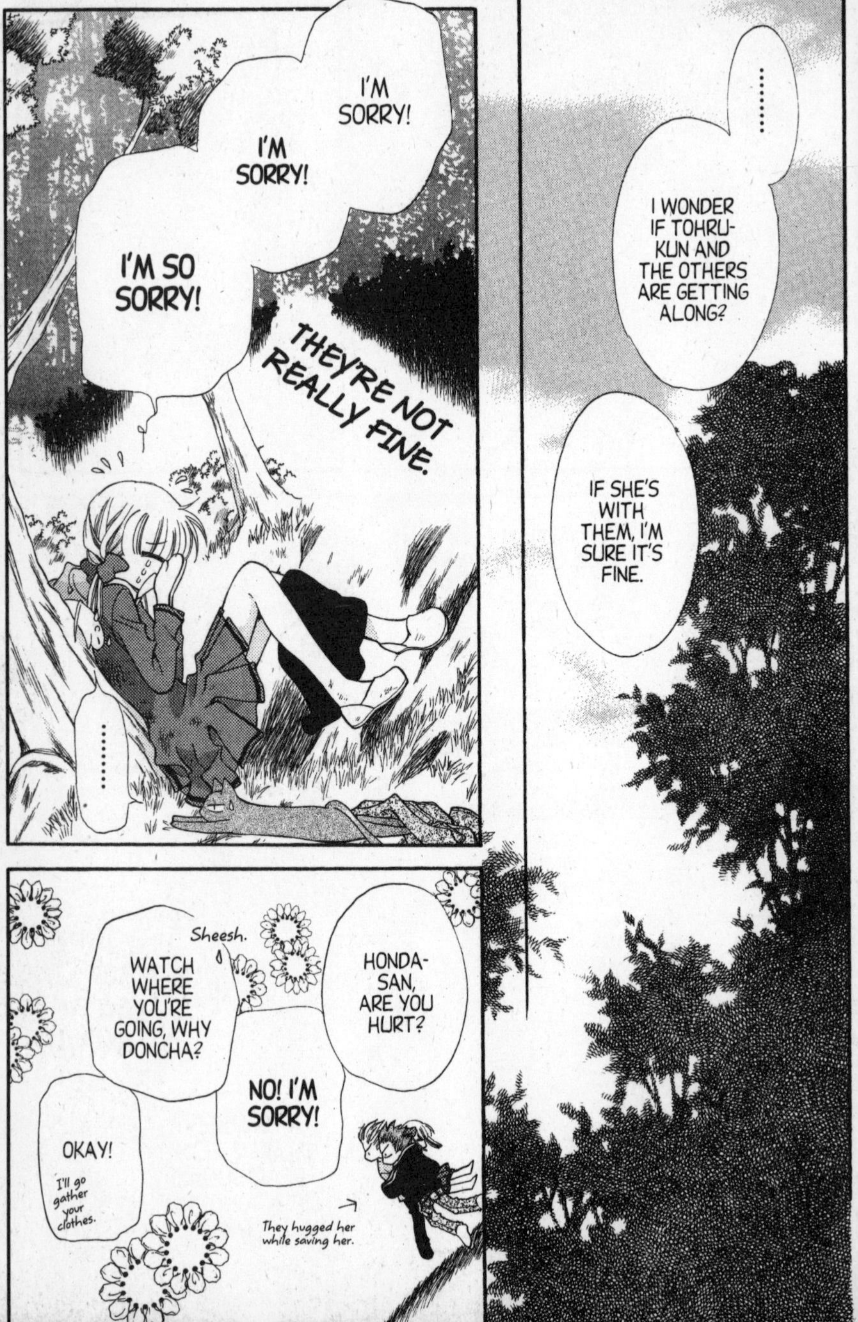
......
I WONDER IF TOHRU-KUN AND THE OTHERS ARE GETTING ALONG?
IF SHE'S WITH THEM, I'M SURE IT'S FINE.
I'M SORRY!
I'M SORRY!
I'M SO SORRY!
THEY'RE NOT REALLY FINE.
......
HONDA-SAN, ARE YOU HURT?
Sheesh.
WATCH WHERE YOU'RE GOING, WHY DONCHA?
NO! I'M SORRY!
OKAY!
I'll go gather your clothes.
They hugged her while saving her.

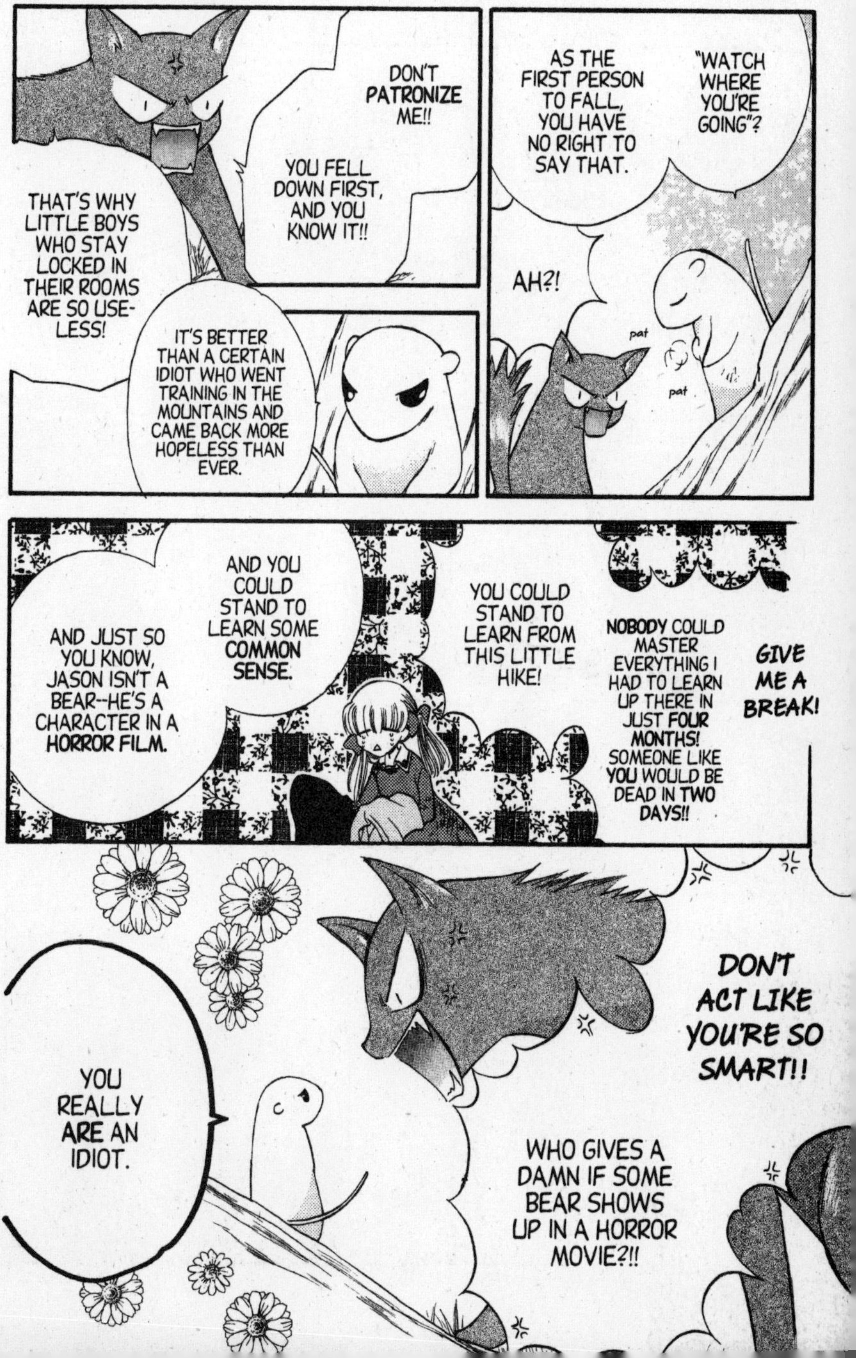
"WATCH WHERE YOU'RE GOING"?
AS THE FIRST PERSON TO FALL, YOU HAVE NO RIGHT TO SAY THAT.
AH?!
pat
pat
DON'T **PATRONIZE** ME!!
YOU FELL DOWN FIRST, AND YOU KNOW IT!!
THAT'S WHY LITTLE BOYS WHO STAY LOCKED IN THEIR ROOMS ARE SO USE-LESS!
IT'S BETTER THAN A CERTAIN IDIOT WHO WENT TRAINING IN THE MOUNTAINS AND CAME BACK MORE HOPELESS THAN EVER.
GIVE ME A BREAK!
**NOBODY** COULD MASTER EVERYTHING I HAD TO LEARN UP THERE IN JUST **FOUR MONTHS!** SOMEONE LIKE **YOU** WOULD BE DEAD IN **TWO DAYS!!**
YOU COULD STAND TO LEARN FROM THIS LITTLE HIKE!
AND YOU COULD STAND TO LEARN SOME **COMMON SENSE.**
AND JUST SO YOU KNOW, JASON ISN'T A BEAR--HE'S A CHARACTER IN A **HORROR FILM.**
DON'T ACT LIKE YOU'RE SO SMART!!
WHO GIVES A DAMN IF SOME BEAR SHOWS UP IN A HORROR MOVIE?!!
YOU REALLY **ARE** AN IDIOT.

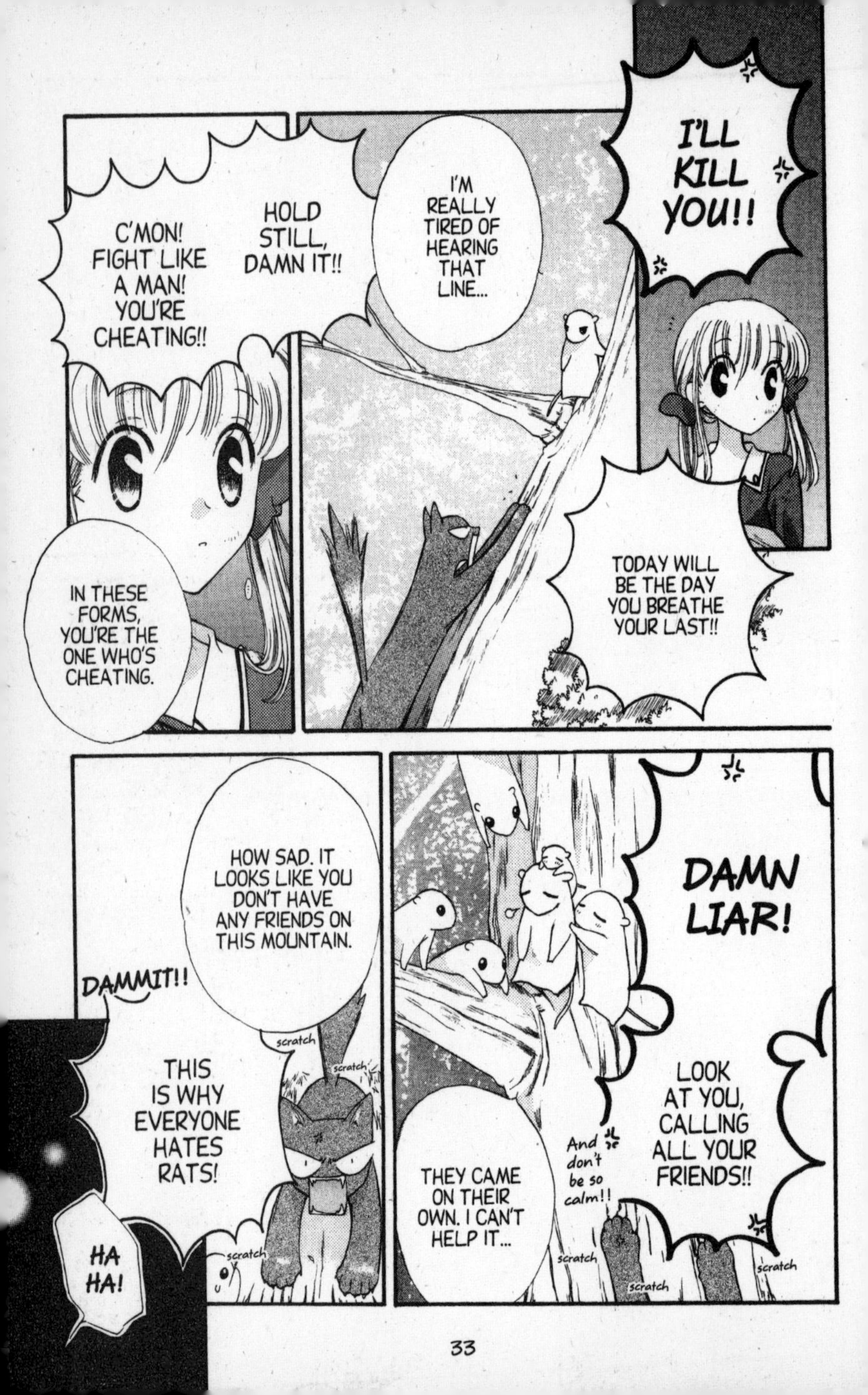

I'LL KILL YOU!!
TODAY WILL BE THE DAY YOU BREATHE YOUR LAST!!
I'M REALLY TIRED OF HEARING THAT LINE...
HOLD STILL, DAMN IT!!
C'MON! FIGHT LIKE A MAN! YOU'RE CHEATING!!
IN THESE FORMS, YOU'RE THE ONE WHO'S CHEATING.
DAMN LIAR!
LOOK AT YOU, CALLING ALL YOUR FRIENDS!!
And don't be so calm!!
THEY CAME ON THEIR OWN. I CAN'T HELP IT...
scratch
scratch
scratch
HOW SAD. IT LOOKS LIKE YOU DON'T HAVE ANY FRIENDS ON THIS MOUNTAIN.
DAMMIT!!
scratch
scratch
THIS IS WHY EVERYONE HATES RATS!
scratch
HA HA!

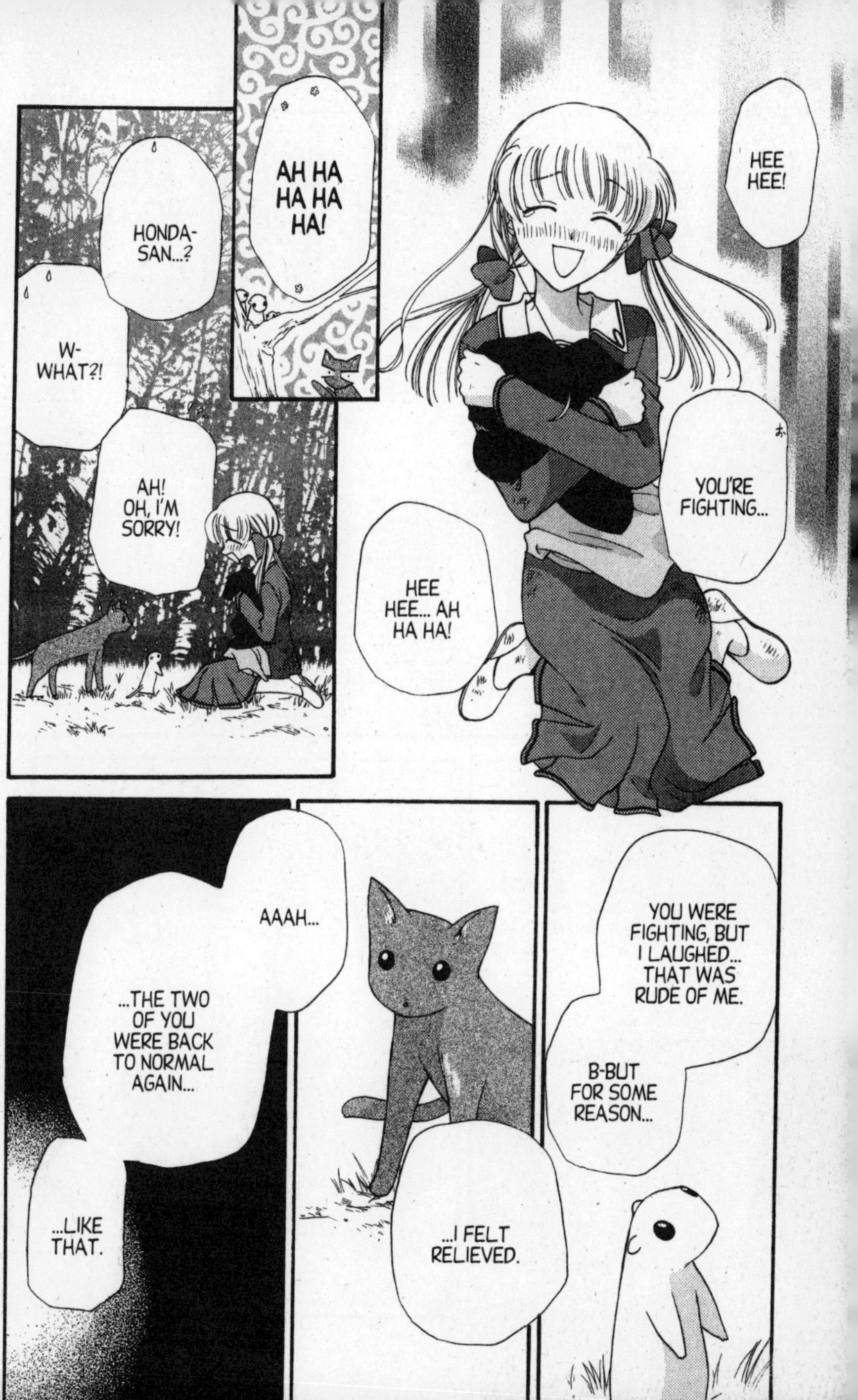
HEE HEE!
YOU'RE FIGHTING...
HEE HEE... AH HA HA!
AH HA HA HA HA!
HONDA-SAN...?
W-WHAT?!
AH! OH, I'M SORRY!
YOU WERE FIGHTING, BUT I LAUGHED... THAT WAS RUDE OF ME.
B-BUT FOR SOME REASON...
...I FELT RELIEVED.
AAAH...
...THE TWO OF YOU WERE BACK TO NORMAL AGAIN...
...LIKE THAT.

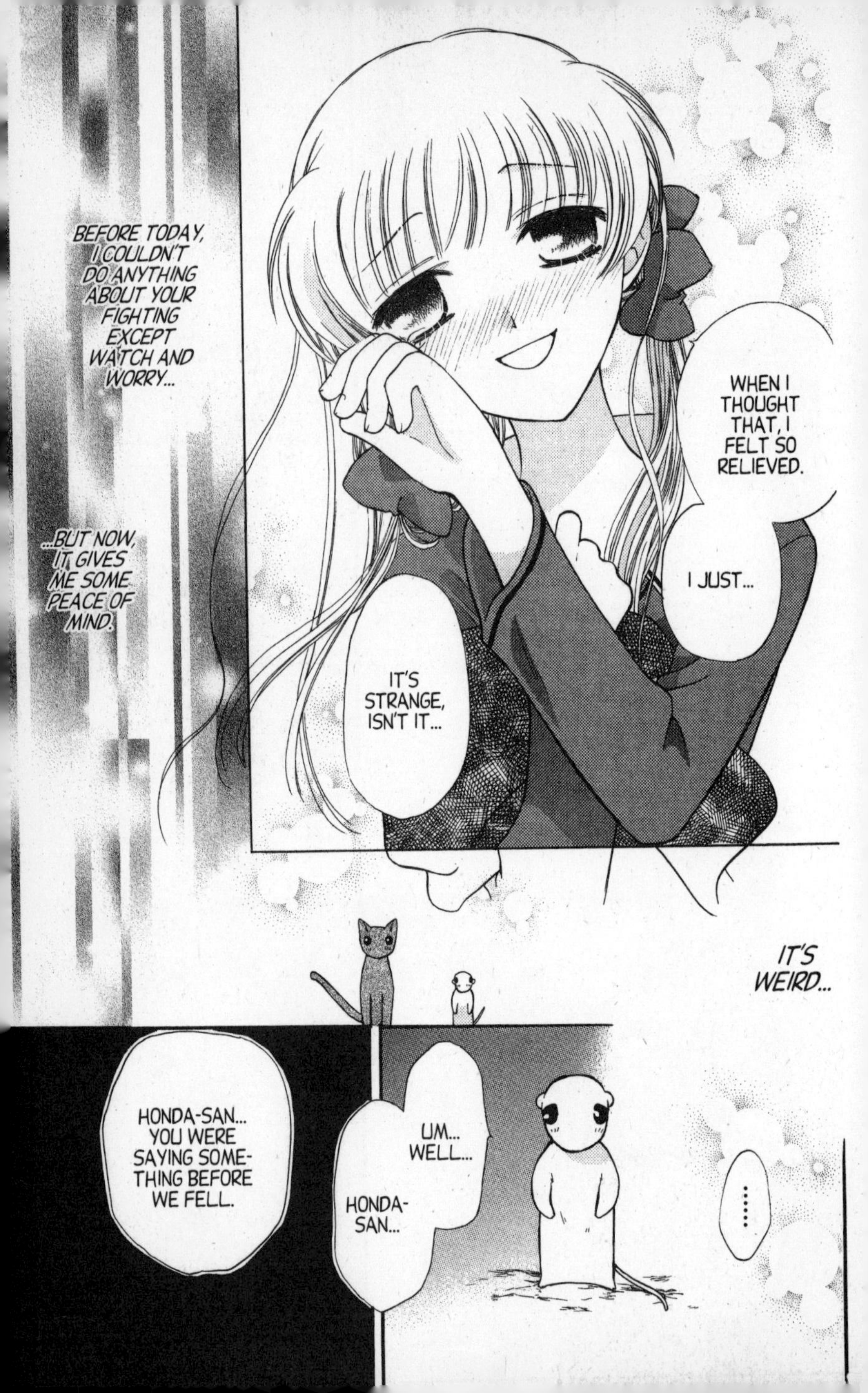
WHEN I THOUGHT THAT, I FELT SO RELIEVED.
I JUST...
IT'S STRANGE, ISN'T IT...
BEFORE TODAY, I COULDN'T DO ANYTHING ABOUT YOUR FIGHTING EXCEPT WATCH AND WORRY...
...BUT NOW, IT GIVES ME SOME PEACE OF MIND.
IT'S WEIRD...
......
UM... WELL...
HONDA-SAN...
HONDA-SAN... YOU WERE SAYING SOME-THING BEFORE WE FELL.

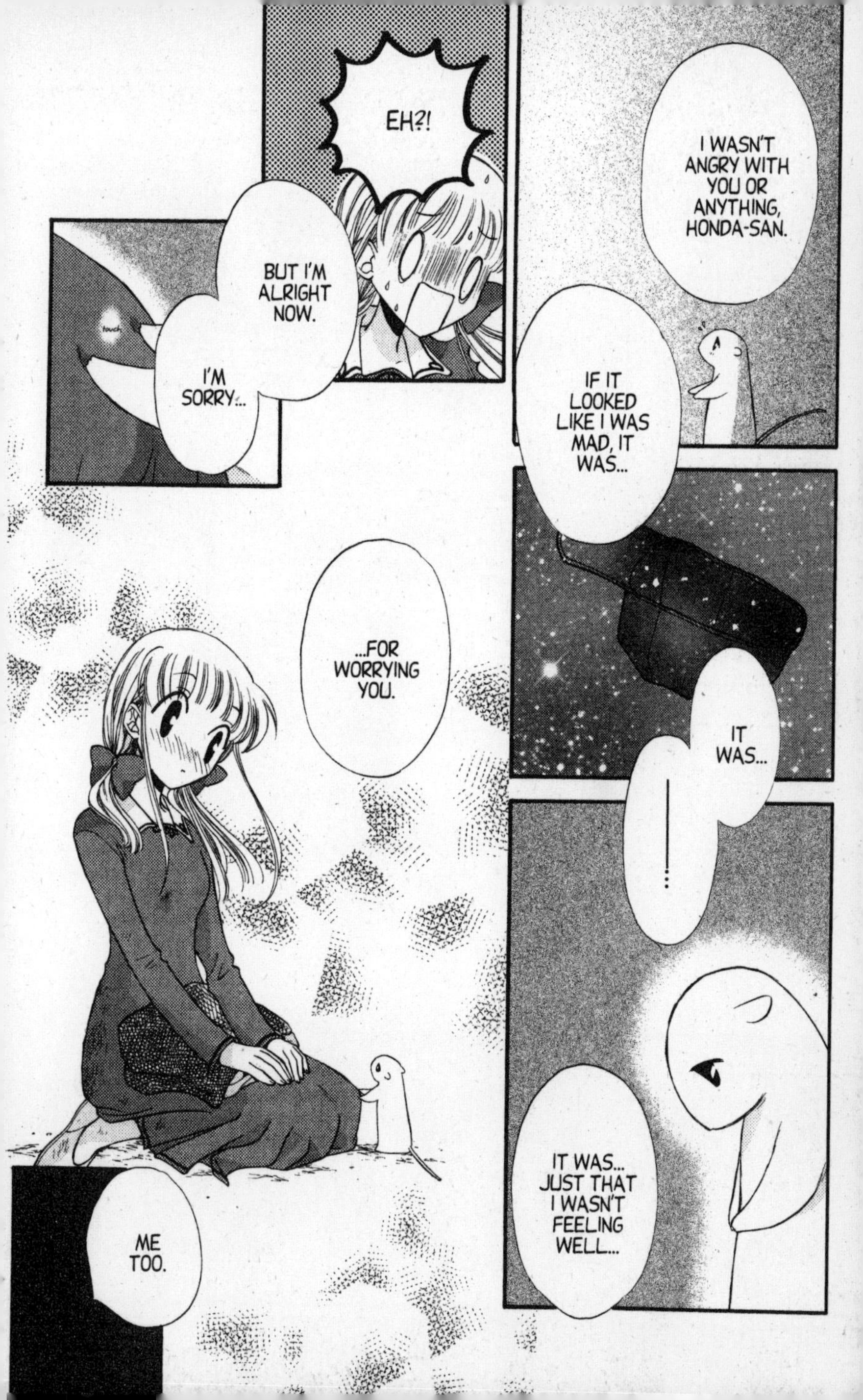
I WASN'T ANGRY WITH YOU OR ANYTHING, HONDA-SAN.
IF IT LOOKED LIKE I WAS MAD, IT WAS...
IT WAS...
—...
IT WAS... JUST THAT I WASN'T FEELING WELL...
EH?!
BUT I'M ALRIGHT NOW.
touch
I'M SORRY...
...FOR WORRYING YOU.
ME TOO.

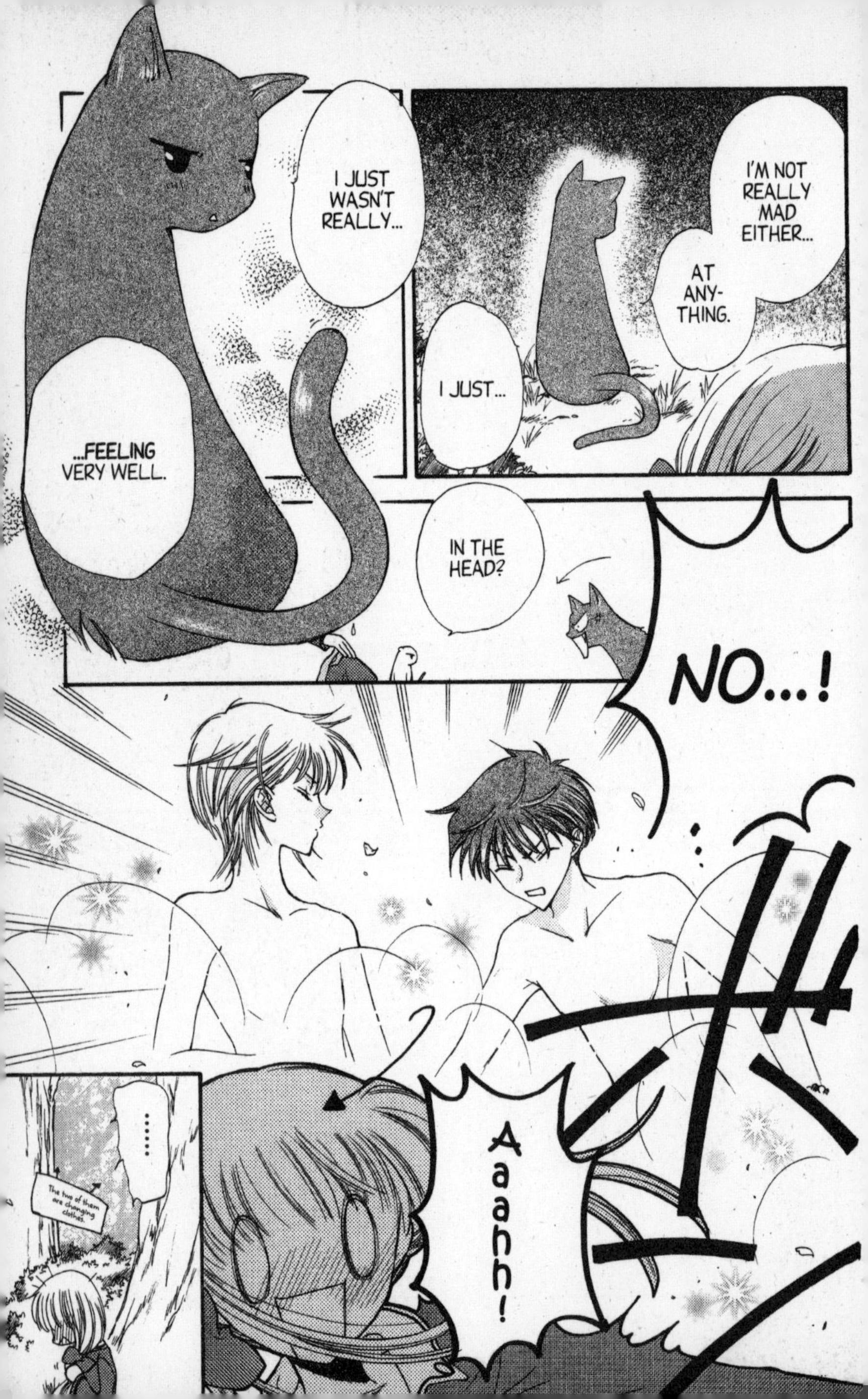
I'M NOT REALLY MAD EITHER...
AT ANY-THING.
I JUST...
I JUST WASN'T REALLY...
...FEELING VERY WELL.
IN THE HEAD?
NO...!
Aaanh!
......
The two of them are changing clothes.

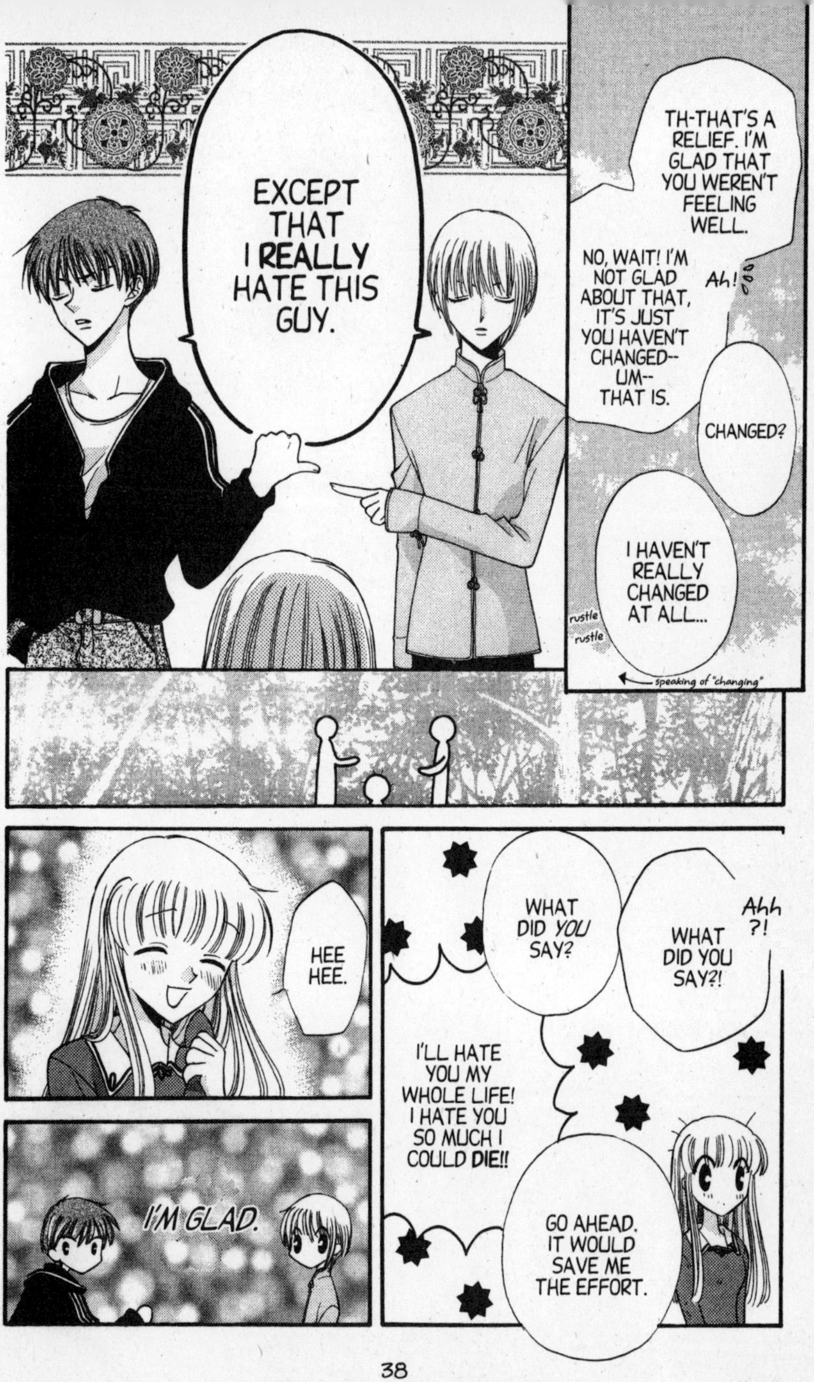
TH-THAT'S A RELIEF. I'M GLAD THAT YOU WEREN'T FEELING WELL.
Ah!
NO, WAIT! I'M NOT GLAD ABOUT THAT, IT'S JUST YOU HAVEN'T CHANGED-- UM-- THAT IS.
CHANGED?
I HAVEN'T REALLY CHANGED AT ALL...
rustle
rustle
speaking of "changing"
EXCEPT THAT I **REALLY** HATE THIS GUY.
Ahh ?!
WHAT DID YOU SAY?!
WHAT DID *YOU* SAY?
I'LL HATE YOU MY WHOLE LIFE! I HATE YOU SO MUCH I COULD **DIE**!!
GO AHEAD. IT WOULD SAVE ME THE EFFORT.
HEE HEE.
I'M GLAD.

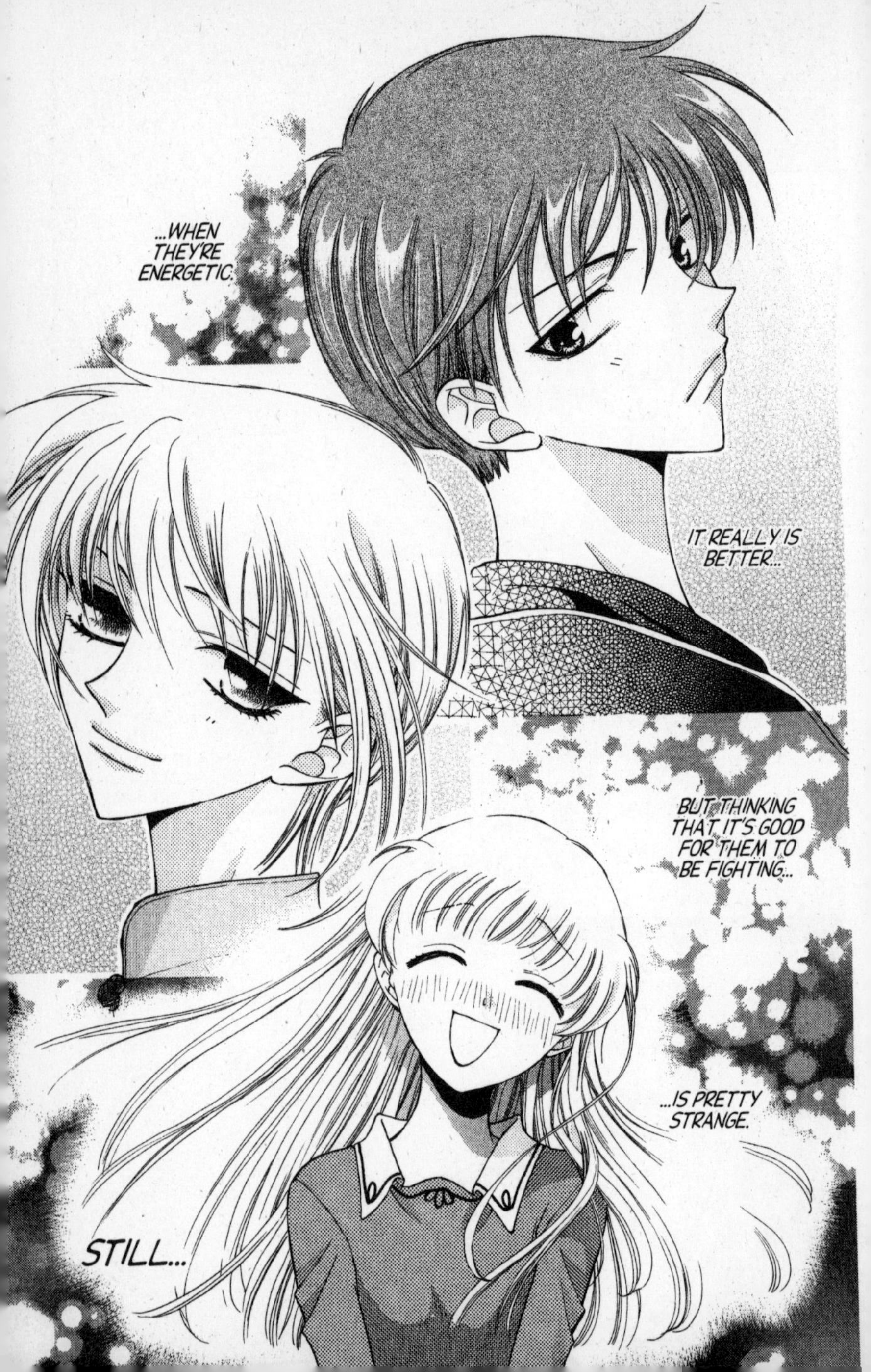

...WHEN THEY'RE ENERGETIC.
IT REALLY IS BETTER...
BUT THINKING THAT IT'S GOOD FOR THEM TO BE FIGHTING...
...IS PRETTY STRANGE.
STILL...

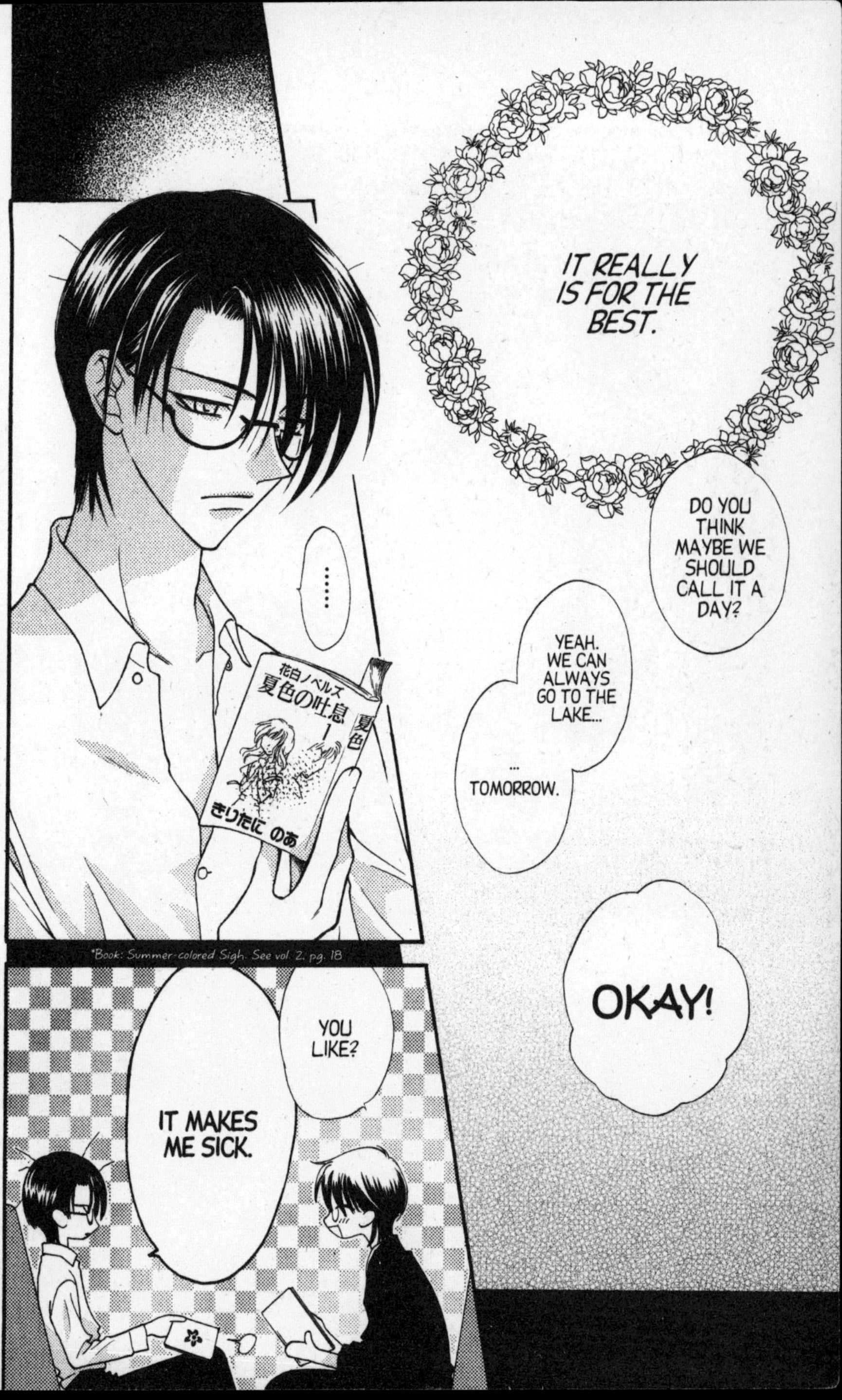
IT REALLY IS FOR THE BEST.
DO YOU THINK MAYBE WE SHOULD CALL IT A DAY?
YEAH. WE CAN ALWAYS GO TO THE LAKE...
... TOMORROW.
OKAY!
......
花白ノベルズ
夏色の吐息 1
夏色
きりたに のあ
*Book: Summer-colored Sigh. See vol. 2, pg. 18
YOU LIKE?
IT MAKES ME SICK.

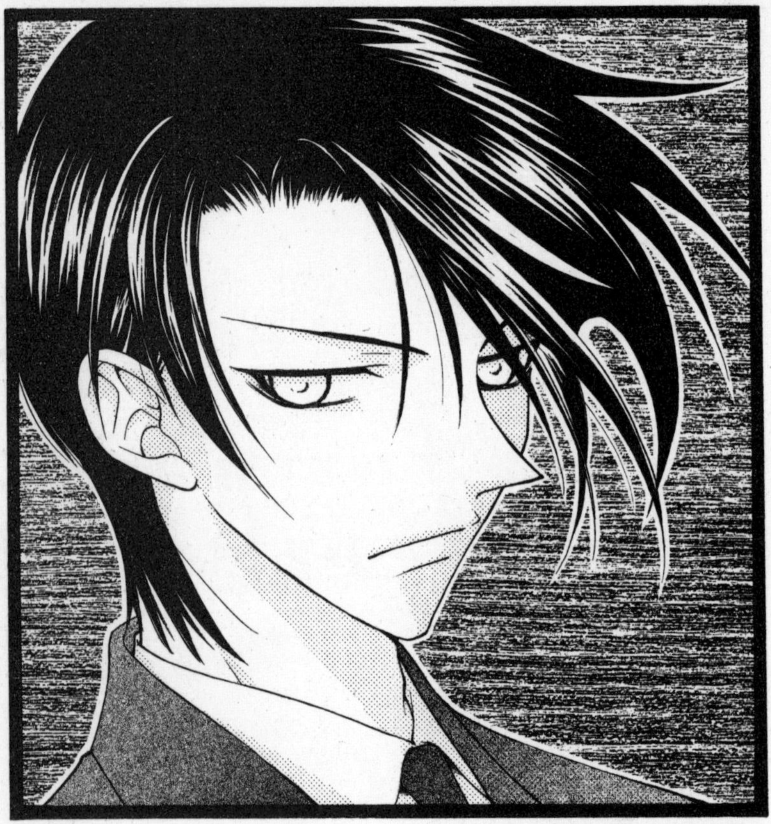

# Chapter 26

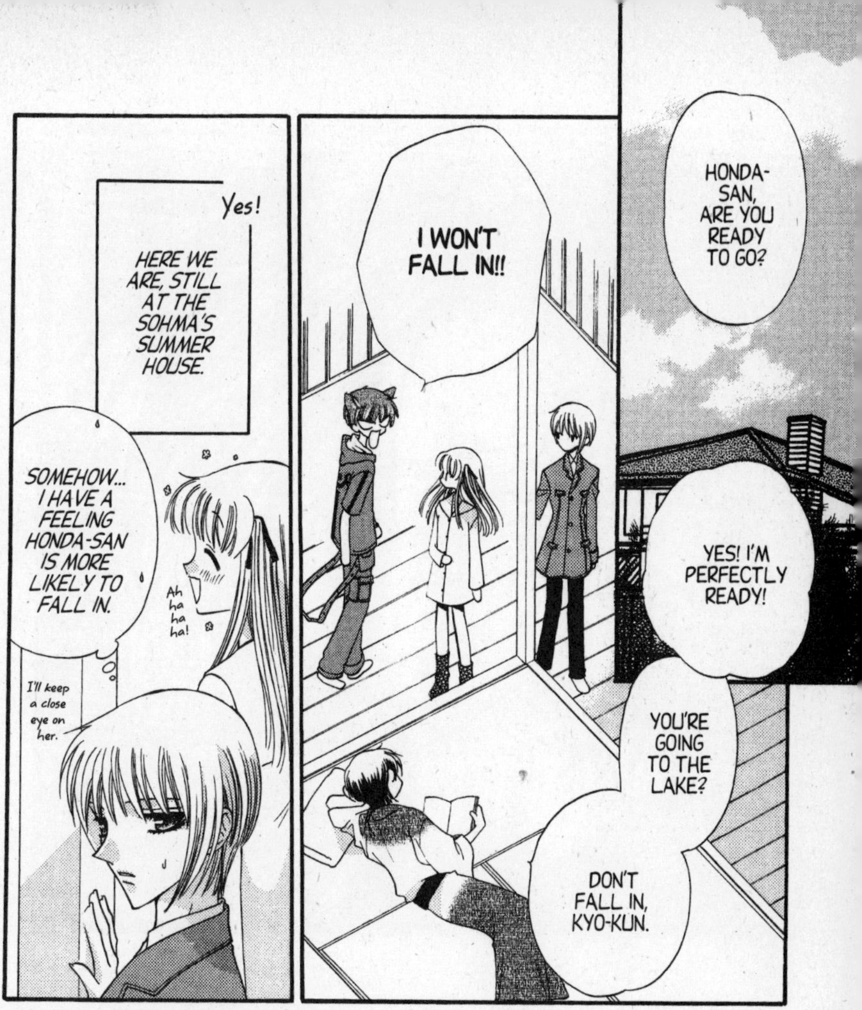
HONDA-SAN, ARE YOU READY TO GO?
YES! I'M PERFECTLY READY!
YOU'RE GOING TO THE LAKE?
DON'T FALL IN, KYO-KUN.
I WON'T FALL IN!!
Yes!
HERE WE ARE, STILL AT THE SOHMA'S SUMMER HOUSE.
SOMEHOW... I HAVE A FEELING HONDA-SAN IS MORE LIKELY TO FALL IN.
Ah ha ha ha!
I'll keep a close eye on her.

## ULTRA SPECIAL BLAH BLAH BLAH 2

Hatori is pretty popular, isn't he? I can say this now, but at first he wasn't liked at all. So now that I've felt his popularity has gone up, I feel like it was worth it to work hard on him.

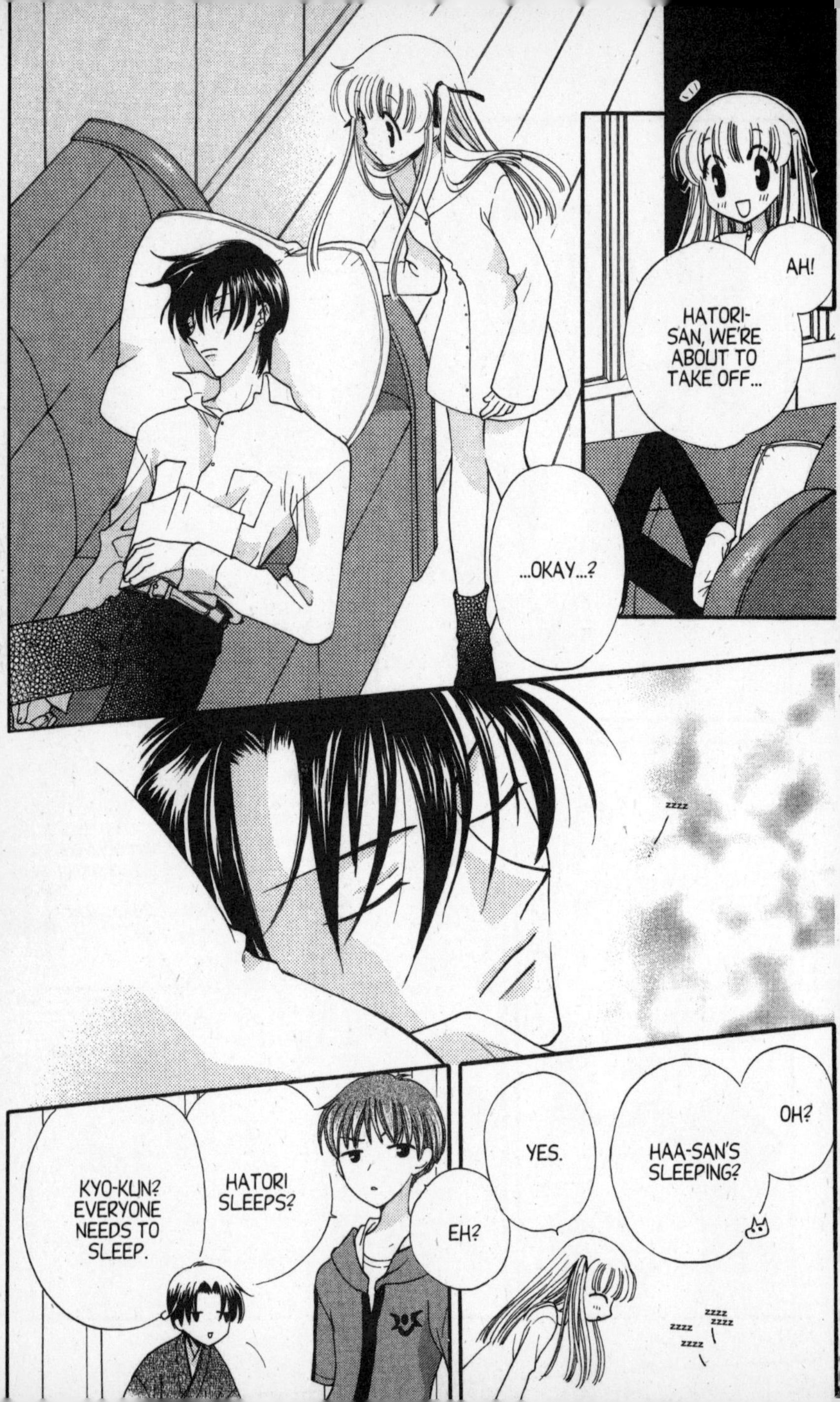
AH!
HATORI-SAN, WE'RE ABOUT TO TAKE OFF...
...OKAY...?
zzzz
OH?
HAA-SAN'S SLEEPING?
YES.
zzzz
zzzz
zzzz
zzzz
EH?
HATORI SLEEPS?
KYO-KUN? EVERYONE NEEDS TO SLEEP.

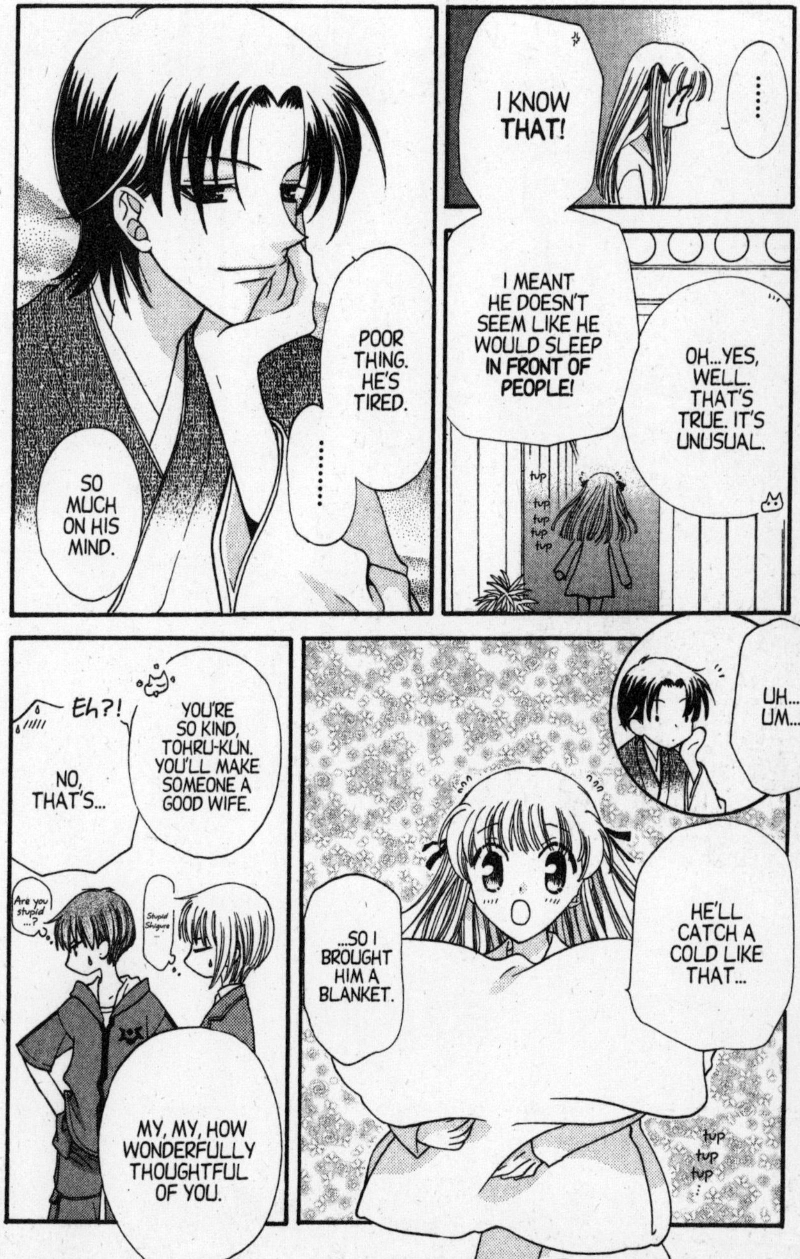

......
I KNOW THAT!
I MEANT HE DOESN'T SEEM LIKE HE WOULD SLEEP IN FRONT OF PEOPLE!
OH...YES, WELL. THAT'S TRUE. IT'S UNUSUAL.
tup tup tup tup tup
POOR THING. HE'S TIRED.
......
SO MUCH ON HIS MIND.
UH... UM...
HE'LL CATCH A COLD LIKE THAT...
...SO I BROUGHT HIM A BLANKET.
tup tup tup ...
YOU'RE SO KIND, TOHRU-KUN. YOU'LL MAKE SOMEONE A GOOD WIFE.
Eh?!
NO, THAT'S...
Stupid Shigure ...
Are you stupid ...?
MY, MY, HOW WONDERFULLY THOUGHTFUL OF YOU.

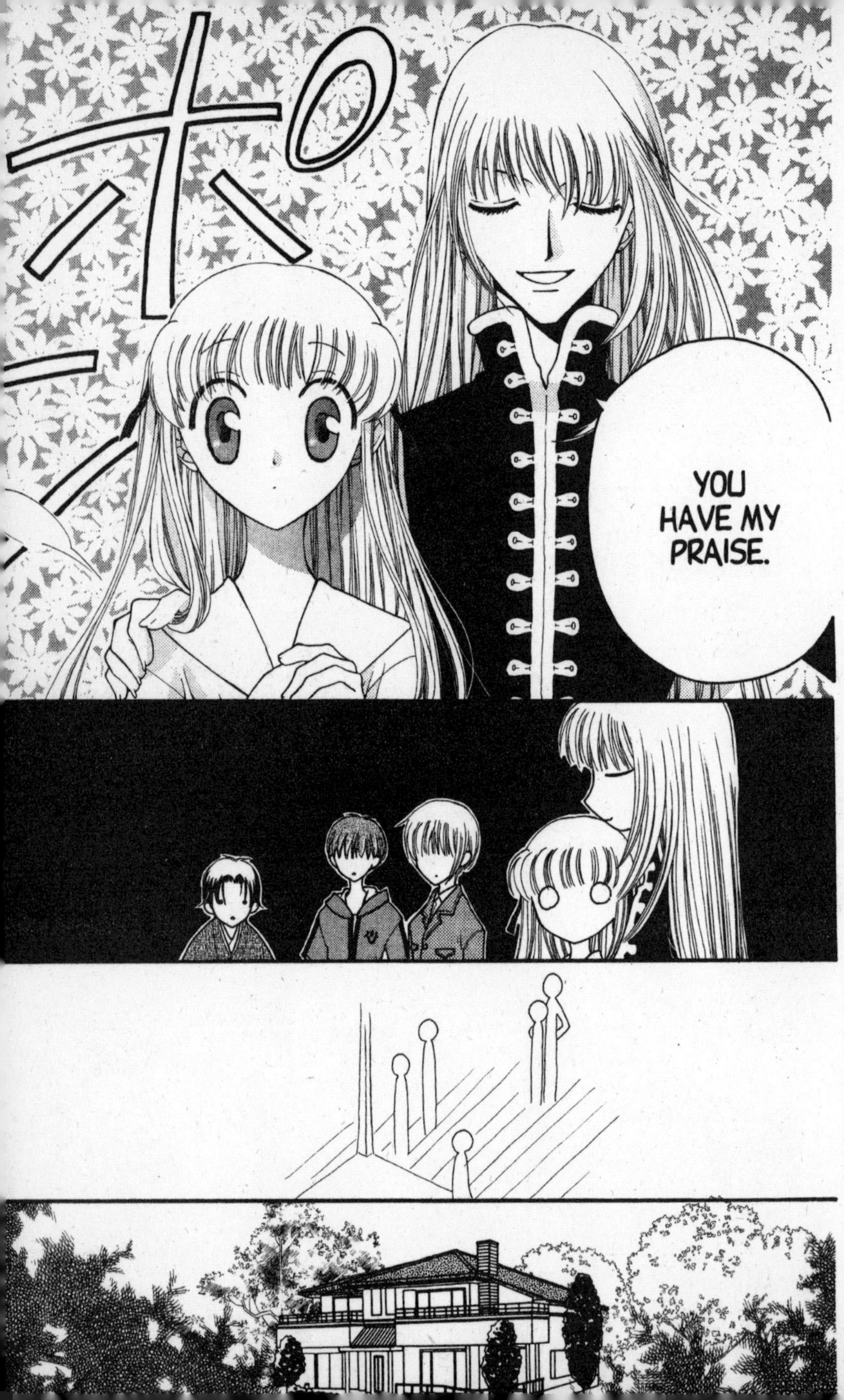
YOU HAVE MY PRAISE.

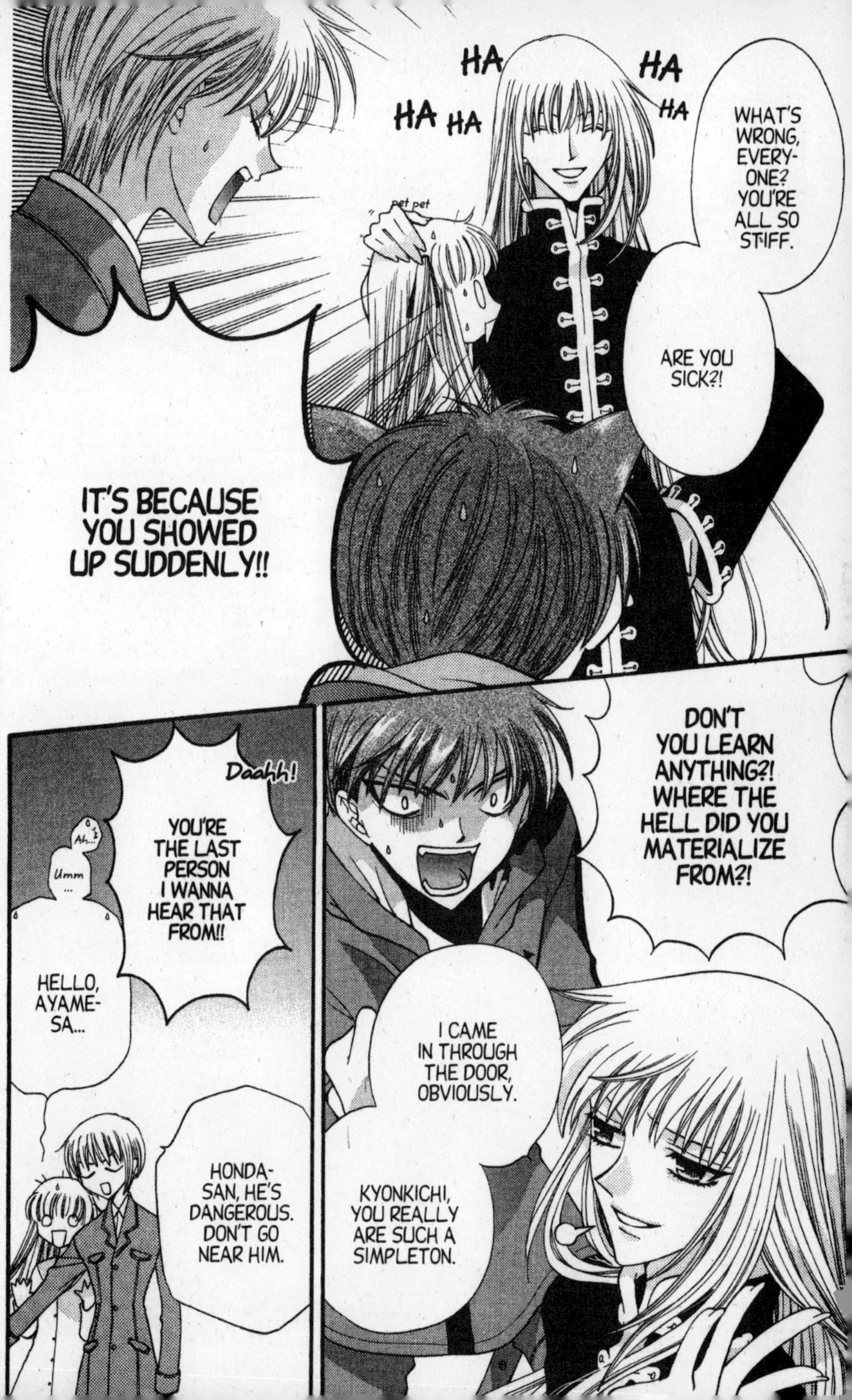
HA HA HA HA HA HA
WHAT'S WRONG, EVERYONE? YOU'RE ALL SO STIFF.
pet pet
ARE YOU SICK?!
IT'S BECAUSE YOU SHOWED UP SUDDENLY!!
DON'T YOU LEARN ANYTHING?! WHERE THE HELL DID YOU MATERIALIZE FROM?!
I CAME IN THROUGH THE DOOR, OBVIOUSLY.
KYONKICHI, YOU REALLY ARE SUCH A SIMPLETON.
Daahh!
YOU'RE THE LAST PERSON I WANNA HEAR THAT FROM!!
Ah...
Umm ...
HELLO, AYAME-SA...
HONDA-SAN, HE'S DANGEROUS. DON'T GO NEAR HIM.

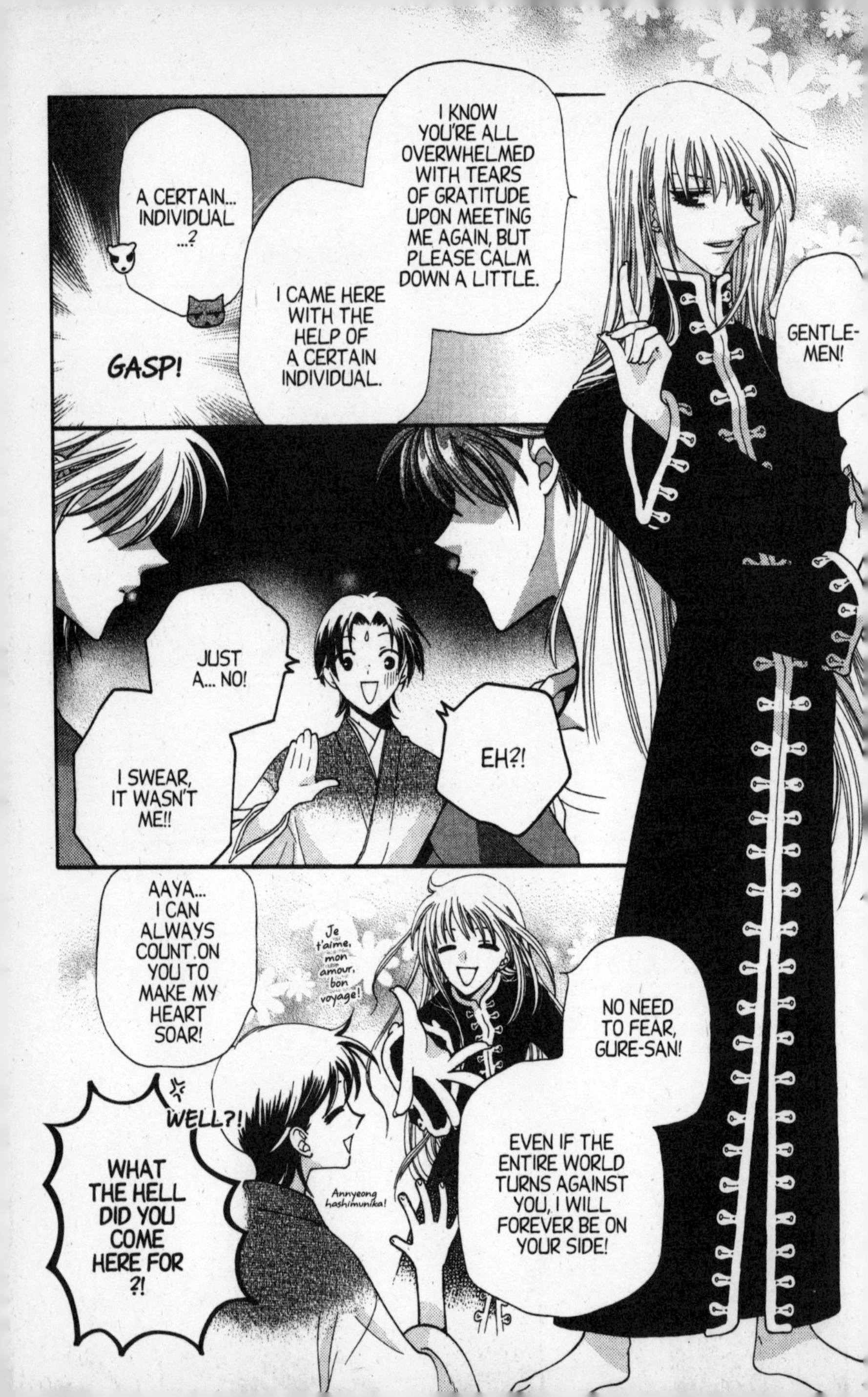
GENTLE-MEN!
I KNOW YOU'RE ALL OVERWHELMED WITH TEARS OF GRATITUDE UPON MEETING ME AGAIN, BUT PLEASE CALM DOWN A LITTLE.
I CAME HERE WITH THE HELP OF A CERTAIN INDIVIDUAL.
A CERTAIN... INDIVIDUAL ...?
GASP!
EH?!
JUST A... NO!
I SWEAR, IT WASN'T ME!!
NO NEED TO FEAR, GURE-SAN!
EVEN IF THE ENTIRE WORLD TURNS AGAINST YOU, I WILL FOREVER BE ON YOUR SIDE!
Je t'aime, mon amour, bon voyage!
AAYA... I CAN ALWAYS COUNT ON YOU TO MAKE MY HEART SOAR!
Annyeong hashimunika!
WELL?!
WHAT THE HELL DID YOU COME HERE FOR ?!

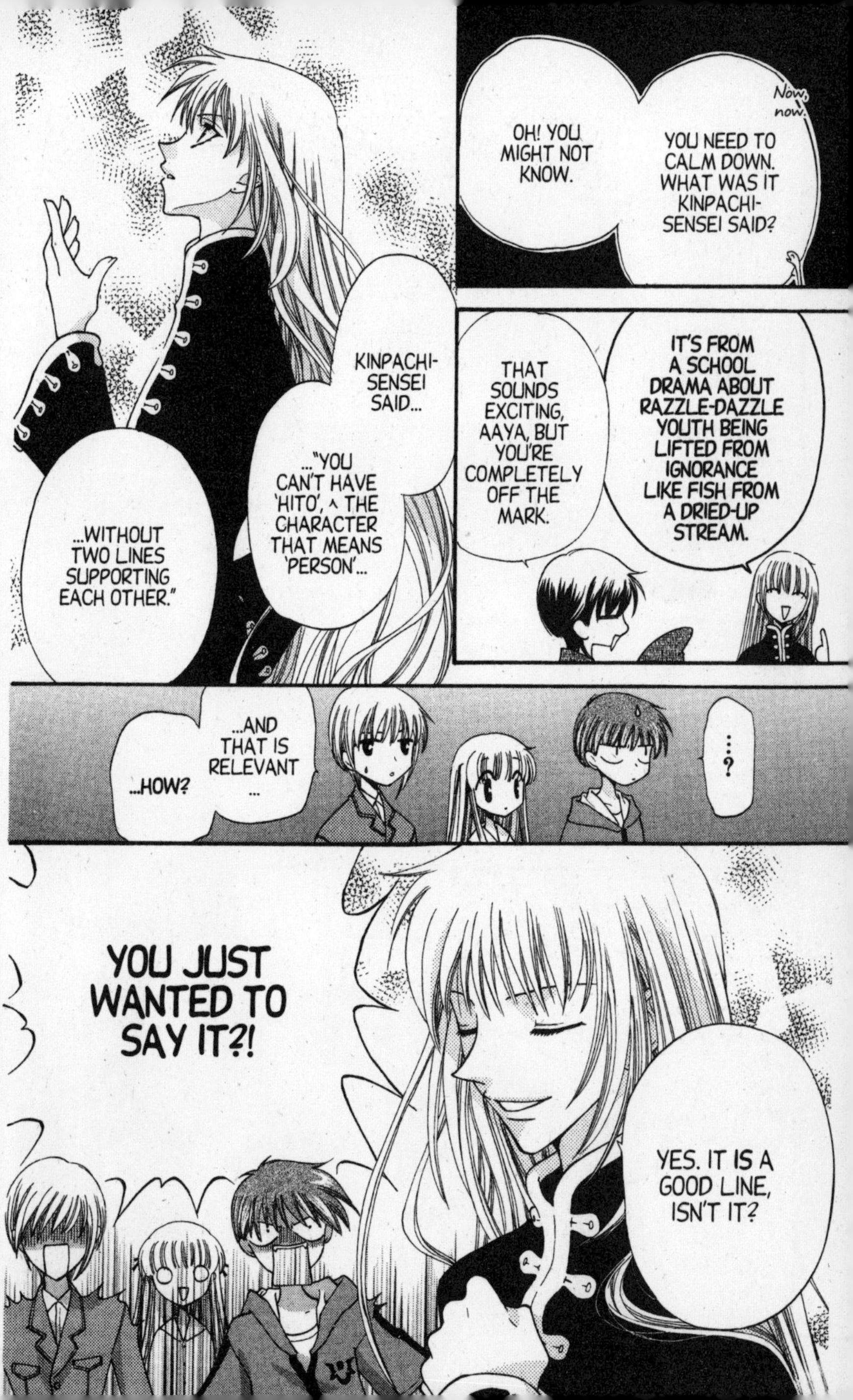
Now, now.
YOU NEED TO CALM DOWN. WHAT WAS IT KINPACHI-SENSEI SAID?
OH! YOU MIGHT NOT KNOW.
IT'S FROM A SCHOOL DRAMA ABOUT RAZZLE-DAZZLE YOUTH BEING LIFTED FROM IGNORANCE LIKE FISH FROM A DRIED-UP STREAM.
THAT SOUNDS EXCITING, AAYA, BUT YOU'RE COMPLETELY OFF THE MARK.
KINPACHI-SENSEI SAID...
..."YOU CAN'T HAVE 'HITO', ^ THE CHARACTER THAT MEANS 'PERSON'...
...WITHOUT TWO LINES SUPPORTING EACH OTHER."
...?
...AND THAT IS RELEVANT ...
...HOW?
YES. IT IS A GOOD LINE, ISN'T IT?
YOU JUST WANTED TO SAY IT?!

**Fruits Basket 5 Part 2:**

I talk about games a lot in this column, but when I do, I get a lot of letters that say, "I don't follow video games, so I don't understand. Talk about something else." But haven't more girls been playing video games lately? I wonder. I wonder... It's the same feeling as turning on the TV, so I feel like maybe it's a part of my life, like what else would I do but playing video games? In other words, when I'm not working, all I would do is play video games. So I didn't have anything to talk about aside from work or video games. (I don't feel sad at all saying that.) I don't even know how many PS memory cards I have anymore.

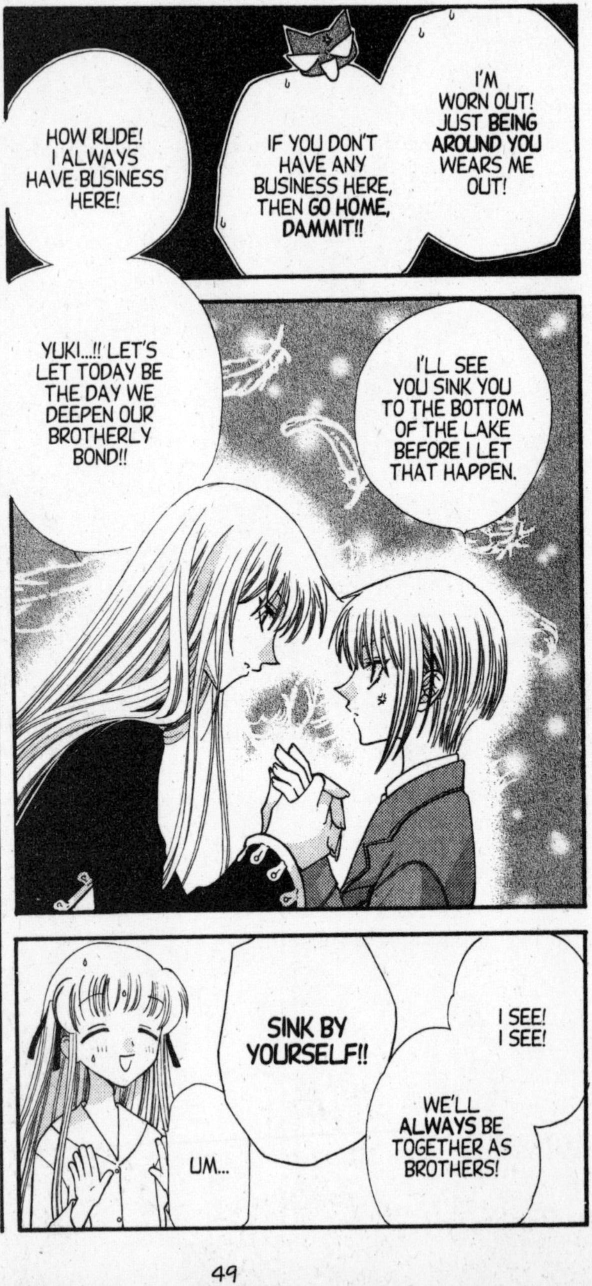
I'M WORN OUT! JUST BEING AROUND YOU WEARS ME OUT!
IF YOU DON'T HAVE ANY BUSINESS HERE, THEN GO HOME, DAMMIT!!
HOW RUDE! I ALWAYS HAVE BUSINESS HERE!
YUKI...!! LET'S LET TODAY BE THE DAY WE DEEPEN OUR BROTHERLY BOND!!
I'LL SEE YOU SINK YOU TO THE BOTTOM OF THE LAKE BEFORE I LET THAT HAPPEN.
I SEE! I SEE!
WE'LL ALWAYS BE TOGETHER AS BROTHERS!
SINK BY YOURSELF!!
UM...

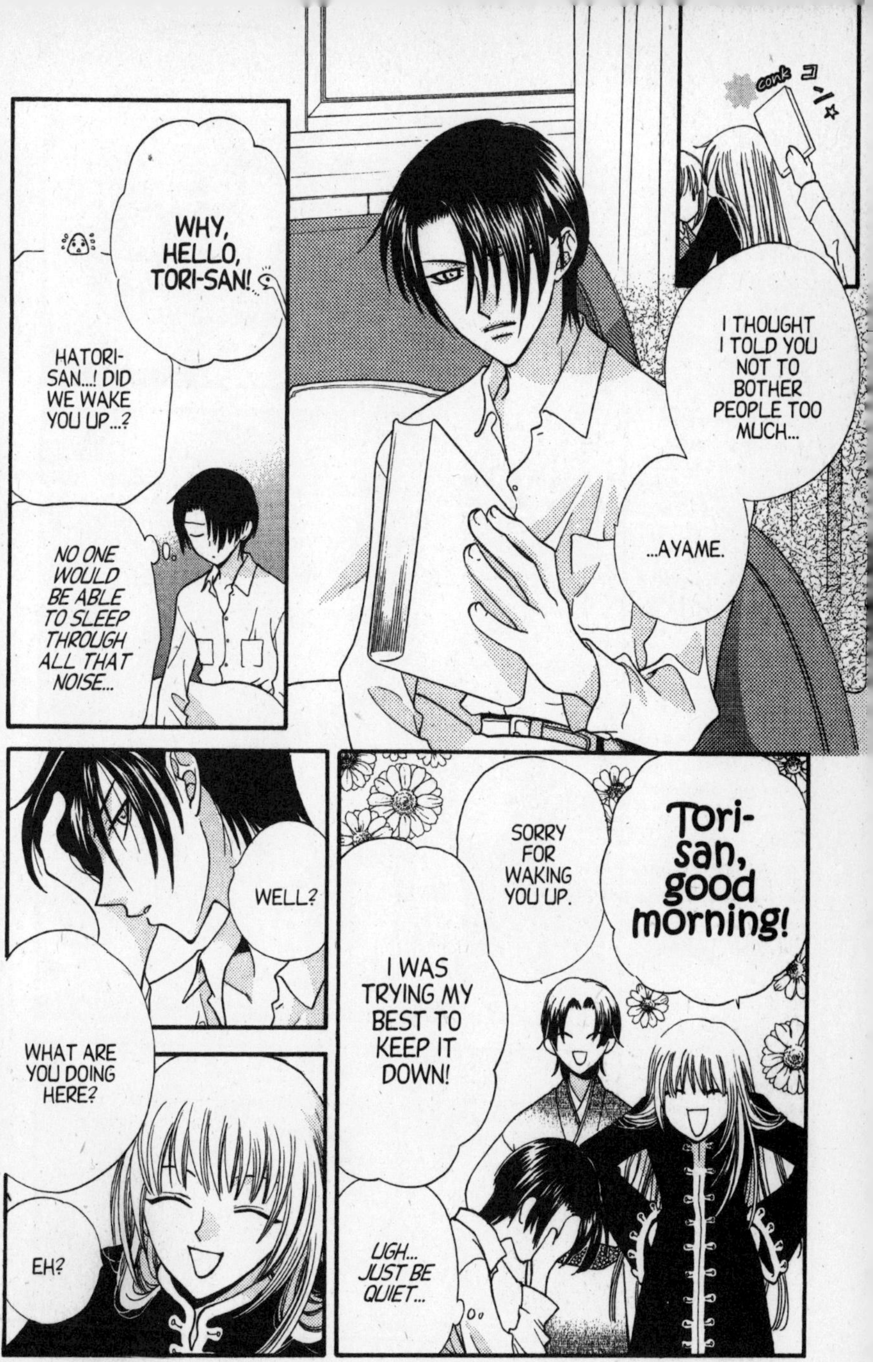
conk
I THOUGHT I TOLD YOU NOT TO BOTHER PEOPLE TOO MUCH...
...AYAME.
WHY, HELLO, TORI-SAN!
HATORI-SAN...! DID WE WAKE YOU UP...?
NO ONE WOULD BE ABLE TO SLEEP THROUGH ALL THAT NOISE...
Tori-san, good morning!
SORRY FOR WAKING YOU UP.
I WAS TRYING MY BEST TO KEEP IT DOWN!
UGH... JUST BE QUIET...
WELL?
WHAT ARE YOU DOING HERE?
EH?

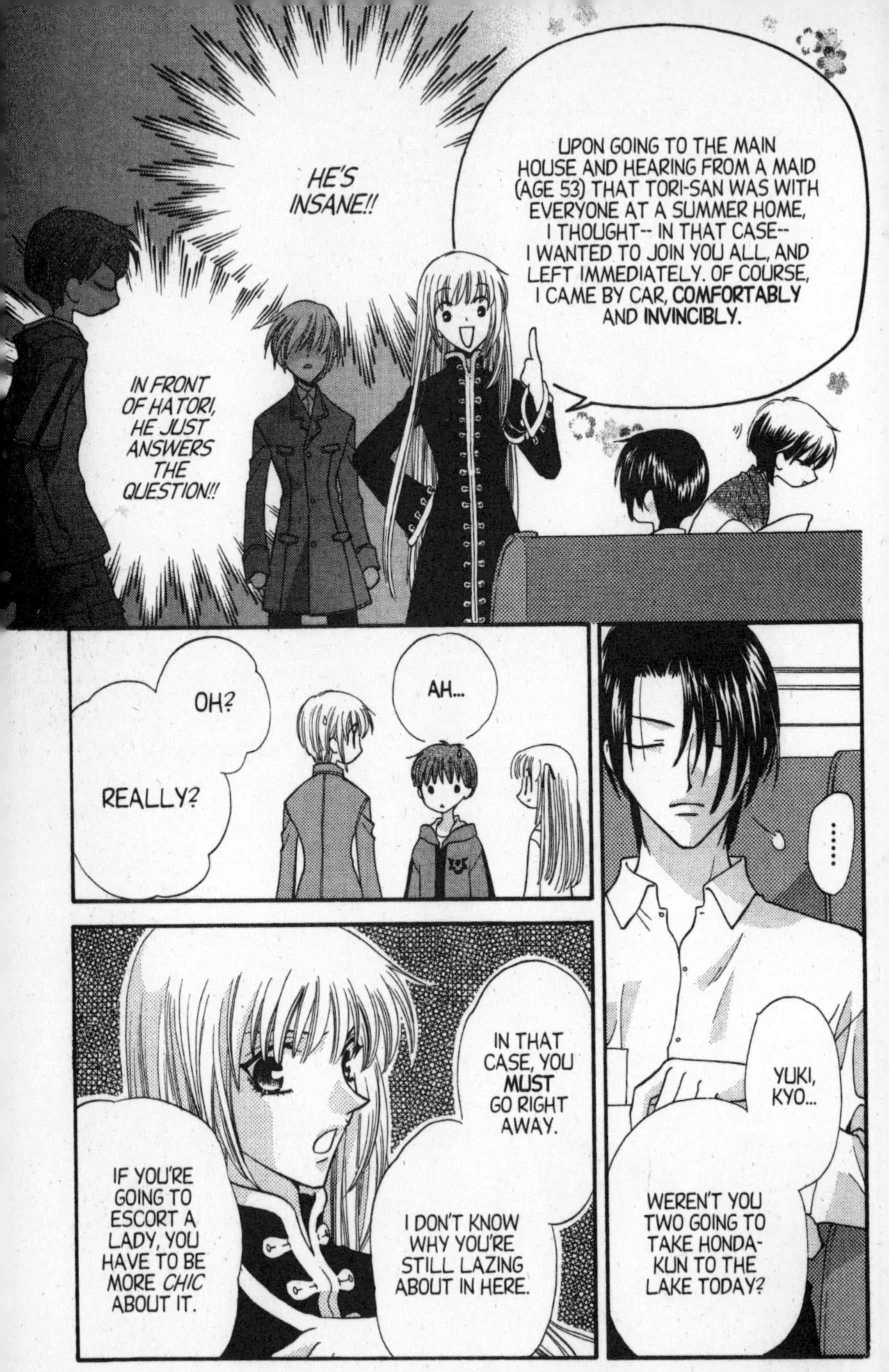

UPON GOING TO THE MAIN HOUSE AND HEARING FROM A MAID (AGE 53) THAT TORI-SAN WAS WITH EVERYONE AT A SUMMER HOME, I THOUGHT-- IN THAT CASE-- I WANTED TO JOIN YOU ALL, AND LEFT IMMEDIATELY. OF COURSE, I CAME BY CAR, **COMFORTABLY** AND **INVINCIBLY.**
HE'S INSANE!!
IN FRONT OF HATORI, HE JUST ANSWERS THE QUESTION!!
......
YUKI, KYO...
WEREN'T YOU TWO GOING TO TAKE HONDA-KUN TO THE LAKE TODAY?
AH...
OH?
REALLY?
IN THAT CASE, YOU **MUST** GO RIGHT AWAY.
I DON'T KNOW WHY YOU'RE STILL LAZING ABOUT IN HERE.
IF YOU'RE GOING TO ESCORT A LADY, YOU HAVE TO BE MORE *CHIC* ABOUT IT.

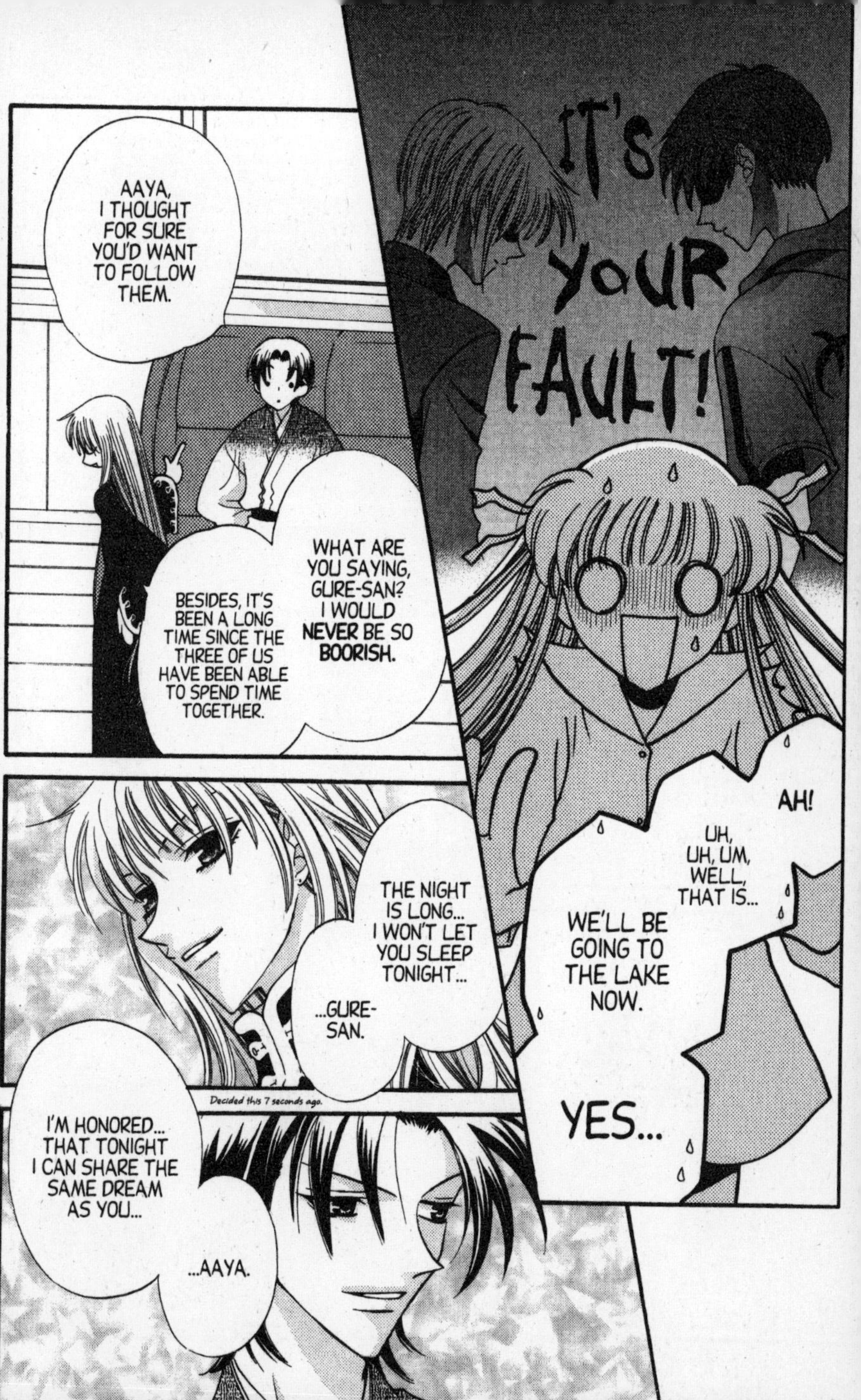
IT'S YOUR FAULT!
AH!
UH, UH, UM, WELL, THAT IS...
WE'LL BE GOING TO THE LAKE NOW.
YES...
AAYA, I THOUGHT FOR SURE YOU'D WANT TO FOLLOW THEM.
WHAT ARE YOU SAYING, GURE-SAN? I WOULD **NEVER** BE SO **BOORISH.**
BESIDES, IT'S BEEN A LONG TIME SINCE THE THREE OF US HAVE BEEN ABLE TO SPEND TIME TOGETHER.
THE NIGHT IS LONG... I WON'T LET YOU SLEEP TONIGHT...
...GURE-SAN.
Decided this 7 seconds ago.
I'M HONORED... THAT TONIGHT I CAN SHARE THE SAME DREAM AS YOU...
...AAYA.

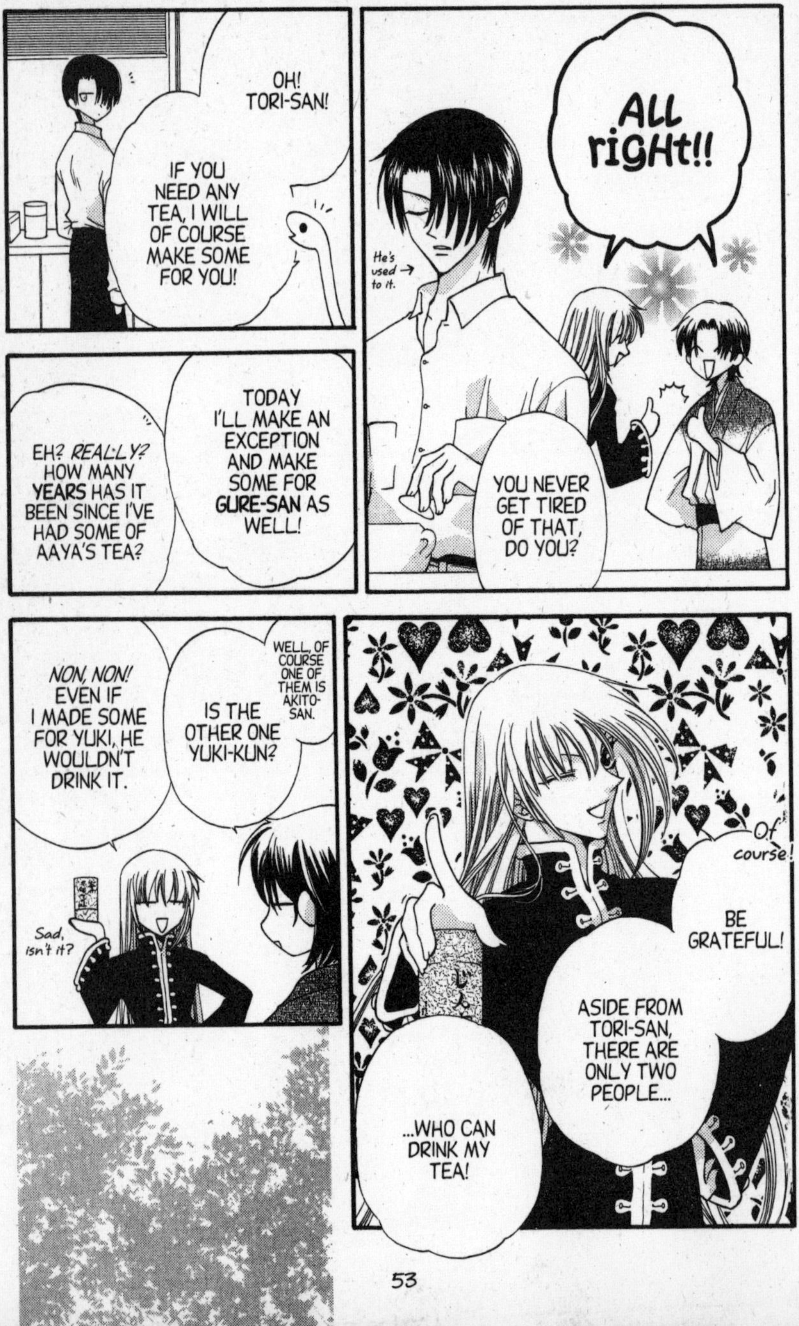
ALL RIGHT!!
He's used to it.
YOU NEVER GET TIRED OF THAT, DO YOU?
OH! TORI-SAN!
IF YOU NEED ANY TEA, I WILL OF COURSE MAKE SOME FOR YOU!
TODAY I'LL MAKE AN EXCEPTION AND MAKE SOME FOR **GURE-SAN** AS WELL!
EH? *REALLY?* HOW MANY **YEARS** HAS IT BEEN SINCE I'VE HAD SOME OF AAYA'S TEA?
Of course!
BE GRATEFUL!
ASIDE FROM TORI-SAN, THERE ARE ONLY TWO PEOPLE...
...WHO CAN DRINK MY TEA!
WELL, OF COURSE ONE OF THEM IS AKITO-SAN.
IS THE OTHER ONE YUKI-KUN?
*NON, NON!* EVEN IF I MADE SOME FOR YUKI, HE WOULDN'T DRINK IT.
Sad, isn't it?

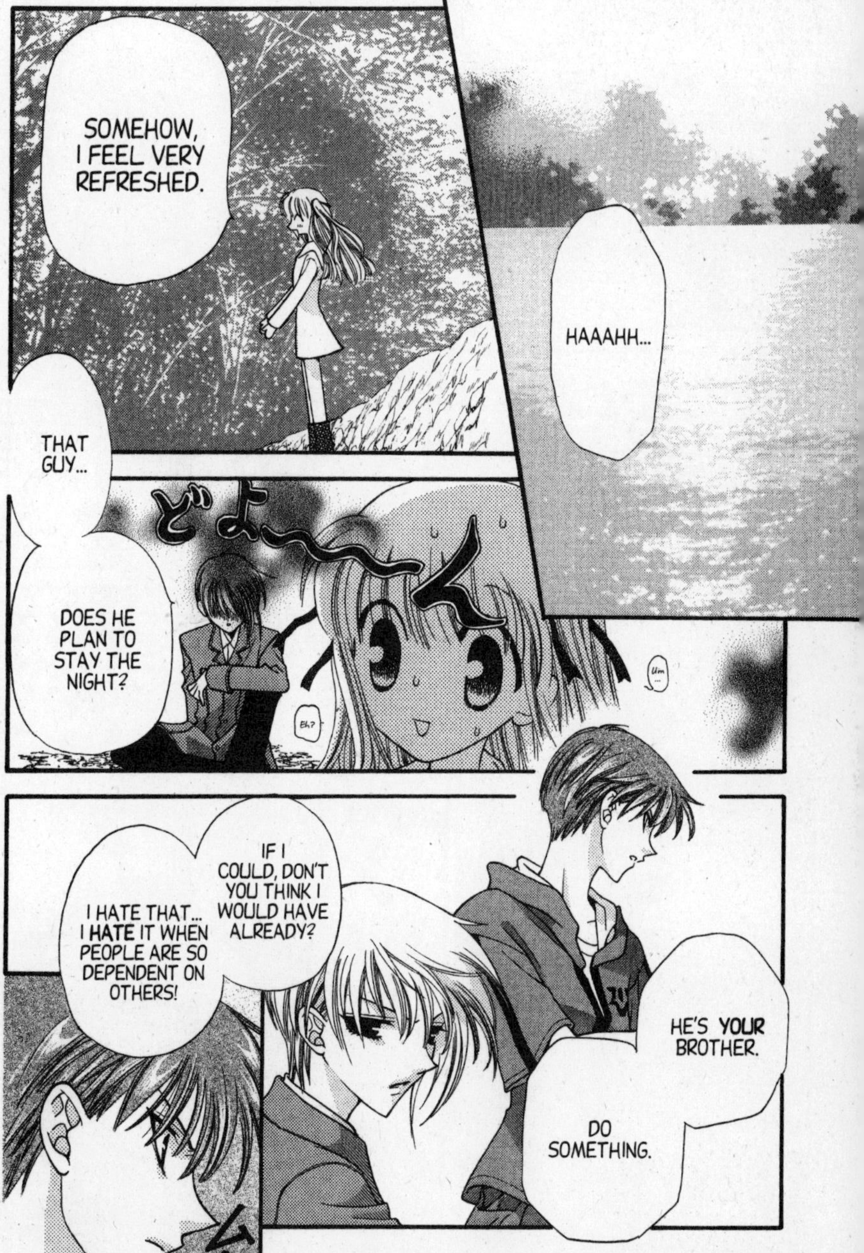
HAAAHH...
SOMEHOW, I FEEL VERY REFRESHED.
どよ〜〜ん
Um...
THAT GUY...
DOES HE PLAN TO STAY THE NIGHT?
Eh?
HE'S **YOUR** BROTHER.
DO SOMETHING.
IF I COULD, DON'T YOU THINK I WOULD HAVE ALREADY?
I HATE THAT... I **HATE** IT WHEN PEOPLE ARE SO DEPENDENT ON OTHERS!
ムカッ

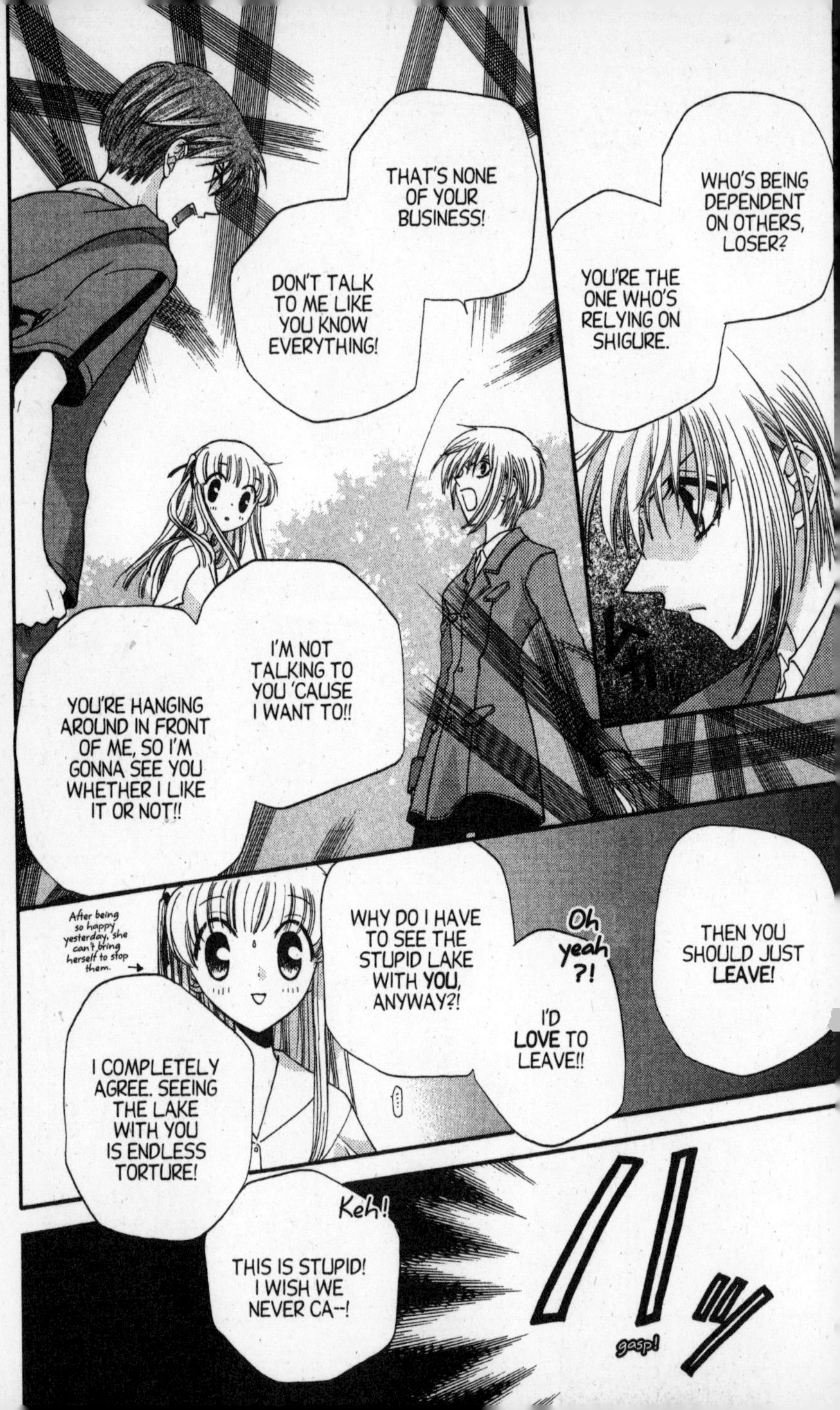
WHO'S BEING DEPENDENT ON OTHERS, LOSER?
YOU'RE THE ONE WHO'S RELYING ON SHIGURE.
THAT'S NONE OF YOUR BUSINESS!
DON'T TALK TO ME LIKE YOU KNOW EVERYTHING!
I'M NOT TALKING TO YOU 'CAUSE I WANT TO!!
YOU'RE HANGING AROUND IN FRONT OF ME, SO I'M GONNA SEE YOU WHETHER I LIKE IT OR NOT!!
THEN YOU SHOULD JUST LEAVE!
Oh yeah?!
I'D LOVE TO LEAVE!!
WHY DO I HAVE TO SEE THE STUPID LAKE WITH YOU, ANYWAY?!
After being so happy yesterday, she can't bring herself to stop them.
I COMPLETELY AGREE. SEEING THE LAKE WITH YOU IS ENDLESS TORTURE!
Keh!
THIS IS STUPID! I WISH WE NEVER CA--!
gasp!

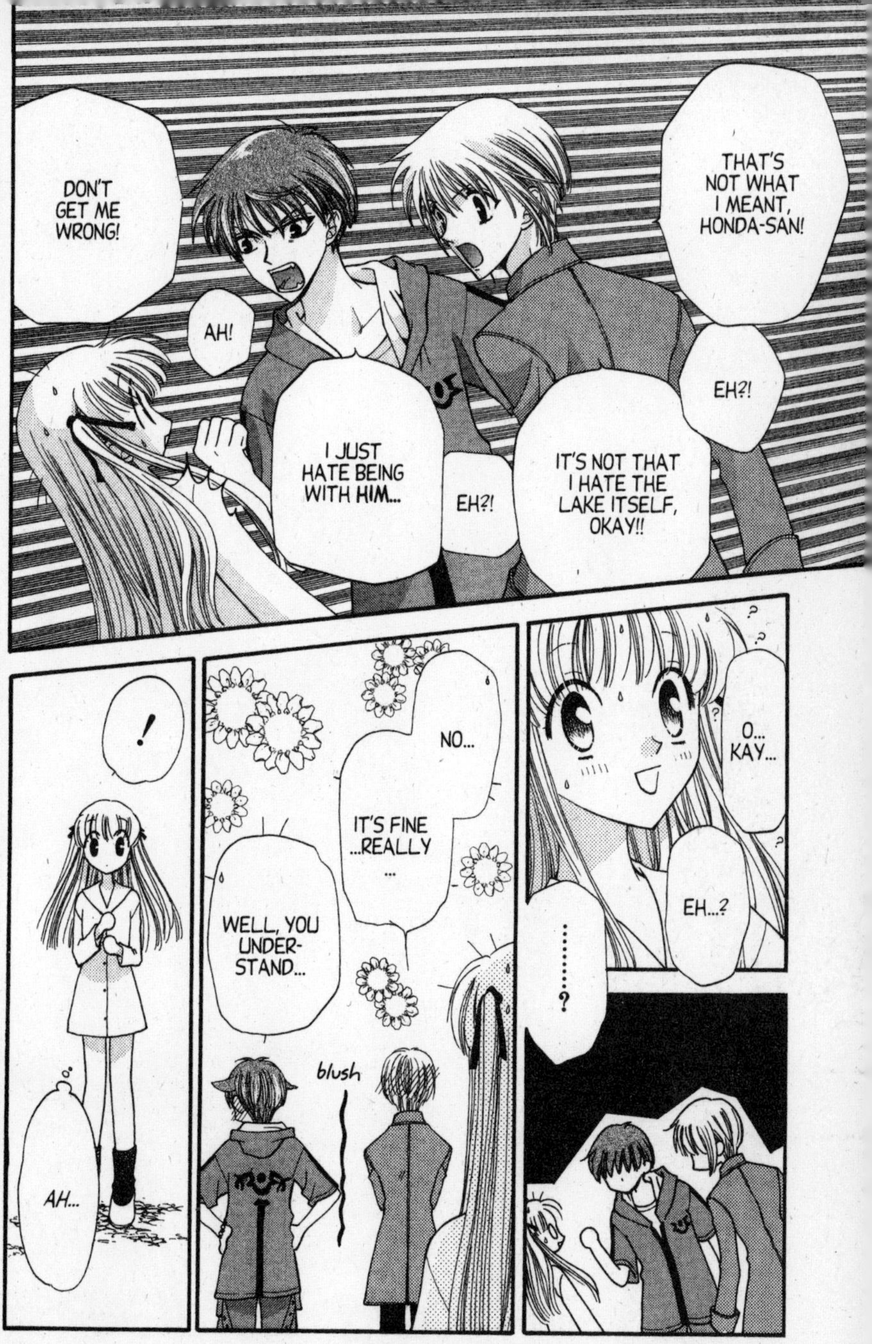
THAT'S NOT WHAT I MEANT, HONDA-SAN!
DON'T GET ME WRONG!
EH?!
AH!
IT'S NOT THAT I HATE THE LAKE ITSELF, OKAY!!
EH?!
I JUST HATE BEING WITH HIM...
O... KAY...
EH...?
......?
NO...
IT'S FINE ...REALLY ...
WELL, YOU UNDER-STAND...
blush
!
AH...

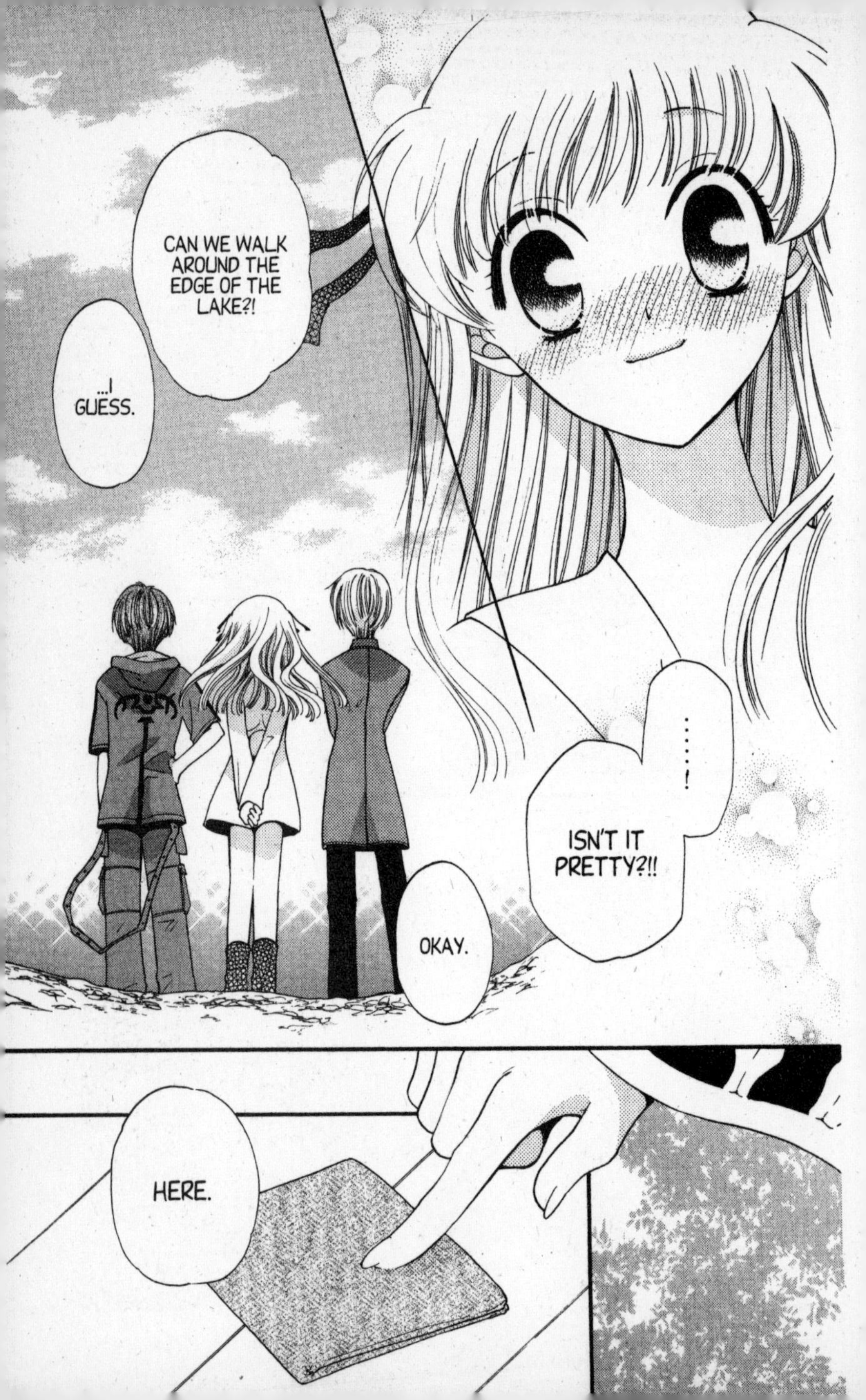
......!
ISN'T IT PRETTY?!!
CAN WE WALK AROUND THE EDGE OF THE LAKE?!
...I GUESS.
OKAY.
HERE.

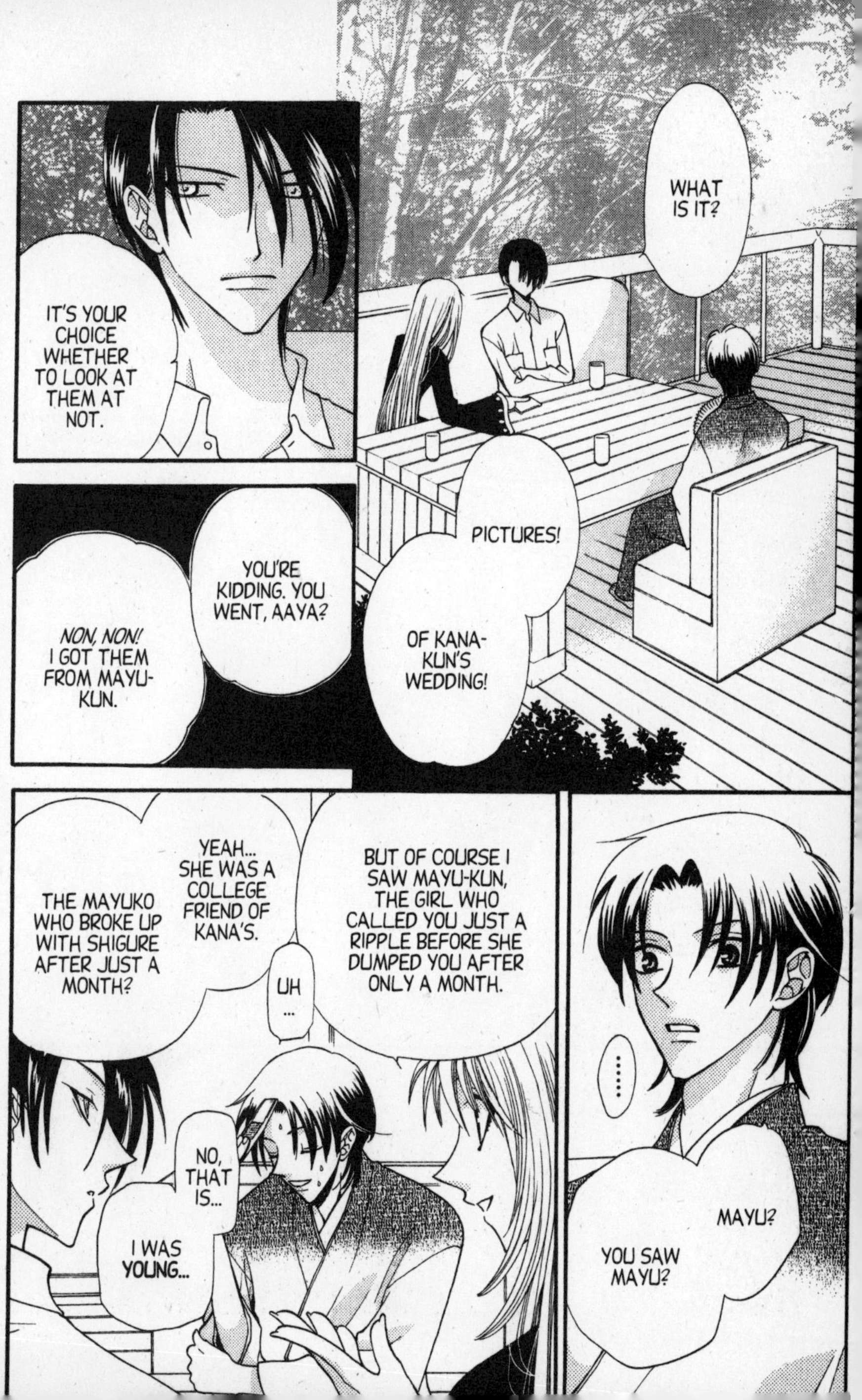
WHAT IS IT?
PICTURES!
OF KANA-KUN'S WEDDING!
IT'S YOUR CHOICE WHETHER TO LOOK AT THEM AT NOT.
YOU'RE KIDDING. YOU WENT, AAYA?
*NON, NON!* I GOT THEM FROM MAYU-KUN.
......
MAYU?
YOU SAW MAYU?
BUT OF COURSE I SAW MAYU-KUN, THE GIRL WHO CALLED YOU JUST A RIPPLE BEFORE SHE DUMPED YOU AFTER ONLY A MONTH.
YEAH... SHE WAS A COLLEGE FRIEND OF KANA'S.
THE MAYUKO WHO BROKE UP WITH SHIGURE AFTER JUST A MONTH?
UH ...
NO, THAT IS...
I WAS YOUNG...

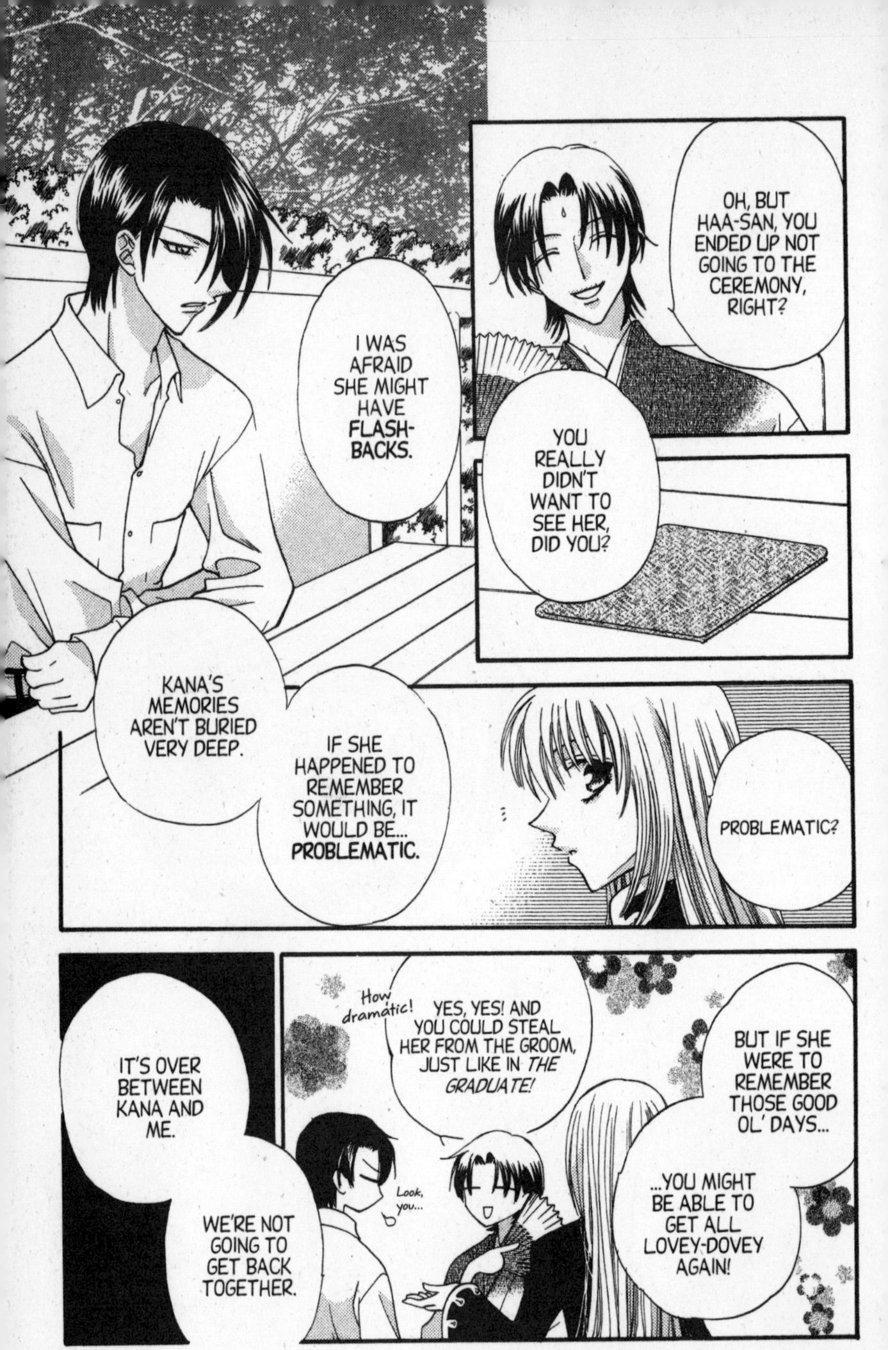
OH, BUT HAA-SAN, YOU ENDED UP NOT GOING TO THE CEREMONY, RIGHT?
YOU REALLY DIDN'T WANT TO SEE HER, DID YOU?
I WAS AFRAID SHE MIGHT HAVE FLASHBACKS.
KANA'S MEMORIES AREN'T BURIED VERY DEEP.
IF SHE HAPPENED TO REMEMBER SOMETHING, IT WOULD BE... PROBLEMATIC.
PROBLEMATIC?
BUT IF SHE WERE TO REMEMBER THOSE GOOD OL' DAYS...
...YOU MIGHT BE ABLE TO GET ALL LOVEY-DOVEY AGAIN!
How dramatic!
YES, YES! AND YOU COULD STEAL HER FROM THE GROOM, JUST LIKE IN THE GRADUATE!
Look, you...
IT'S OVER BETWEEN KANA AND ME.
WE'RE NOT GOING TO GET BACK TOGETHER.

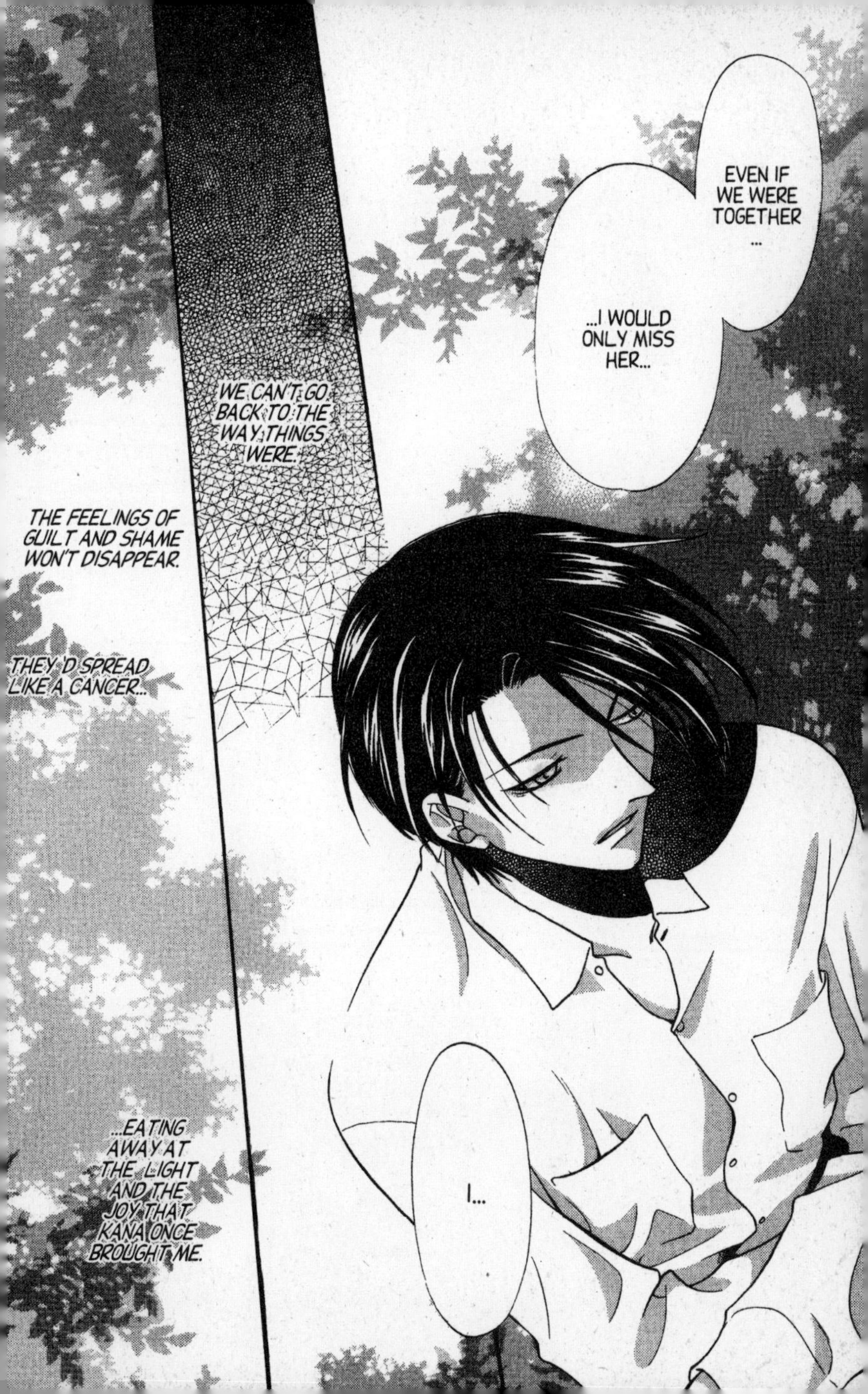
EVEN IF WE WERE TOGETHER ...
...I WOULD ONLY MISS HER...
WE CAN'T GO BACK TO THE WAY THINGS WERE.
THE FEELINGS OF GUILT AND SHAME WON'T DISAPPEAR.
THEY'D SPREAD LIKE A CANCER...
...EATING AWAY AT THE LIGHT AND THE JOY THAT KANA ONCE BROUGHT ME.
I...

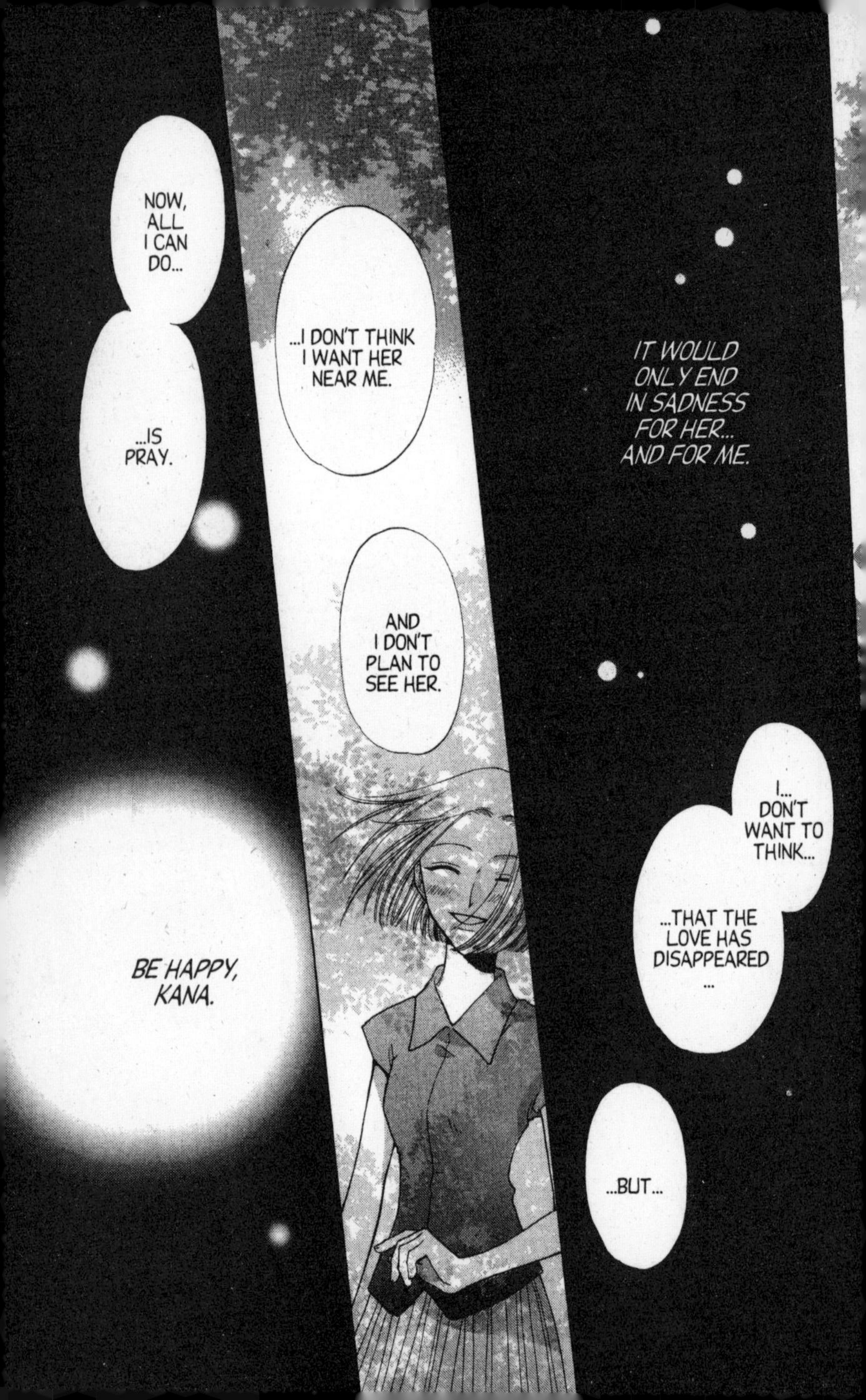
IT WOULD ONLY END IN SADNESS FOR HER... AND FOR ME.
I... DON'T WANT TO THINK...
...THAT THE LOVE HAS DISAPPEARED ...
...BUT...
...I DON'T THINK I WANT HER NEAR ME.
AND I DON'T PLAN TO SEE HER.
NOW, ALL I CAN DO...
...IS PRAY.
BE HAPPY, KANA.

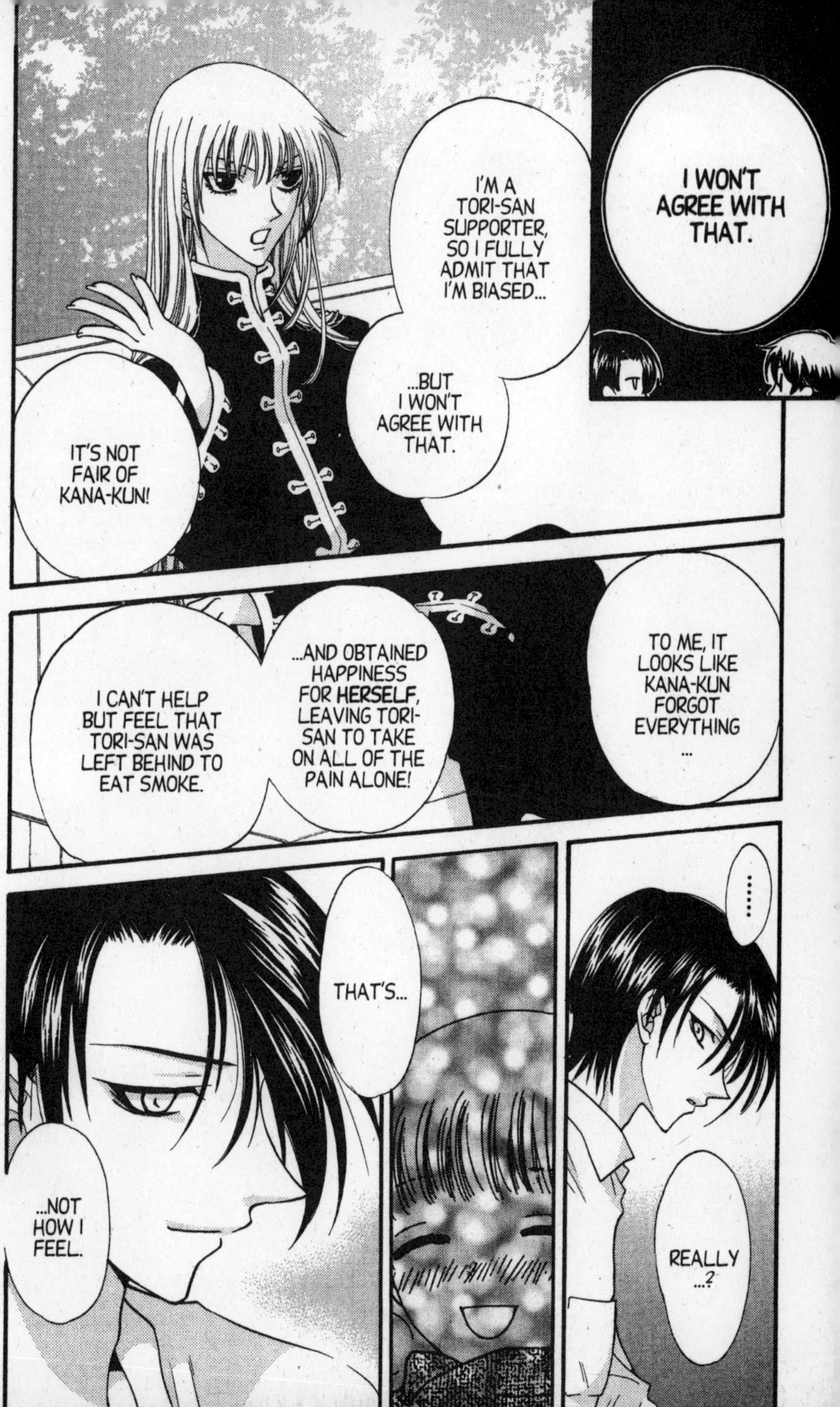
I WON'T AGREE WITH THAT.
I'M A TORI-SAN SUPPORTER, SO I FULLY ADMIT THAT I'M BIASED...
...BUT I WON'T AGREE WITH THAT.
IT'S NOT FAIR OF KANA-KUN!
TO ME, IT LOOKS LIKE KANA-KUN FORGOT EVERYTHING ...
...AND OBTAINED HAPPINESS FOR **HERSELF**, LEAVING TORI-SAN TO TAKE ON ALL OF THE PAIN ALONE!
I CAN'T HELP BUT FEEL THAT TORI-SAN WAS LEFT BEHIND TO EAT SMOKE.
......
REALLY ...?
THAT'S...
...NOT HOW I FEEL.

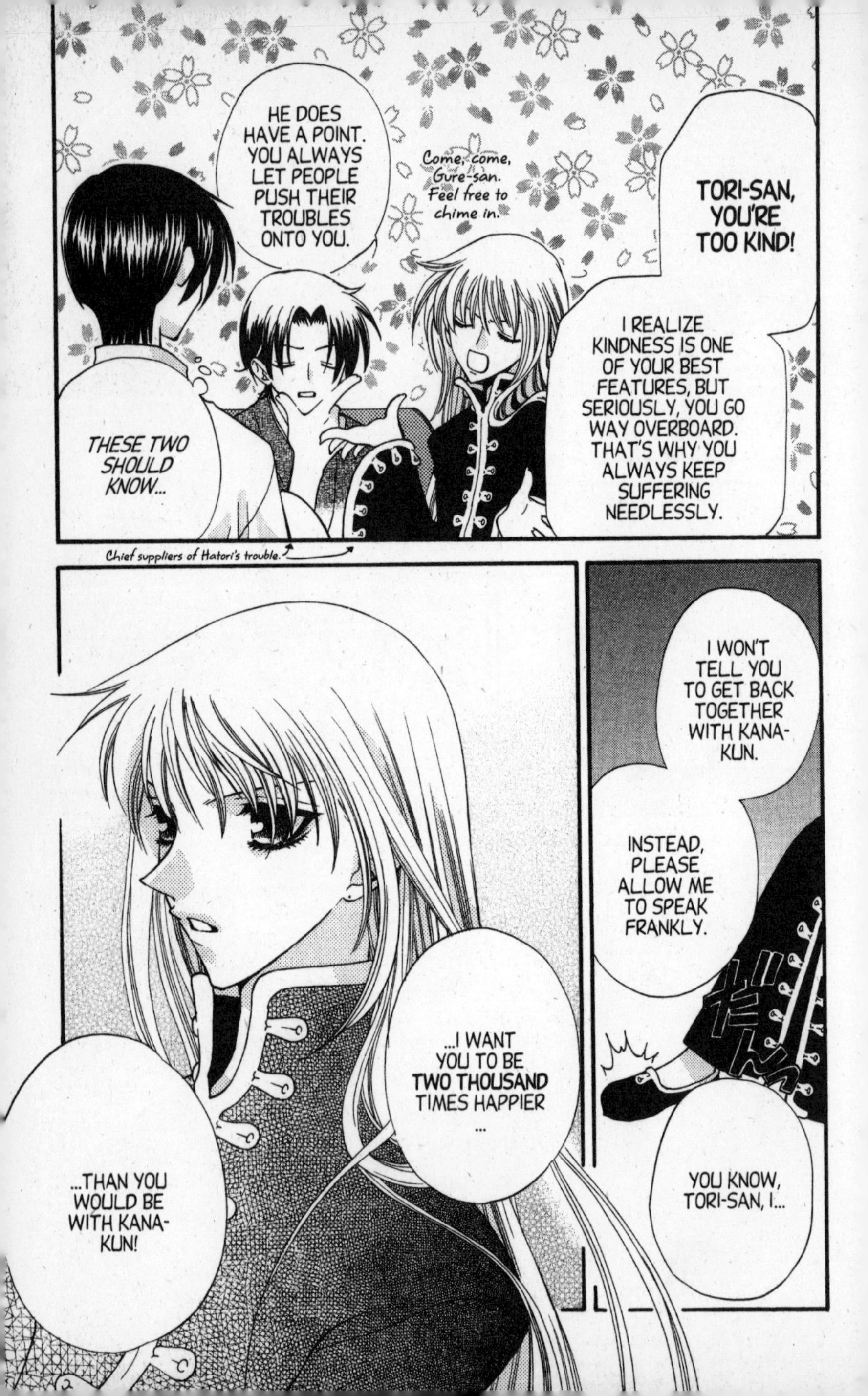
TORI-SAN, YOU'RE TOO KIND!
I REALIZE KINDNESS IS ONE OF YOUR BEST FEATURES, BUT SERIOUSLY, YOU GO WAY OVERBOARD. THAT'S WHY YOU ALWAYS KEEP SUFFERING NEEDLESSLY.
Come, come, Gure-san. Feel free to chime in.
HE DOES HAVE A POINT. YOU ALWAYS LET PEOPLE PUSH THEIR TROUBLES ONTO YOU.
THESE TWO SHOULD KNOW...
Chief suppliers of Hatori's trouble.
I WON'T TELL YOU TO GET BACK TOGETHER WITH KANA-KUN.
INSTEAD, PLEASE ALLOW ME TO SPEAK FRANKLY.
YOU KNOW, TORI-SAN, I...
...I WANT YOU TO BE TWO THOUSAND TIMES HAPPIER ...
...THAN YOU WOULD BE WITH KANA-KUN!

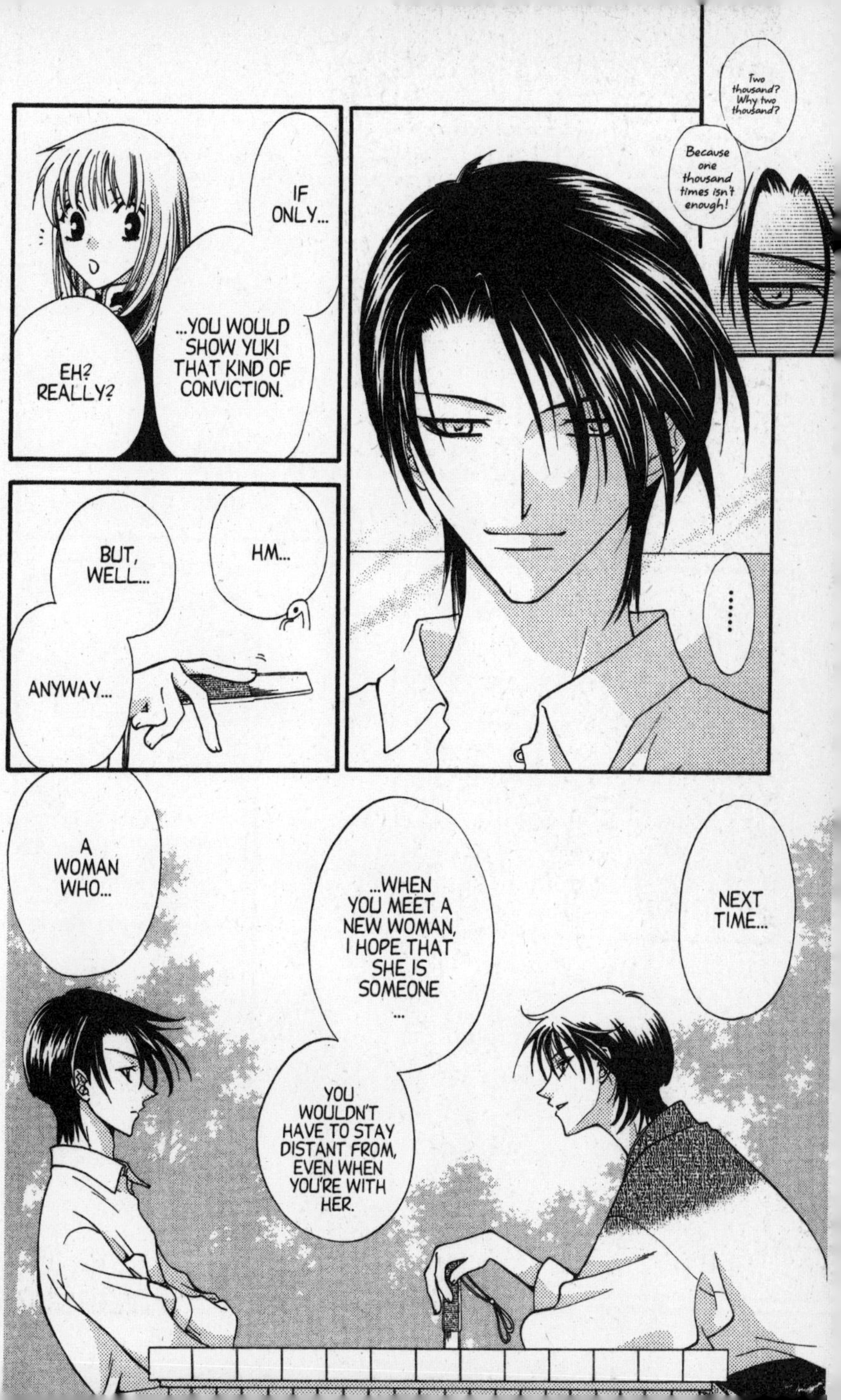
Two thousand? Why two thousand?
Because one thousand times isn't enough!
......
IF ONLY...
...YOU WOULD SHOW YUKI THAT KIND OF CONVICTION.
EH? REALLY?
HM...
BUT, WELL...
ANYWAY...
NEXT TIME...
...WHEN YOU MEET A NEW WOMAN, I HOPE THAT SHE IS SOMEONE ...
YOU WOULDN'T HAVE TO STAY DISTANT FROM, EVEN WHEN YOU'RE WITH HER.
A WOMAN WHO...

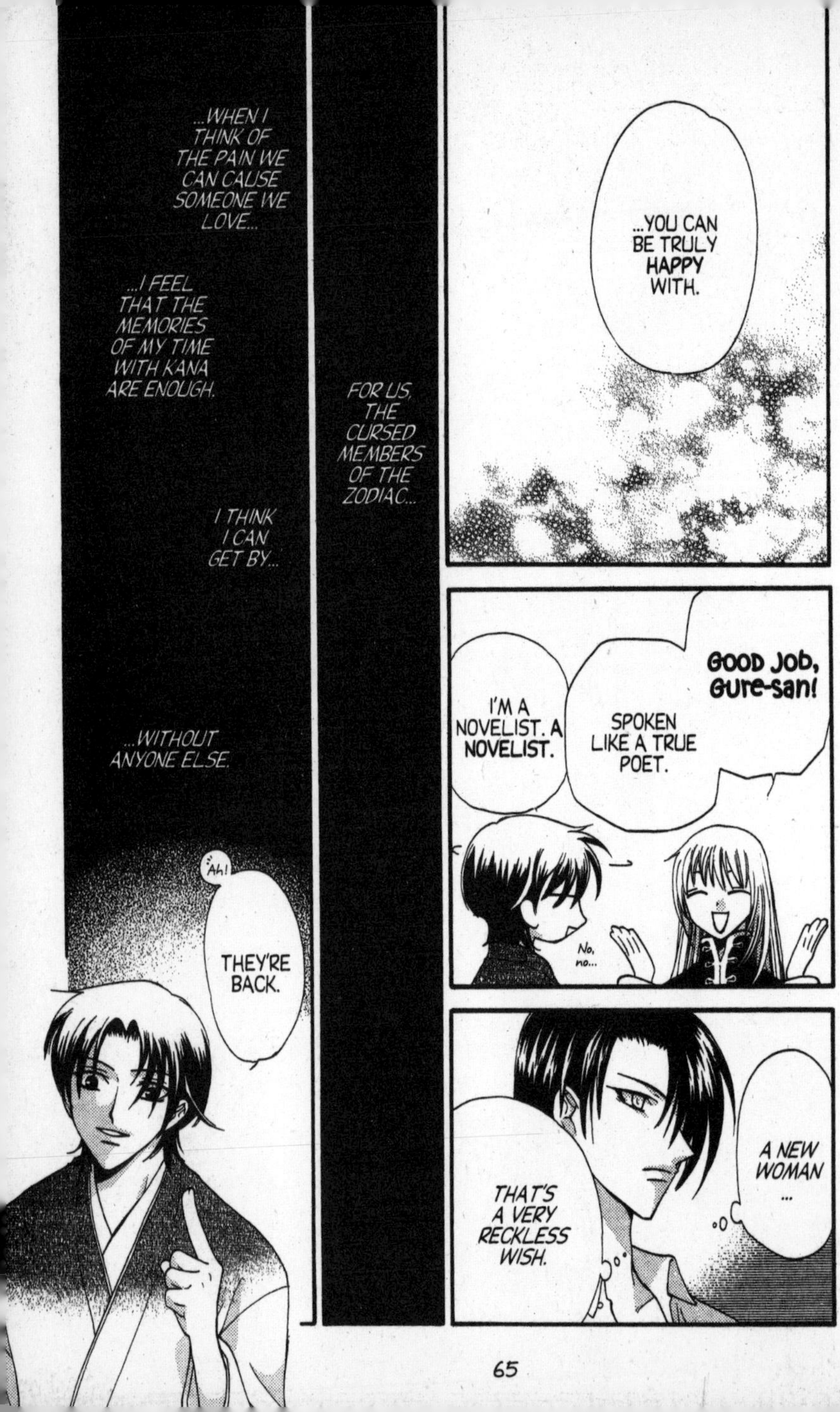
...YOU CAN BE TRULY HAPPY WITH.
GOOD JOB, GURE-SAN!
SPOKEN LIKE A TRUE POET.
I'M A NOVELIST. A NOVELIST.
No, no...
A NEW WOMAN...
THAT'S A VERY RECKLESS WISH.
FOR US, THE CURSED MEMBERS OF THE ZODIAC...
...WHEN I THINK OF THE PAIN WE CAN CAUSE SOMEONE WE LOVE...
...I FEEL THAT THE MEMORIES OF MY TIME WITH KANA ARE ENOUGH.
I THINK I CAN GET BY...
...WITHOUT ANYONE ELSE.
Ah!
THEY'RE BACK.

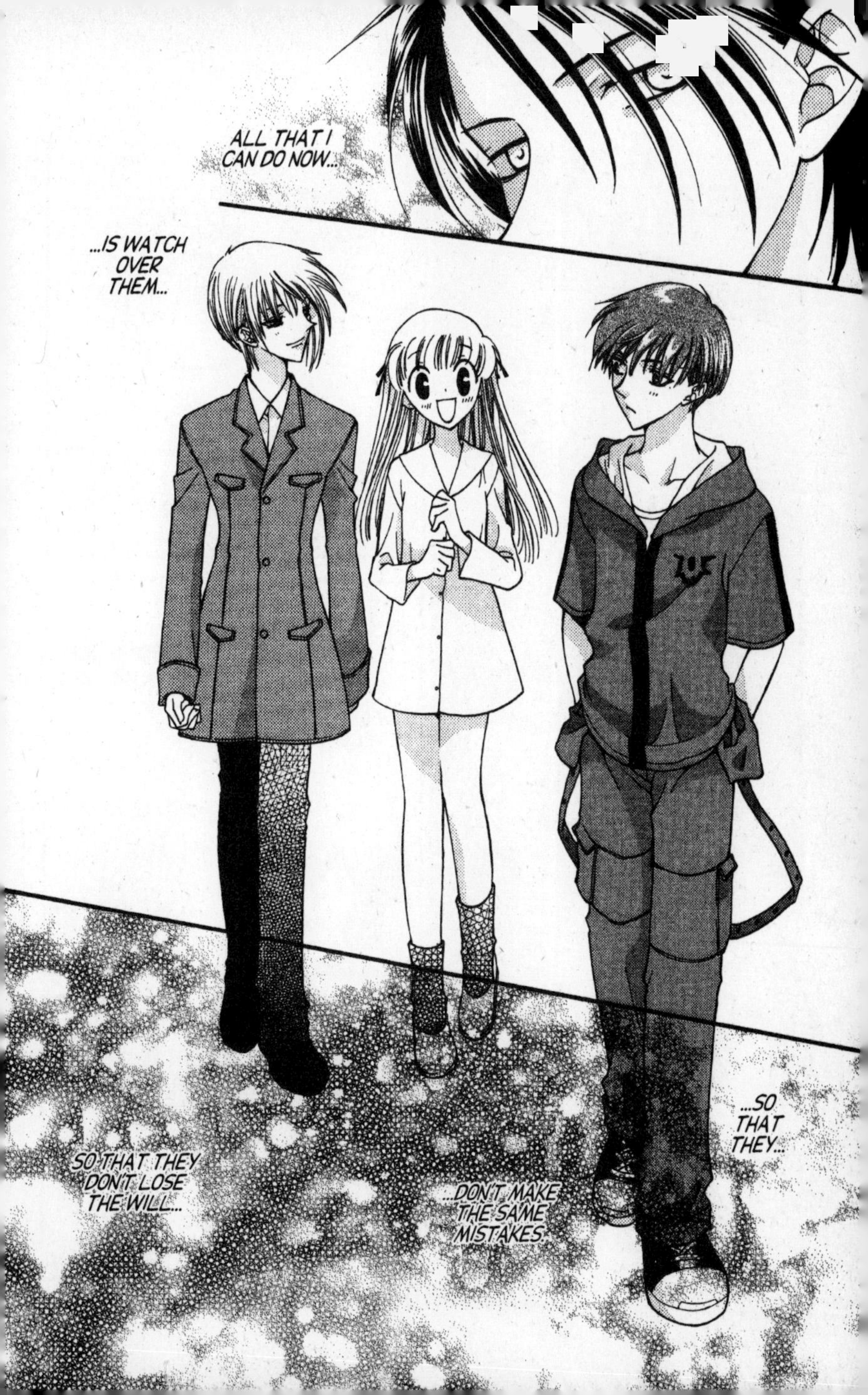
ALL THAT I CAN DO NOW...
...IS WATCH OVER THEM...
...SO THAT THEY...
...DON'T MAKE THE SAME MISTAKES.
SO THAT THEY DON'T LOSE THE WILL...

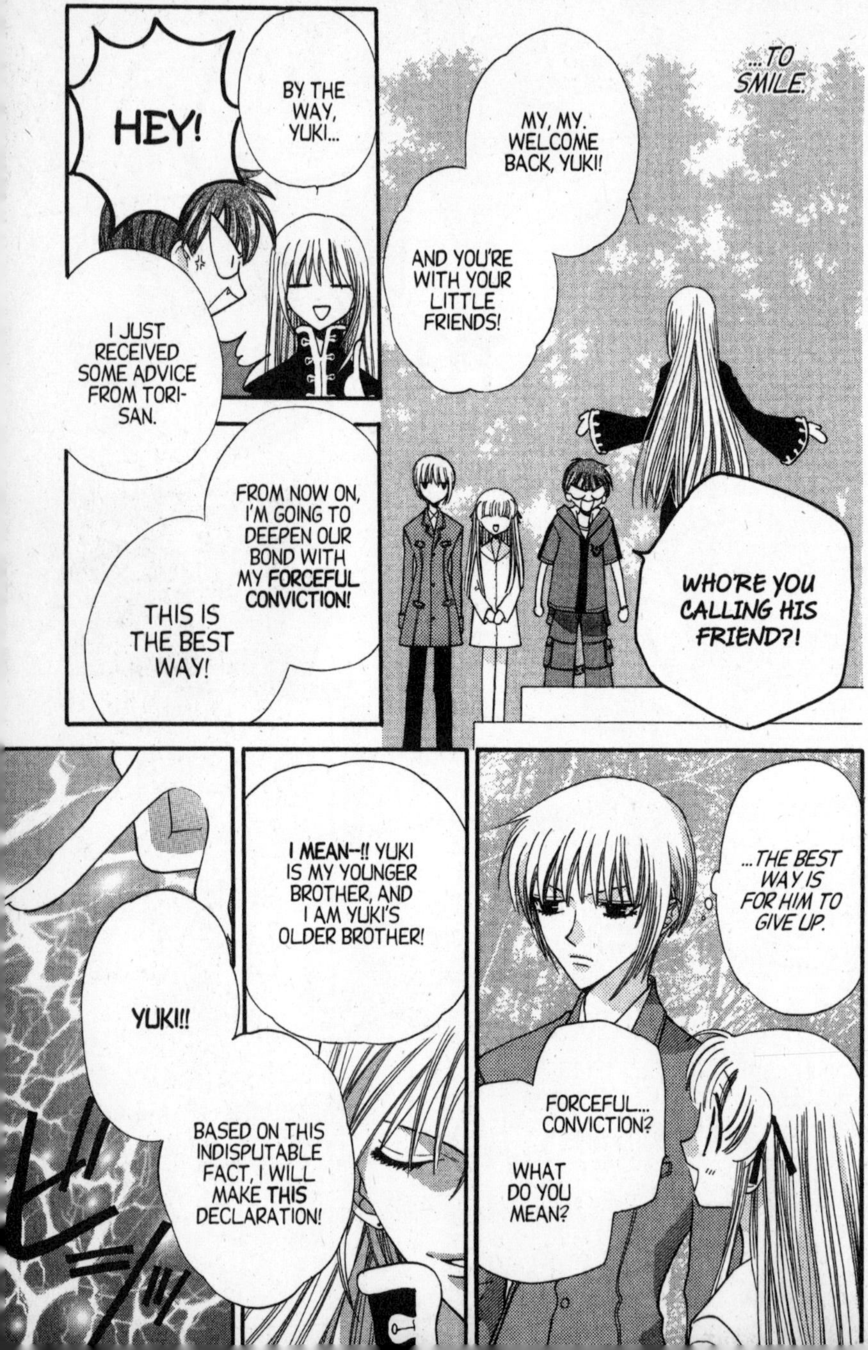
...TO SMILE.
MY, MY. WELCOME BACK, YUKI!
AND YOU'RE WITH YOUR LITTLE FRIENDS!
WHO'RE YOU CALLING HIS FRIEND?!
BY THE WAY, YUKI...
HEY!
I JUST RECEIVED SOME ADVICE FROM TORI-SAN.
FROM NOW ON, I'M GOING TO DEEPEN OUR BOND WITH MY FORCEFUL CONVICTION!
THIS IS THE BEST WAY!
...THE BEST WAY IS FOR HIM TO GIVE UP.
FORCEFUL... CONVICTION?
WHAT DO YOU MEAN?
I MEAN--!! YUKI IS MY YOUNGER BROTHER, AND I AM YUKI'S OLDER BROTHER!
BASED ON THIS INDISPUTABLE FACT, I WILL MAKE THIS DECLARATION!
YUKI!!

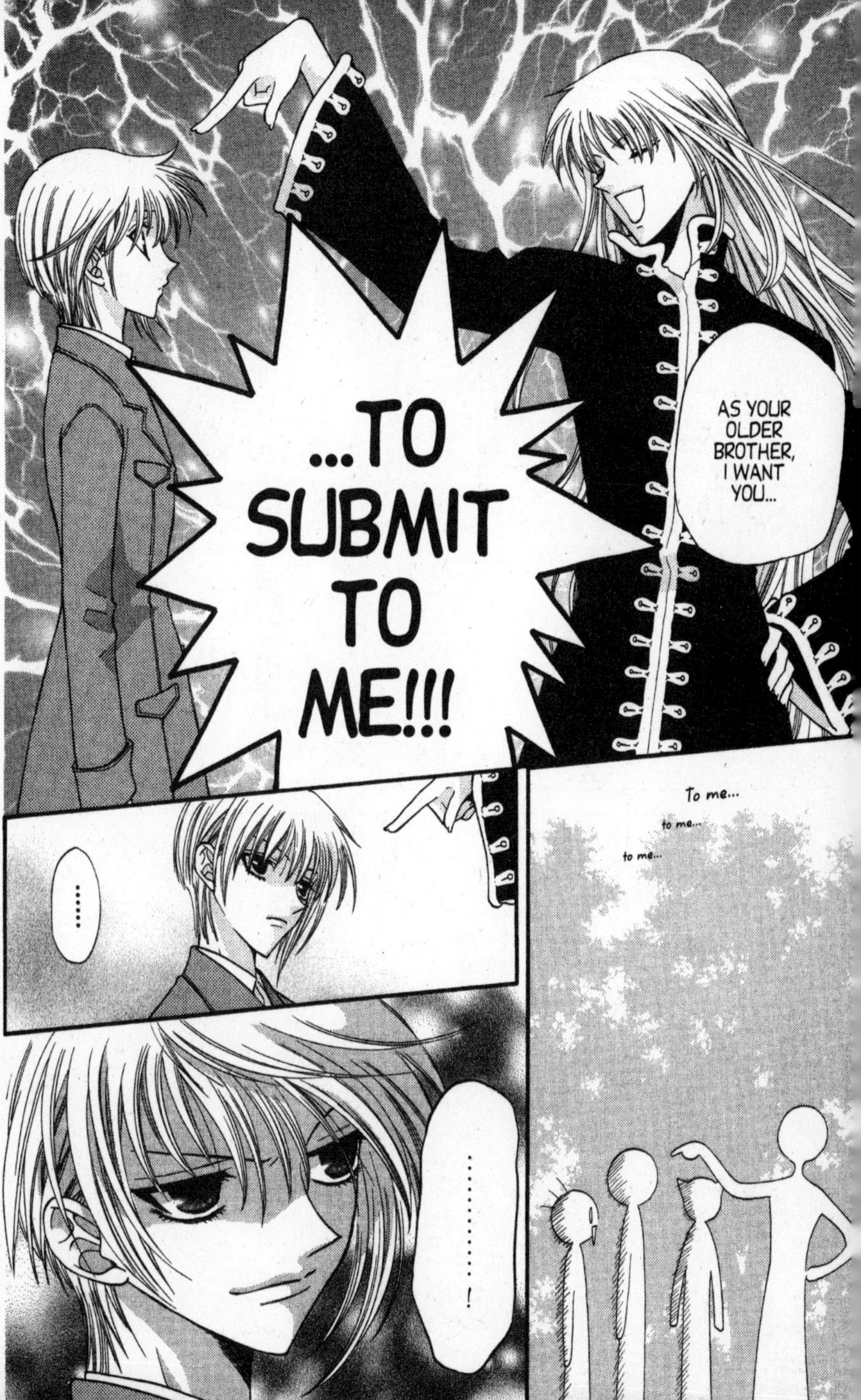
AS YOUR OLDER BROTHER, I WANT YOU...
...TO SUBMIT TO ME!!!
To me...
to me...
to me...
......
..........!

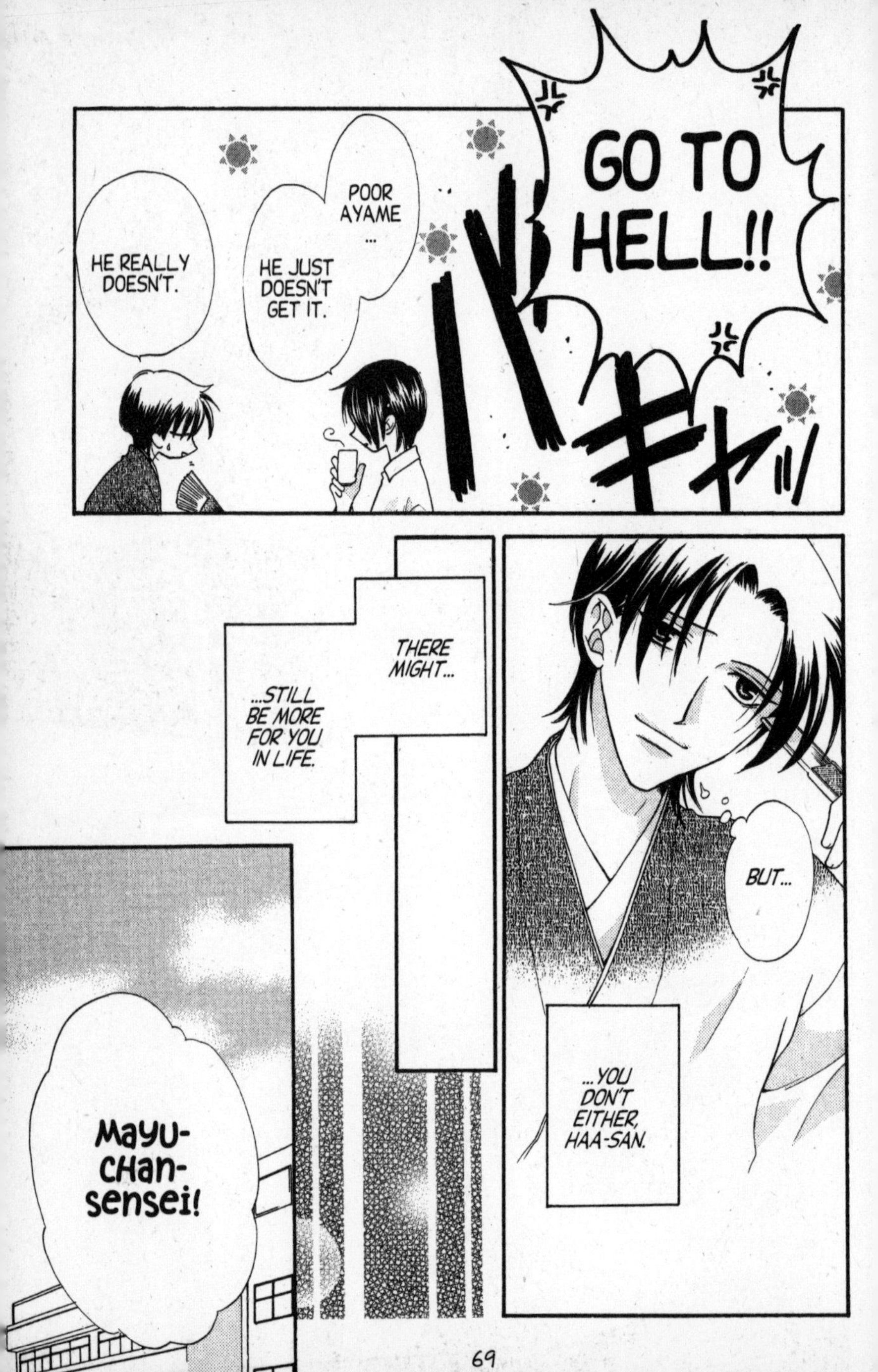
GO TO HELL!!
バキャッ
POOR AYAME ...
HE JUST DOESN'T GET IT.
HE REALLY DOESN'T.
BUT...
...YOU DON'T EITHER, HAA-SAN.
THERE MIGHT...
...STILL BE MORE FOR YOU IN LIFE.
Mayu-chan-sensei!

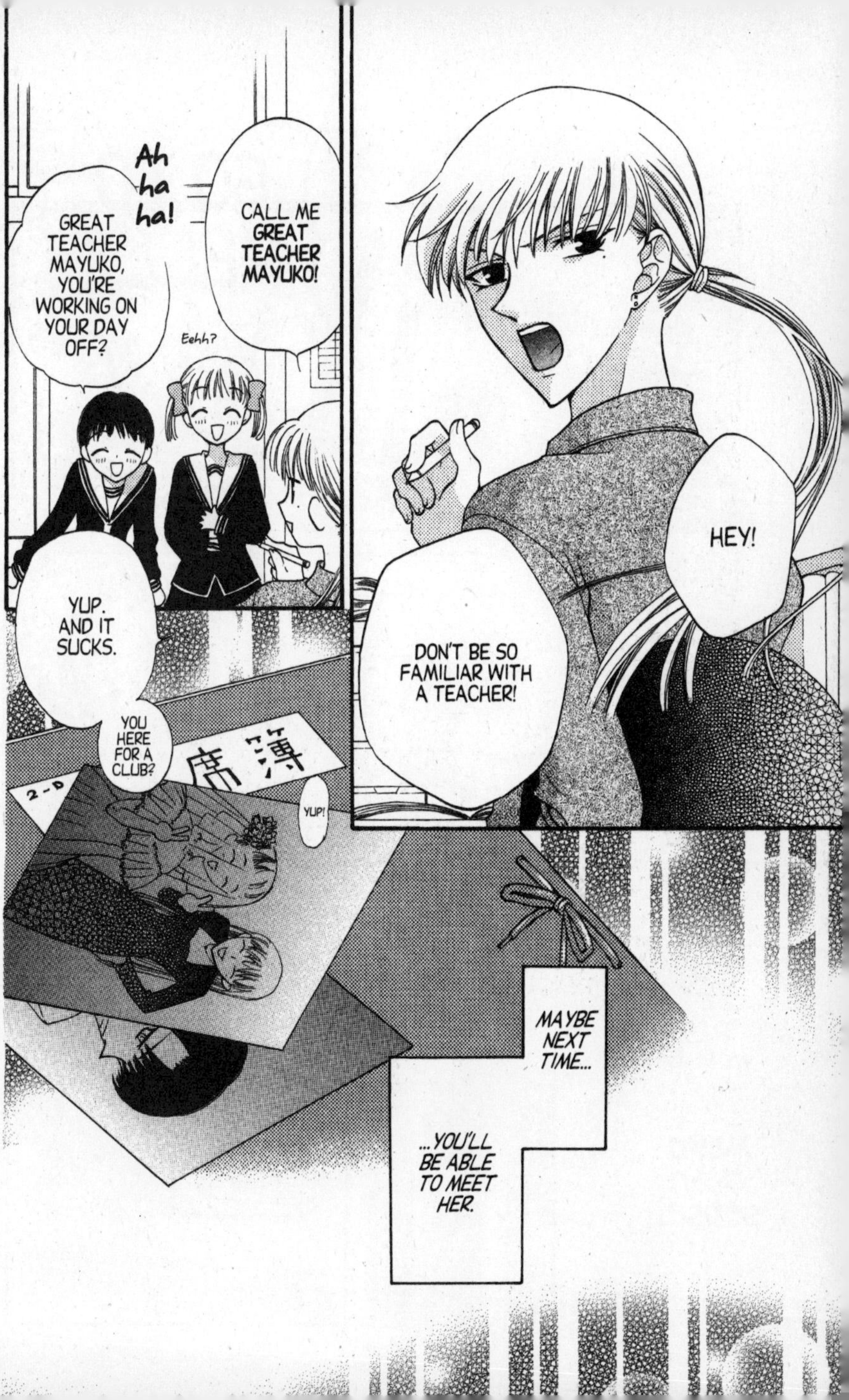
HEY!
DON'T BE SO FAMILIAR WITH A TEACHER!
CALL ME GREAT TEACHER MAYUKO!
Ah ha ha!
GREAT TEACHER MAYUKO, YOU'RE WORKING ON YOUR DAY OFF?
Eehh?
YUP. AND IT SUCKS.
YOU HERE FOR A CLUB?
YUP!
2-D
MAYBE NEXT TIME...
...YOU'LL BE ABLE TO MEET HER.

## Chapter 27

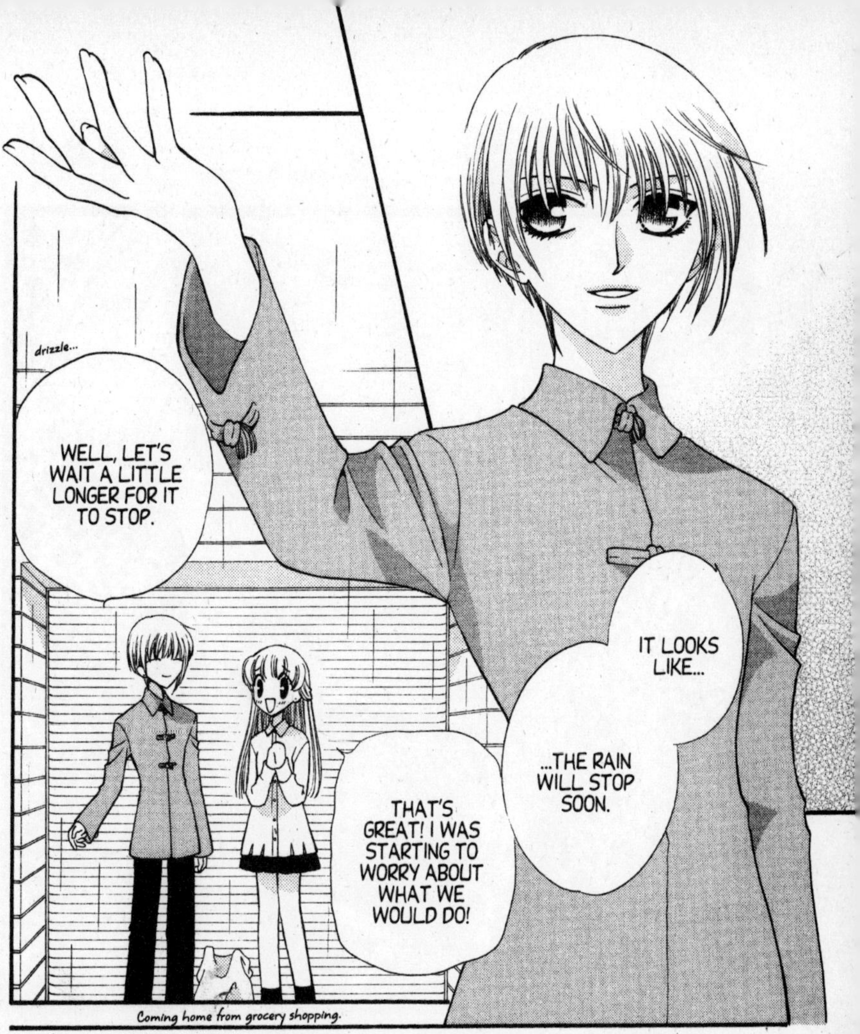
drizzle...
IT LOOKS LIKE...
...THE RAIN WILL STOP SOON.
THAT'S GREAT! I WAS STARTING TO WORRY ABOUT WHAT WE WOULD DO!
WELL, LET'S WAIT A LITTLE LONGER FOR IT TO STOP.
Coming home from grocery shopping.

## ULTRA SPECIAL BLAH BLAH BLAH 3

I feel like it's high time I introduce Kisa... Actually, now that I think of it, it's more like Yuki somehow summoned her. The way I see it, the hardships in our lives never disappear completely. There must be an exit waiting for us somewhere at the end. ...Well...I want to think that. Hmm, I wonder.

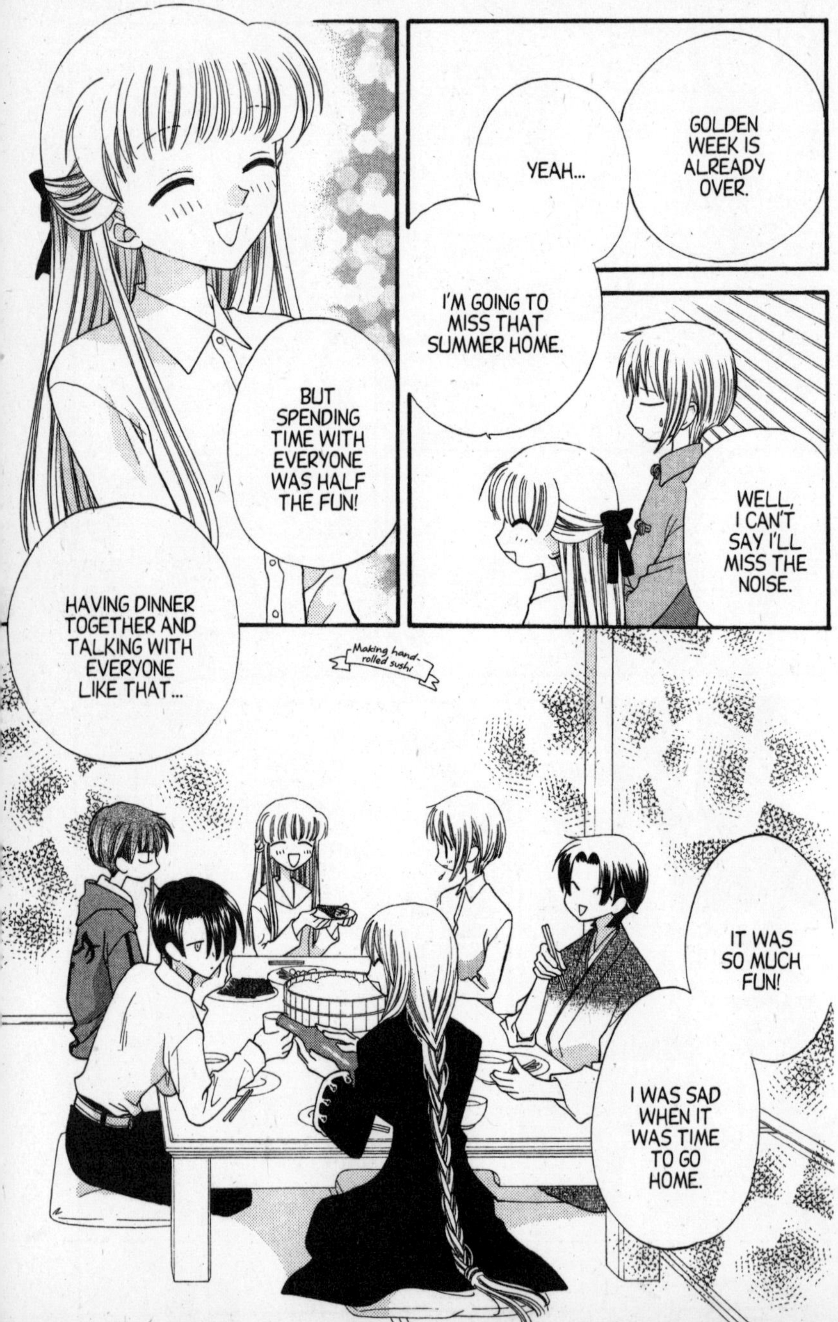
GOLDEN WEEK IS ALREADY OVER.
YEAH...
I'M GOING TO MISS THAT SUMMER HOME.
WELL, I CAN'T SAY I'LL MISS THE NOISE.
BUT SPENDING TIME WITH EVERYONE WAS HALF THE FUN!
HAVING DINNER TOGETHER AND TALKING WITH EVERYONE LIKE THAT...
Making hand-rolled sushi
IT WAS SO MUCH FUN!
I WAS SAD WHEN IT WAS TIME TO GO HOME.

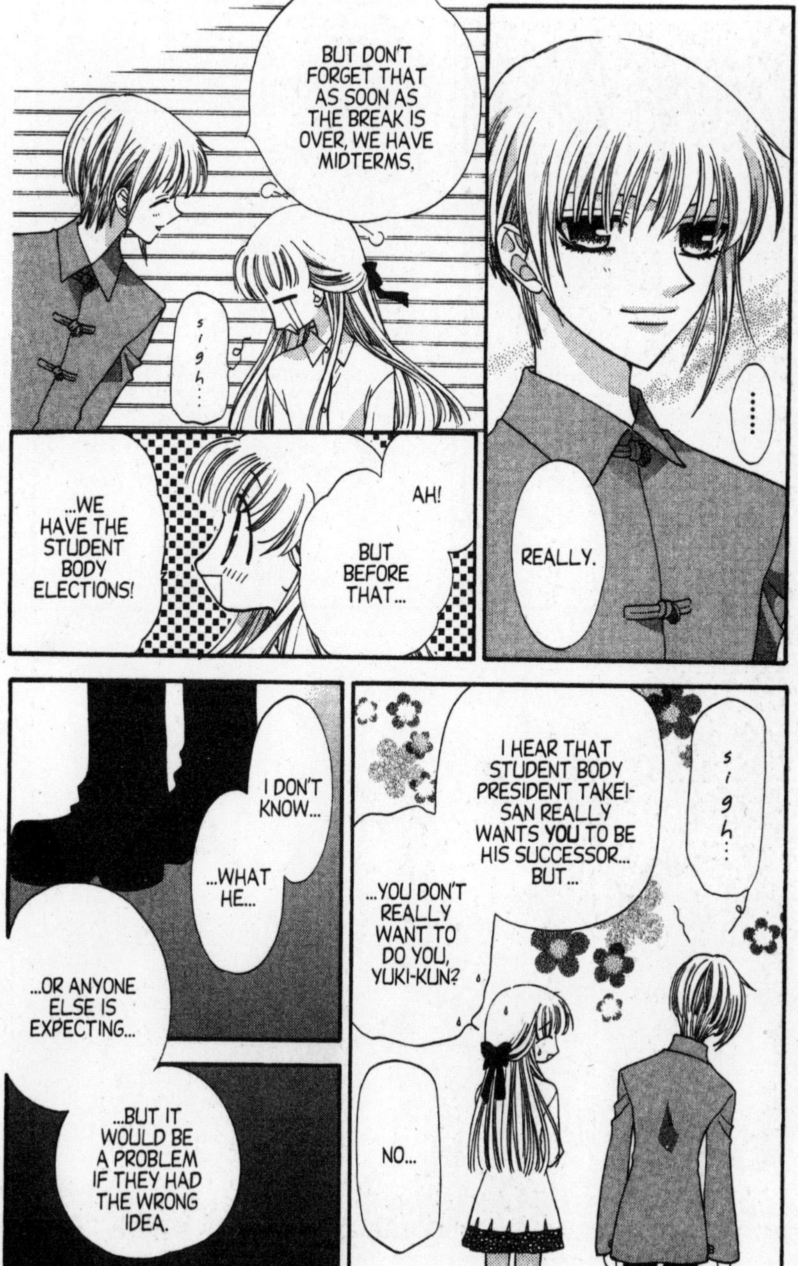
......
REALLY.
BUT DON'T FORGET THAT AS SOON AS THE BREAK IS OVER, WE HAVE MIDTERMS.
sigh...
AH!
BUT BEFORE THAT...
...WE HAVE THE STUDENT BODY ELECTIONS!
sigh...
I HEAR THAT STUDENT BODY PRESIDENT TAKEI-SAN REALLY WANTS YOU TO BE HIS SUCCESSOR... BUT...
...YOU DON'T REALLY WANT TO DO YOU, YUKI-KUN?
NO...
I DON'T KNOW...
...WHAT HE...
...OR ANYONE ELSE IS EXPECTING...
...BUT IT WOULD BE A PROBLEM IF THEY HAD THE WRONG IDEA.

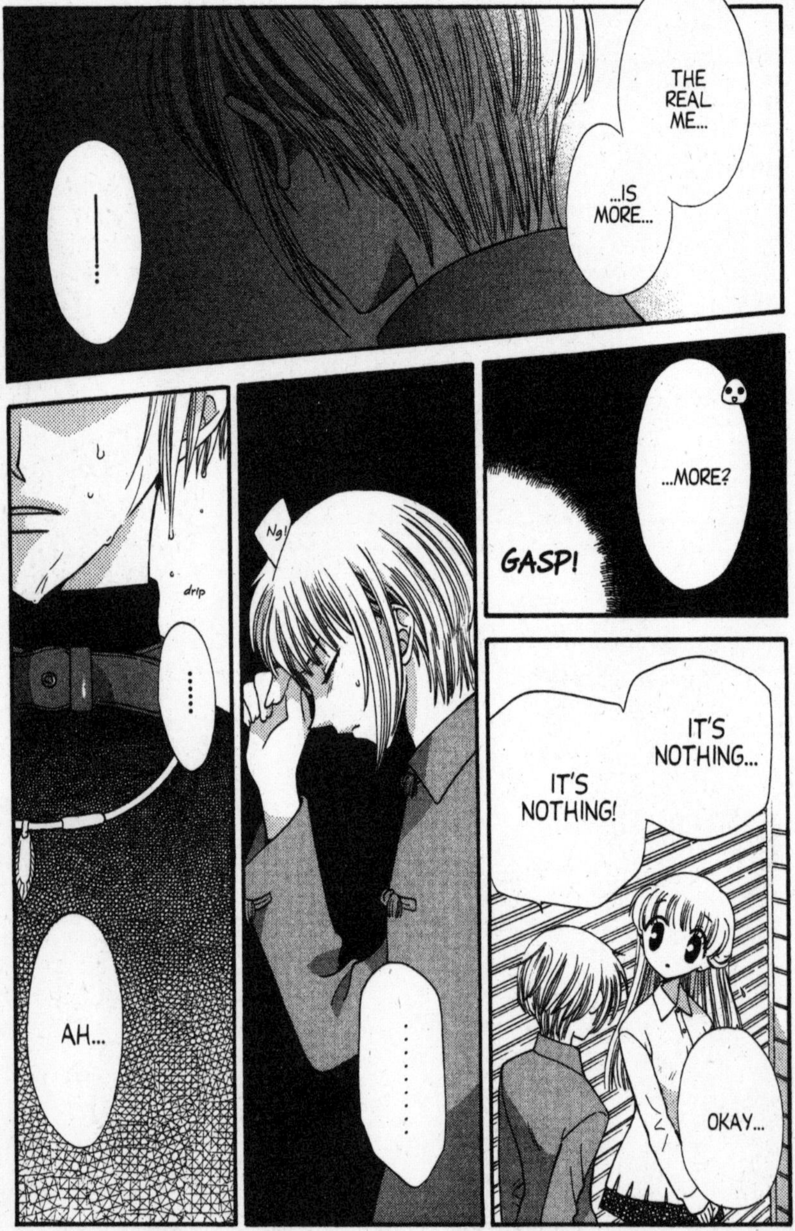
THE REAL ME...
...IS MORE...
......!
...MORE?
GASP!
IT'S NOTHING...
IT'S NOTHING!
OKAY...
Ng!
......
drip
......
AH...

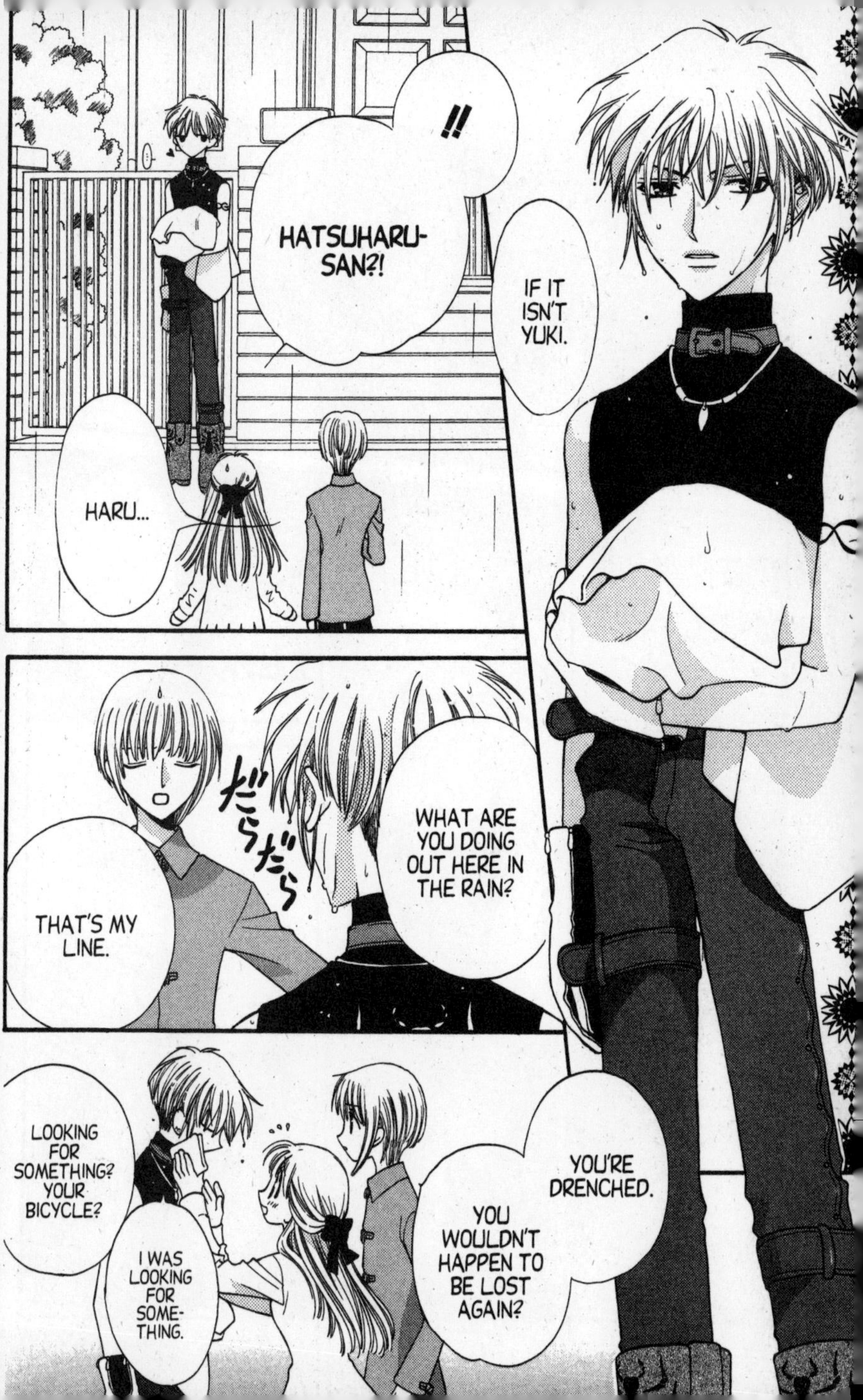
IF IT ISN'T YUKI.
!!
HATSUHARU-SAN?!
HARU...
WHAT ARE YOU DOING OUT HERE IN THE RAIN?
だらだら
THAT'S MY LINE.
YOU'RE DRENCHED.
YOU WOULDN'T HAPPEN TO BE LOST AGAIN?
LOOKING FOR SOMETHING? YOUR BICYCLE?
I WAS LOOKING FOR SOMETHING.

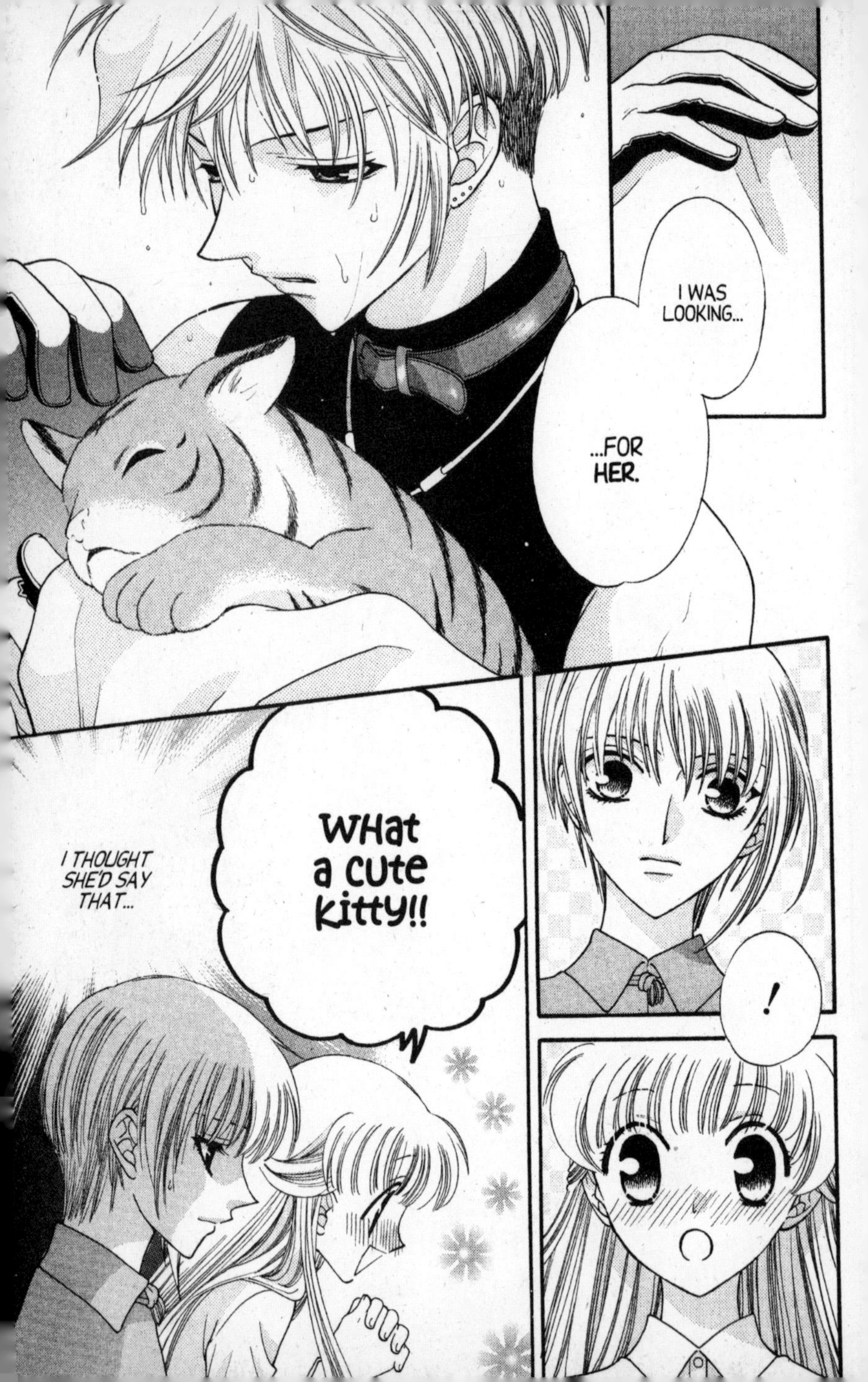
I WAS LOOKING...
...FOR HER.
!
WHAT a CUTE KITTY!!
I THOUGHT SHE'D SAY THAT...

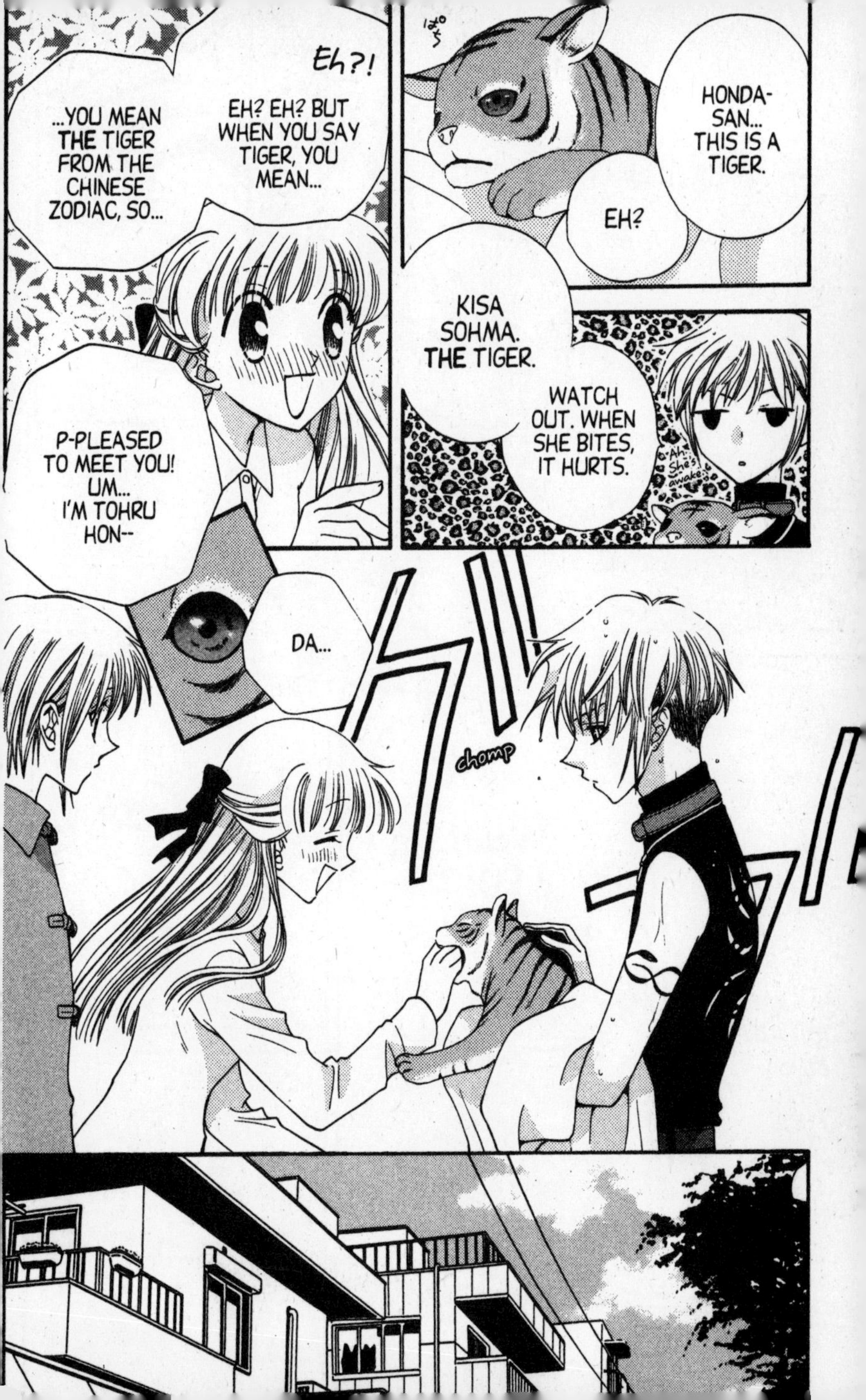

HONDA-SAN... THIS IS A TIGER.
EH?
KISA SOHMA. THE TIGER.
WATCH OUT. WHEN SHE BITES, IT HURTS.
Ah. She's awake.
Eh?!
EH? EH? BUT WHEN YOU SAY TIGER, YOU MEAN...
...YOU MEAN THE TIGER FROM THE CHINESE ZODIAC, SO...
P-PLEASED TO MEET YOU! UM... I'M TOHRU HON--
DA...
chomp

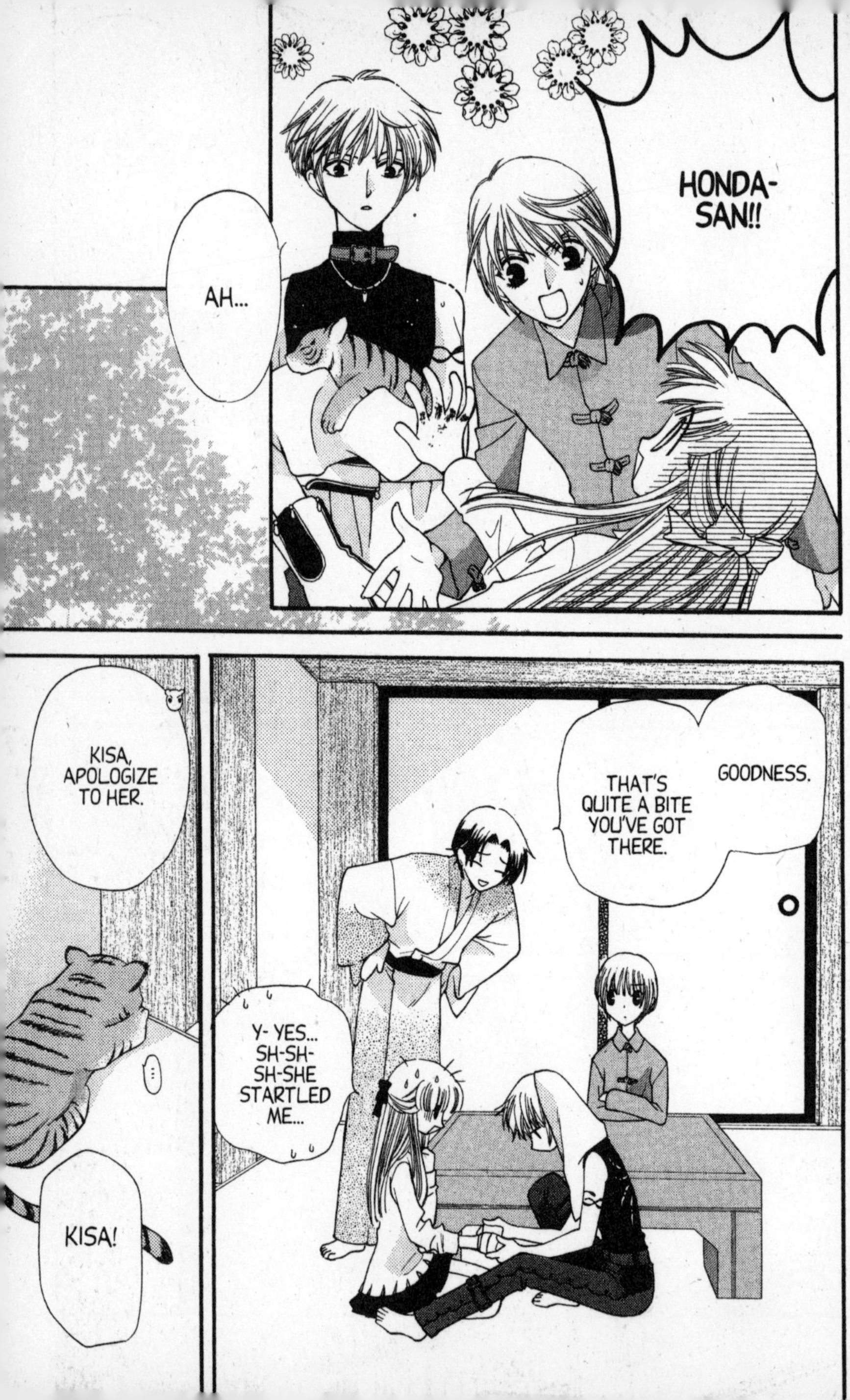
HONDA-SAN!!
AH...
GOODNESS.
THAT'S QUITE A BITE YOU'VE GOT THERE.
Y- YES... SH-SH-SH-SHE STARTLED ME...
KISA, APOLOGIZE TO HER.
...
KISA!

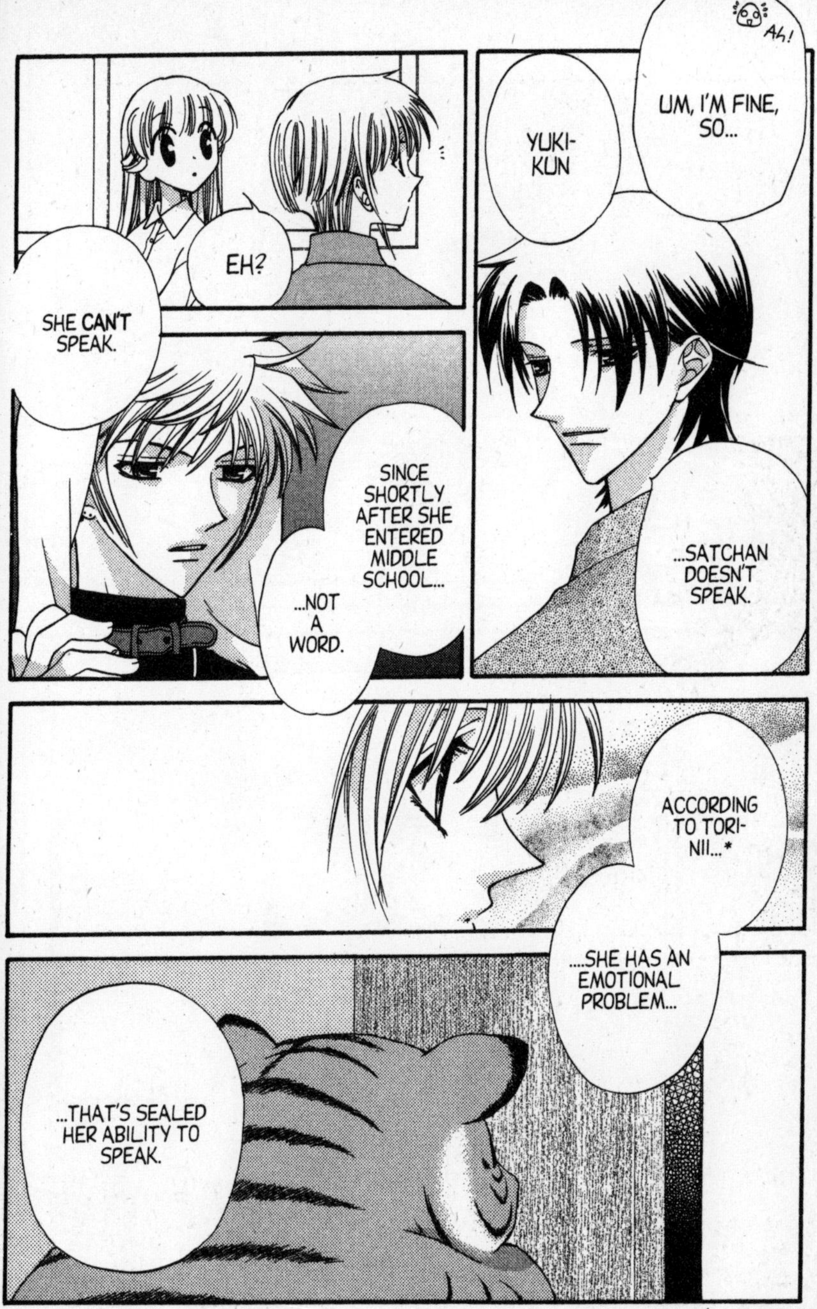
Ah!
UM, I'M FINE, SO...
YUKI-KUN
...SATCHAN DOESN'T SPEAK.
EH?
SHE CAN'T SPEAK.
SINCE SHORTLY AFTER SHE ENTERED MIDDLE SCHOOL...
...NOT A WORD.
ACCORDING TO TORI-NII...*
....SHE HAS AN EMOTIONAL PROBLEM...
...THAT'S SEALED HER ABILITY TO SPEAK.

*Tori-nii: Hatori. "nii" is short for "older brother."

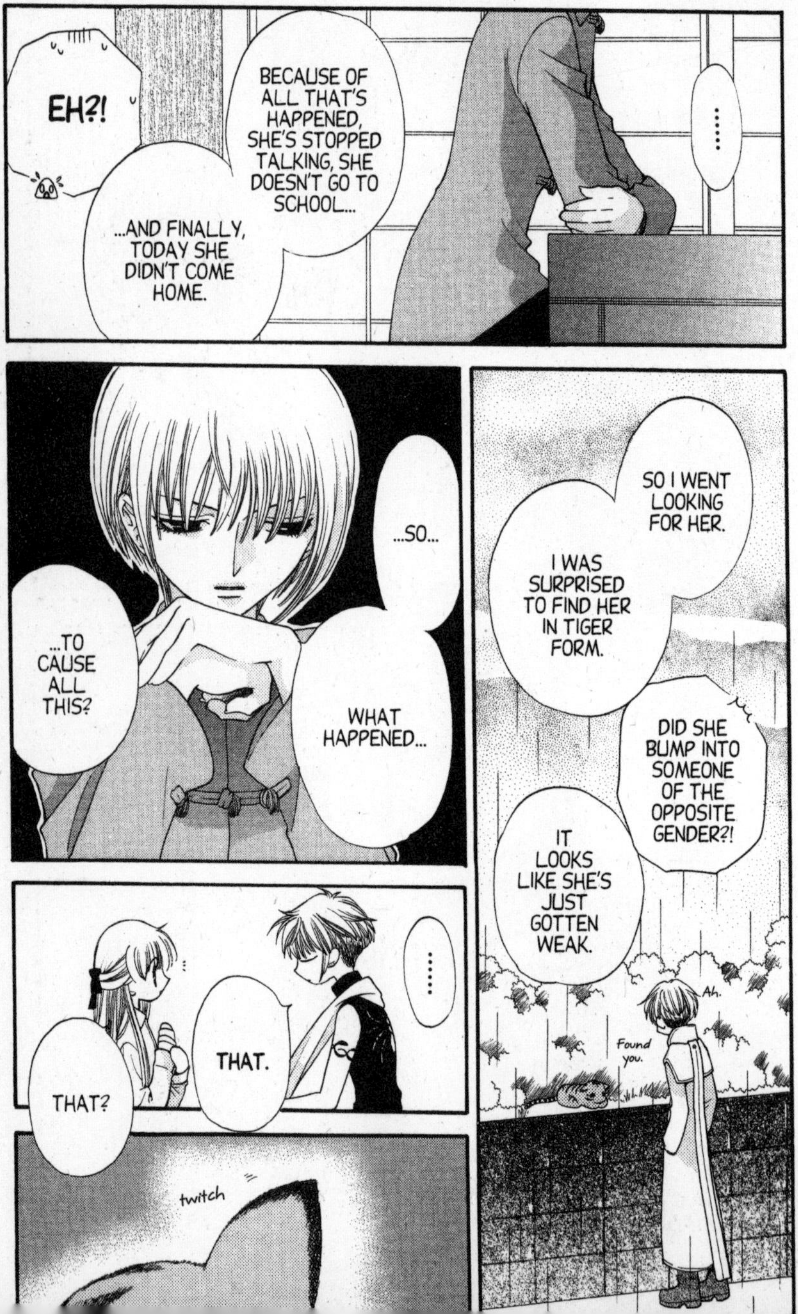
......
BECAUSE OF ALL THAT'S HAPPENED, SHE'S STOPPED TALKING, SHE DOESN'T GO TO SCHOOL...
...AND FINALLY, TODAY SHE DIDN'T COME HOME.
EH?!
SO I WENT LOOKING FOR HER.
I WAS SURPRISED TO FIND HER IN TIGER FORM.
DID SHE BUMP INTO SOMEONE OF THE OPPOSITE GENDER?!
IT LOOKS LIKE SHE'S JUST GOTTEN WEAK.
Ah.
Found you.
...SO...
WHAT HAPPENED...
...TO CAUSE ALL THIS?
......
THAT.
THAT?
twitch

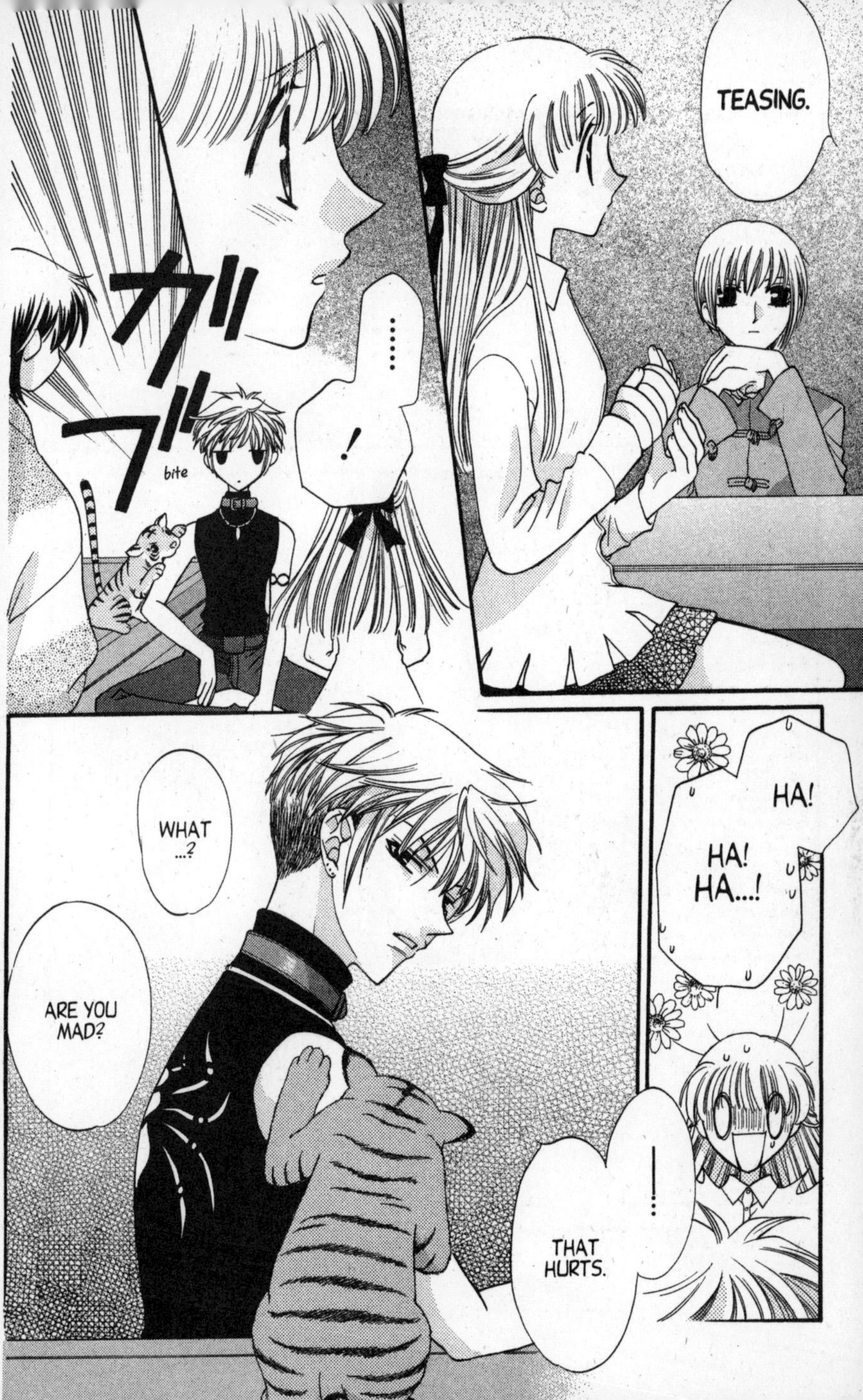
TEASING.
......
!
bite
HA!
HA! HA...!
...!
THAT HURTS.
WHAT ...?
ARE YOU MAD?

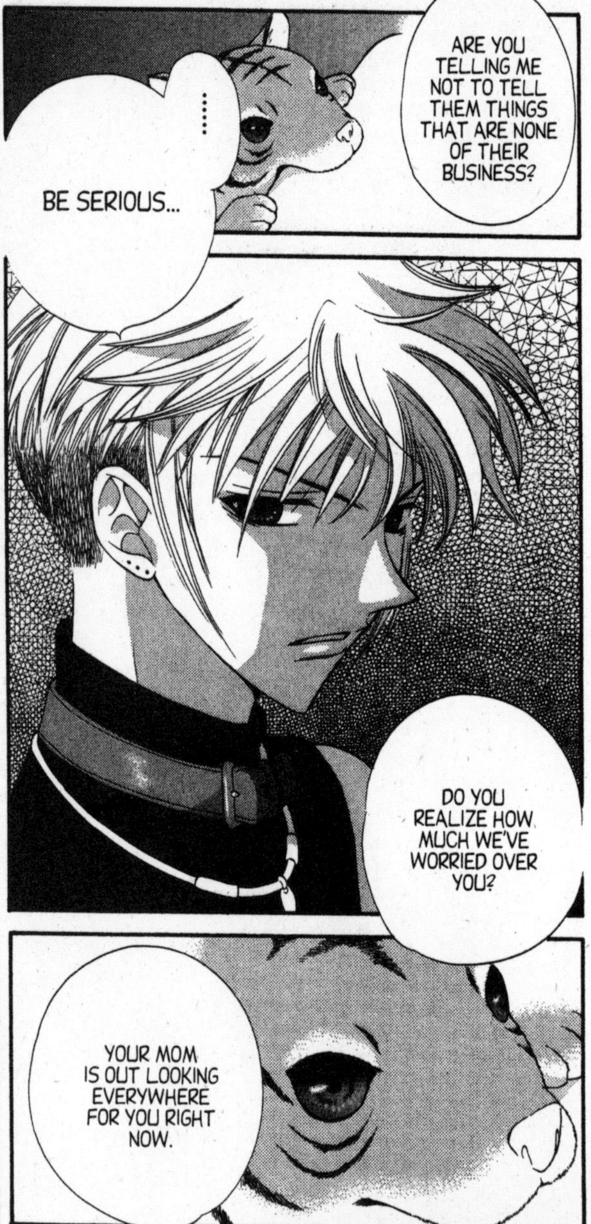
ARE YOU TELLING ME NOT TO TELL THEM THINGS THAT ARE NONE OF THEIR BUSINESS?
......
BE SERIOUS...
DO YOU REALIZE HOW MUCH WE'VE WORRIED OVER YOU?
YOUR MOM IS OUT LOOKING EVERYWHERE FOR YOU RIGHT NOW.

**Fruits Basket 5 Part 3:**

I played Tokimeki Memorial 2. I wanted... a limited edition one... Although I'm ashamed to admit it. (Oops! I just admitted it!) Instead of Takaya-kun, I got Hikari-chan to call me Natsuki-kun. But no matter what happened, the pronunciation was weird, so in the middle I changed it to my real name. I thought, "Whoa, she said my name!" (laugh). Leave it to me to win goldfish for you!! (laugh) (That's a lie. Truth be told, I suck at it.) As for Kotoko-chan, for no reason, I face the screen and tell her I'm sorry. And I sing along with the opening. (Big Mistake.) My voice is low and I have a small range, so I'm no good at singing. I end up in falsetto. Macky's songs are so high I can't sing them very well either. Basically, I'm tone-deaf.

Editor's note: Tokimeki Memorial (TokiMemo for short) is a super-popular Japanese dating simulator series. TokiMemo 2 for the Playstation featured an "Emotional Voice System" that allowed two of the girls to actually call out the player's name. TokiMemo 2 has a sequel which incorporates Dance Dance Revolution!

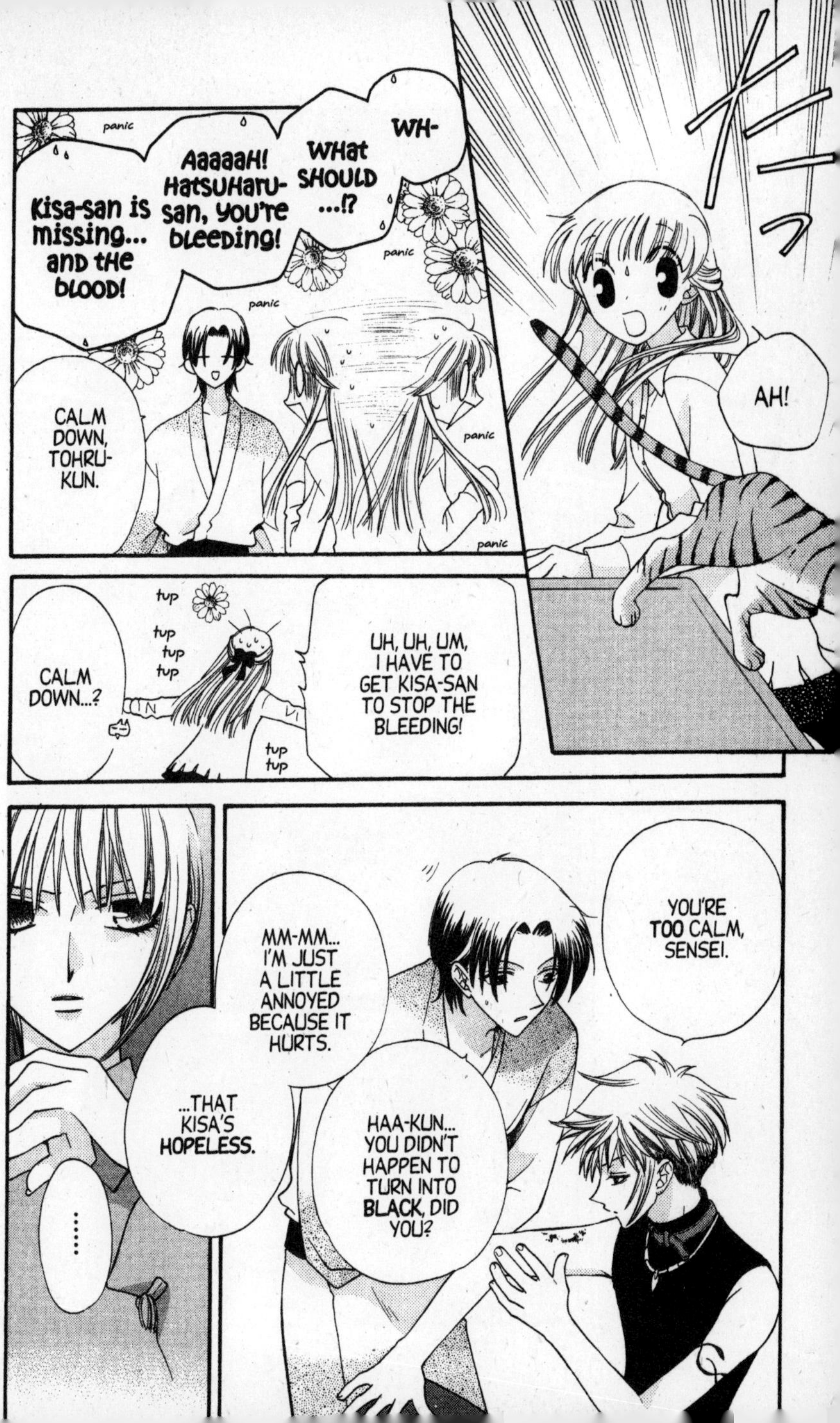
AH!
WH- WHAT SHOULD ...!?
AaaaaH! HatsuHaru-san, you're bleeding!
Kisa-san is missing... and the blood!
panic
panic
panic
panic
panic
CALM DOWN, TOHRU-KUN.
UH, UH, UM, I HAVE TO GET KISA-SAN TO STOP THE BLEEDING!
tup
tup tup tup
tup tup
CALM DOWN...?
YOU'RE TOO CALM, SENSEI.
MM-MM... I'M JUST A LITTLE ANNOYED BECAUSE IT HURTS.
HAA-KUN... YOU DIDN'T HAPPEN TO TURN INTO BLACK, DID YOU?
...THAT KISA'S HOPELESS.
......

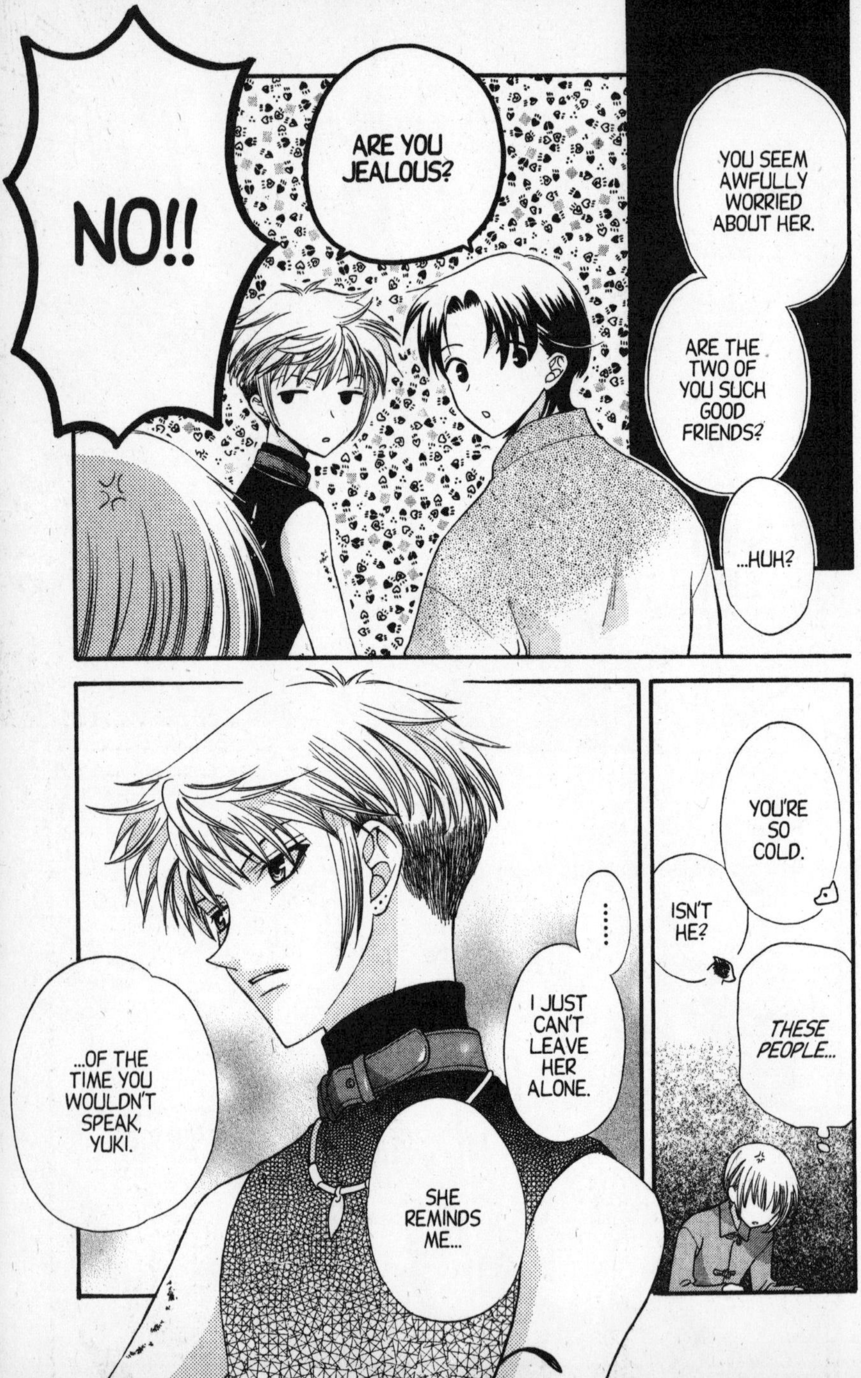
YOU SEEM AWFULLY WORRIED ABOUT HER.
ARE THE TWO OF YOU SUCH GOOD FRIENDS?
...HUH?
ARE YOU JEALOUS?
NO!!
YOU'RE SO COLD.
ISN'T HE?
THESE PEOPLE...
......
I JUST CAN'T LEAVE HER ALONE.
SHE REMINDS ME...
...OF THE TIME YOU WOULDN'T SPEAK, YUKI.

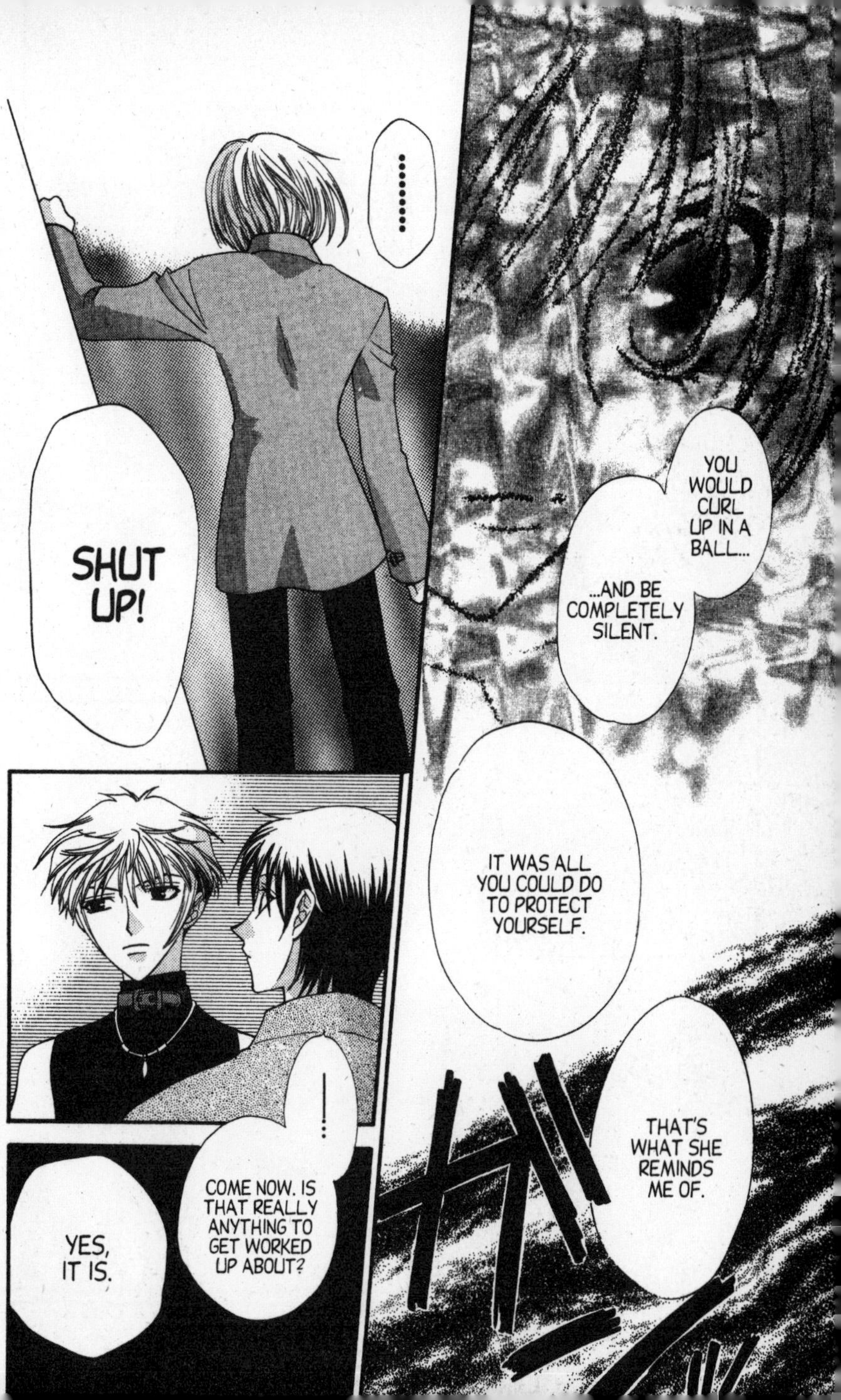
YOU WOULD CURL UP IN A BALL...
...AND BE COMPLETELY SILENT.
IT WAS ALL YOU COULD DO TO PROTECT YOURSELF.
THAT'S WHAT SHE REMINDS ME OF.
......
SHUT UP!
!...
COME NOW. IS THAT REALLY ANYTHING TO GET WORKED UP ABOUT?
YES, IT IS.

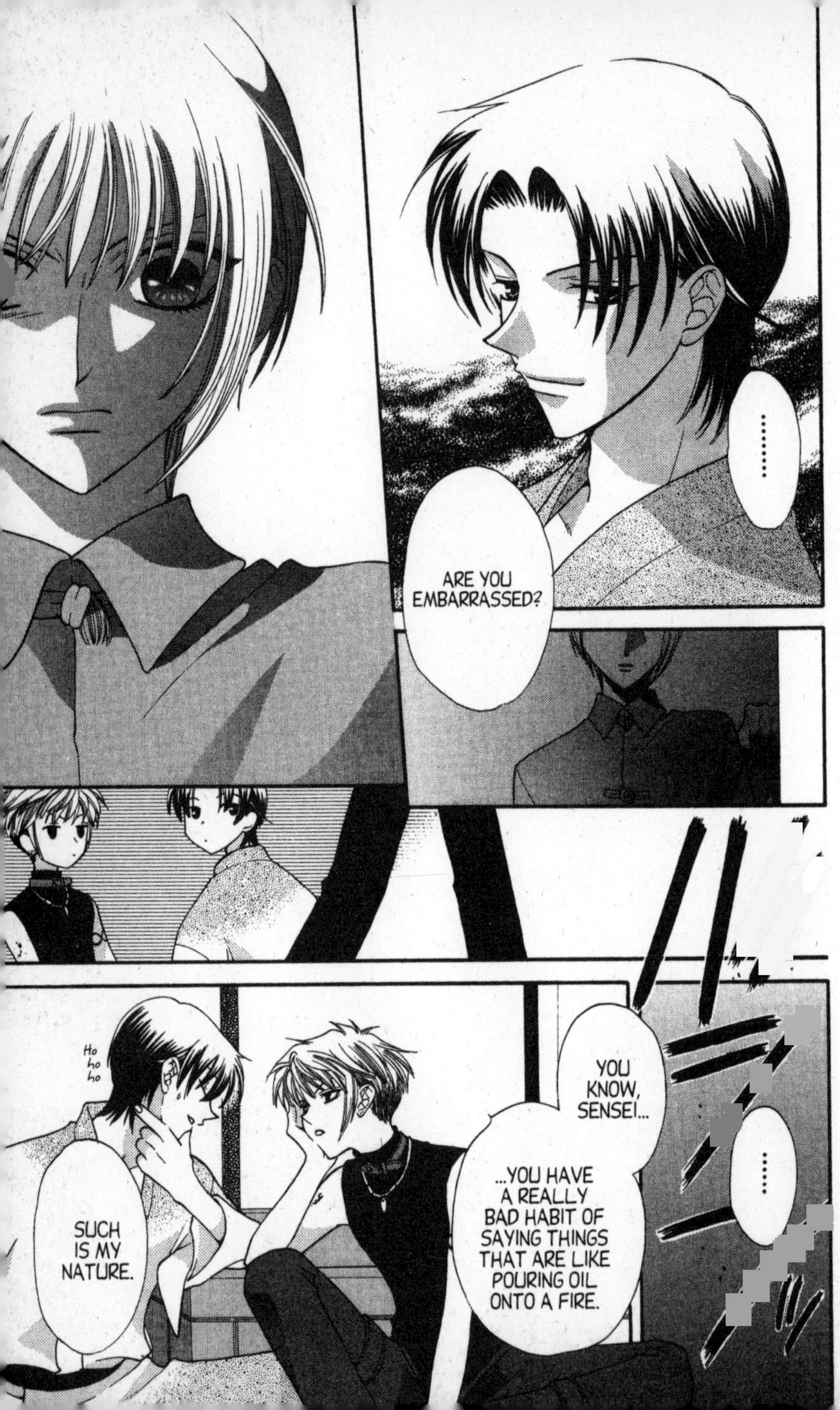
……
ARE YOU EMBARRASSED?
YOU KNOW, SENSEI...
……
...YOU HAVE A REALLY BAD HABIT OF SAYING THINGS THAT ARE LIKE POURING OIL ONTO A FIRE.
Ho ho ho
SUCH IS MY NATURE.

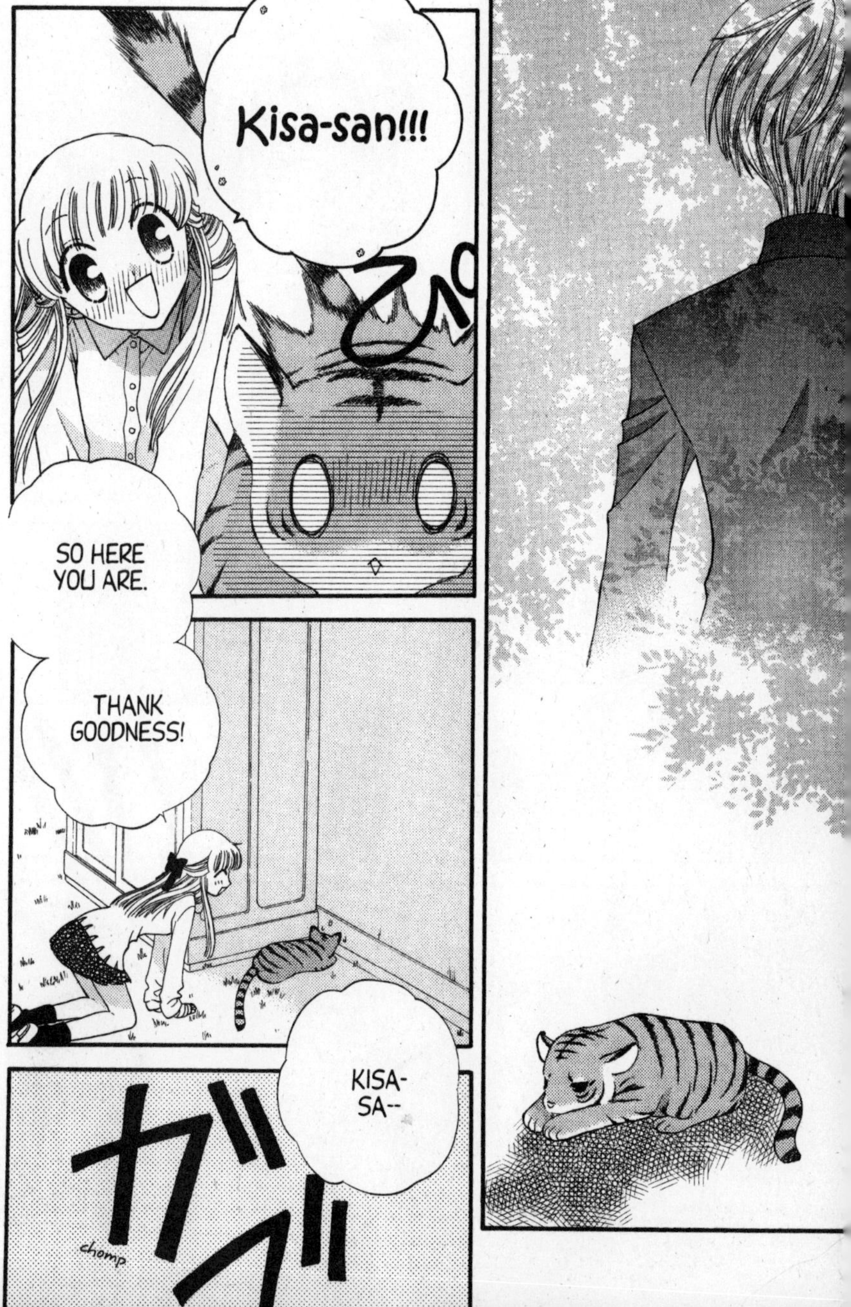
Kisa-san!!!
SO HERE YOU ARE.
THANK GOODNESS!
KISA-SA--
ガブ
chomp

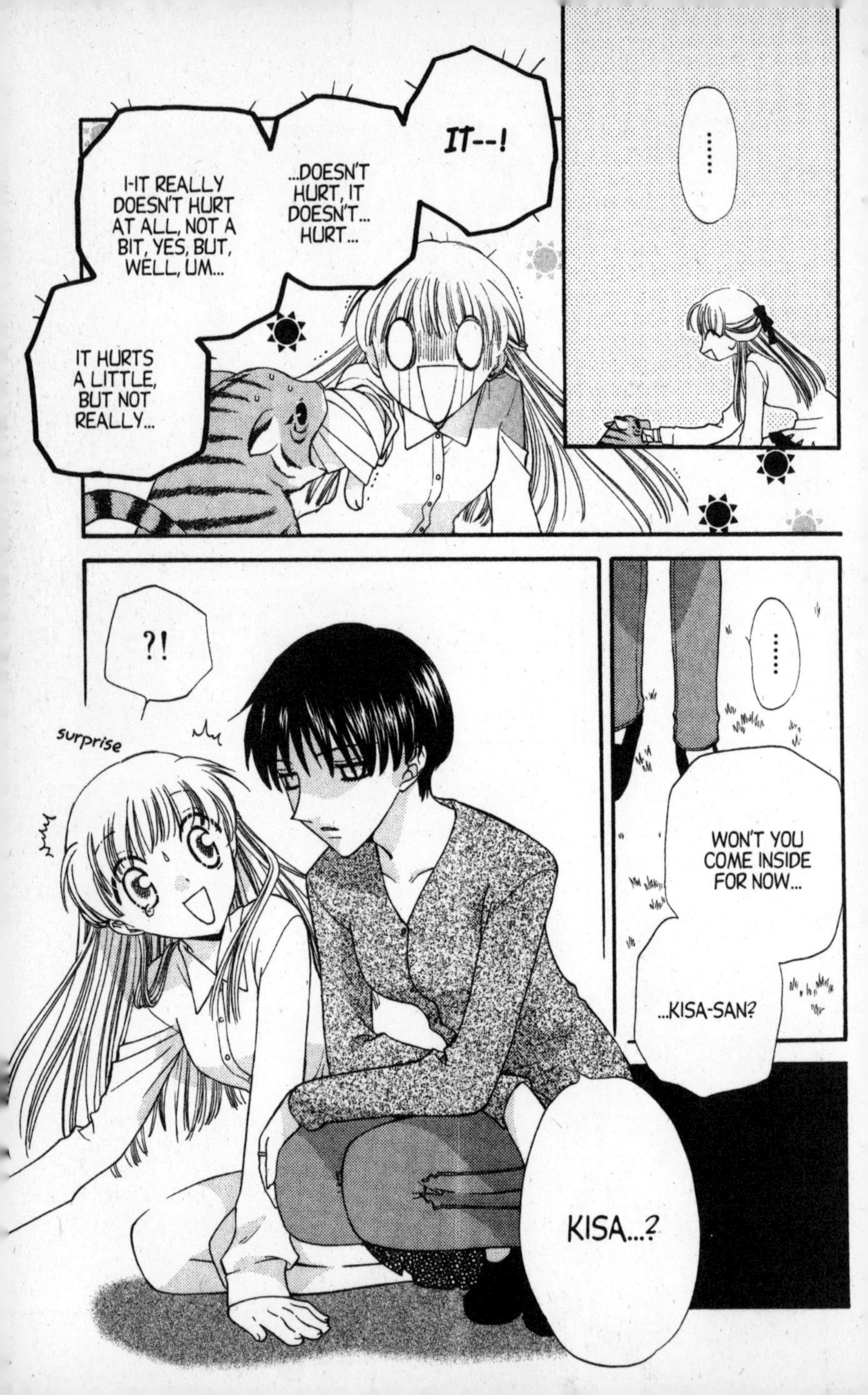
......
IT--!
...DOESN'T HURT, IT DOESN'T... HURT...
I-IT REALLY DOESN'T HURT AT ALL, NOT A BIT, YES, BUT, WELL, UM...
IT HURTS A LITTLE, BUT NOT REALLY...
......
WON'T YOU COME INSIDE FOR NOW...
...KISA-SAN?
?!
surprise
KISA...?

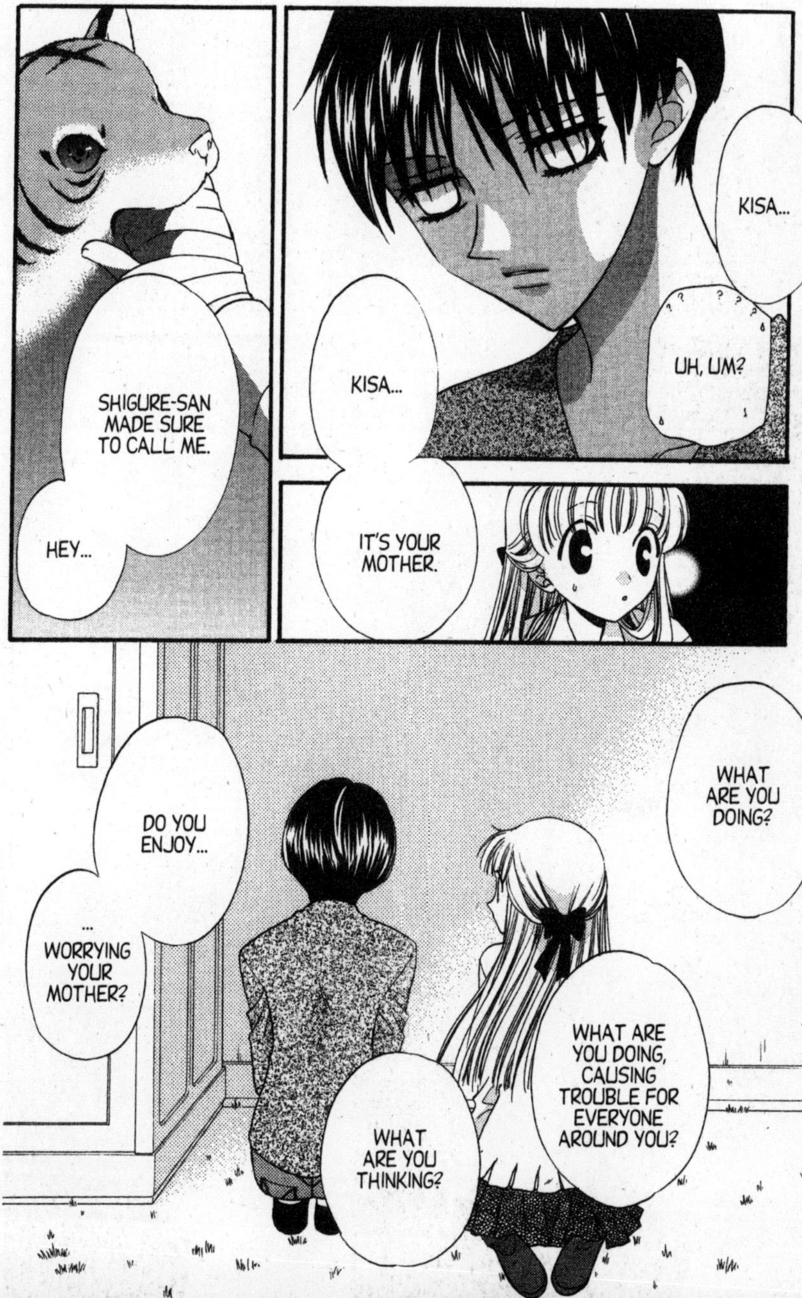
KISA...
UH, UM?
KISA...
IT'S YOUR MOTHER.
SHIGURE-SAN MADE SURE TO CALL ME.
HEY...
WHAT ARE YOU DOING?
WHAT ARE YOU DOING, CAUSING TROUBLE FOR EVERYONE AROUND YOU?
WHAT ARE YOU THINKING?
DO YOU ENJOY...
... WORRYING YOUR MOTHER?

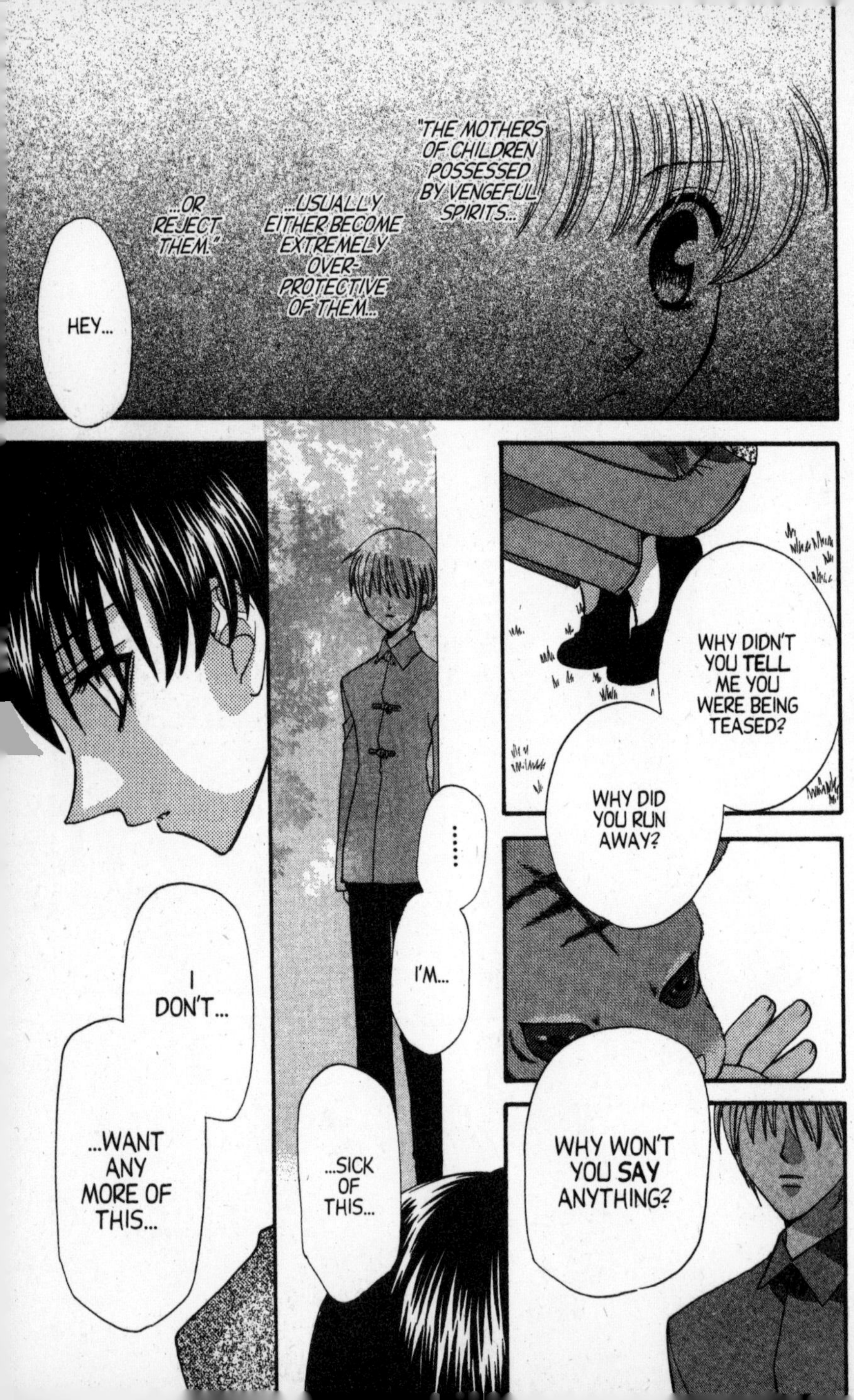
"THE MOTHERS OF CHILDREN POSSESSED BY VENGEFUL SPIRITS...
...USUALLY EITHER BECOME EXTREMELY OVER-PROTECTIVE OF THEM...
...OR REJECT THEM."
HEY...
WHY DIDN'T YOU TELL ME YOU WERE BEING TEASED?
WHY DID YOU RUN AWAY?
WHY WON'T YOU SAY ANYTHING?
......
I'M...
...SICK OF THIS...
I DON'T...
...WANT ANY MORE OF THIS...

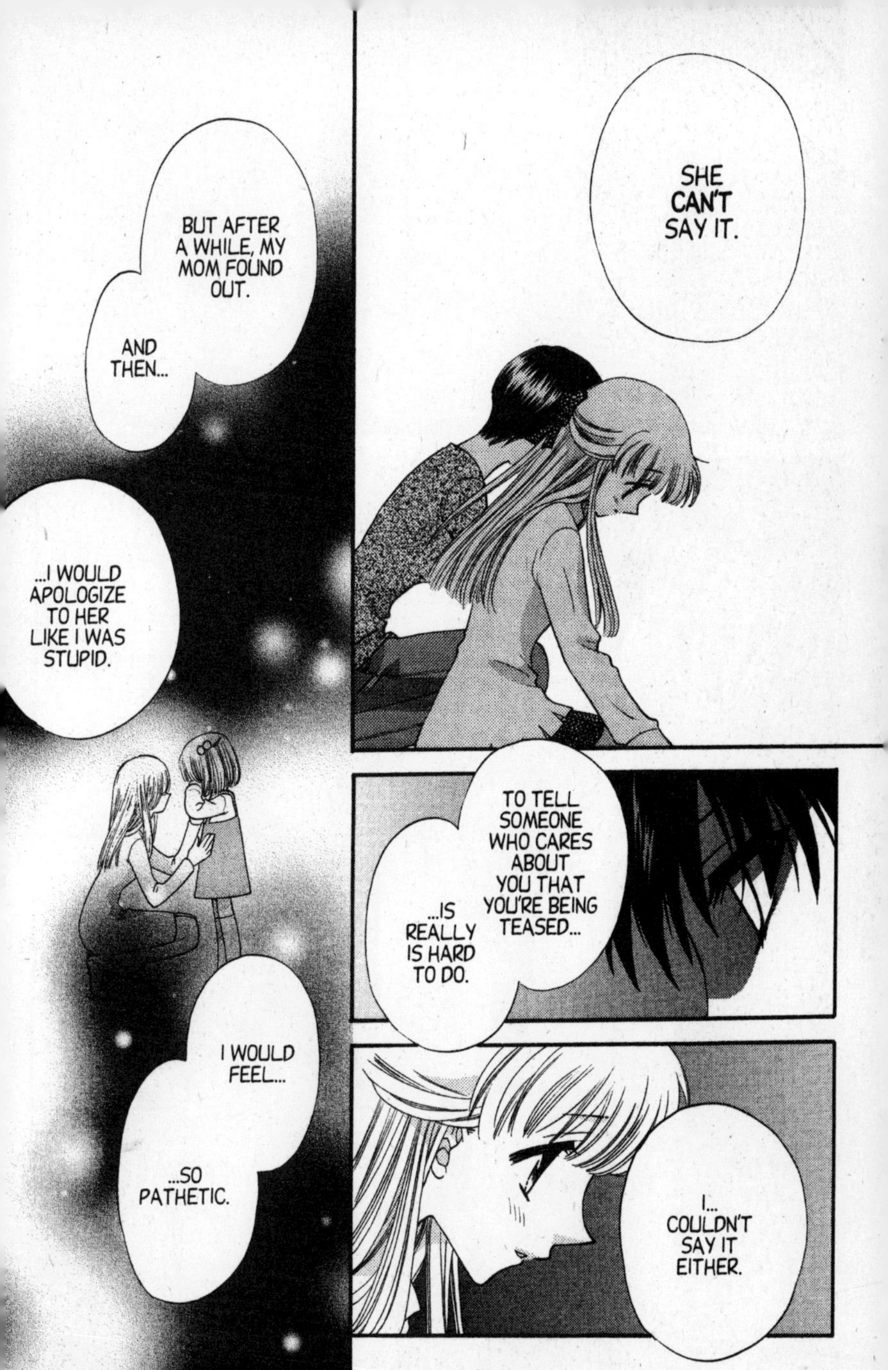
SHE CAN'T SAY IT.
TO TELL SOMEONE WHO CARES ABOUT YOU THAT YOU'RE BEING TEASED...
...IS REALLY IS HARD TO DO.
I... COULDN'T SAY IT EITHER.
BUT AFTER A WHILE, MY MOM FOUND OUT.
AND THEN...
...I WOULD APOLOGIZE TO HER LIKE I WAS STUPID.
I WOULD FEEL...
...SO PATHETIC.

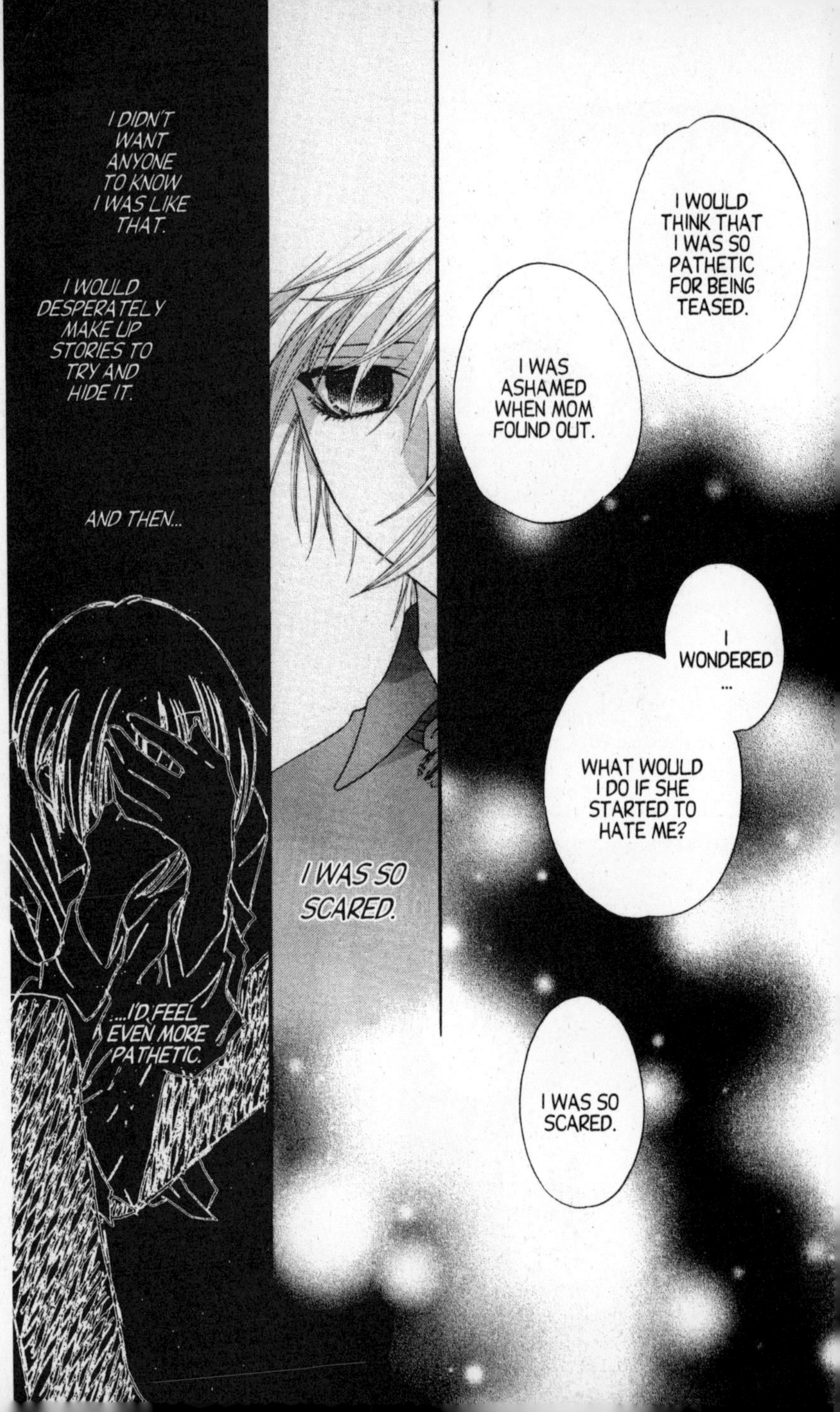

I WOULD THINK THAT I WAS SO PATHETIC FOR BEING TEASED.
I WAS ASHAMED WHEN MOM FOUND OUT.
I WONDERED...
WHAT WOULD I DO IF SHE STARTED TO HATE ME?
I WAS SO SCARED.
I WAS SO SCARED.
I DIDN'T WANT ANYONE TO KNOW I WAS LIKE THAT.
I WOULD DESPERATELY MAKE UP STORIES TO TRY AND HIDE IT.
AND THEN...
...I'D FEEL EVEN MORE PATHETIC.

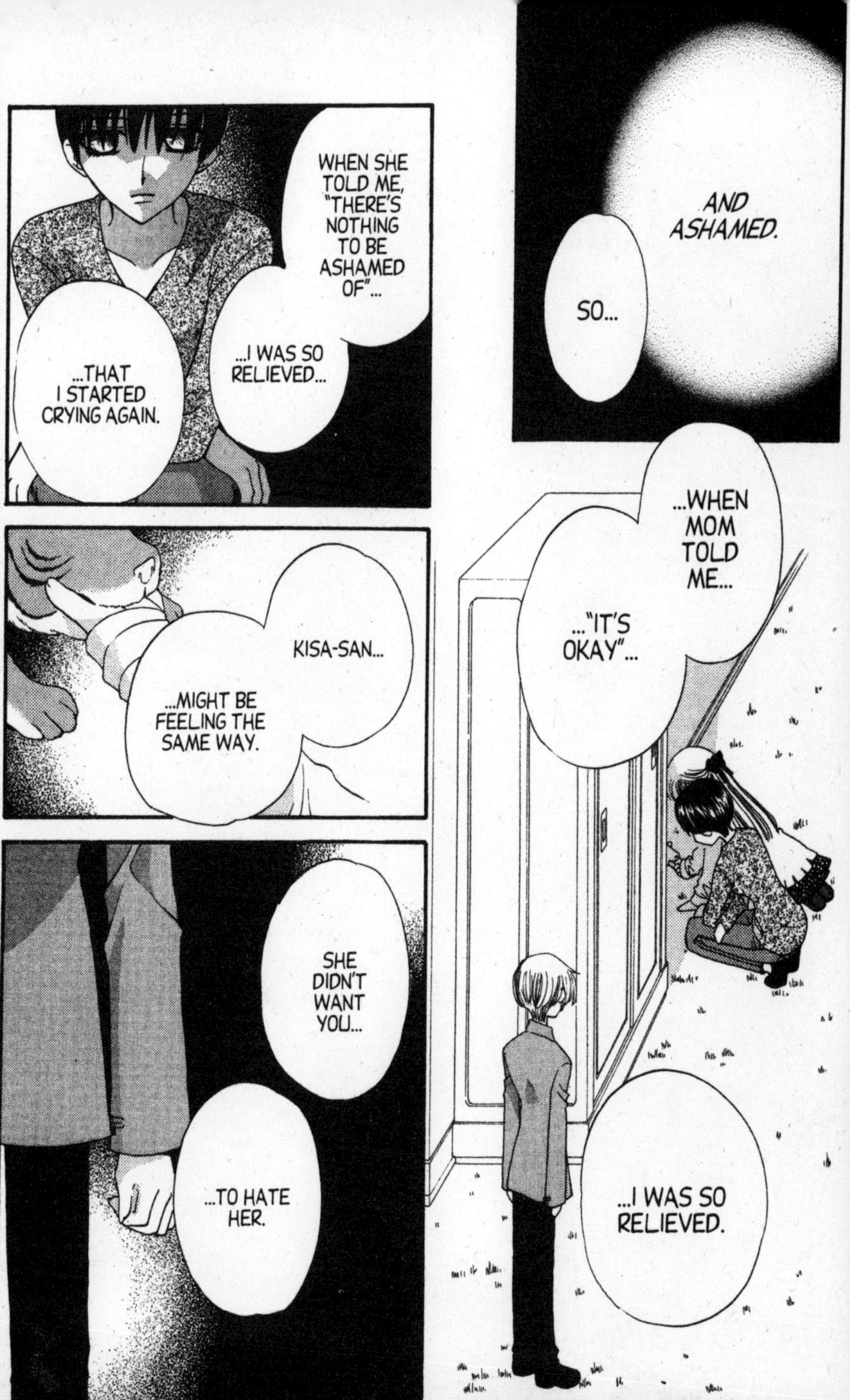
AND ASHAMED.
SO...
...WHEN MOM TOLD ME...
..."IT'S OKAY"...
...I WAS SO RELIEVED.
WHEN SHE TOLD ME, "THERE'S NOTHING TO BE ASHAMED OF"...
...I WAS SO RELIEVED...
...THAT I STARTED CRYING AGAIN.
KISA-SAN...
...MIGHT BE FEELING THE SAME WAY.
SHE DIDN'T WANT YOU...
...TO HATE HER.

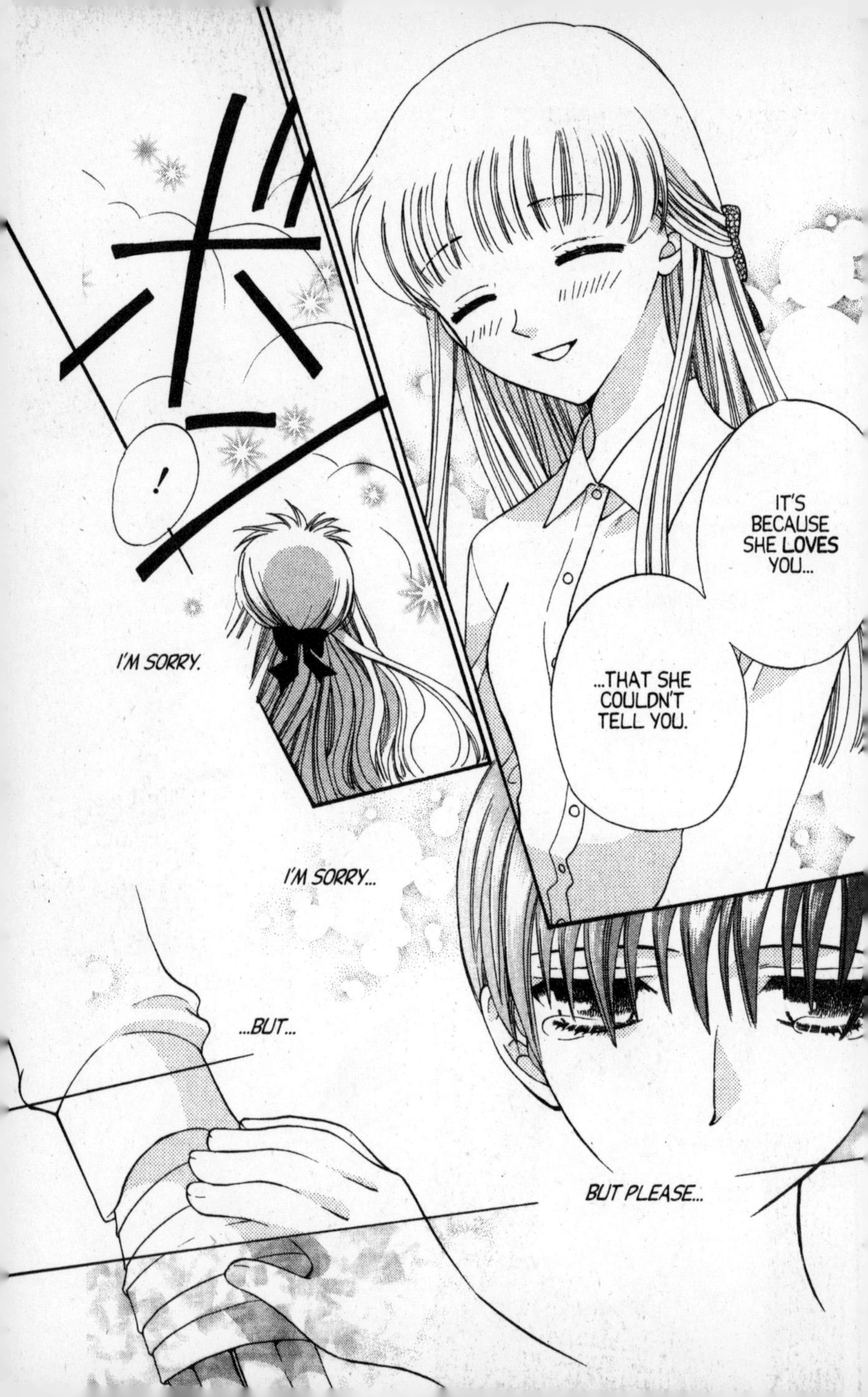
IT'S BECAUSE SHE LOVES YOU...
...THAT SHE COULDN'T TELL YOU.
!
I'M SORRY.
I'M SORRY...
...BUT...
BUT PLEASE...

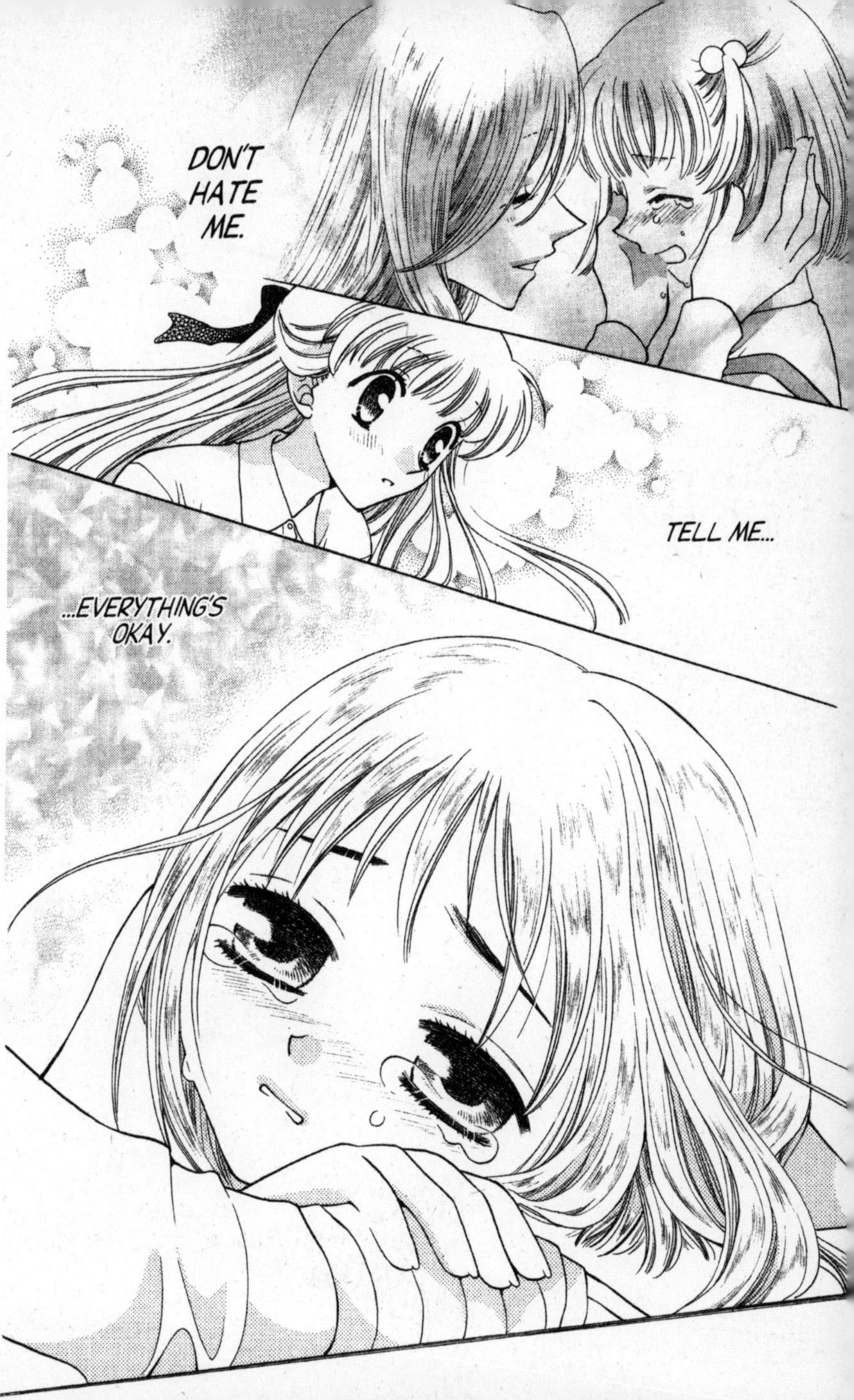
DON'T HATE ME.
TELL ME...
...EVERYTHING'S OKAY.

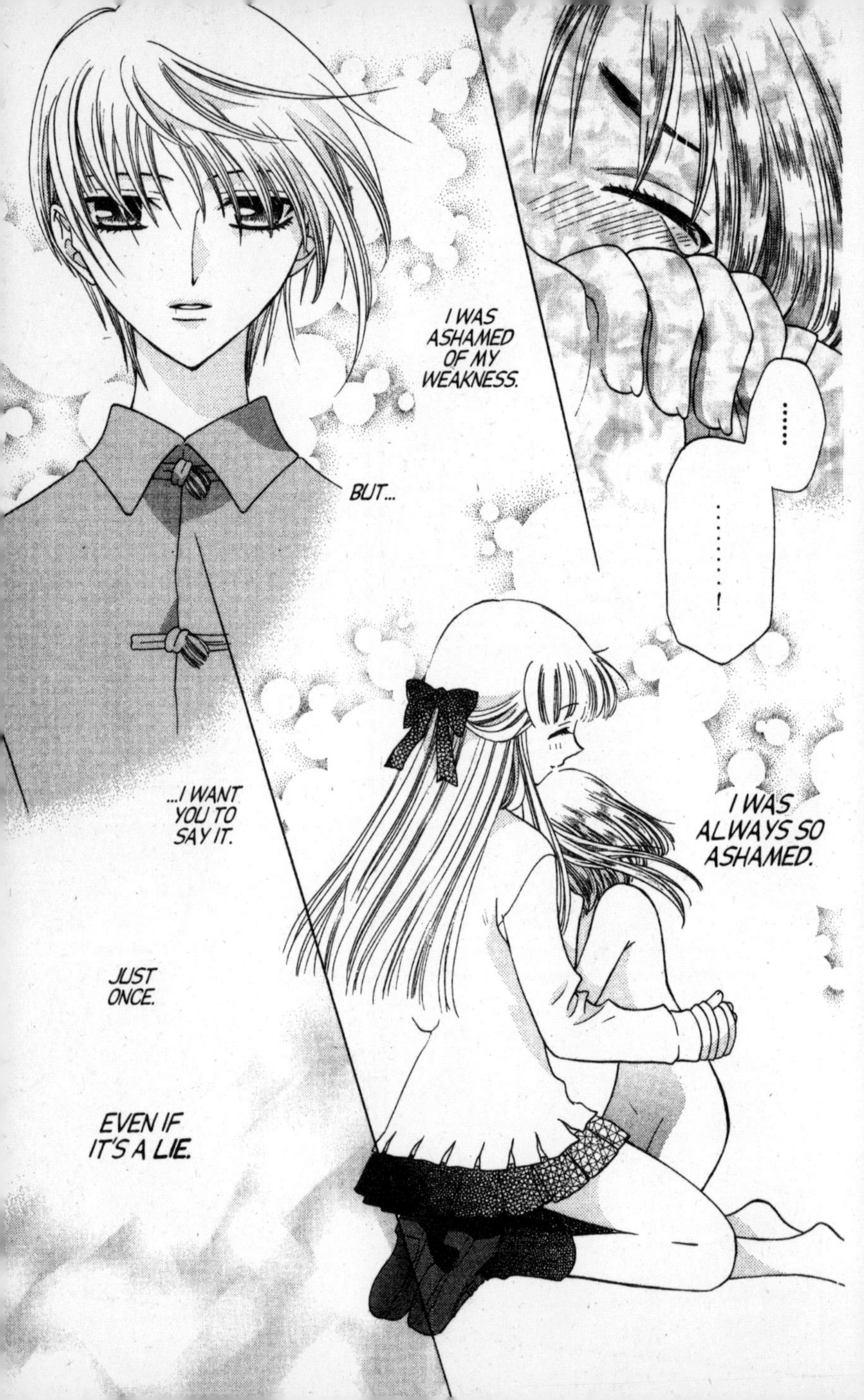
.....
......!
I WAS ASHAMED OF MY WEAKNESS.
I WAS ALWAYS SO ASHAMED.
BUT...
...I WANT YOU TO SAY IT.
JUST ONCE.
EVEN IF IT'S A LIE.

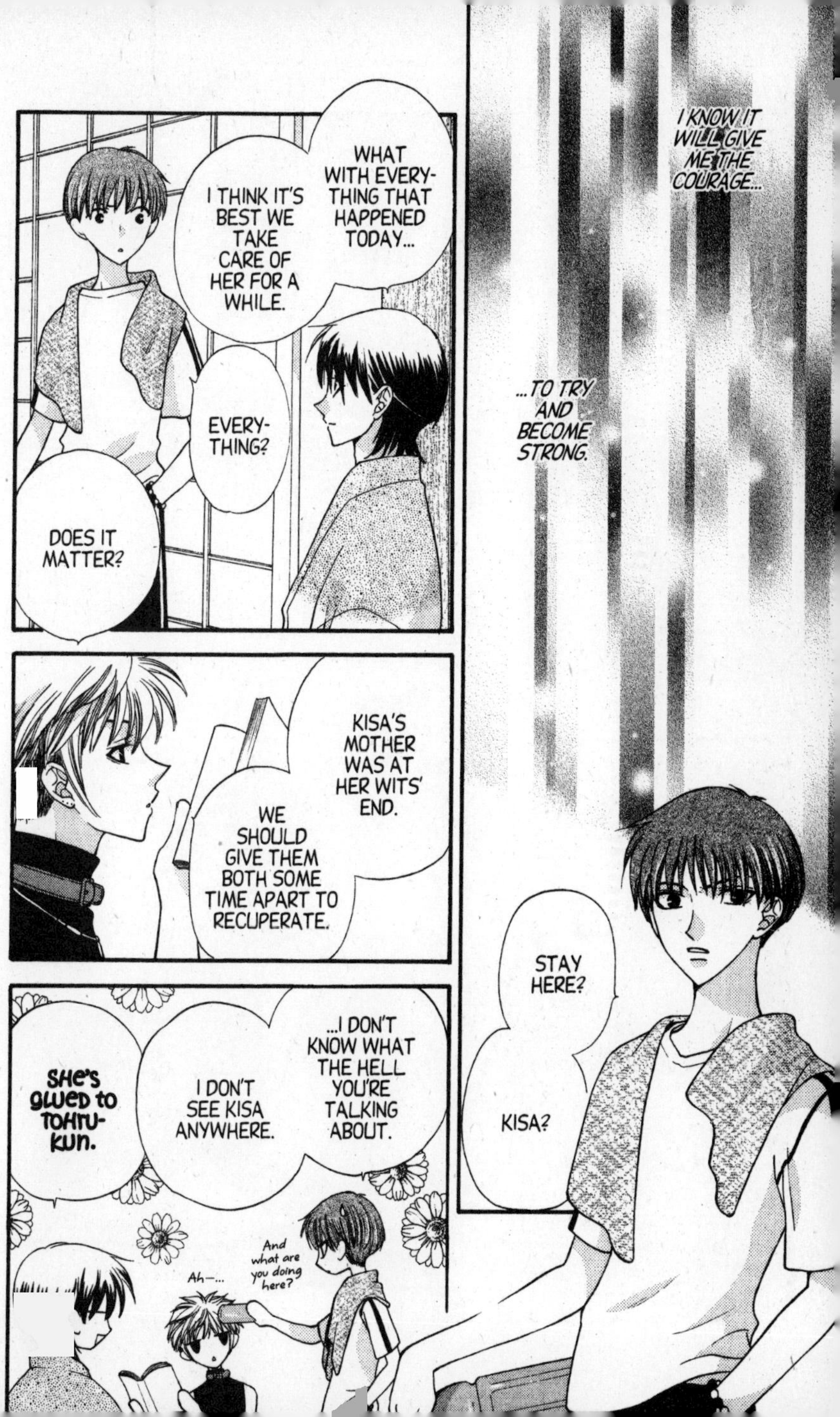
I KNOW IT WILL GIVE ME THE COURAGE...
...TO TRY AND BECOME STRONG.
STAY HERE?
KISA?
WHAT WITH EVERY-THING THAT HAPPENED TODAY...
I THINK IT'S BEST WE TAKE CARE OF HER FOR A WHILE.
EVERY-THING?
DOES IT MATTER?
KISA'S MOTHER WAS AT HER WITS' END.
WE SHOULD GIVE THEM BOTH SOME TIME APART TO RECUPERATE.
...I DON'T KNOW WHAT THE HELL YOU'RE TALKING ABOUT.
I DON'T SEE KISA ANYWHERE.
SHE'S GLUED TO TOHRU-KUN.
And what are you doing here?
Ah—...

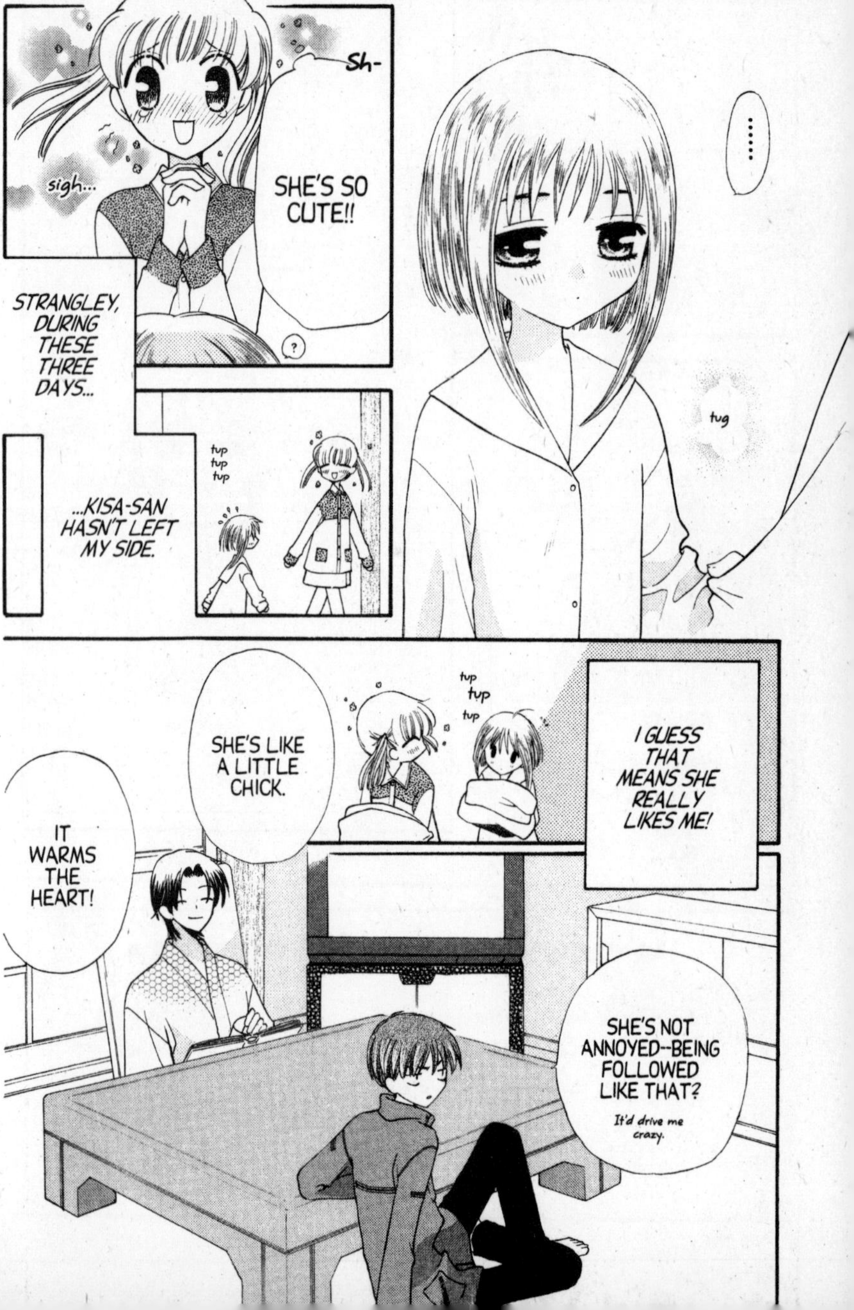

......
tug
Sh-
SHE'S SO CUTE!!
sigh...
?
STRANGLEY, DURING THESE THREE DAYS...
...KISA-SAN HASN'T LEFT MY SIDE.
tup tup tup
I GUESS THAT MEANS SHE REALLY LIKES ME!
tup tup tup
SHE'S LIKE A LITTLE CHICK.
IT WARMS THE HEART!
SHE'S NOT ANNOYED--BEING FOLLOWED LIKE THAT?
It'd drive me crazy.

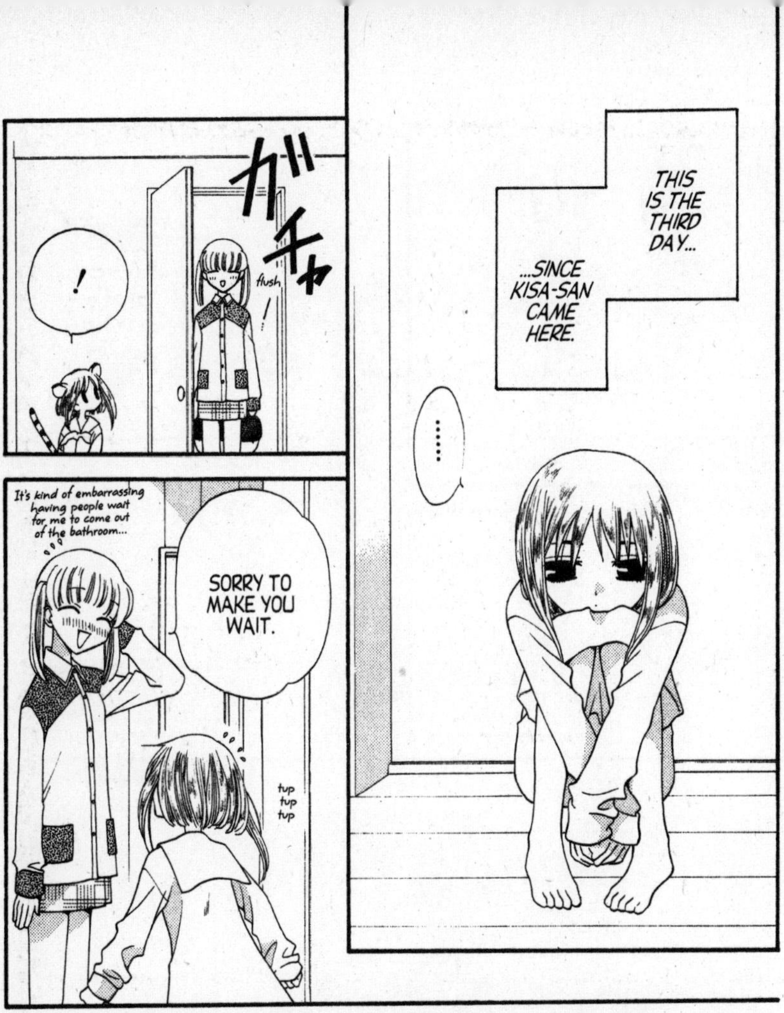
THIS IS THE THIRD DAY...
...SINCE KISA-SAN CAME HERE.
......
ガチャ
!
flush
!
It's kind of embarrassing having people wait for me to come out of the bathroom...
SORRY TO MAKE YOU WAIT.
tup tup tup

## ULTRA SPECIAL BLAH BLAH BLAH 4

So people want to know what song Tohru was singing... Maybe it was "A*daba*a"...Would Tohru be too young to know it? Do all of you know it?

Sometimes they're gone for good...

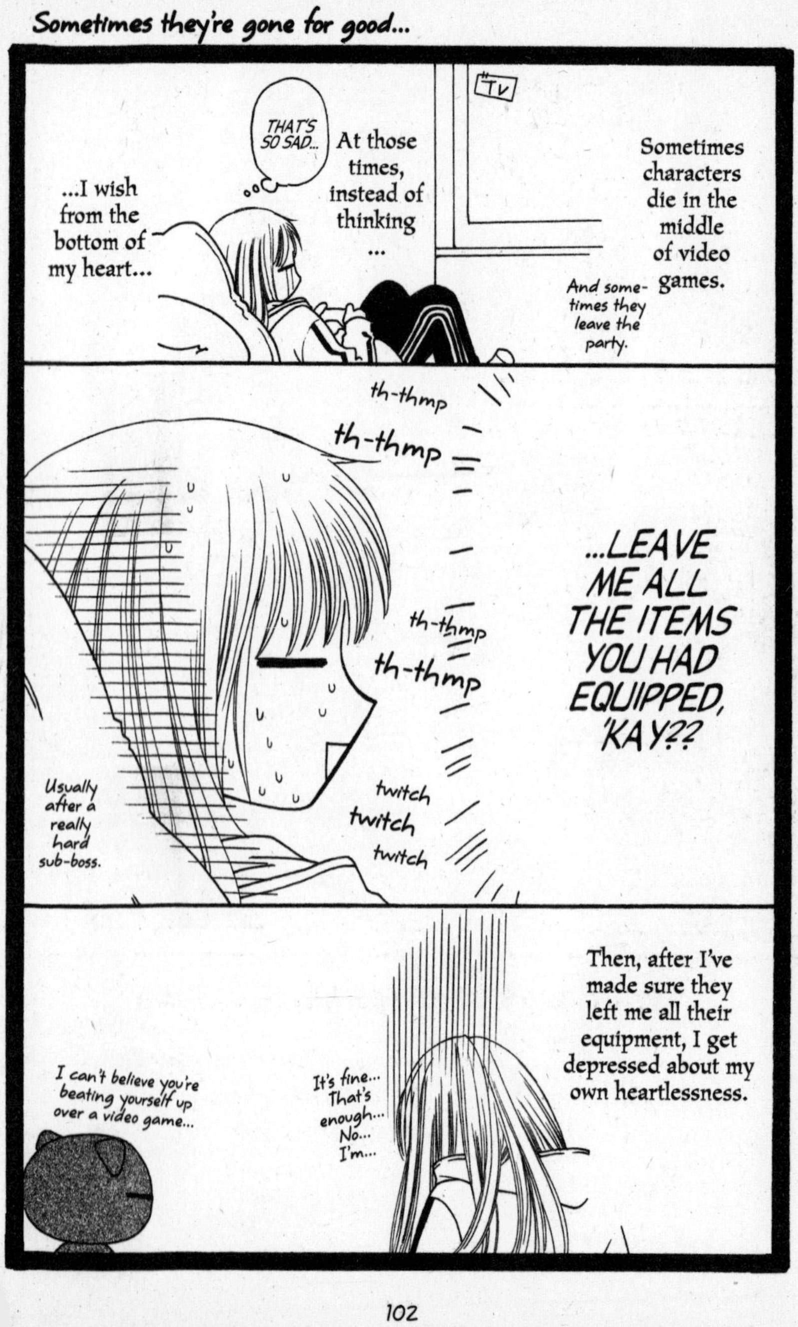
TV
Sometimes characters die in the middle of video games.
And sometimes they leave the party.
At those times, instead of thinking ...
THAT'S SO SAD...
...I wish from the bottom of my heart...
th-thmp
th-thmp
...LEAVE ME ALL THE ITEMS YOU HAD EQUIPPED, 'KAY??
th-thmp
th-thmp
twitch
twitch
twitch
Usually after a really hard sub-boss.
Then, after I've made sure they left me all their equipment, I get depressed about my own heartlessness.
It's fine... That's enough... No... I'm...
I can't believe you're beating yourself up over a video game...

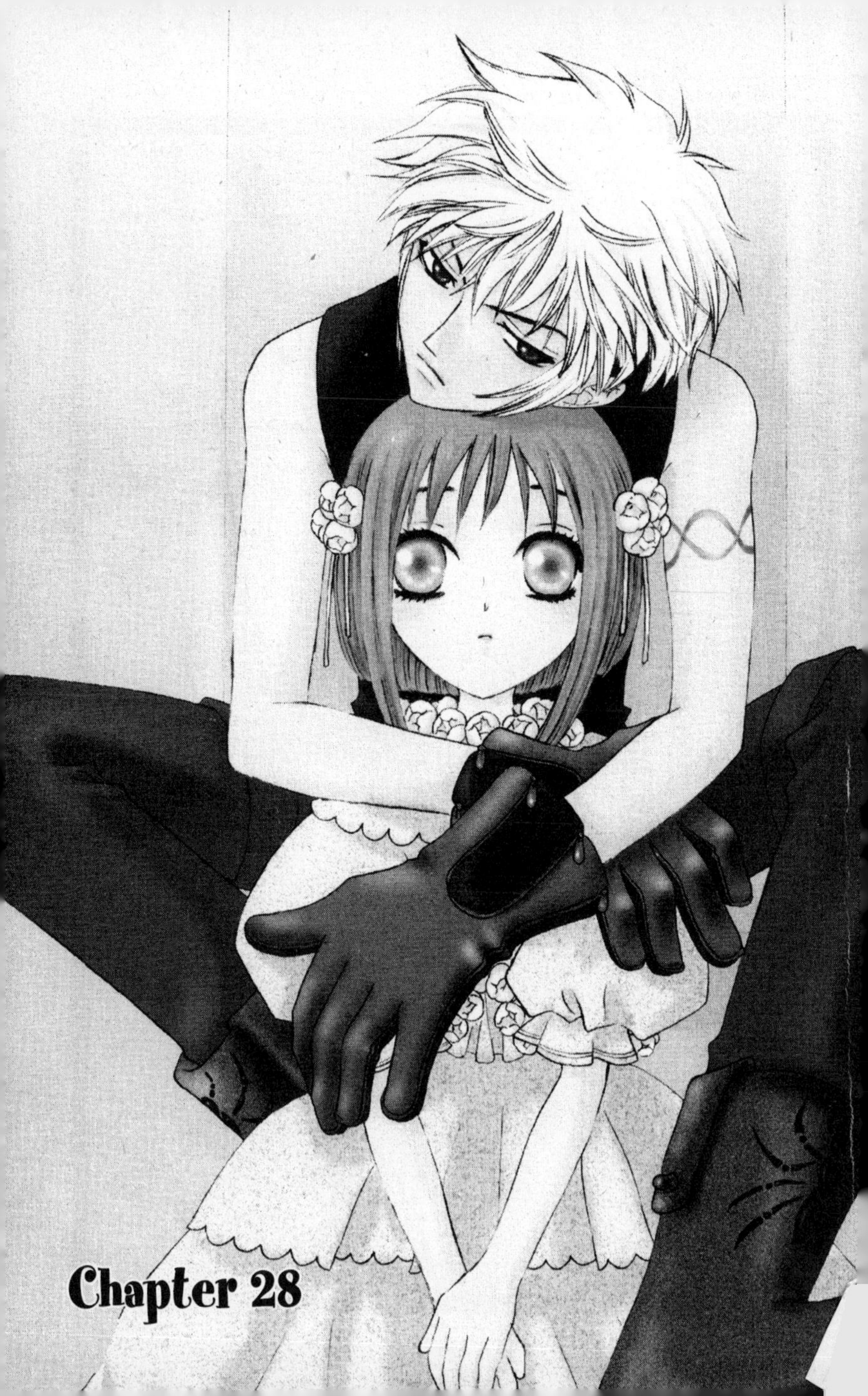
Chapter 28

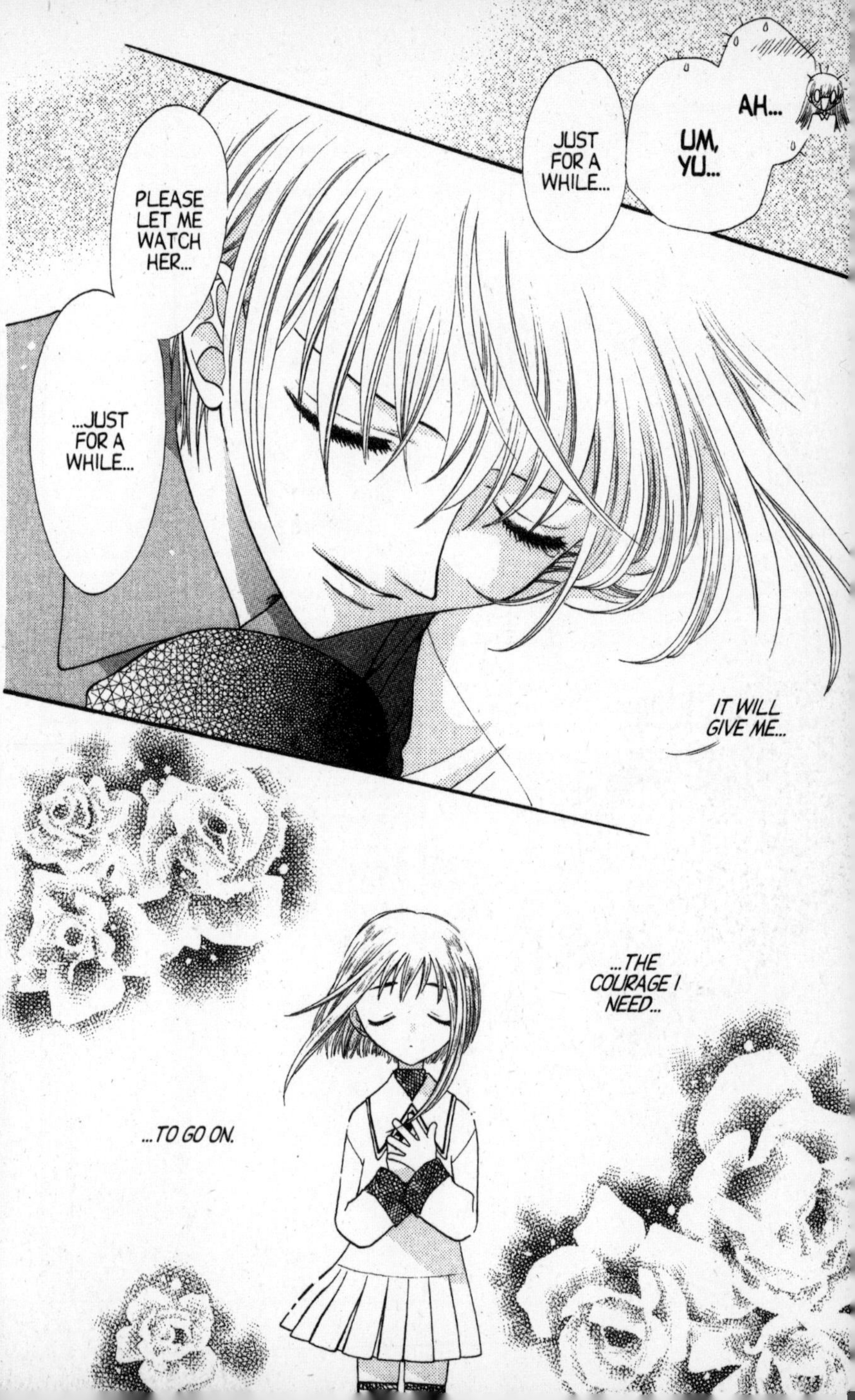
AH... UM, YU...
JUST FOR A WHILE...
PLEASE LET ME WATCH HER...
...JUST FOR A WHILE...
IT WILL GIVE ME...
...THE COURAGE I NEED...
...TO GO ON.

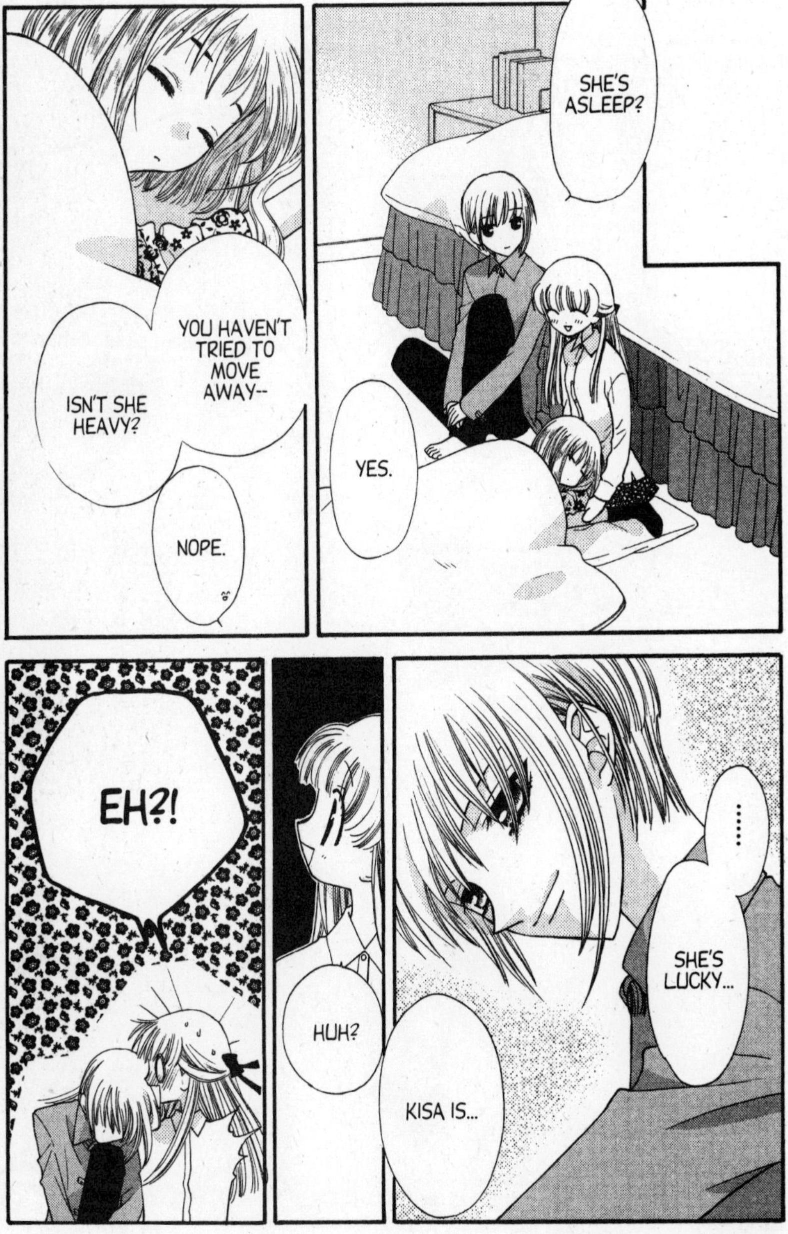
SHE'S ASLEEP?
YES.
YOU HAVEN'T TRIED TO MOVE AWAY--
ISN'T SHE HEAVY?
NOPE.
......
SHE'S LUCKY...
KISA IS...
HUH?
EH?!

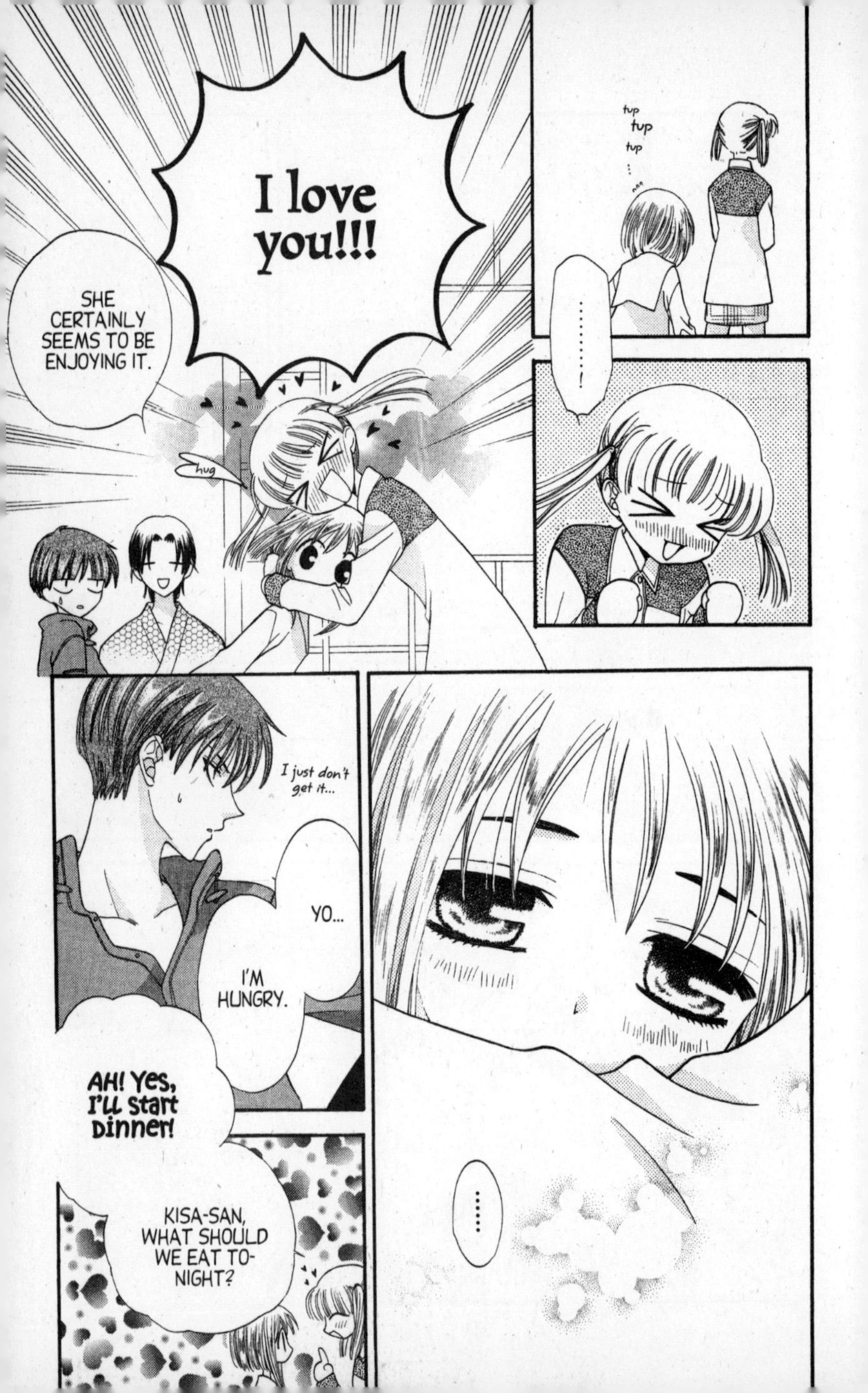
tup
tup
tup
........!
I love you!!!
hug
SHE CERTAINLY SEEMS TO BE ENJOYING IT.
......
I just don't get it...
YO...
I'M HUNGRY.
AH! Yes, I'll start Dinner!
KISA-SAN, WHAT SHOULD WE EAT TO-NIGHT?

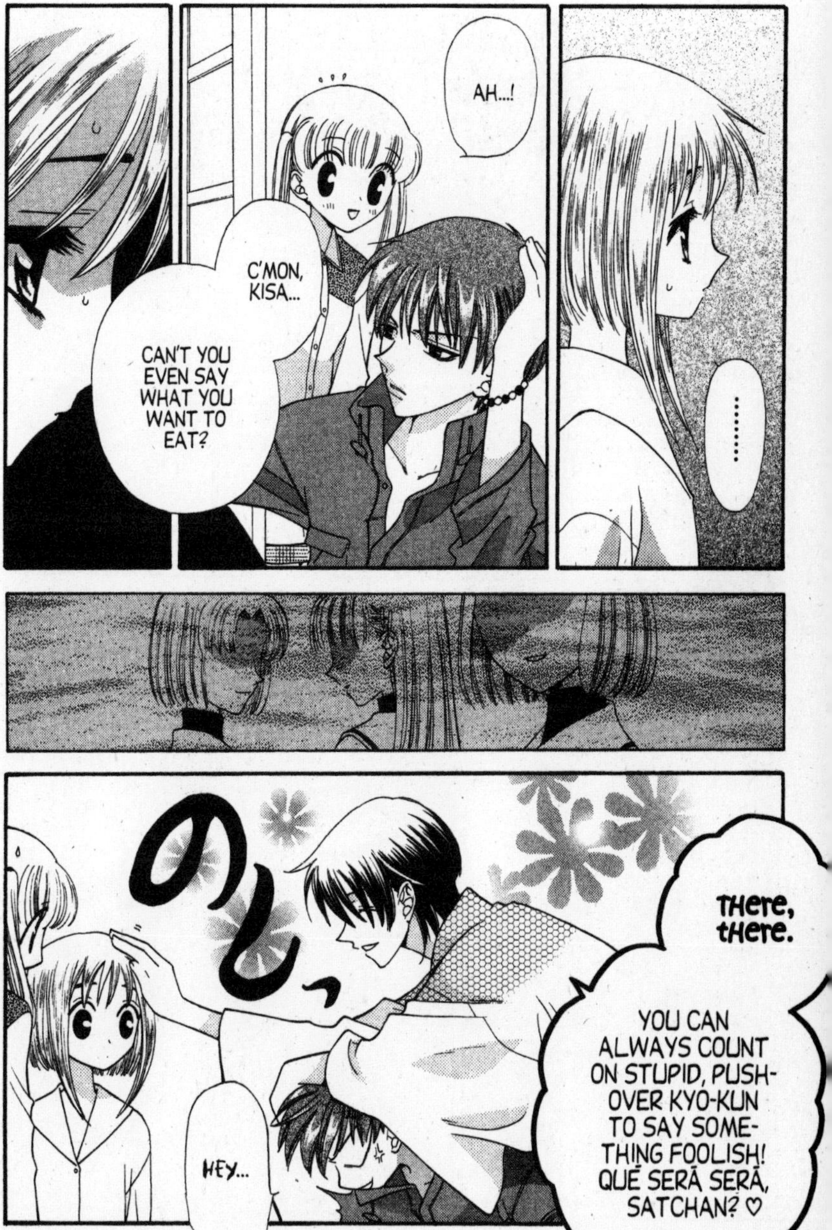
........
AH...!
C'MON, KISA...
CAN'T YOU EVEN SAY WHAT YOU WANT TO EAT?
There, there.
YOU CAN ALWAYS COUNT ON STUPID, PUSH-OVER KYO-KUN TO SAY SOME-THING FOOLISH! QUÉ SERÁ SERÁ, SATCHAN? ♡
のしっ
HEY...

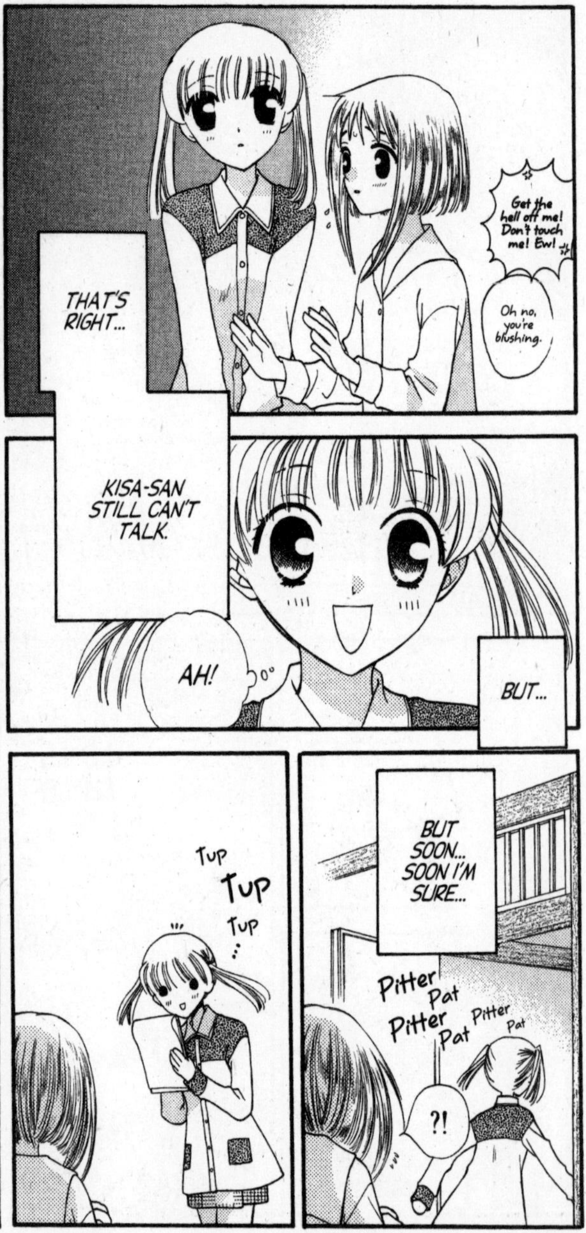
Get the hell off me! Don't touch me! Ew!
Oh no, you're blushing.
THAT'S RIGHT...
KISA-SAN STILL CAN'T TALK.
AH!
BUT...
BUT SOON... SOON I'M SURE...
Pitter Pat Pitter Pat Pitter Pat
?!
Tup Tup Tup

**Fruits Basket 5 Part 4:**

I played Hanagumi Columns 2*. (I'm still talking about games...) At first, I thought, "Why don't they fall on their side...?" (That's Puyo Puyo.) Once I figured out the game play, I piled practice upon practice (laugh), and on Progression Mode I beat all but the highest level without incident. Anyway, it's hard!! That highest level is a killer! (laugh) Even my Sakura Wars mentor K-chan was saying "Hmm" about it...
But we were both talking excitedly, saying, "That thing from that thing? It's so great?!" (Thanks for always teaching me so many things, K-chan. I'm in your debt.) Puzzle games make my mind go blank. It feels as if only half of my brain is working. It's like exercise. And I'm in love with Mogiri! (laugh)

*Editor's note: Hanagumi Columns 2 is a Tetris-like puzzle game based on the Sakura Taisen franchise.

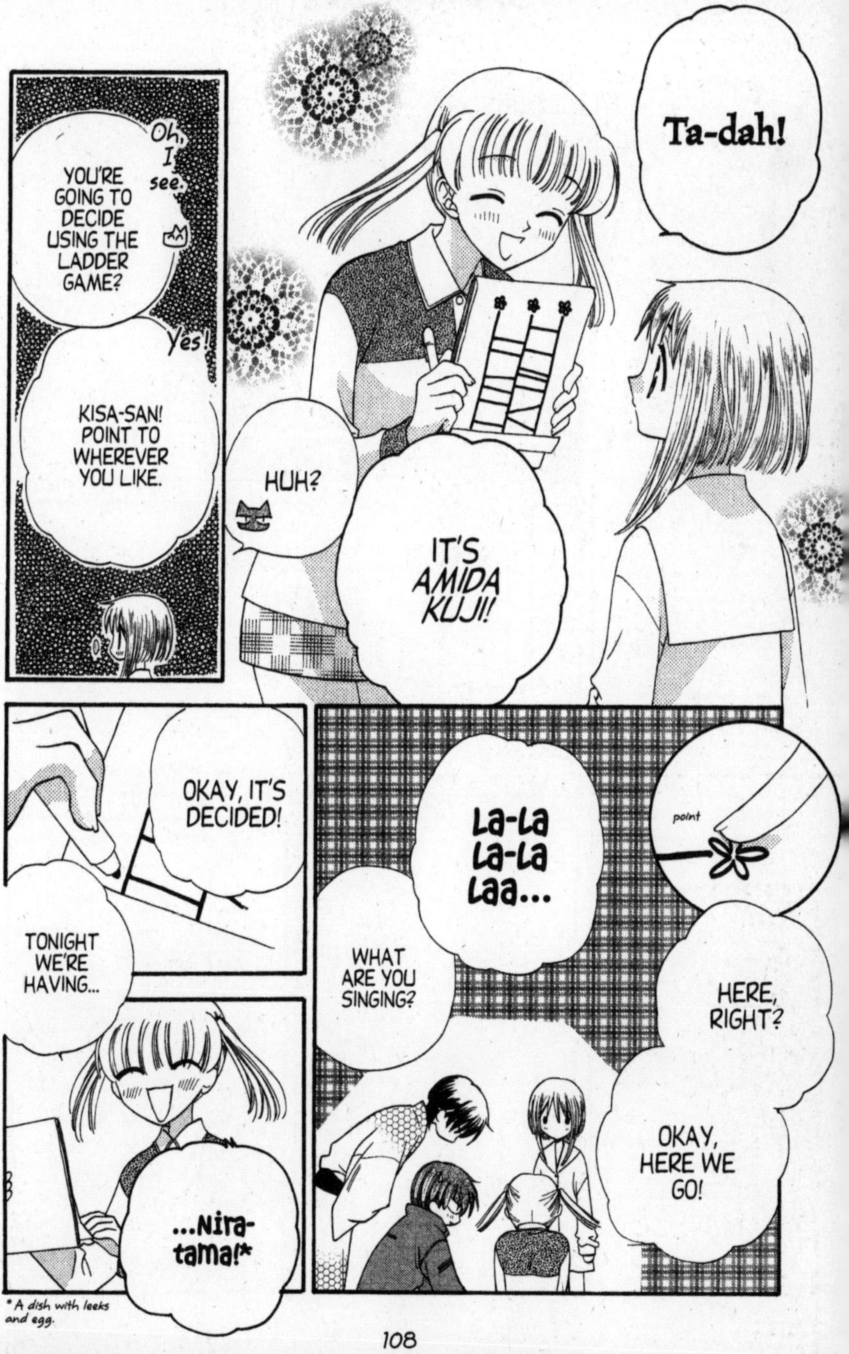
Ta-dah!
HUH?
IT'S AMIDA KUJI!
Oh, I see.
YOU'RE GOING TO DECIDE USING THE LADDER GAME?
Yes!
KISA-SAN! POINT TO WHEREVER YOU LIKE.
point
La-la la-la laa...
HERE, RIGHT?
WHAT ARE YOU SINGING?
OKAY, HERE WE GO!
OKAY, IT'S DECIDED!
TONIGHT WE'RE HAVING...
...Nira-tama!*

* A dish with leeks and egg.

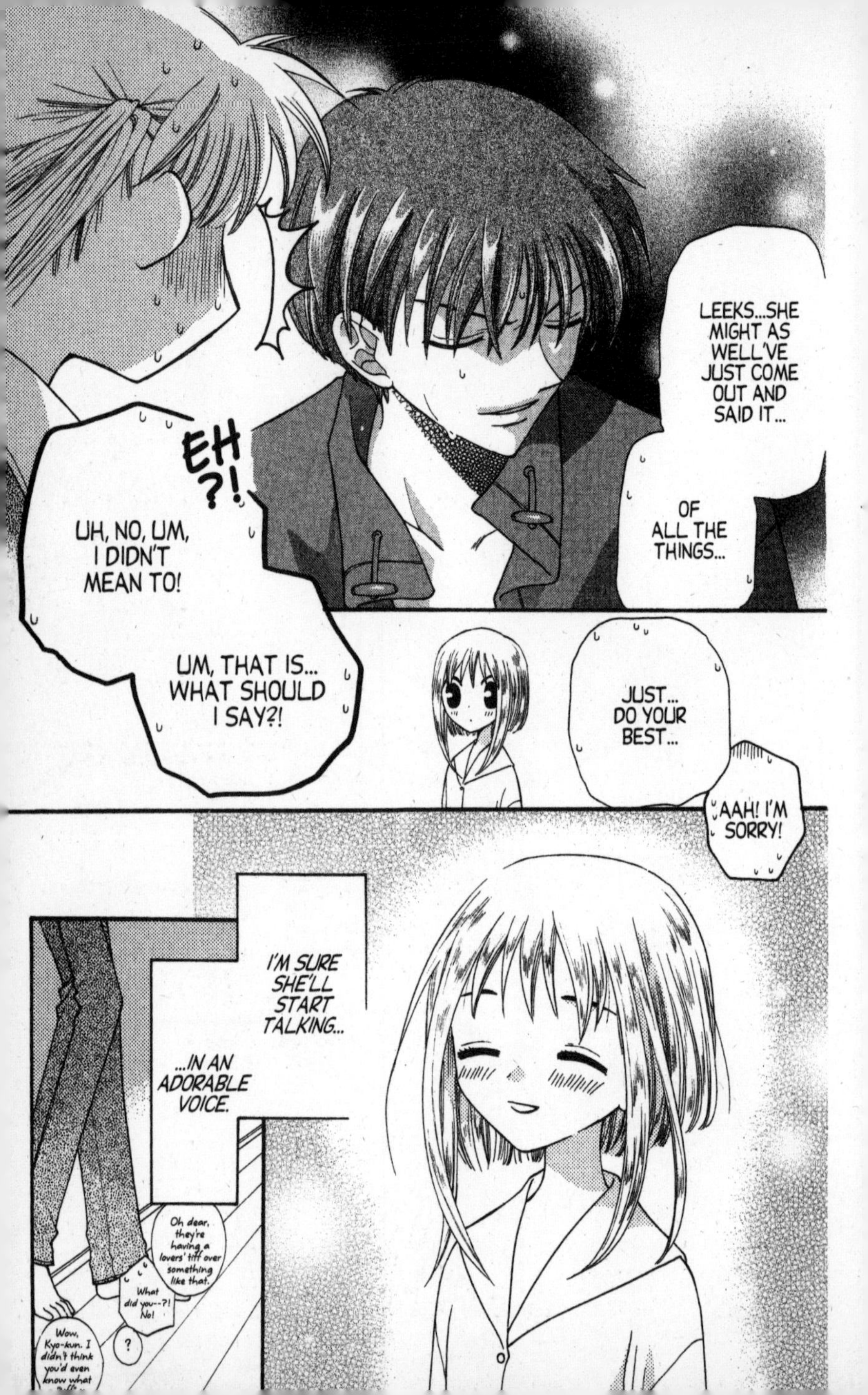
LEEKS...SHE MIGHT AS WELL'VE JUST COME OUT AND SAID IT...
OF ALL THE THINGS...
EH?!
UH, NO, UM, I DIDN'T MEAN TO!
UM, THAT IS... WHAT SHOULD I SAY?!
JUST... DO YOUR BEST...
AAH! I'M SORRY!
I'M SURE SHE'LL START TALKING...
...IN AN ADORABLE VOICE.
Oh dear, they're having a lovers' tiff over something like that.
What did you--?! No!
?
Wow, Kyo-kun. I didn't think you'd even know what

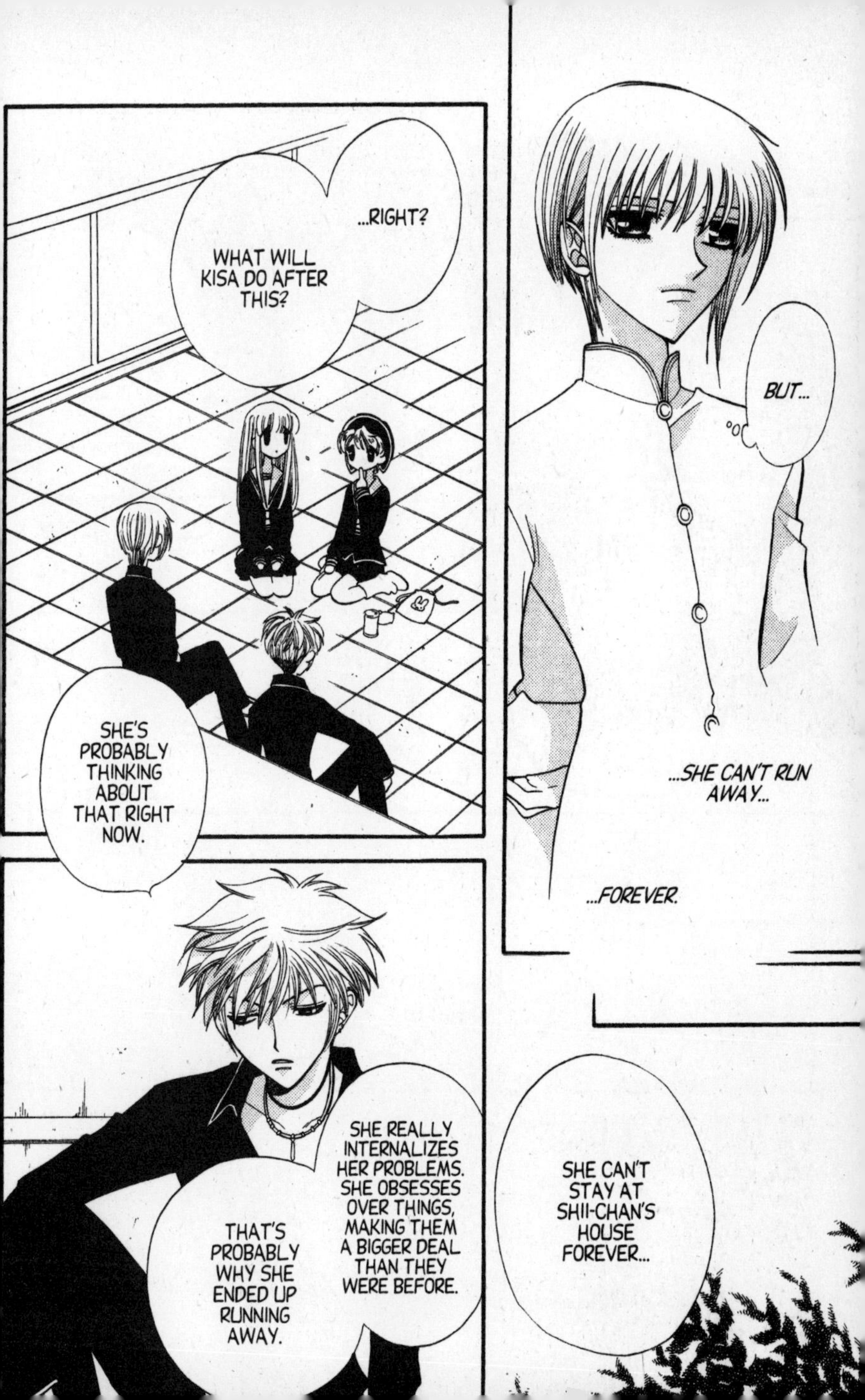
WHAT WILL KISA DO AFTER THIS?
...RIGHT?
SHE'S PROBABLY THINKING ABOUT THAT RIGHT NOW.
SHE REALLY INTERNALIZES HER PROBLEMS. SHE OBSESSES OVER THINGS, MAKING THEM A BIGGER DEAL THAN THEY WERE BEFORE.
THAT'S PROBABLY WHY SHE ENDED UP RUNNING AWAY.
SHE CAN'T STAY AT SHII-CHAN'S HOUSE FOREVER...
BUT...
...SHE CAN'T RUN AWAY...
...FOREVER.

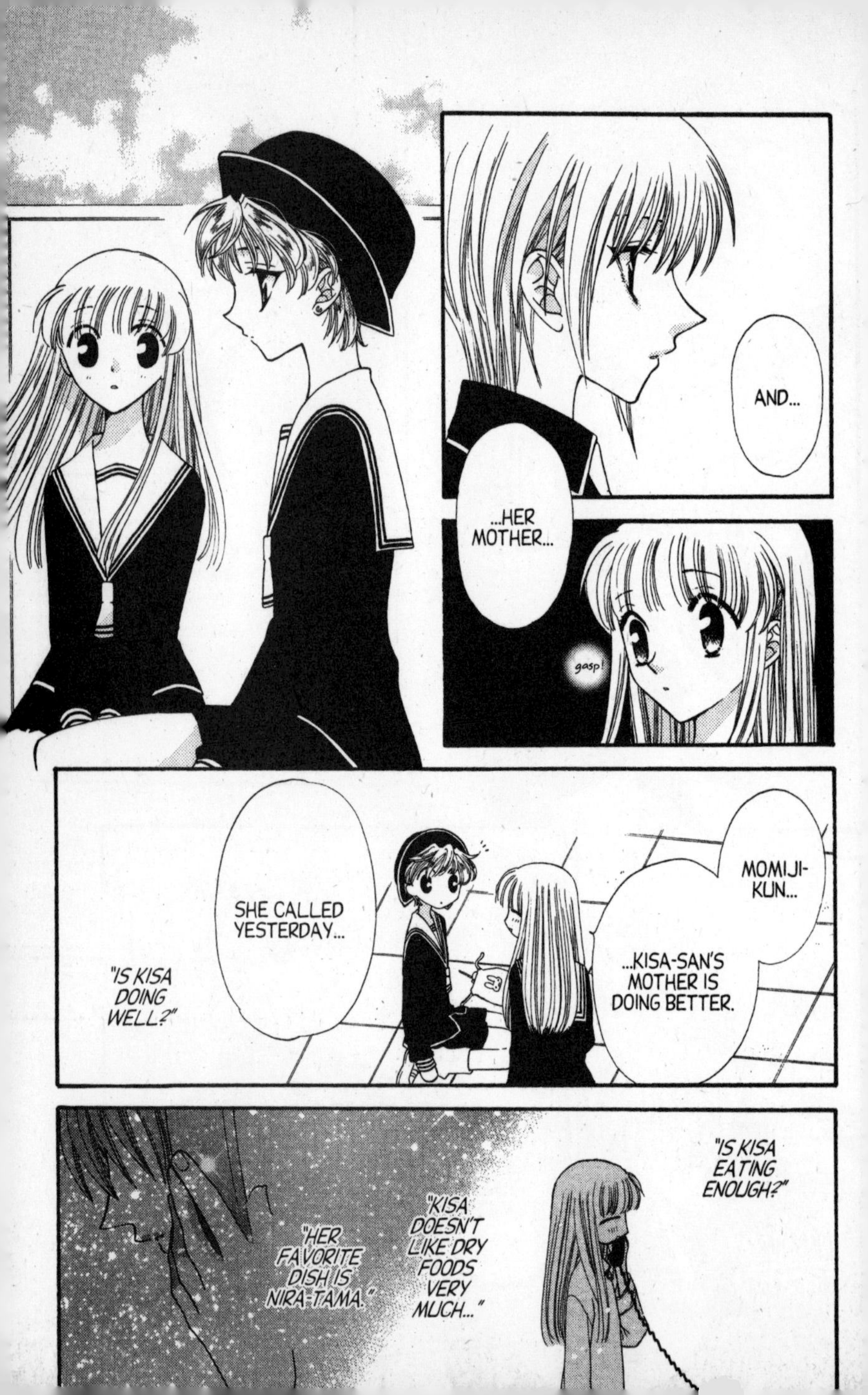
AND...
...HER MOTHER...
gasp!
MOMIJI-KUN...
...KISA-SAN'S MOTHER IS DOING BETTER.
SHE CALLED YESTERDAY...
"IS KISA DOING WELL?"
"IS KISA EATING ENOUGH?"
"KISA DOESN'T LIKE DRY FOODS VERY MUCH..."
"HER FAVORITE DISH IS NIRA-TAMA."

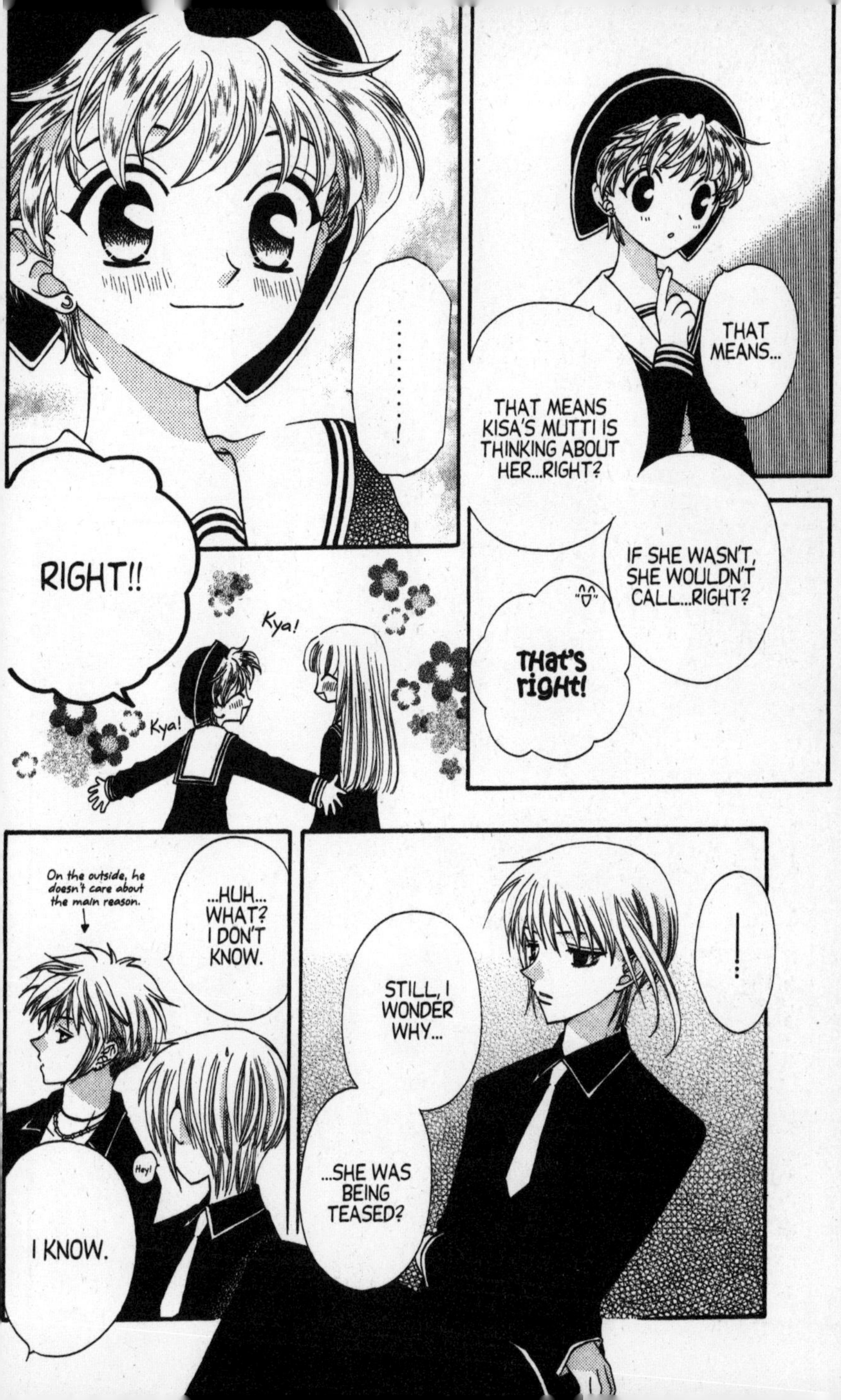
THAT MEANS...
THAT MEANS KISA'S MUTTI IS THINKING ABOUT HER...RIGHT?
......!
IF SHE WASN'T, SHE WOULDN'T CALL...RIGHT?
That's right!
RIGHT!!
Kya!
Kya!
...!
STILL, I WONDER WHY...
...SHE WAS BEING TEASED?
...HUH... WHAT? I DON'T KNOW.
On the outside, he doesn't care about the main reason.
Hey!
I KNOW.

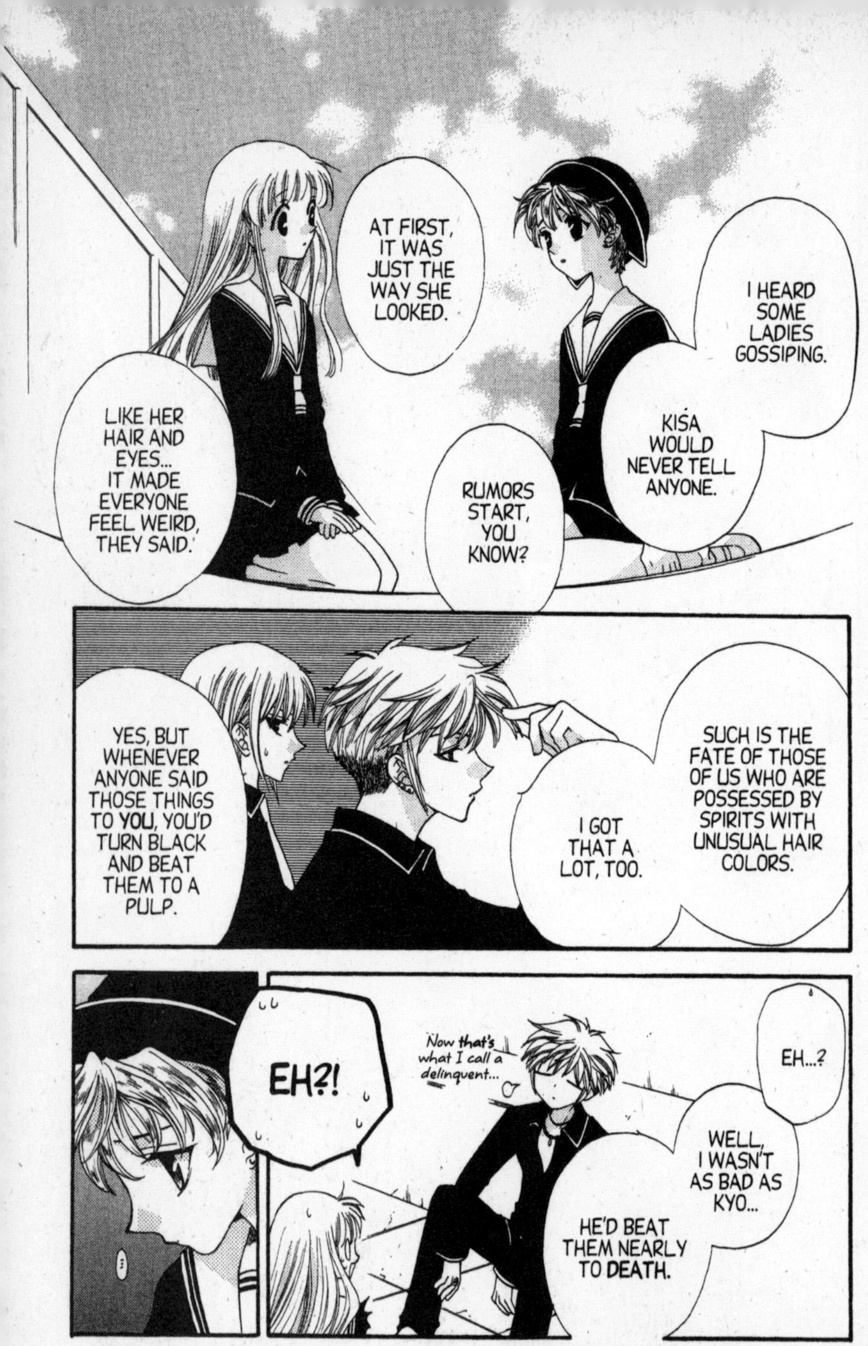
I HEARD SOME LADIES GOSSIPING.
AT FIRST, IT WAS JUST THE WAY SHE LOOKED.
KISA WOULD NEVER TELL ANYONE.
RUMORS START, YOU KNOW?
LIKE HER HAIR AND EYES... IT MADE EVERYONE FEEL WEIRD, THEY SAID.
SUCH IS THE FATE OF THOSE OF US WHO ARE POSSESSED BY SPIRITS WITH UNUSUAL HAIR COLORS.
I GOT THAT A LOT, TOO.
YES, BUT WHENEVER ANYONE SAID THOSE THINGS TO YOU, YOU'D TURN BLACK AND BEAT THEM TO A PULP.
EH...?
WELL, I WASN'T AS BAD AS KYO...
HE'D BEAT THEM NEARLY TO DEATH.
Now that's what I call a delinquent...
EH?!
...

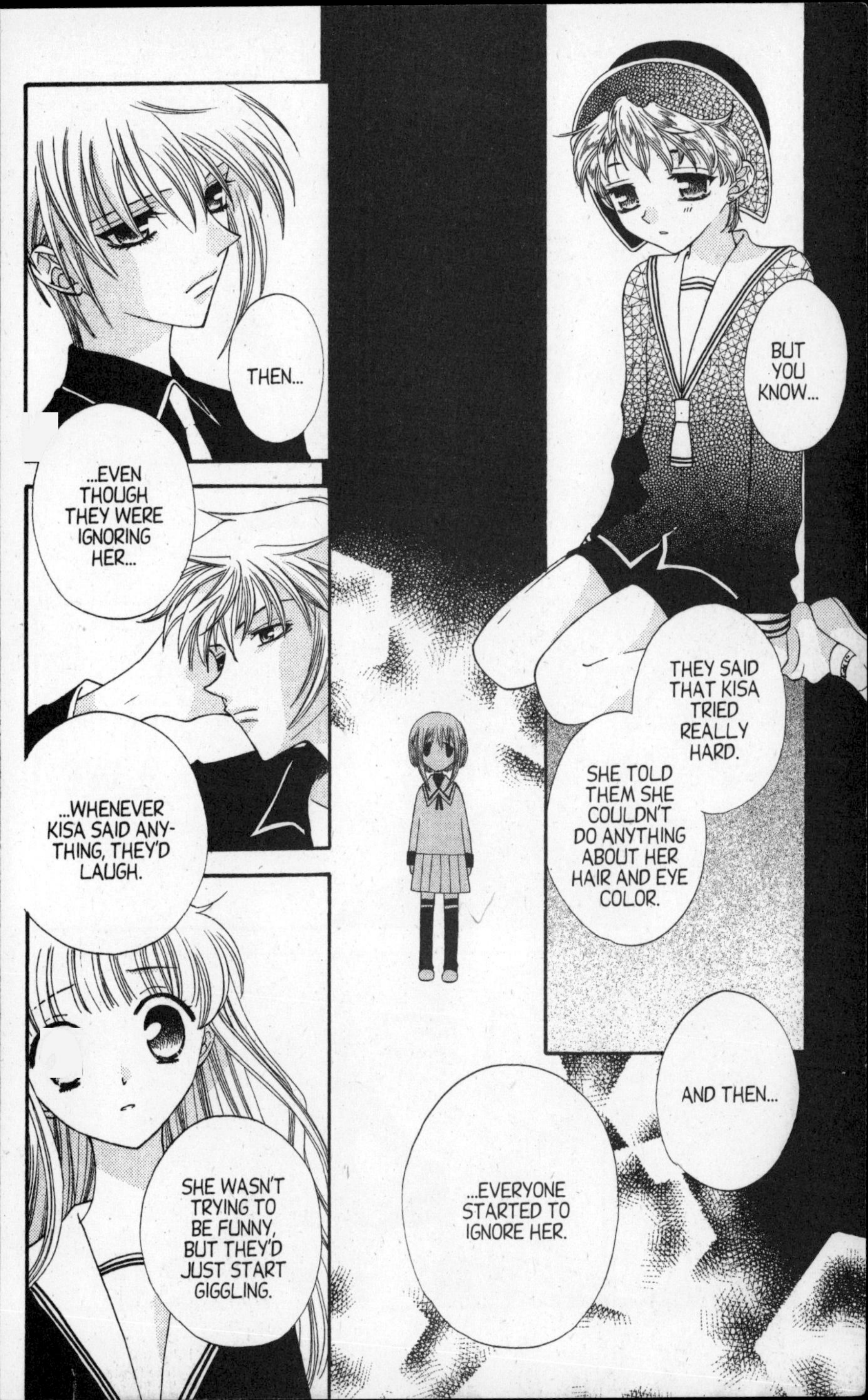
BUT YOU KNOW...
THEY SAID THAT KISA TRIED REALLY HARD.
SHE TOLD THEM SHE COULDN'T DO ANYTHING ABOUT HER HAIR AND EYE COLOR.
AND THEN...
...EVERYONE STARTED TO IGNORE HER.
THEN...
...EVEN THOUGH THEY WERE IGNORING HER...
...WHENEVER KISA SAID ANY-THING, THEY'D LAUGH.
SHE WASN'T TRYING TO BE FUNNY, BUT THEY'D JUST START GIGGLING.

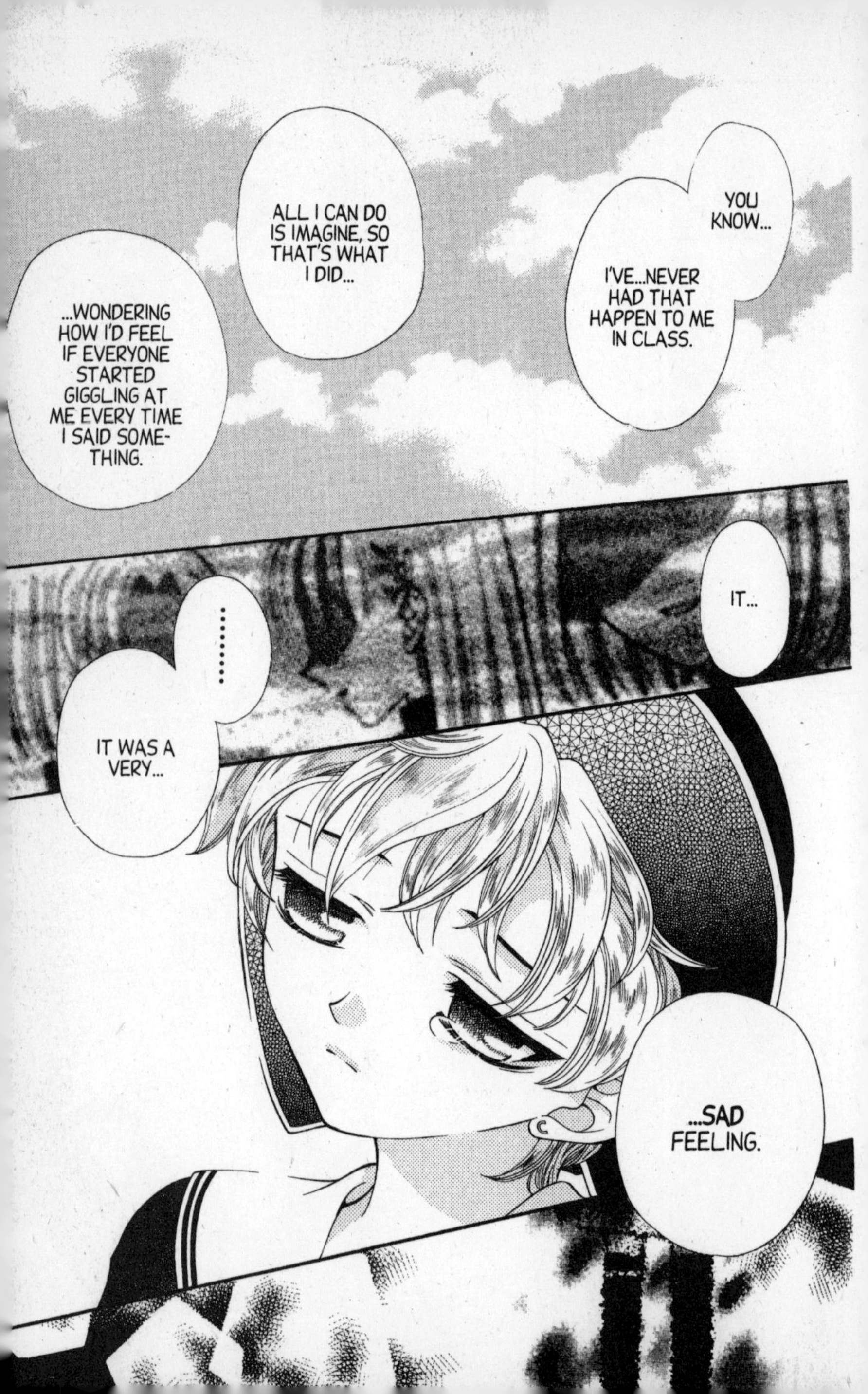
YOU KNOW...
I'VE...NEVER HAD THAT HAPPEN TO ME IN CLASS.
ALL I CAN DO IS IMAGINE, SO THAT'S WHAT I DID...
...WONDERING HOW I'D FEEL IF EVERYONE STARTED GIGGLING AT ME EVERY TIME I SAID SOME-THING.
IT...
......
IT WAS A VERY...
...SAD FEELING.

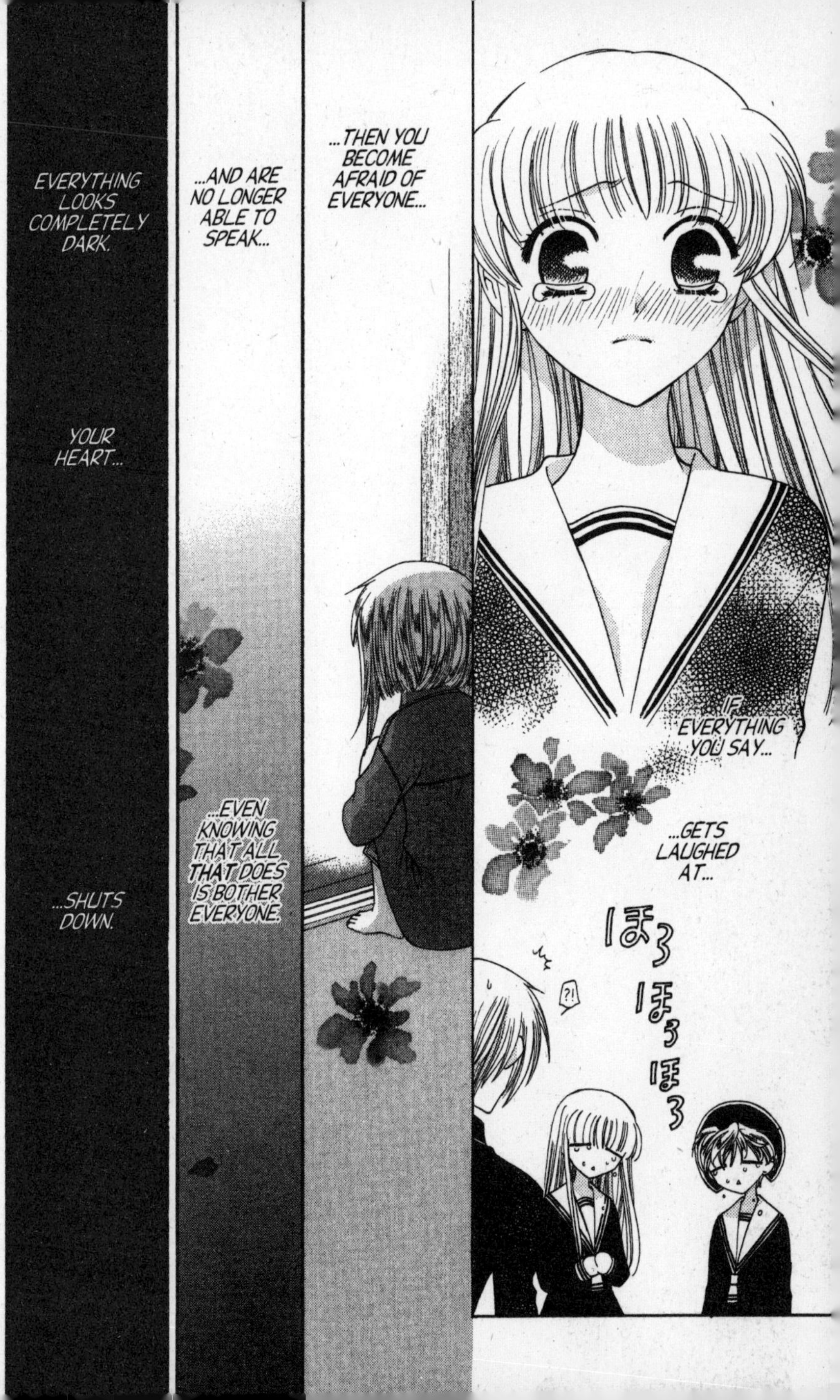
IF EVERYTHING YOU SAY...
...GETS LAUGHED AT...
?!
ほろほろほろ
...THEN YOU BECOME AFRAID OF EVERYONE...
...AND ARE NO LONGER ABLE TO SPEAK...
...EVEN KNOWING THAT ALL THAT DOES IS BOTHER EVERYONE.
EVERYTHING LOOKS COMPLETELY DARK.
YOUR HEART...
...SHUTS DOWN.

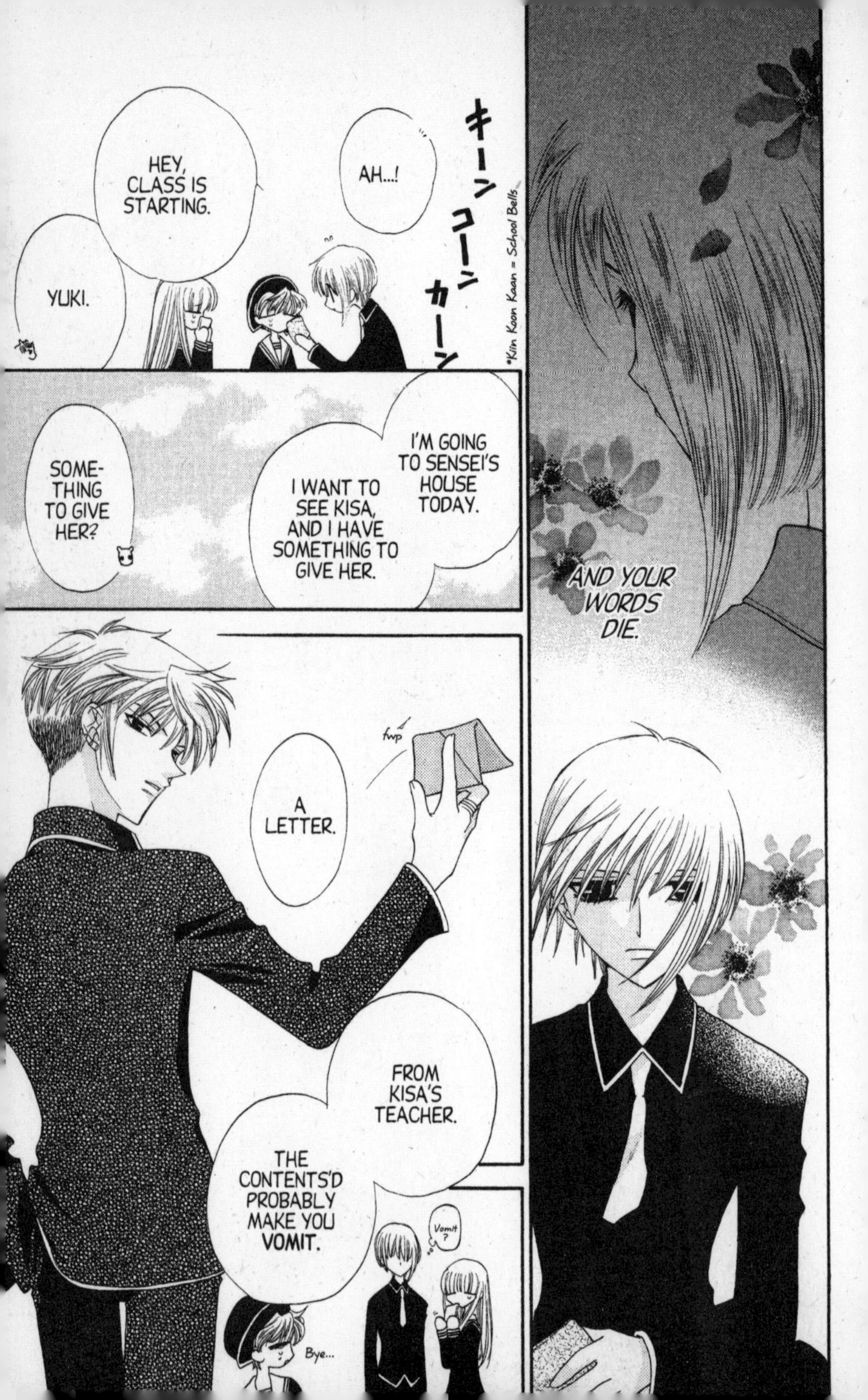
AND YOUR WORDS DIE.
キーンコーンカーン
*Kiin Koon Kaan = School Bells
AH...!
HEY, CLASS IS STARTING.
YUKI.
I'M GOING TO SENSEI'S HOUSE TODAY.
I WANT TO SEE KISA, AND I HAVE SOMETHING TO GIVE HER.
SOME-THING TO GIVE HER?
fwp
A LETTER.
FROM KISA'S TEACHER.
THE CONTENTS'D PROBABLY MAKE YOU VOMIT.
Vomit?
Bye...

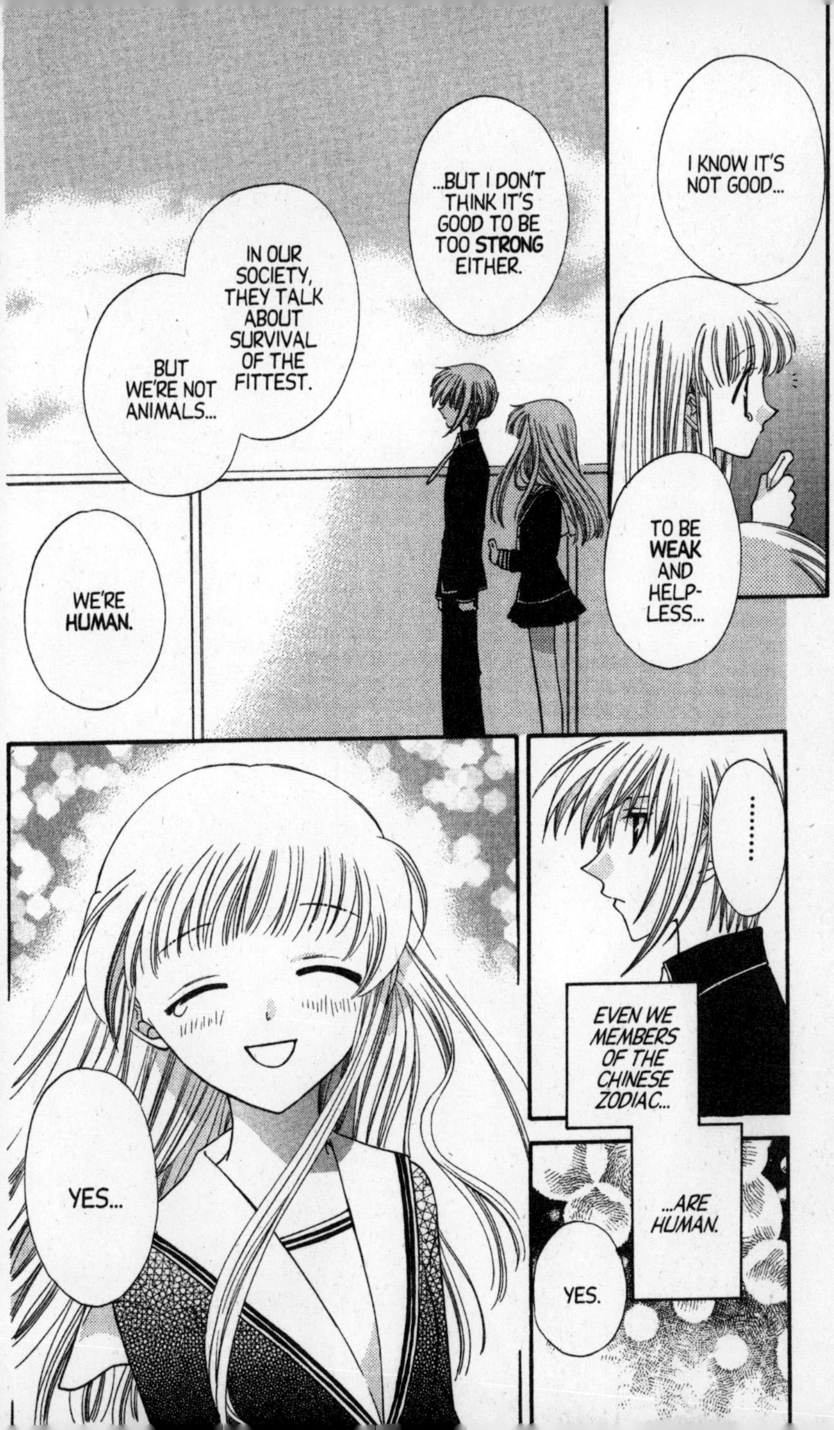
I KNOW IT'S NOT GOOD...
TO BE WEAK AND HELPLESS...
...BUT I DON'T THINK IT'S GOOD TO BE TOO STRONG EITHER.
IN OUR SOCIETY, THEY TALK ABOUT SURVIVAL OF THE FITTEST.
BUT WE'RE NOT ANIMALS...
WE'RE HUMAN.
......
EVEN WE MEMBERS OF THE CHINESE ZODIAC...
...ARE HUMAN.
YES.
YES...

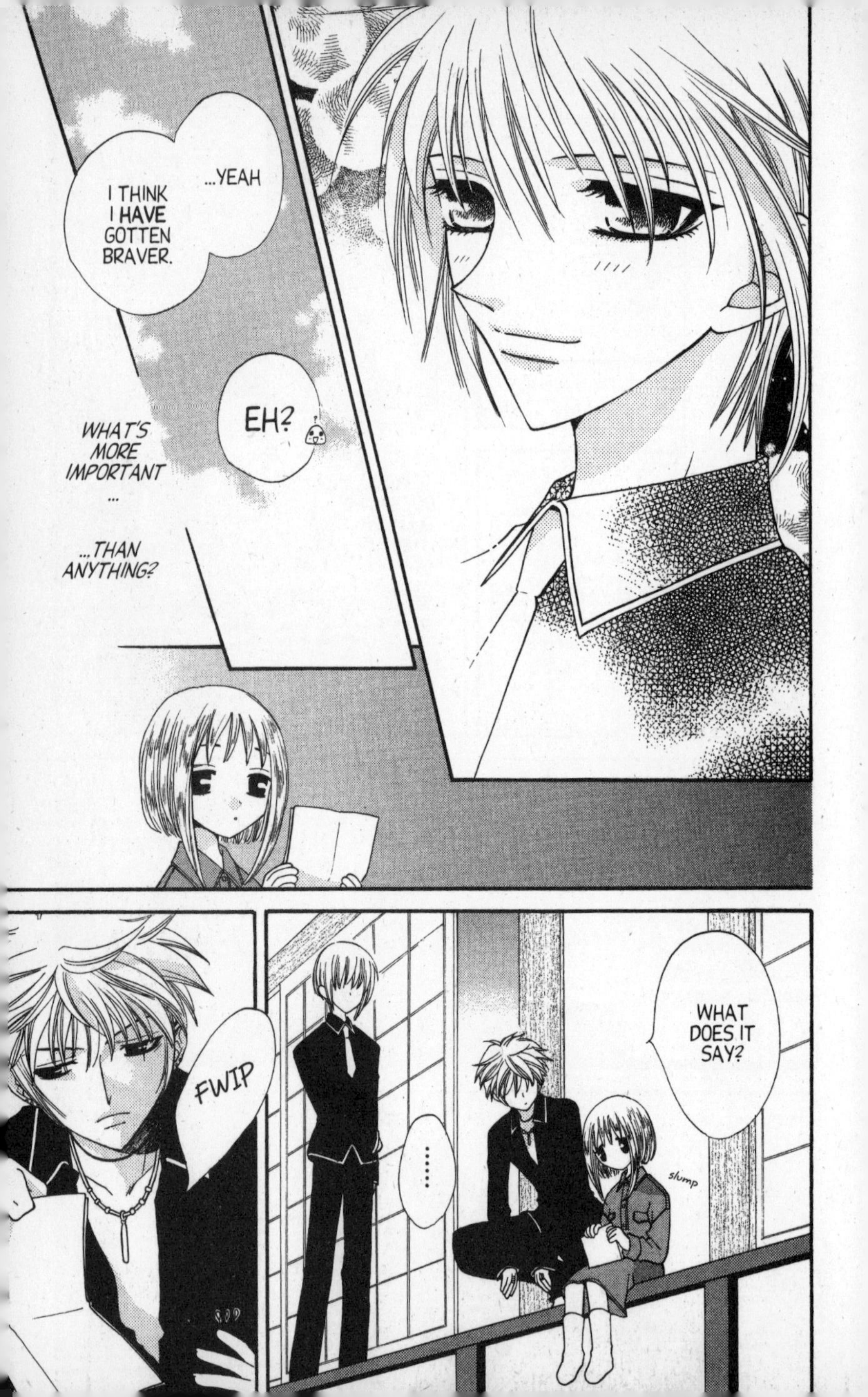

...YEAH
I THINK I HAVE GOTTEN BRAVER.
EH?
WHAT'S MORE IMPORTANT ...
...THAN ANYTHING?
WHAT DOES IT SAY?
slump
......
FWIP

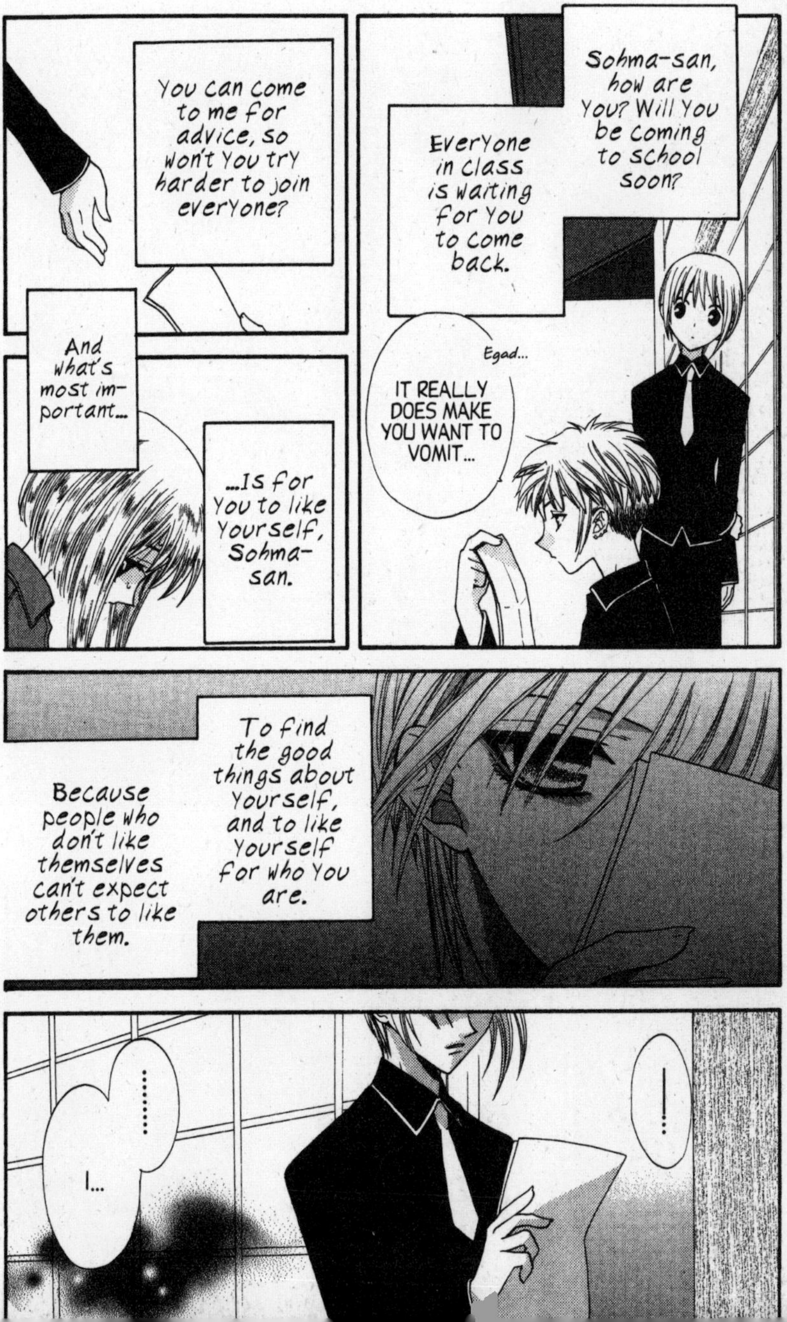
Sohma-san, how are You? Will You be coming to school soon?
EverYone in class is waiting for You to come back.
Egad...
IT REALLY DOES MAKE YOU WANT TO VOMIT...
You can come to me for advice, so won't You try harder to join everYone?
And what's most important...
...Is for You to like Yourself, Sohma-san.
To find the good things about Yourself, and to like Yourself for who You are.
Because people who don't like themselves can't expect others to like them.
......!
......
I...

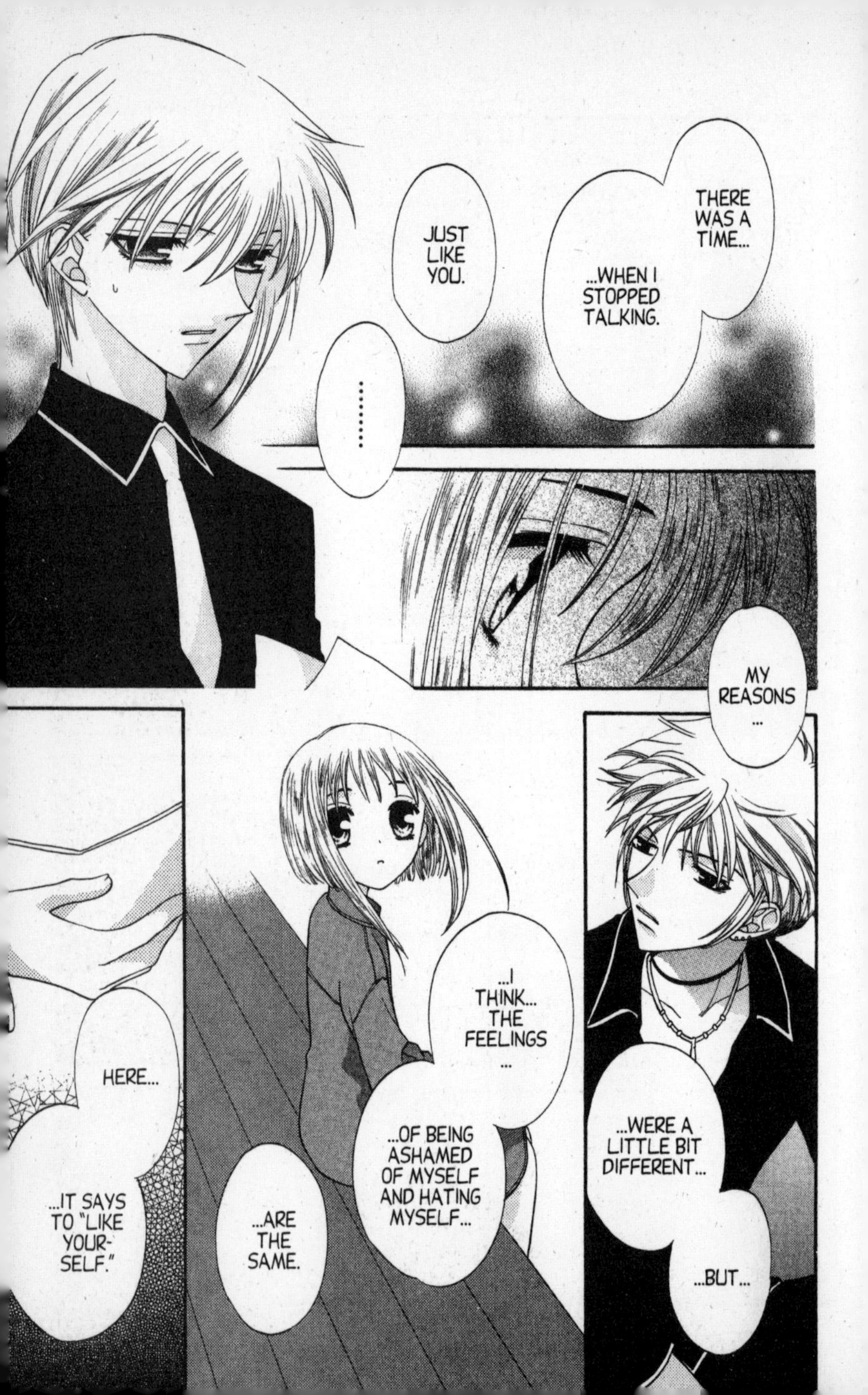
THERE WAS A TIME...
...WHEN I STOPPED TALKING.
JUST LIKE YOU.
......
MY REASONS ...
...WERE A LITTLE BIT DIFFERENT...
...BUT...
...I THINK... THE FEELINGS ...
...OF BEING ASHAMED OF MYSELF AND HATING MYSELF...
...ARE THE SAME.
HERE...
...IT SAYS TO "LIKE YOUR-SELF."

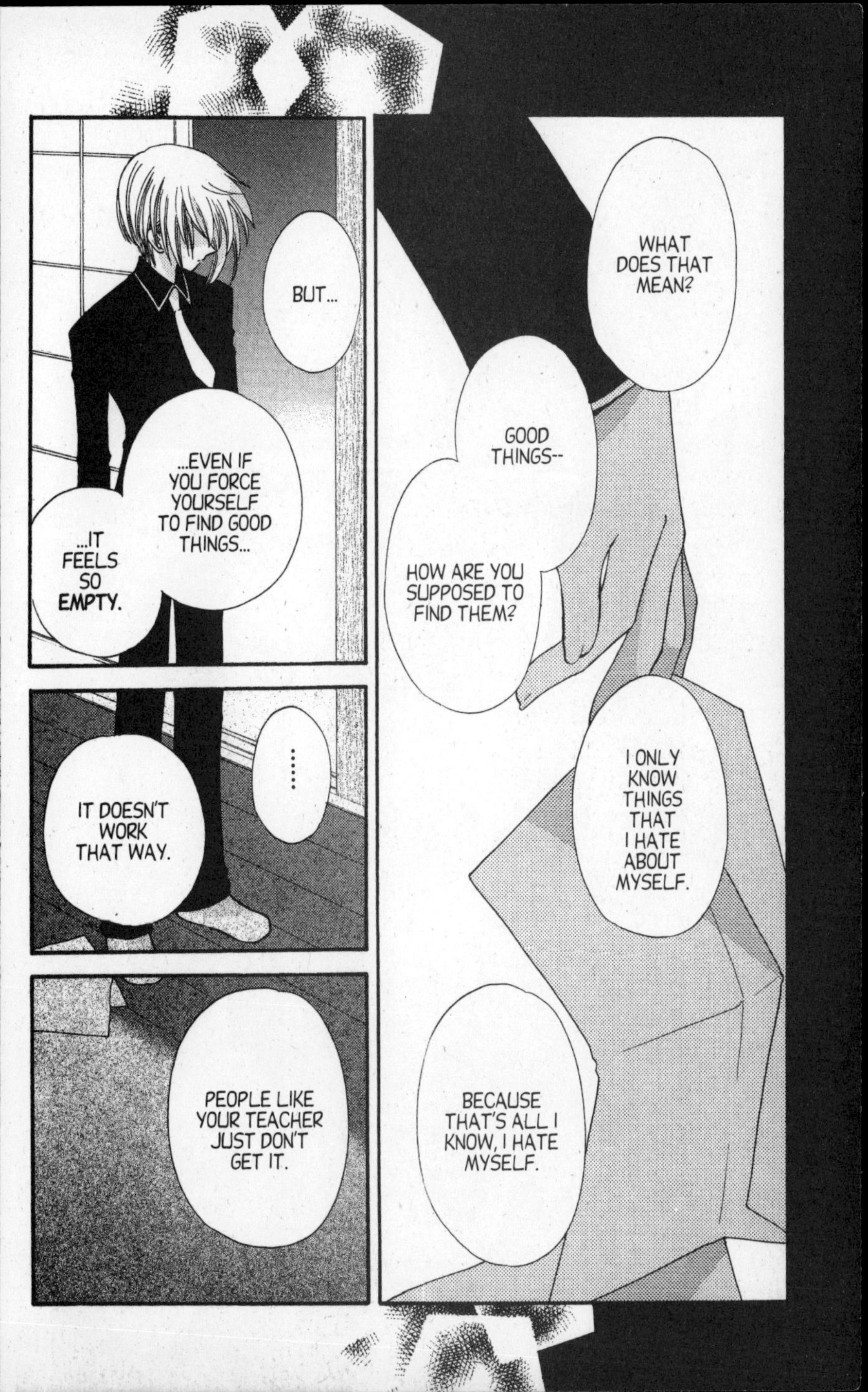
WHAT DOES THAT MEAN?
GOOD THINGS--
HOW ARE YOU SUPPOSED TO FIND THEM?
I ONLY KNOW THINGS THAT I HATE ABOUT MYSELF.
BECAUSE THAT'S ALL I KNOW, I HATE MYSELF.
BUT...
...EVEN IF YOU FORCE YOURSELF TO FIND GOOD THINGS...
...IT FEELS SO EMPTY.
......
IT DOESN'T WORK THAT WAY.
PEOPLE LIKE YOUR TEACHER JUST DON'T GET IT.

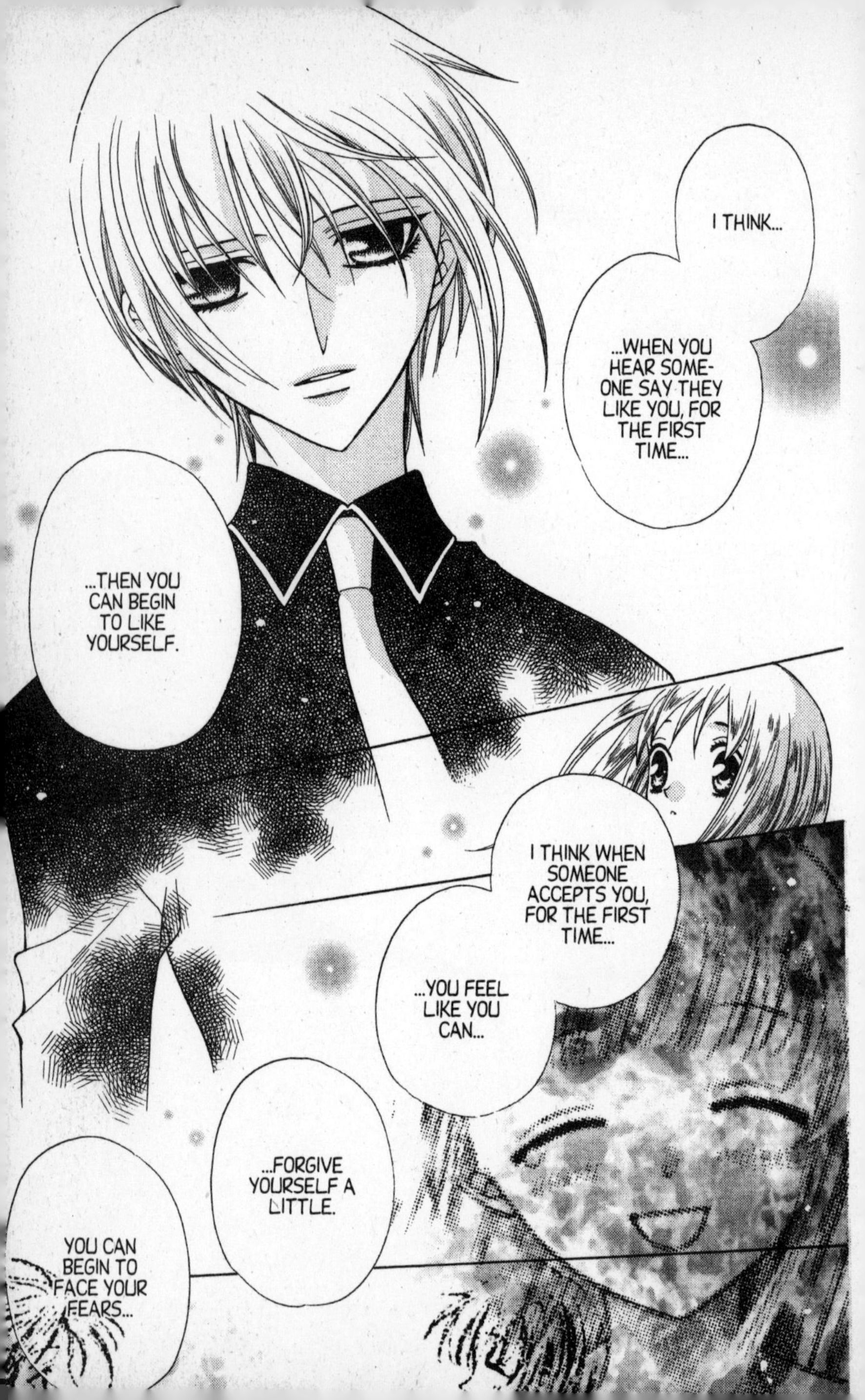
I THINK...
...WHEN YOU HEAR SOME-ONE SAY THEY LIKE YOU, FOR THE FIRST TIME...
...THEN YOU CAN BEGIN TO LIKE YOURSELF.
I THINK WHEN SOMEONE ACCEPTS YOU, FOR THE FIRST TIME...
...YOU FEEL LIKE YOU CAN...
...FORGIVE YOURSELF A LITTLE.
YOU CAN BEGIN TO FACE YOUR FEARS...

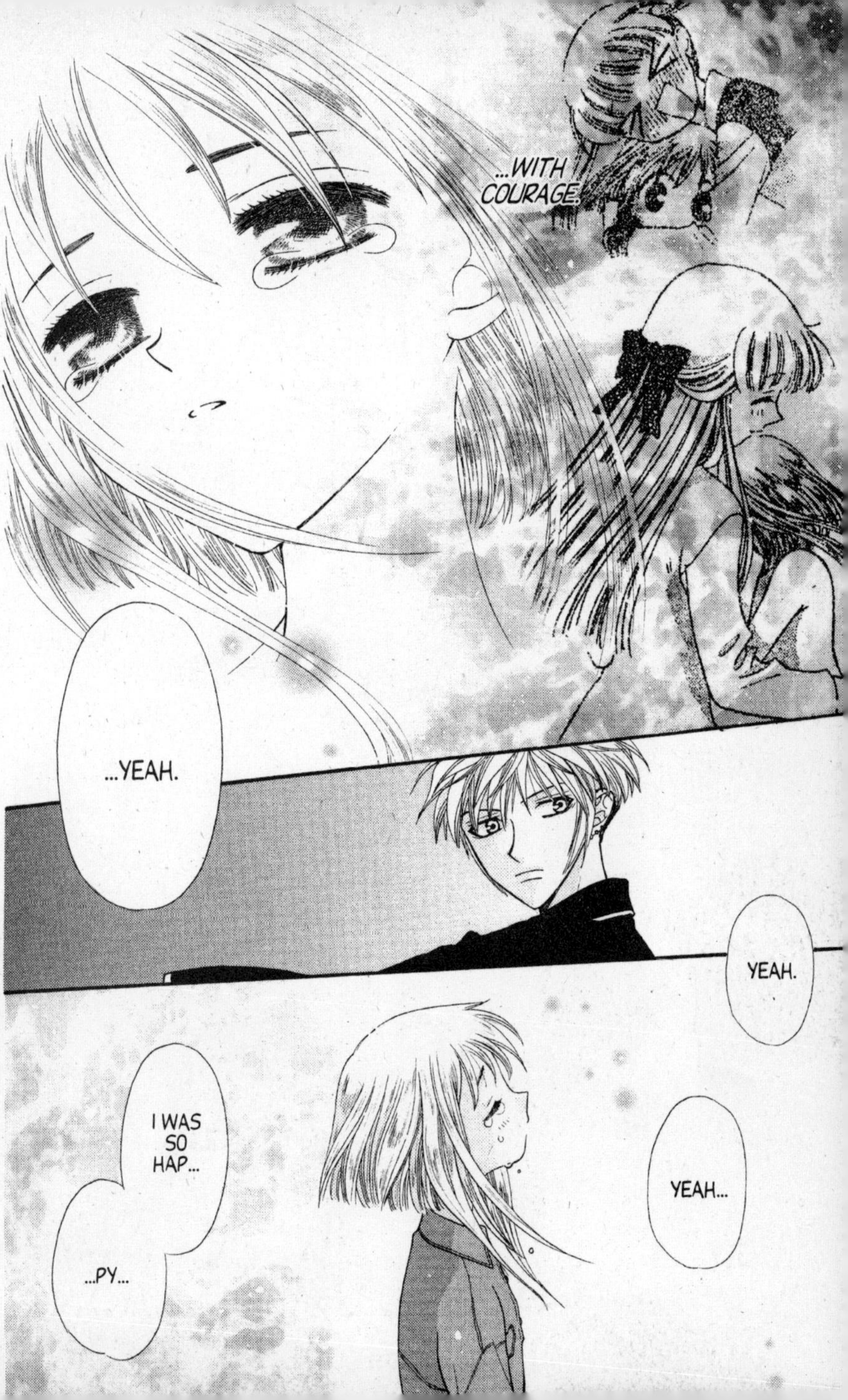
...WITH COURAGE.
...YEAH.
YEAH.
YEAH...
I WAS SO HAP...
...PY...

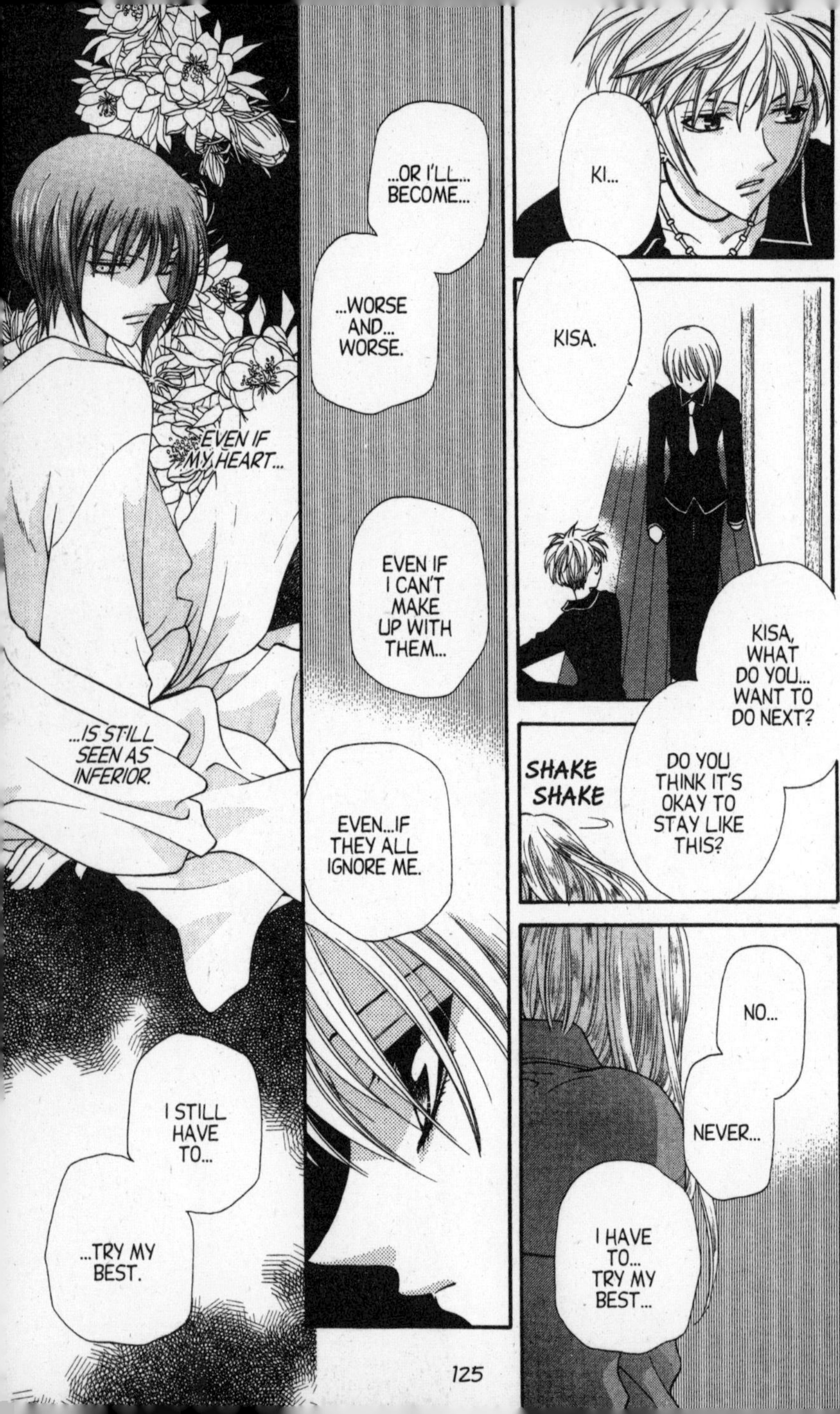
KI...
KISA.
KISA, WHAT DO YOU... WANT TO DO NEXT?
DO YOU THINK IT'S OKAY TO STAY LIKE THIS?
SHAKE SHAKE
NO...
NEVER...
I HAVE TO... TRY MY BEST...
...OR I'LL... BECOME...
...WORSE AND... WORSE.
EVEN IF I CAN'T MAKE UP WITH THEM...
EVEN...IF THEY ALL IGNORE ME.
EVEN IF MY HEART...
...IS STILL SEEN AS INFERIOR.
I STILL HAVE TO...
...TRY MY BEST.

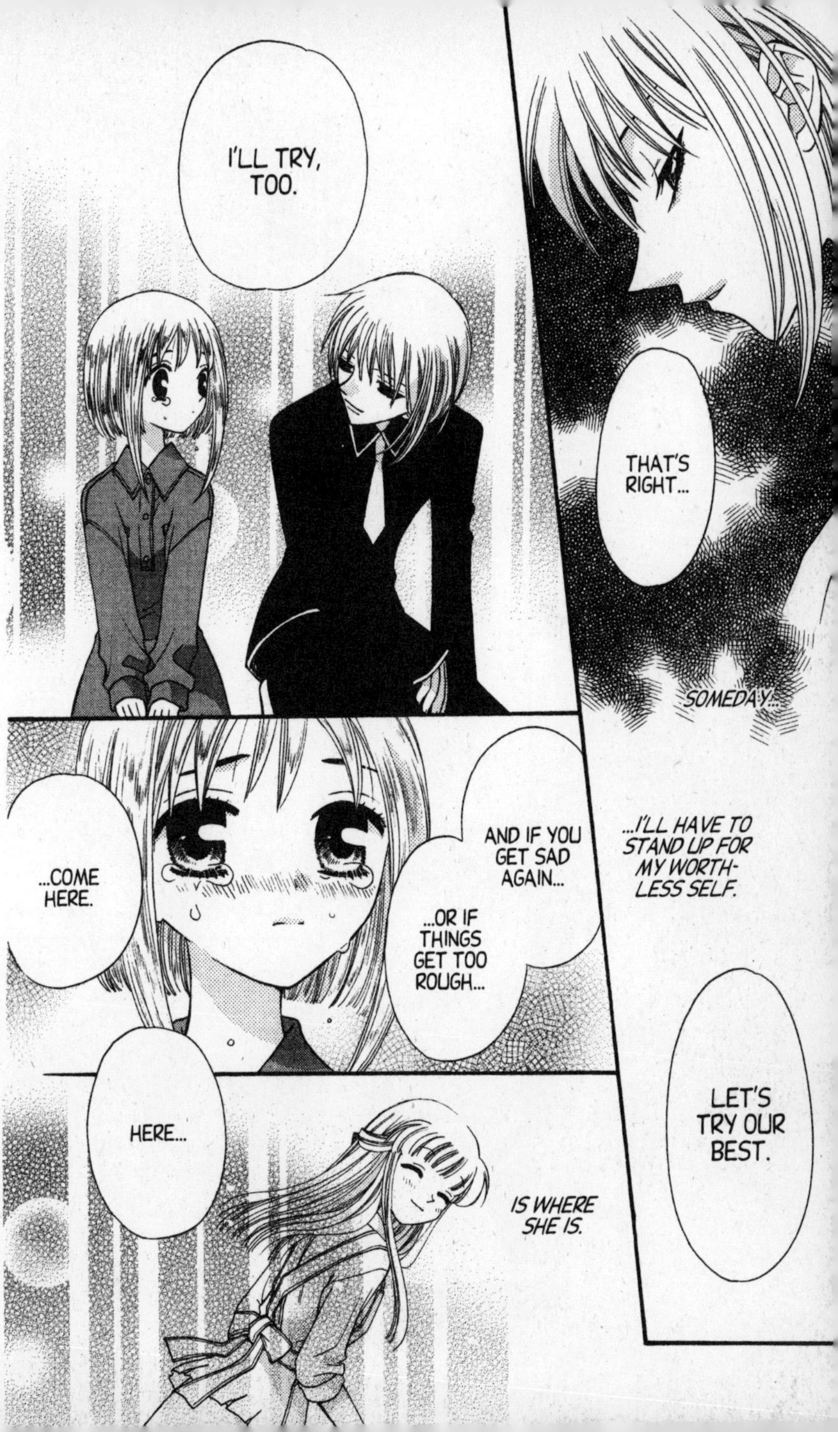
THAT'S RIGHT...
SOMEDAY...
...I'LL HAVE TO STAND UP FOR MY WORTH-LESS SELF.
LET'S TRY OUR BEST.
I'LL TRY, TOO.
AND IF YOU GET SAD AGAIN...
...OR IF THINGS GET TOO ROUGH...
...COME HERE.
HERE...
IS WHERE SHE IS.

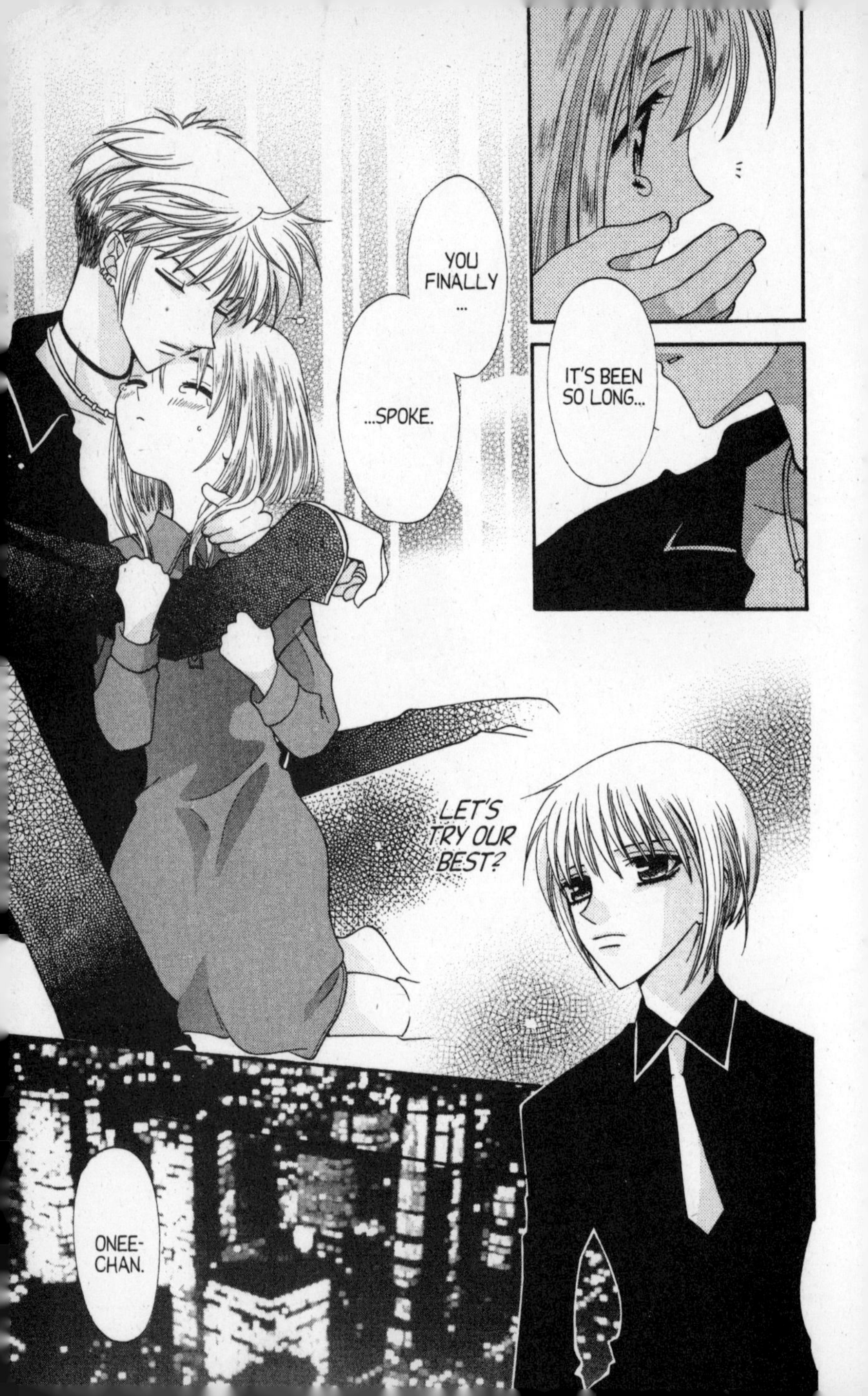
IT'S BEEN SO LONG...
YOU FINALLY ...
...SPOKE.
LET'S TRY OUR BEST?
ONEE-CHAN.

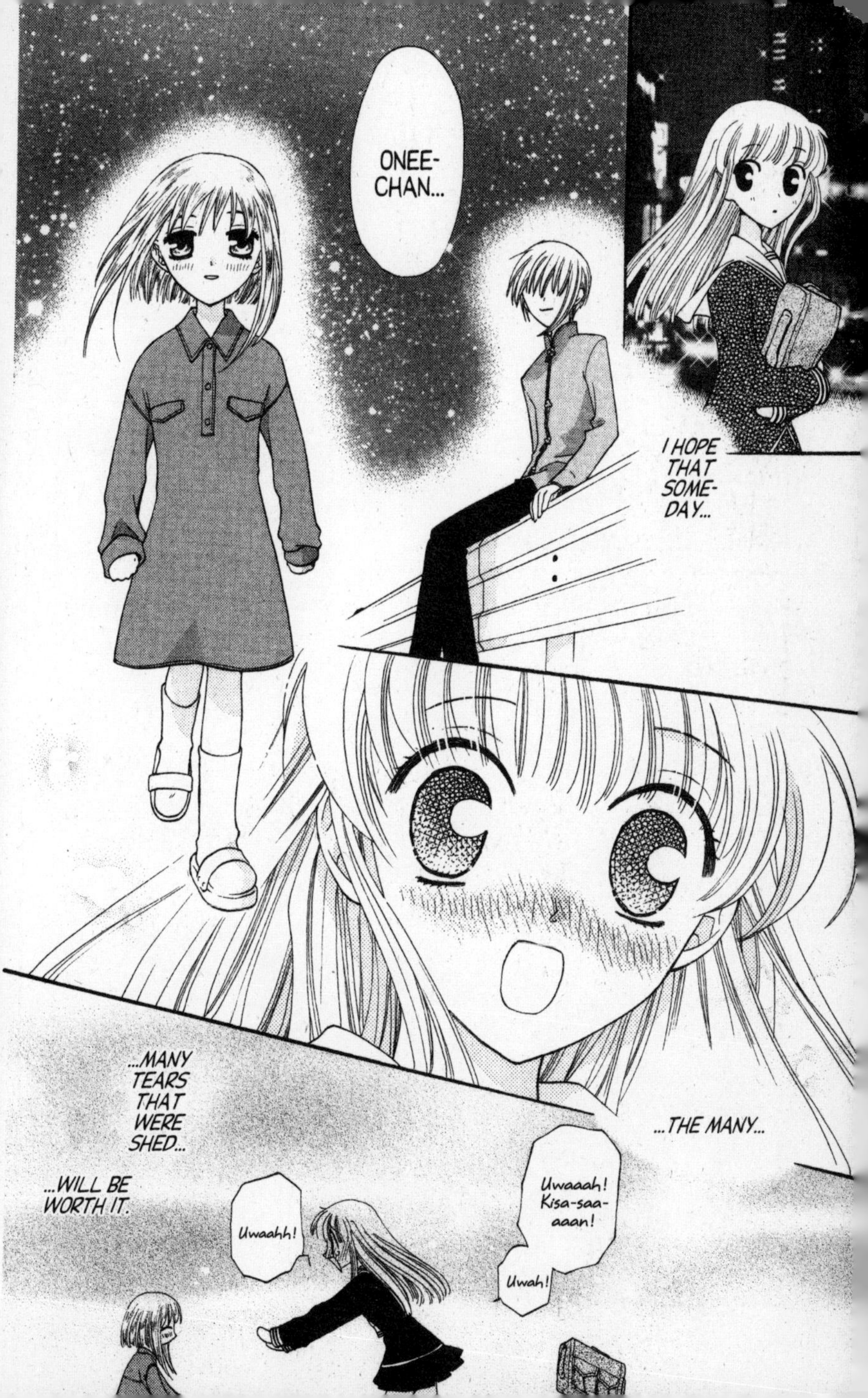
I HOPE THAT SOME-DAY...
ONEE-CHAN...
...THE MANY...
Uwaaah! Kisa-saa-aaan!
Uwah!
...MANY TEARS THAT WERE SHED...
Uwaahh!
...WILL BE WORTH IT.

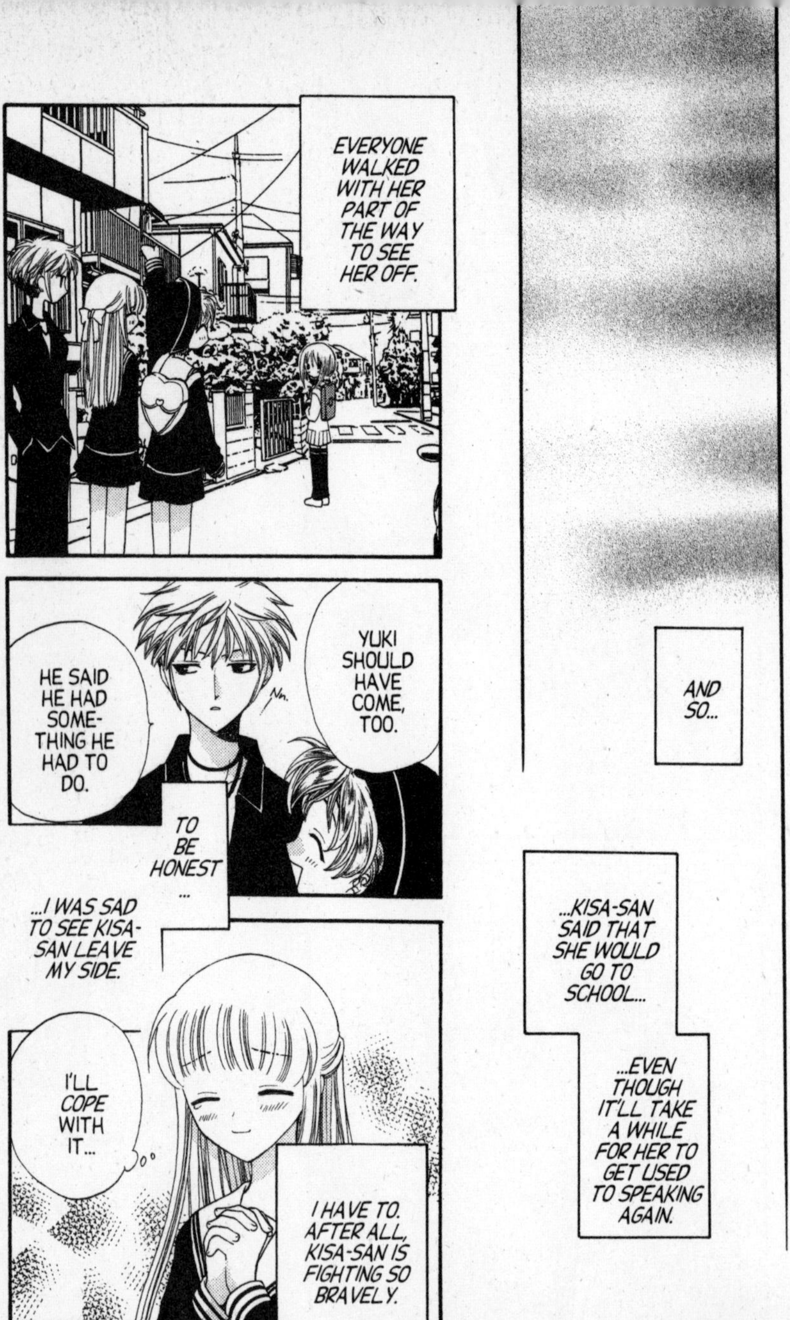
AND SO...
...KISA-SAN SAID THAT SHE WOULD GO TO SCHOOL...
...EVEN THOUGH IT'LL TAKE A WHILE FOR HER TO GET USED TO SPEAKING AGAIN.
EVERYONE WALKED WITH HER PART OF THE WAY TO SEE HER OFF.
YUKI SHOULD HAVE COME, TOO.
Nn.
HE SAID HE HAD SOME-THING HE HAD TO DO.
TO BE HONEST...
...I WAS SAD TO SEE KISA-SAN LEAVE MY SIDE.
I'LL COPE WITH IT...
I HAVE TO. AFTER ALL, KISA-SAN IS FIGHTING SO BRAVELY.

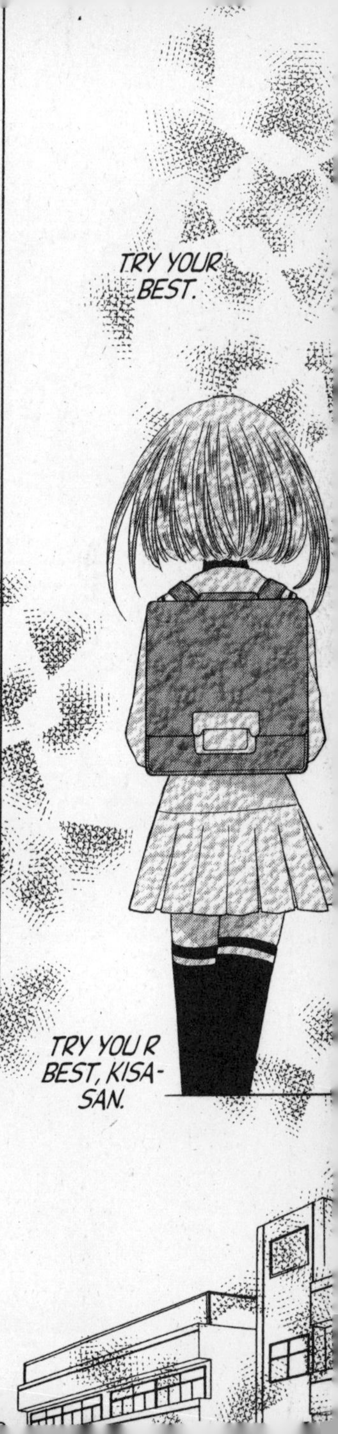
TRY YOUR BEST.
TRY YOU R BEST, KISA-SAN.
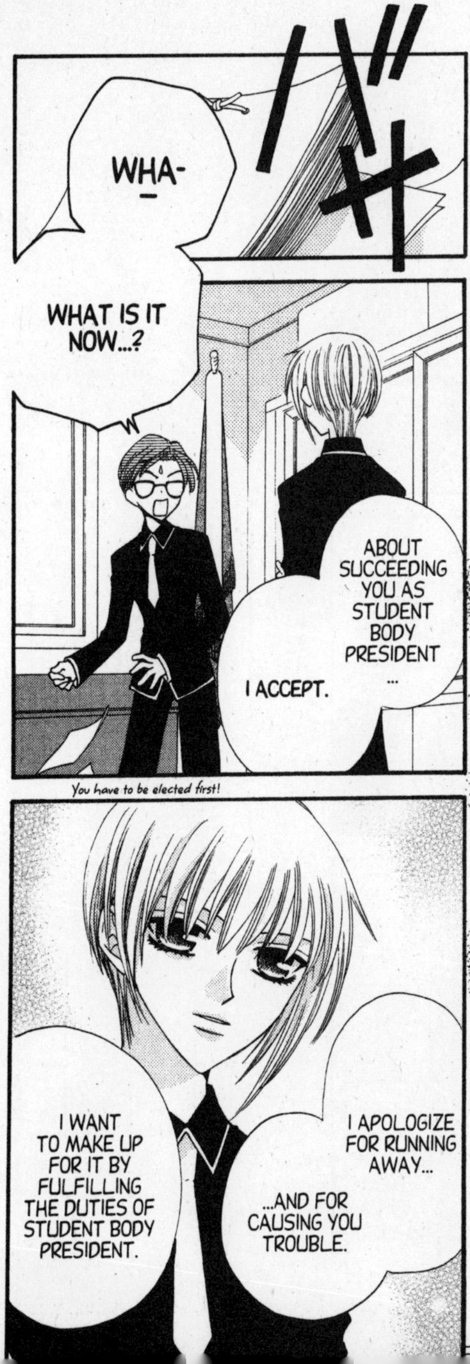
バサ
WHA-
WHAT IS IT NOW...?
ABOUT SUCCEEDING YOU AS STUDENT BODY PRESIDENT ...
I ACCEPT.
You have to be elected first!
I APOLOGIZE FOR RUNNING AWAY...
...AND FOR CAUSING YOU TROUBLE.
I WANT TO MAKE UP FOR IT BY FULFILLING THE DUTIES OF STUDENT BODY PRESIDENT.

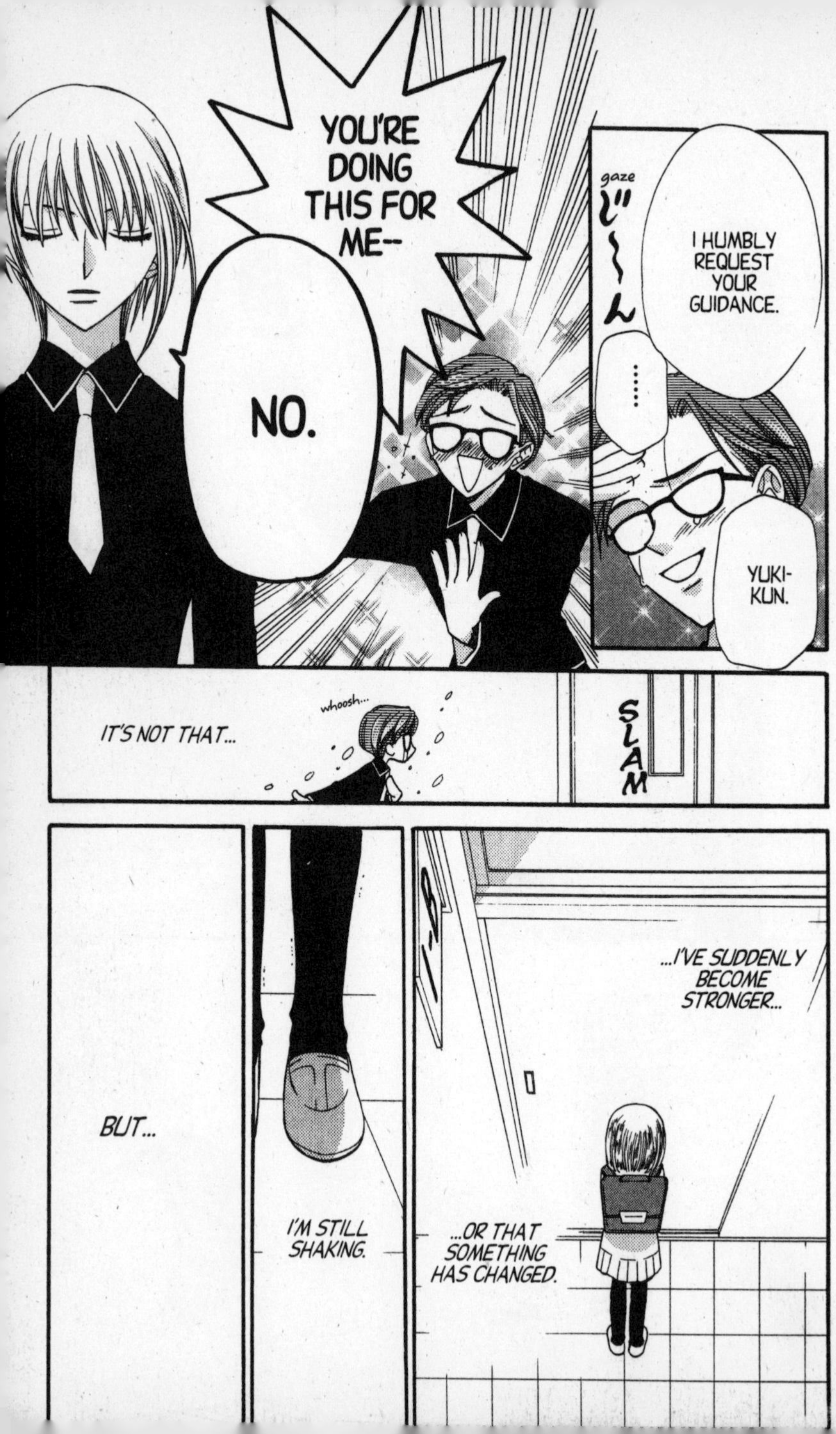
I HUMBLY REQUEST YOUR GUIDANCE.
gaze
じ~ん
......
YUKI-KUN.
YOU'RE DOING THIS FOR ME--
NO.
SLAM
whoosh...
IT'S NOT THAT...
...I'VE SUDDENLY BECOME STRONGER...
...OR THAT SOMETHING HAS CHANGED.
I'M STILL SHAKING.
BUT...

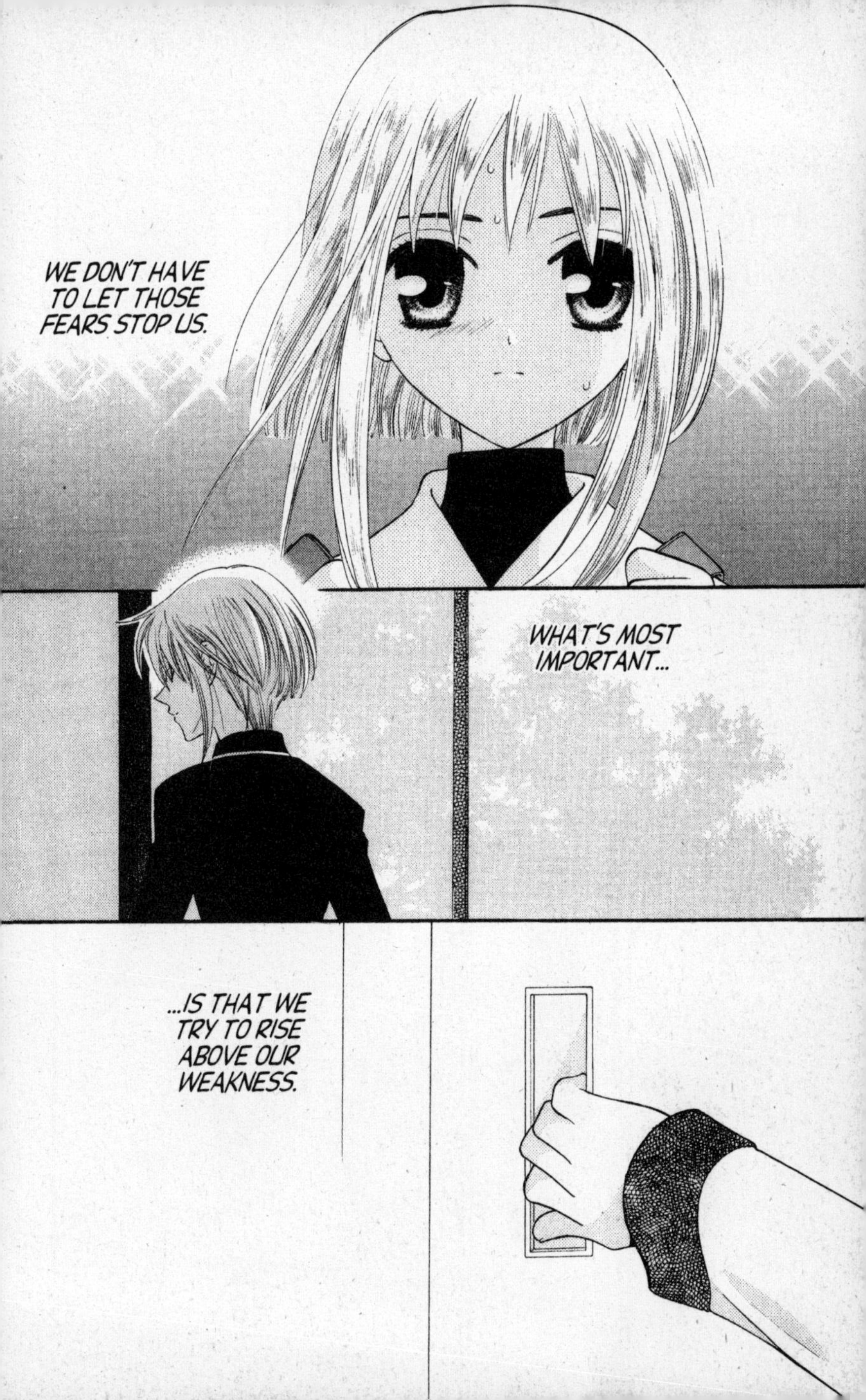
WE DON'T HAVE TO LET THOSE FEARS STOP US.
WHAT'S MOST IMPORTANT...
...IS THAT WE TRY TO RISE ABOVE OUR WEAKNESS.

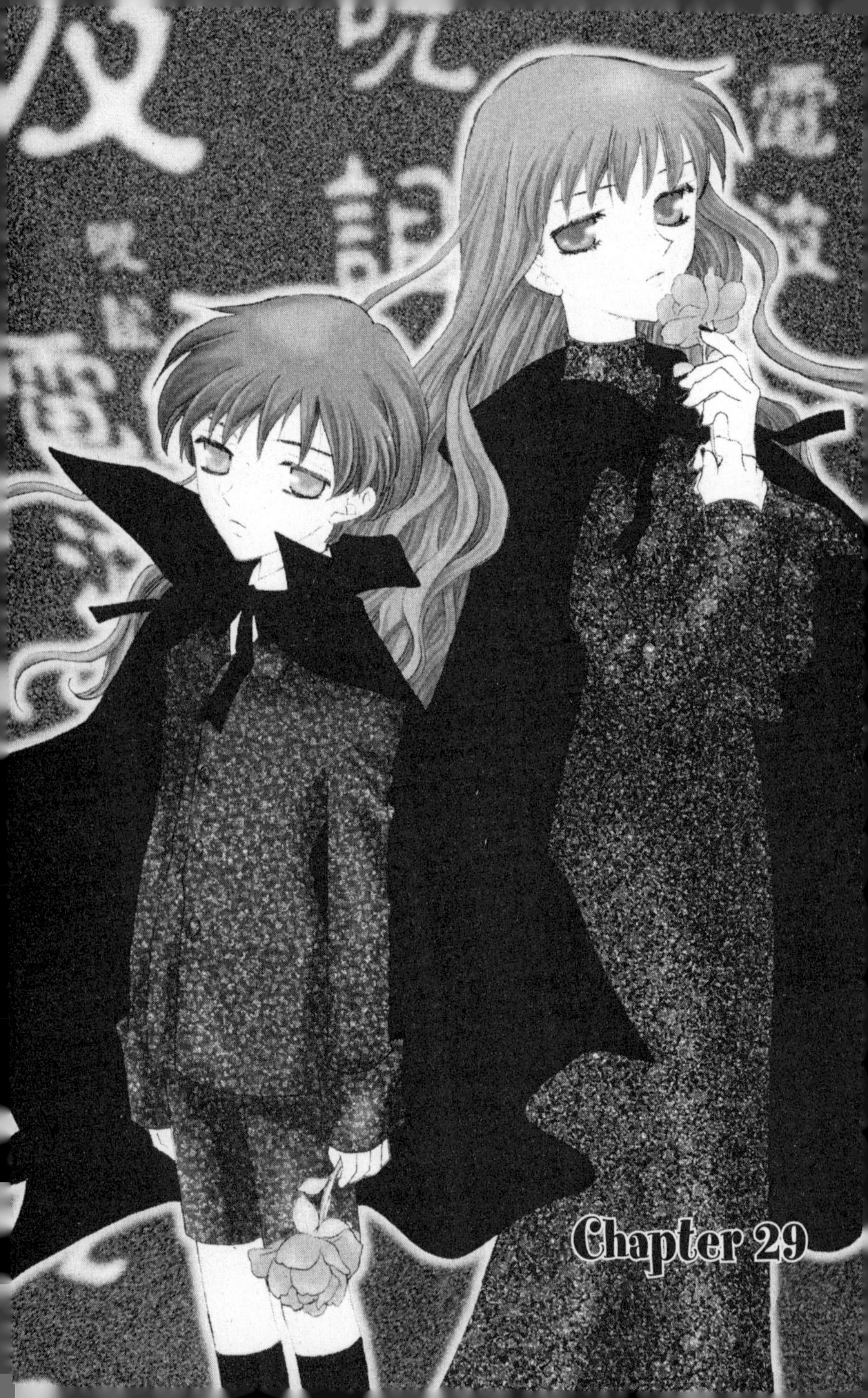
Chapter 29

# I feel so grateful!

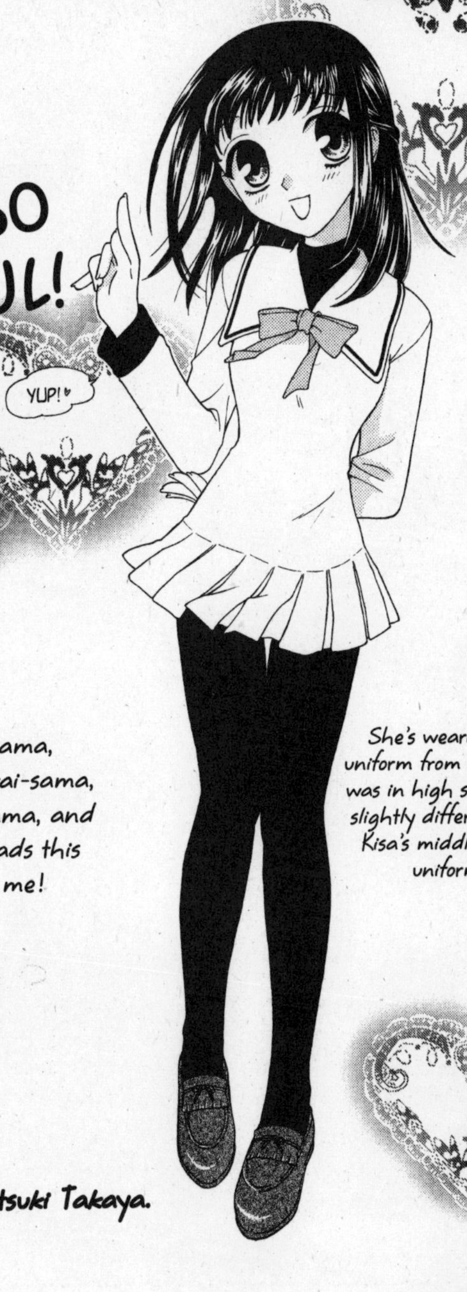
YUP!

For Harada-sama, Araki-sama, Kawai-sama, Mother, Editor-sama, and everyone who reads this and supports me!

She's wearing her uniform from when she was in high school. It's slightly different from Kisa's middle school uniform.

Next is Momitchi.

**This has been Natsuki Takaya.**

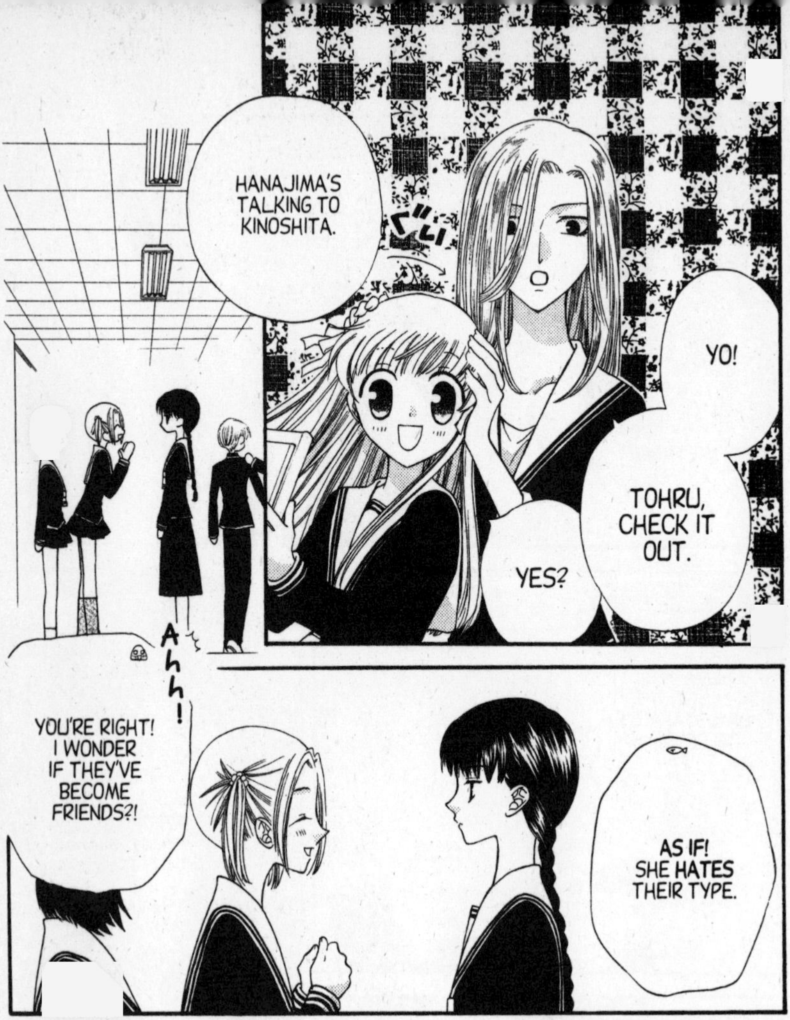
YO!
TOHRU, CHECK IT OUT.
YES?
HANAJIMA'S TALKING TO KINOSHITA.
Ahh!
YOU'RE RIGHT! I WONDER IF THEY'VE BECOME FRIENDS?!
AS IF! SHE HATES THEIR TYPE.

## ULTRA SPECIAL BLAH BLAH BLAH 5

I don't know if they're good people or not, but every time Motoko-chan and company try to do something and it backfires, it makes me laugh so much that I can't help but like them. (Like Shouka*.) Is that a mean thing to say? (laugh) I want to draw Megumi again. The strongest combo in Furuba, Saki & Megumi. (laugh)

* A character in Takaya-sensei's previous series, Tsubasa o Motsumono.

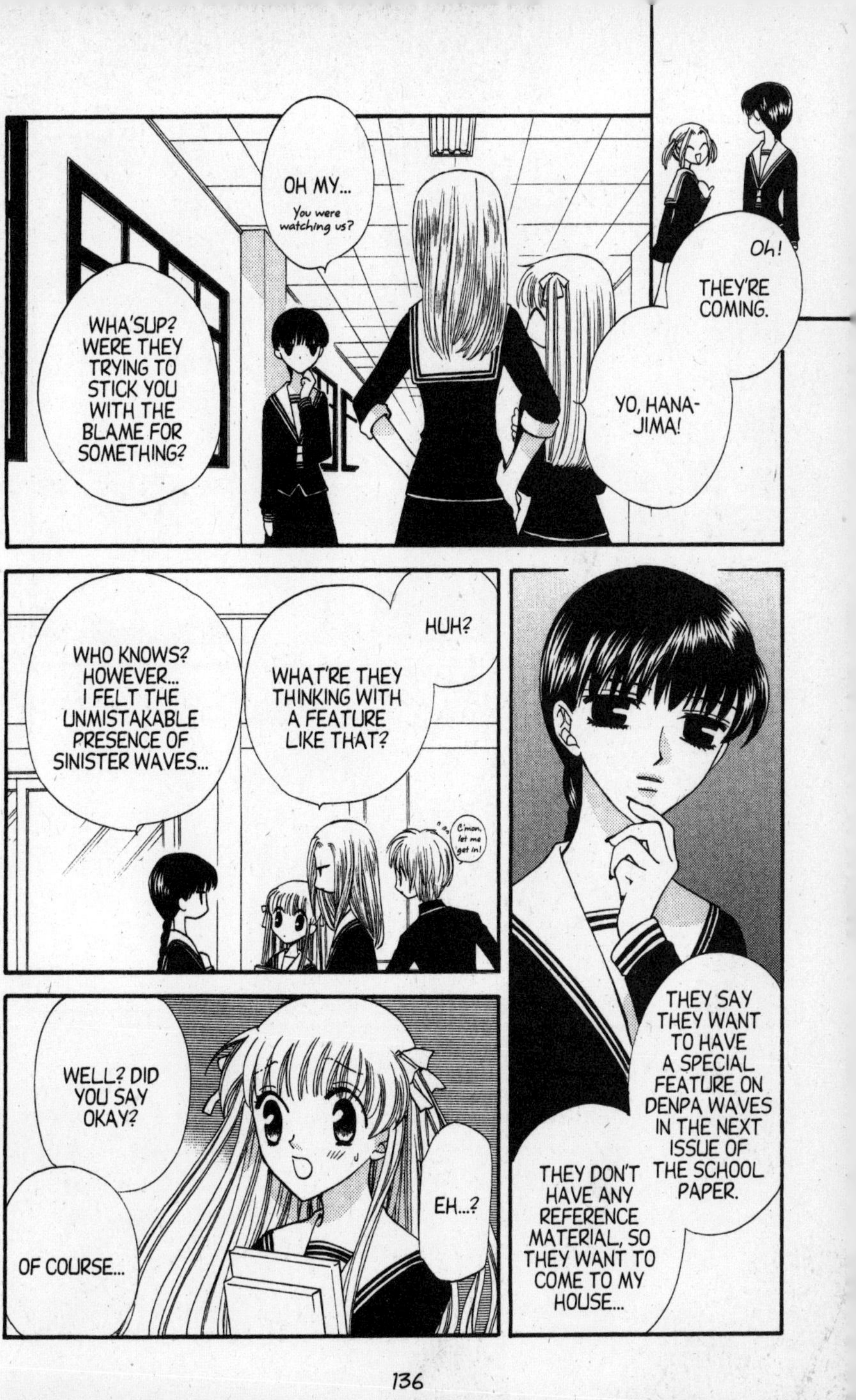
Oh! THEY'RE COMING.
YO, HANA-JIMA!
OH MY... You were watching us?
WHA'SUP? WERE THEY TRYING TO STICK YOU WITH THE BLAME FOR SOMETHING?
THEY SAY THEY WANT TO HAVE A SPECIAL FEATURE ON DENPA WAVES IN THE NEXT ISSUE OF THE SCHOOL PAPER.
THEY DON'T HAVE ANY REFERENCE MATERIAL, SO THEY WANT TO COME TO MY HOUSE...
HUH?
WHAT'RE THEY THINKING WITH A FEATURE LIKE THAT?
C'mon, let me get in!
WHO KNOWS? HOWEVER... I FELT THE UNMISTAKABLE PRESENCE OF SINISTER WAVES...
EH...?
WELL? DID YOU SAY OKAY?
OF COURSE...

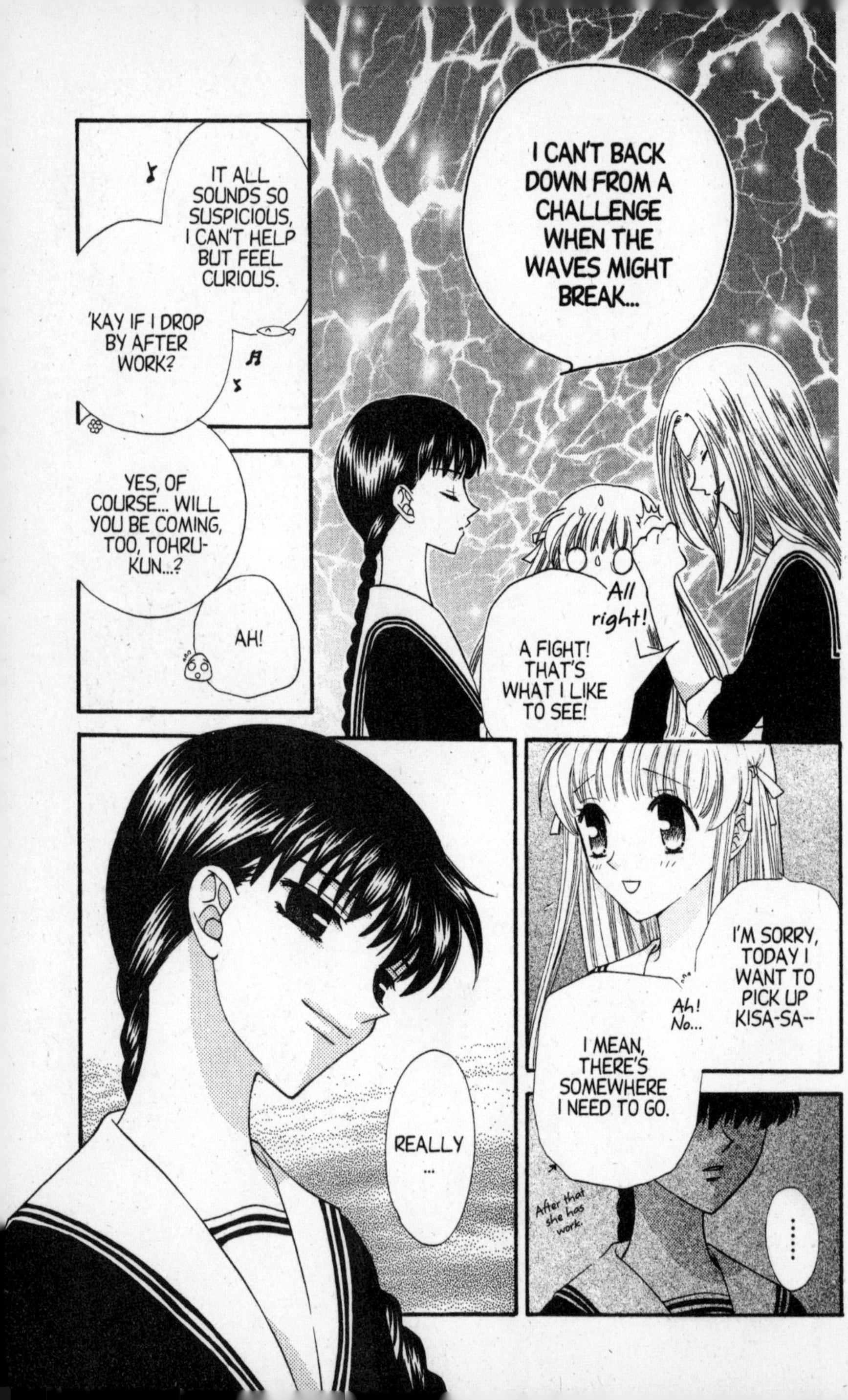
I CAN'T BACK DOWN FROM A CHALLENGE WHEN THE WAVES MIGHT BREAK...
All right!
A FIGHT! THAT'S WHAT I LIKE TO SEE!
IT ALL SOUNDS SO SUSPICIOUS, I CAN'T HELP BUT FEEL CURIOUS.
'KAY IF I DROP BY AFTER WORK?
YES, OF COURSE... WILL YOU BE COMING, TOO, TOHRU-KUN...?
AH!
I'M SORRY, TODAY I WANT TO PICK UP KISA-SA--
Ah! No...
I MEAN, THERE'S SOMEWHERE I NEED TO GO.
After that she has work.
......
REALLY ...

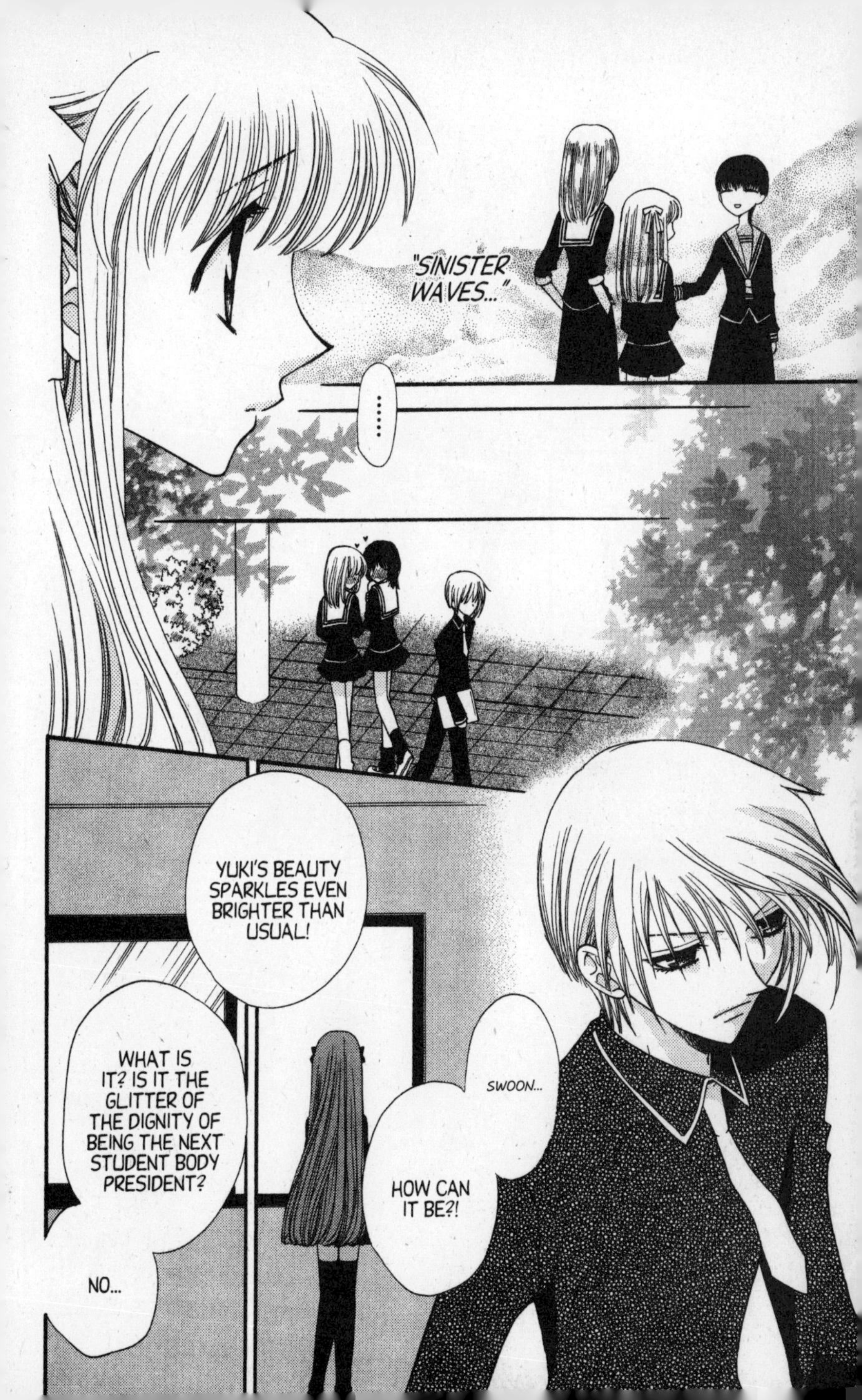
"SINISTER WAVES..."
......
YUKI'S BEAUTY SPARKLES EVEN BRIGHTER THAN USUAL!
SWOON...
WHAT IS IT? IS IT THE GLITTER OF THE DIGNITY OF BEING THE NEXT STUDENT BODY PRESIDENT?
HOW CAN IT BE?!
NO...

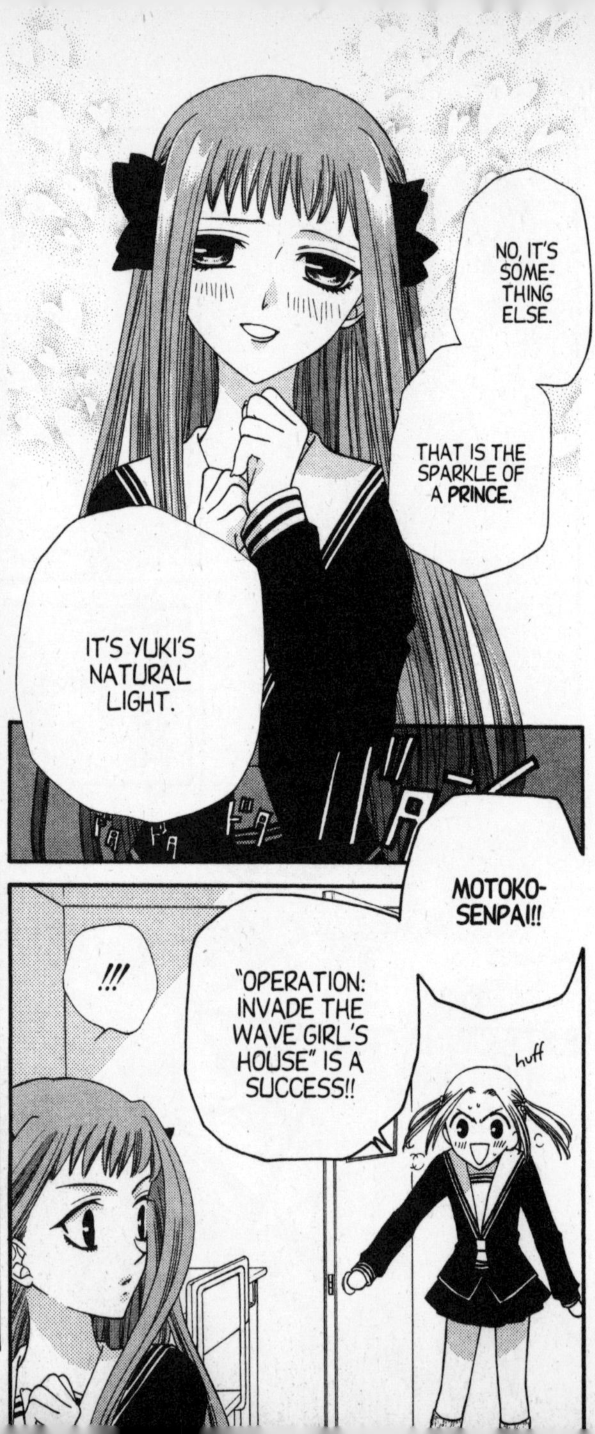
NO, IT'S SOME-THING ELSE.
THAT IS THE SPARKLE OF A PRINCE.
IT'S YUKI'S NATURAL LIGHT.
MOTOKO-SENPAI!!!
"OPERATION: INVADE THE WAVE GIRL'S HOUSE" IS A SUCCESS!!
huff
!!!

**Fruits Basket 5 Part 5:**

Also, lately I've played... (Yup. Here she goes again about her video games...) I finished Chrono Cross. I thought of a lot of things. (Not about the game.) I finally got through Resident Evil: Code Veronica, too. By far, the monsters I hate the most are the Hunters... Whenever a Hunter turned up, I screamed. I'm still in the middle of Legend of Dragoon. Better hurry up because Grandia 2 is coming out, and in the summer is Final Fantasy (isn't that wrong?). I have so much to do (laugh). When a FF game comes out, I drop everything to play it, so it's very dangerous. Will the Crystals be revived, or not? (Am I wrong?) Aahh, those were the days. The Crystal was shattered; it brings back memories... (She gazes off into the distance...) The darkness with the paladin and Gilgamesh and Excalibur and the fresh fish... (Gazing even farther into the distance...)

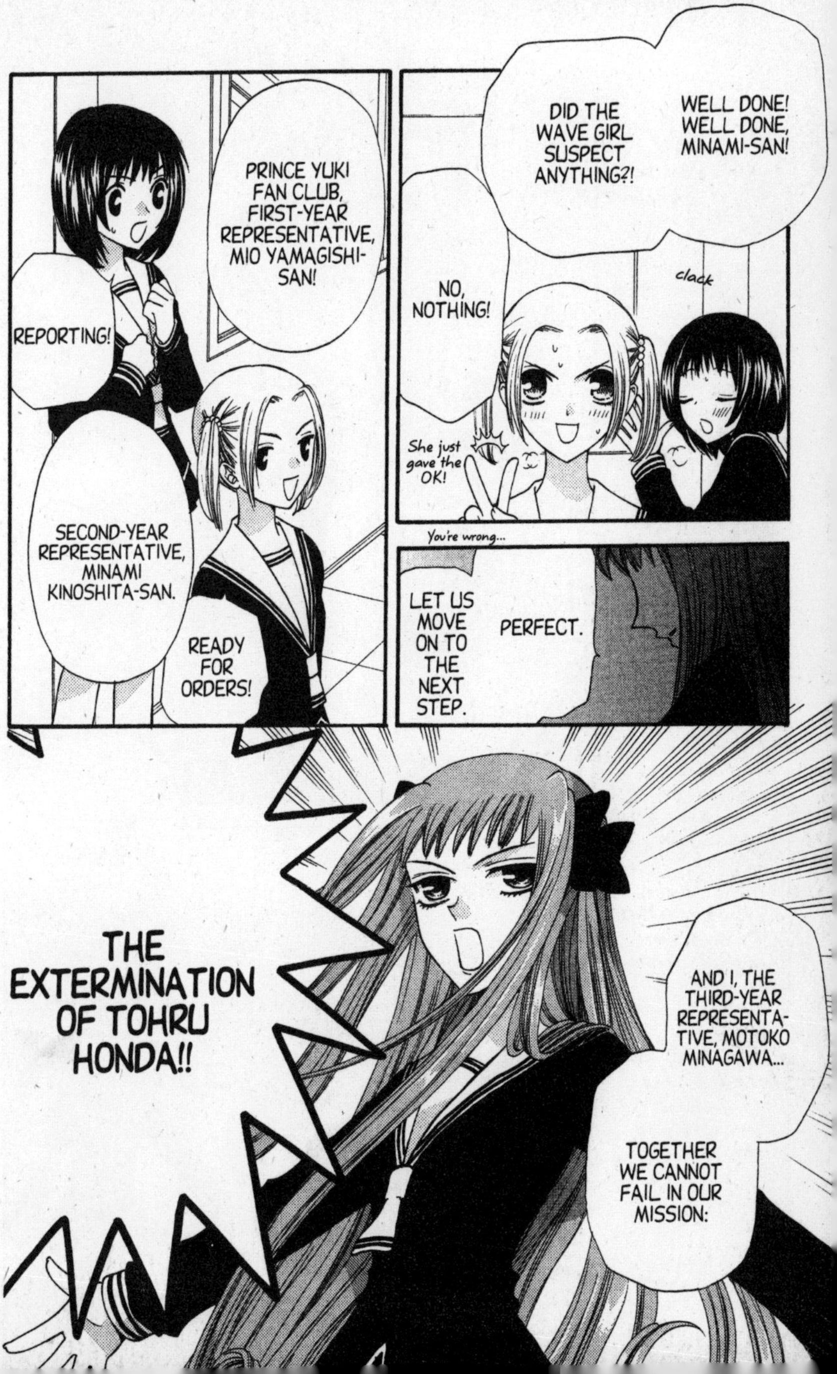
WELL DONE! WELL DONE, MINAMI-SAN!
DID THE WAVE GIRL SUSPECT ANYTHING?!
clack
NO, NOTHING!
She just gave the OK!
You're wrong...
PERFECT.
LET US MOVE ON TO THE NEXT STEP.
PRINCE YUKI FAN CLUB, FIRST-YEAR REPRESENTATIVE, MIO YAMAGISHI-SAN!
REPORTING!
SECOND-YEAR REPRESENTATIVE, MINAMI KINOSHITA-SAN.
READY FOR ORDERS!
AND I, THE THIRD-YEAR REPRESENTATIVE, MOTOKO MINAGAWA...
TOGETHER WE CANNOT FAIL IN OUR MISSION:
THE EXTERMINATION OF TOHRU HONDA!!

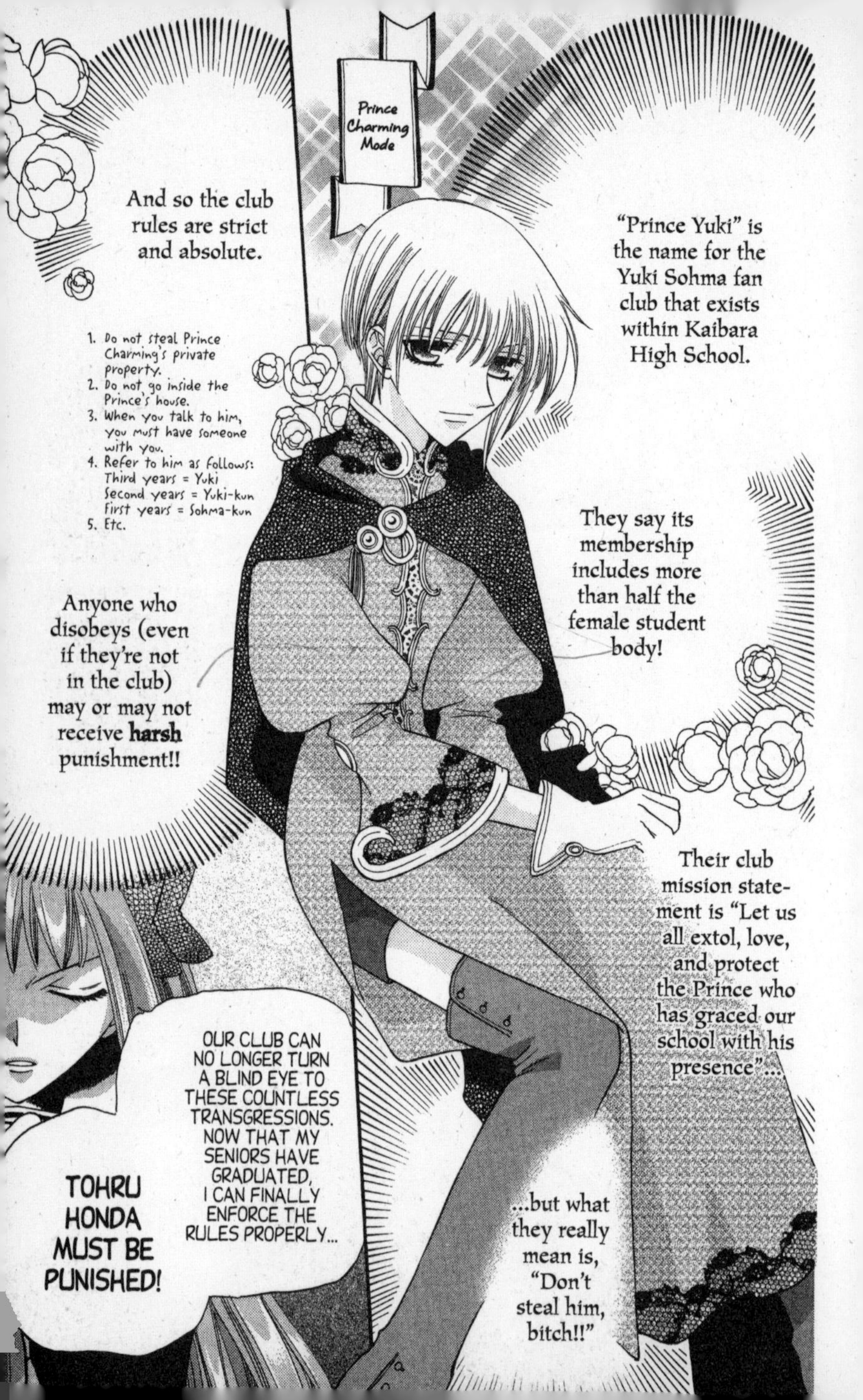

Prince Charming Mode
"Prince Yuki" is the name for the Yuki Sohma fan club that exists within Kaibara High School.
And so the club rules are strict and absolute.
1. Do not steal Prince Charming's private property.
2. Do not go inside the Prince's house.
3. When you talk to him, you must have someone with you.
4. Refer to him as follows: Third years = Yuki Second years = Yuki-kun First years = Sohma-kun
5. Etc.
They say its membership includes more than half the female student body!
Anyone who disobeys (even if they're not in the club) may or may not receive **harsh** punishment!!
Their club mission state-ment is "Let us all extol, love, and protect the Prince who has graced our school with his presence"...
...but what they really mean is, "Don't steal him, bitch!!"
OUR CLUB CAN NO LONGER TURN A BLIND EYE TO THESE COUNTLESS TRANSGRESSIONS. NOW THAT MY SENIORS HAVE GRADUATED, I CAN FINALLY ENFORCE THE RULES PROPERLY...
TOHRU HONDA MUST BE PUNISHED!

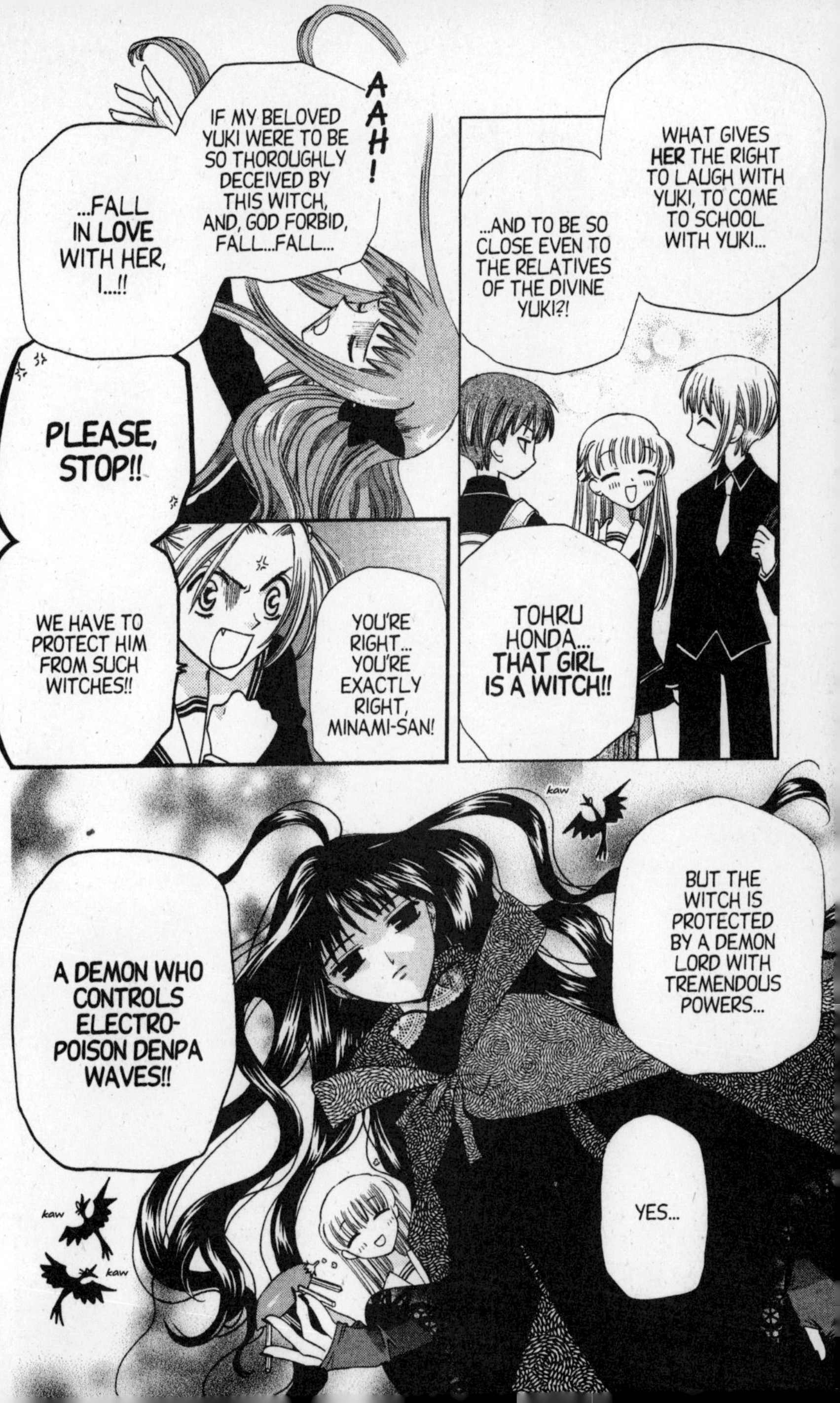
WHAT GIVES HER THE RIGHT TO LAUGH WITH YUKI, TO COME TO SCHOOL WITH YUKI...
...AND TO BE SO CLOSE EVEN TO THE RELATIVES OF THE DIVINE YUKI?!
TOHRU HONDA... THAT GIRL IS A WITCH!!
AAH!
IF MY BELOVED YUKI WERE TO BE SO THOROUGHLY DECEIVED BY THIS WITCH, AND, GOD FORBID, FALL...FALL...
...FALL IN LOVE WITH HER, I...!!
PLEASE, STOP!!
YOU'RE RIGHT... YOU'RE EXACTLY RIGHT, MINAMI-SAN!
WE HAVE TO PROTECT HIM FROM SUCH WITCHES!!
kaw
BUT THE WITCH IS PROTECTED BY A DEMON LORD WITH TREMENDOUS POWERS...
A DEMON WHO CONTROLS ELECTRO-POISON DENPA WAVES!!
YES...
kaw
kaw

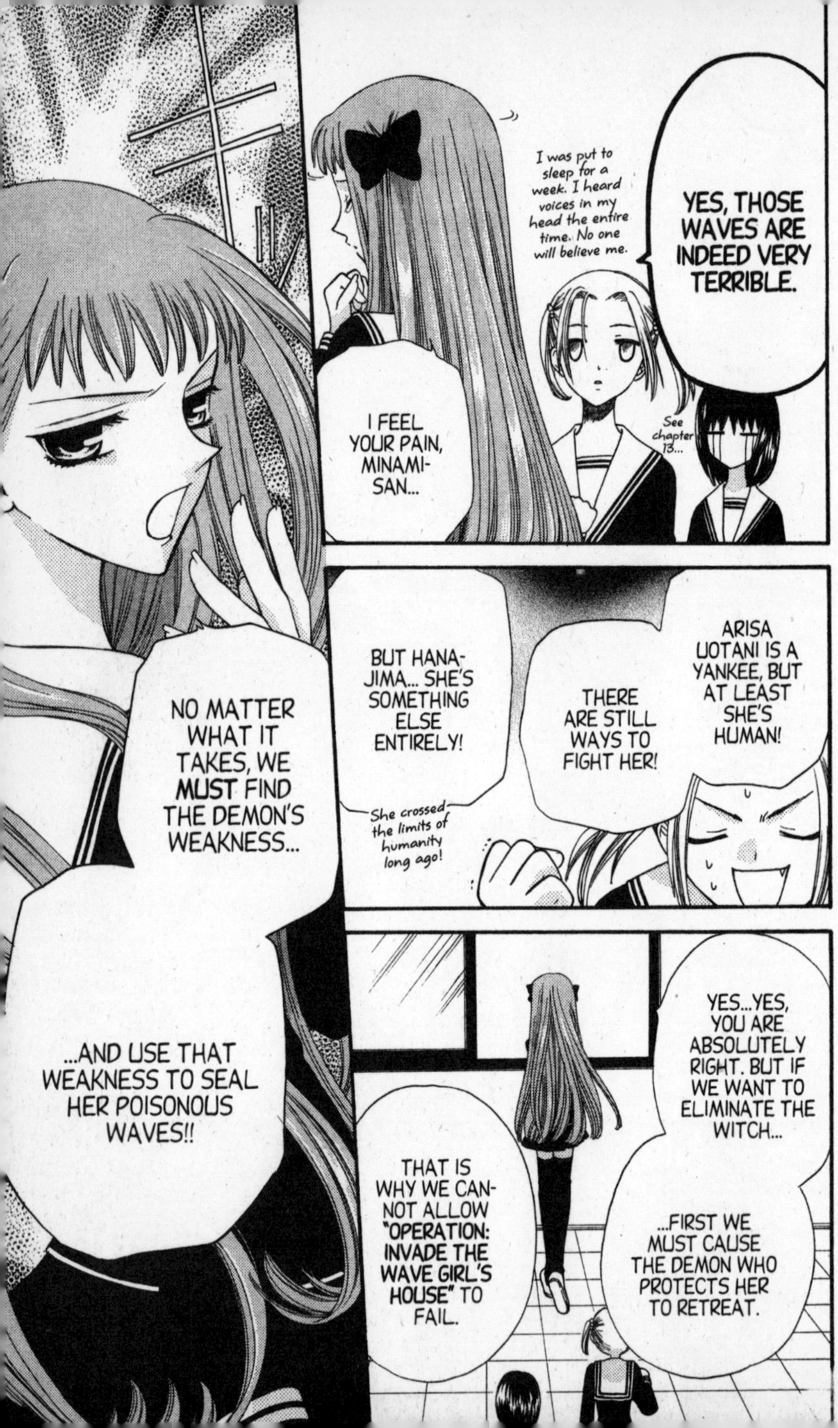
YES, THOSE WAVES ARE INDEED VERY TERRIBLE.
I was put to sleep for a week. I heard voices in my head the entire time. No one will believe me.
See chapter 13...
I FEEL YOUR PAIN, MINAMI-SAN...
ARISA UOTANI IS A YANKEE, BUT AT LEAST SHE'S HUMAN!
THERE ARE STILL WAYS TO FIGHT HER!
BUT HANA-JIMA... SHE'S SOMETHING ELSE ENTIRELY!
She crossed the limits of humanity long ago!
YES...YES, YOU ARE ABSOLUTELY RIGHT. BUT IF WE WANT TO ELIMINATE THE WITCH...
...FIRST WE MUST CAUSE THE DEMON WHO PROTECTS HER TO RETREAT.
THAT IS WHY WE CAN-NOT ALLOW "OPERATION: INVADE THE WAVE GIRL'S HOUSE" TO FAIL.
NO MATTER WHAT IT TAKES, WE MUST FIND THE DEMON'S WEAKNESS...
...AND USE THAT WEAKNESS TO SEAL HER POISONOUS WAVES!!

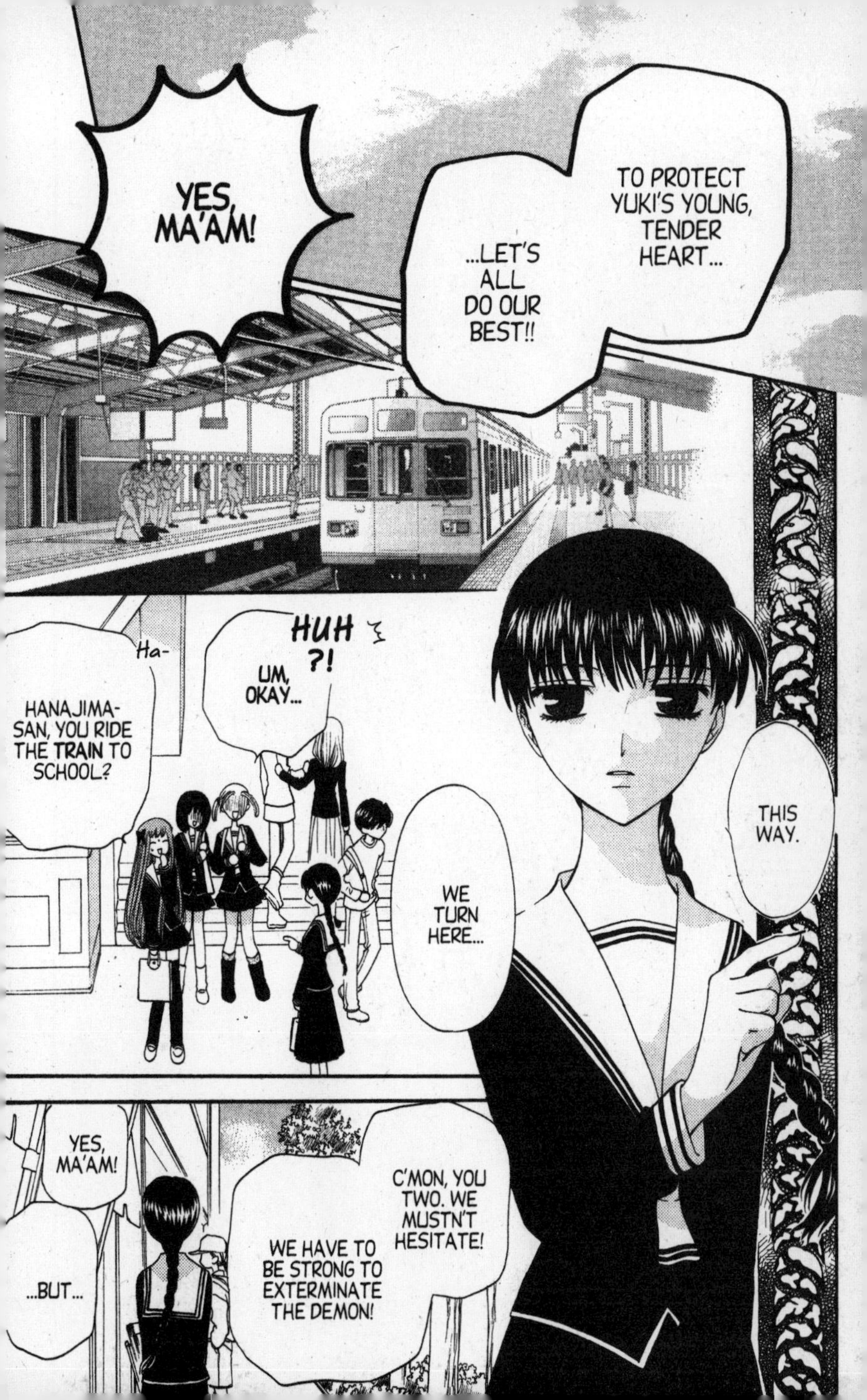
TO PROTECT YUKI'S YOUNG, TENDER HEART...
...LET'S ALL DO OUR BEST!!
YES, MA'AM!
THIS WAY.
WE TURN HERE...
UM, OKAY...
HUH ?!
Ha-
HANAJIMA-SAN, YOU RIDE THE TRAIN TO SCHOOL?
C'MON, YOU TWO. WE MUSTN'T HESITATE!
WE HAVE TO BE STRONG TO EXTERMINATE THE DEMON!
YES, MA'AM!
...BUT...

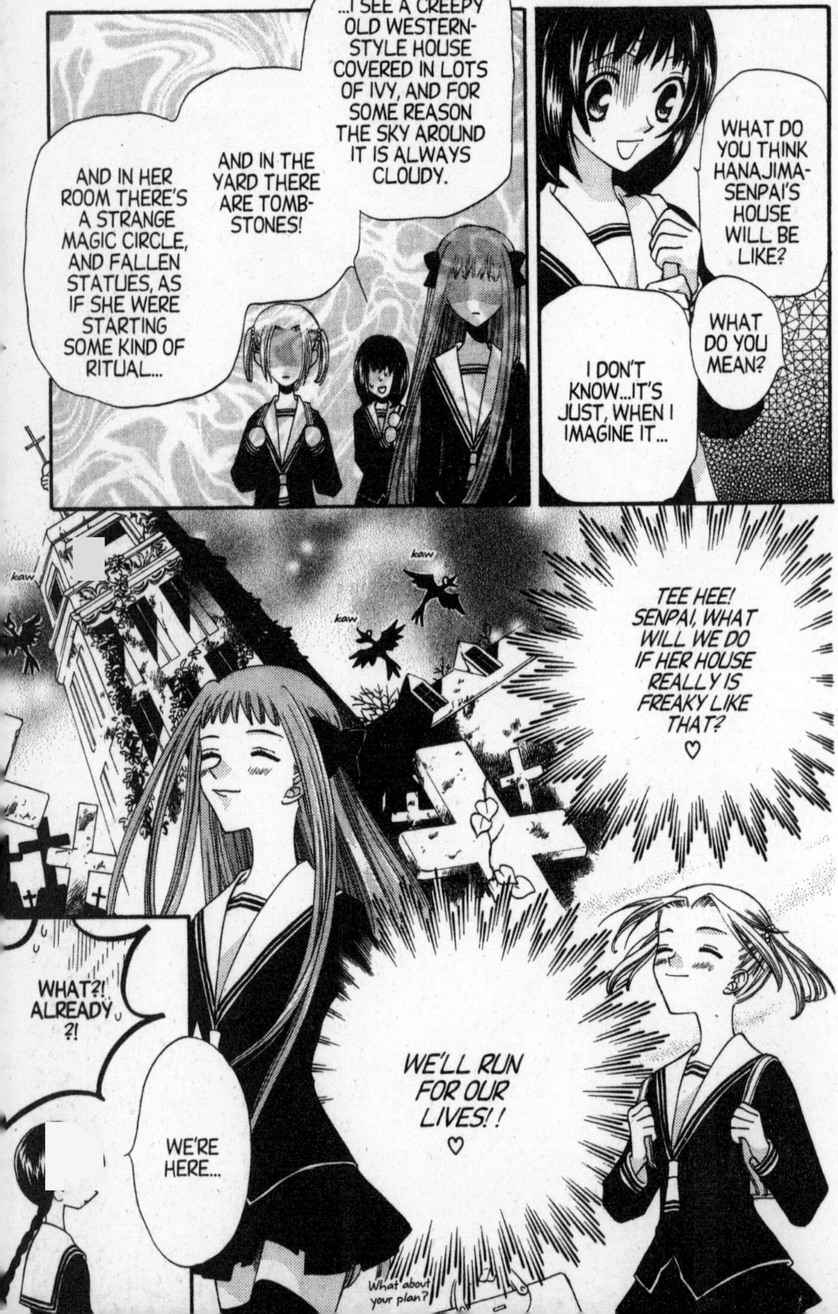
WHAT DO YOU THINK HANAJIMA-SENPAI'S HOUSE WILL BE LIKE?
WHAT DO YOU MEAN?
I DON'T KNOW...IT'S JUST, WHEN I IMAGINE IT...
...I SEE A CREEPY OLD WESTERN-STYLE HOUSE COVERED IN LOTS OF IVY, AND FOR SOME REASON THE SKY AROUND IT IS ALWAYS CLOUDY.
AND IN THE YARD THERE ARE TOMB-STONES!
AND IN HER ROOM THERE'S A STRANGE MAGIC CIRCLE, AND FALLEN STATUES, AS IF SHE WERE STARTING SOME KIND OF RITUAL...
kaw
kaw
kaw
TEE HEE! SENPAI, WHAT WILL WE DO IF HER HOUSE REALLY IS FREAKY LIKE THAT? ♡
WE'LL RUN FOR OUR LIVES!! ♡
WE'RE HERE...
WHAT?! ALREADY?!
What about your plan?

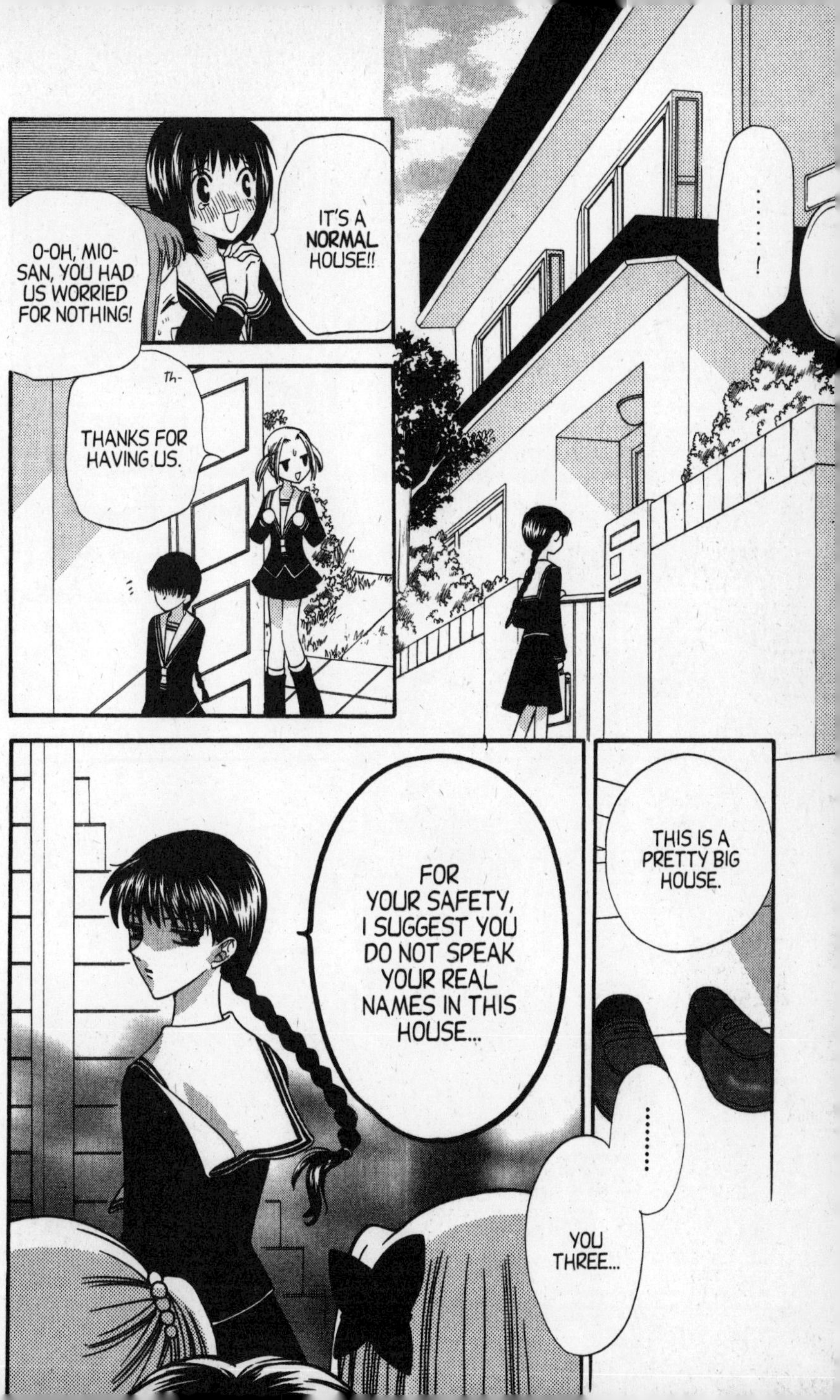
......!
IT'S A NORMAL HOUSE!!
O-OH, MIO-SAN, YOU HAD US WORRIED FOR NOTHING!
Th-
THANKS FOR HAVING US.
THIS IS A PRETTY BIG HOUSE.
......
YOU THREE...
FOR YOUR SAFETY, I SUGGEST YOU DO NOT SPEAK YOUR REAL NAMES IN THIS HOUSE...

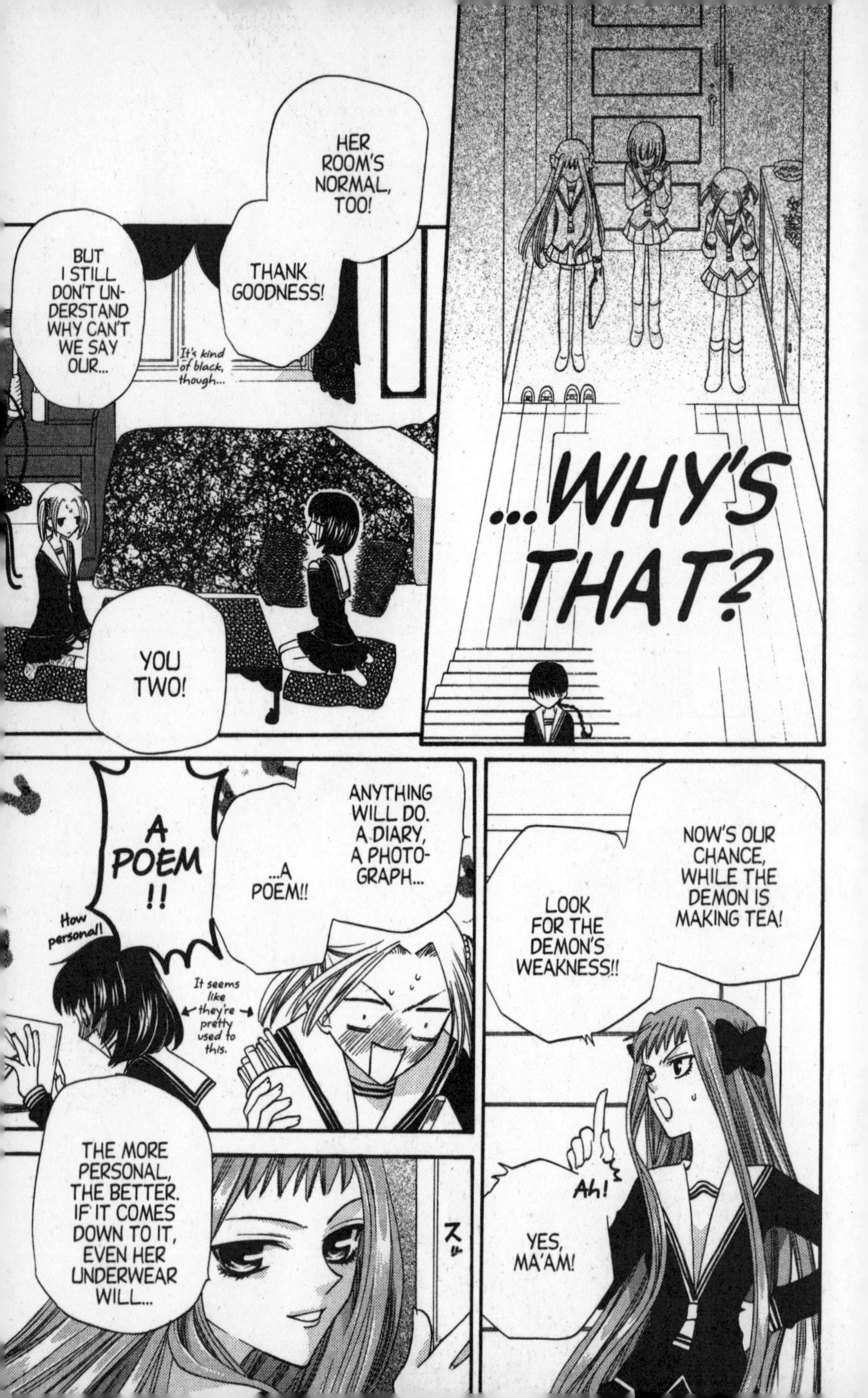
...WHY'S THAT?
HER ROOM'S NORMAL, TOO!
THANK GOODNESS!
BUT I STILL DON'T UNDERSTAND WHY CAN'T WE SAY OUR...
It's kind of black, though...
YOU TWO!
NOW'S OUR CHANCE, WHILE THE DEMON IS MAKING TEA!
LOOK FOR THE DEMON'S WEAKNESS!!
Ah!
YES, MA'AM!
ANYTHING WILL DO. A DIARY, A PHOTOGRAPH...
...A POEM!!
A POEM !!
How personal!
It seems like they're pretty used to this.
THE MORE PERSONAL, THE BETTER. IF IT COMES DOWN TO IT, EVEN HER UNDERWEAR WILL...
スッ

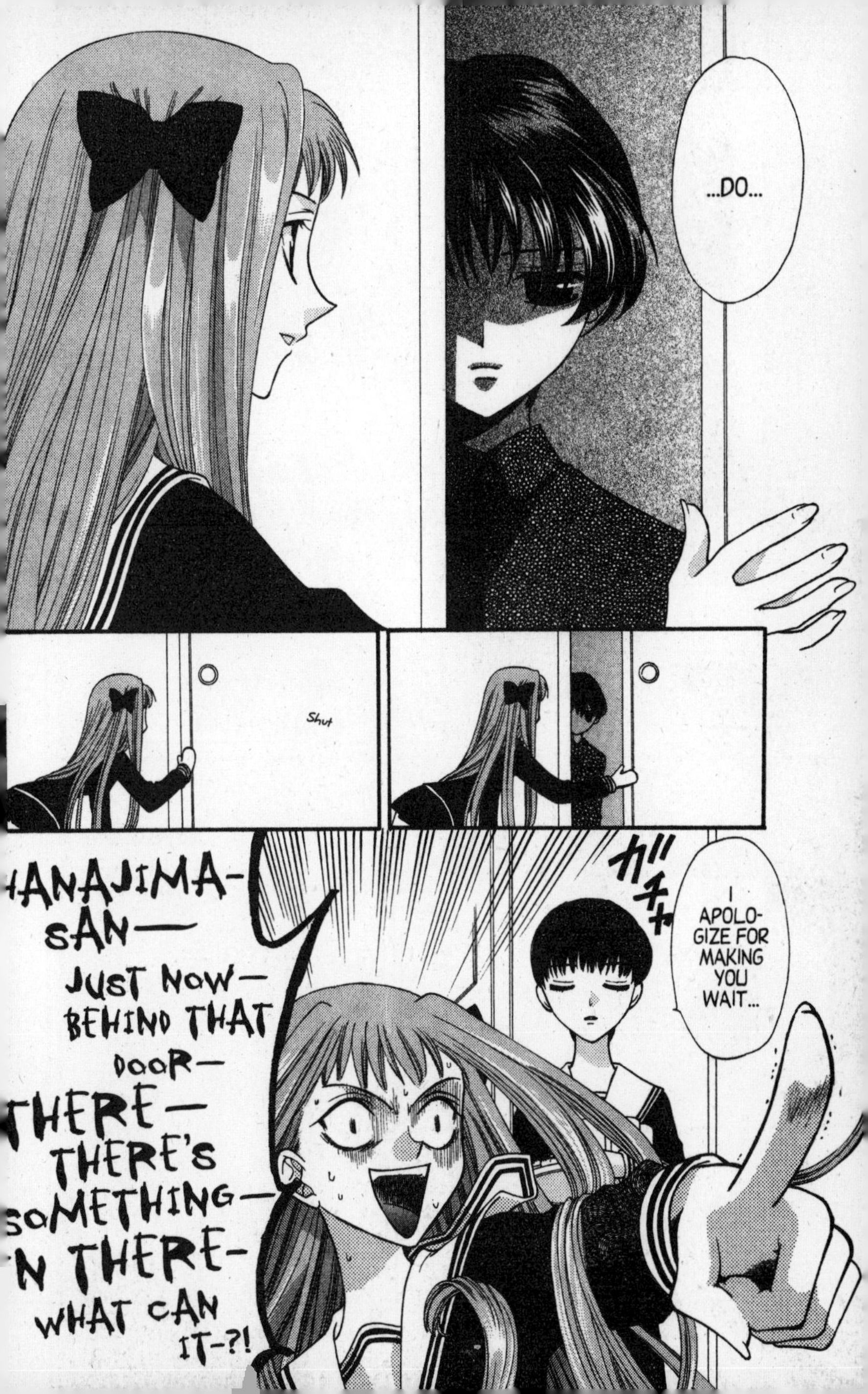
...DO...
Shut
I APOLOGIZE FOR MAKING YOU WAIT...
ガチャ
HANAJIMA-SAN—
JUST NOW—
BEHIND THAT DOOR—
THERE—
THERE'S SOMETHING—
SOMETHING—
N THERE-
WHAT CAN IT-?!

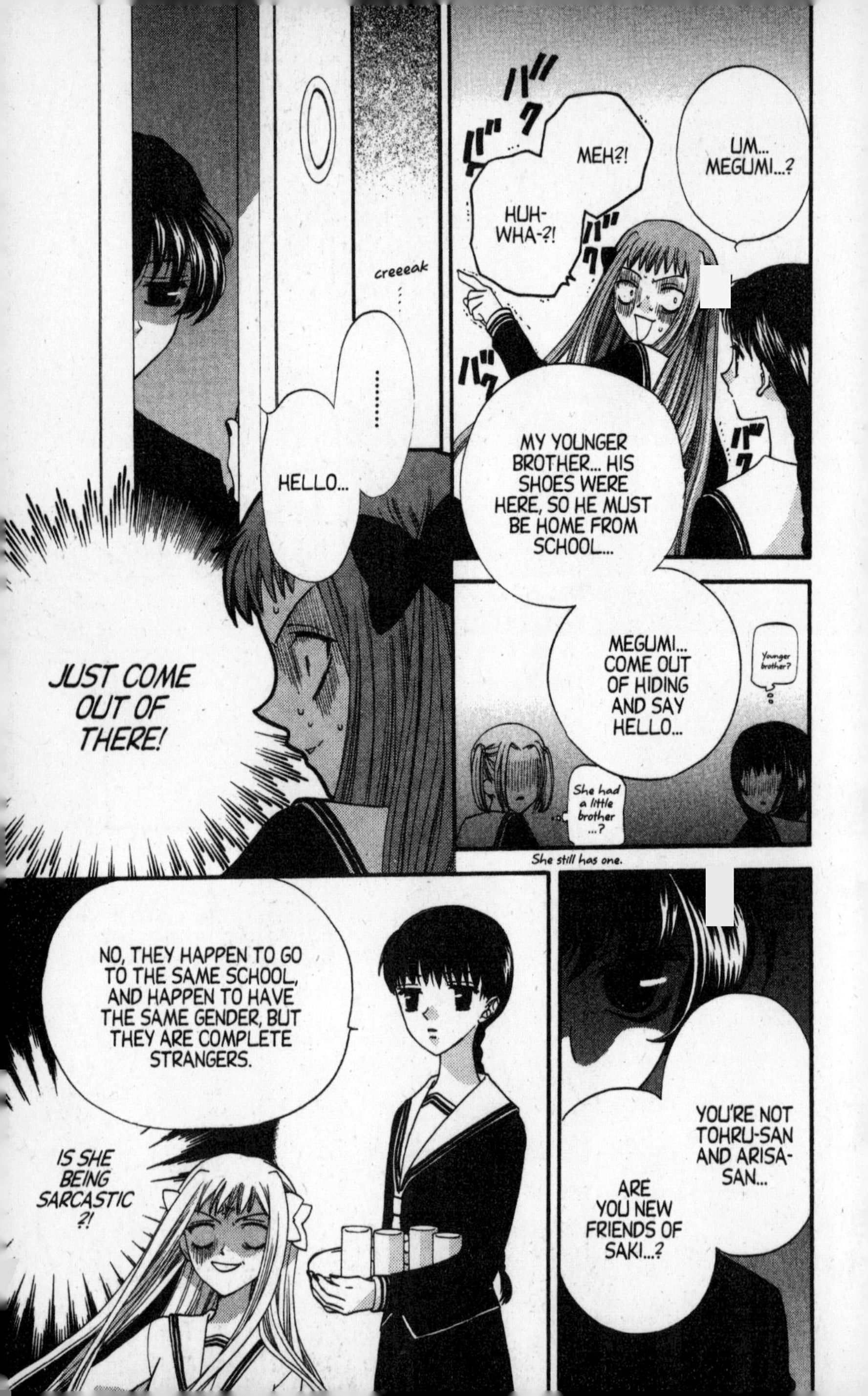
UM... MEGUMI...?
MEH?!
HUH-WHA-?!
MY YOUNGER BROTHER... HIS SHOES WERE HERE, SO HE MUST BE HOME FROM SCHOOL...
MEGUMI... COME OUT OF HIDING AND SAY HELLO...
Younger brother?
She had a little brother ...?
She still has one.
creeeak
......
HELLO...
JUST COME OUT OF THERE!
YOU'RE NOT TOHRU-SAN AND ARISA-SAN...
ARE YOU NEW FRIENDS OF SAKI...?
NO, THEY HAPPEN TO GO TO THE SAME SCHOOL, AND HAPPEN TO HAVE THE SAME GENDER, BUT THEY ARE COMPLETE STRANGERS.
IS SHE BEING SARCASTIC?!

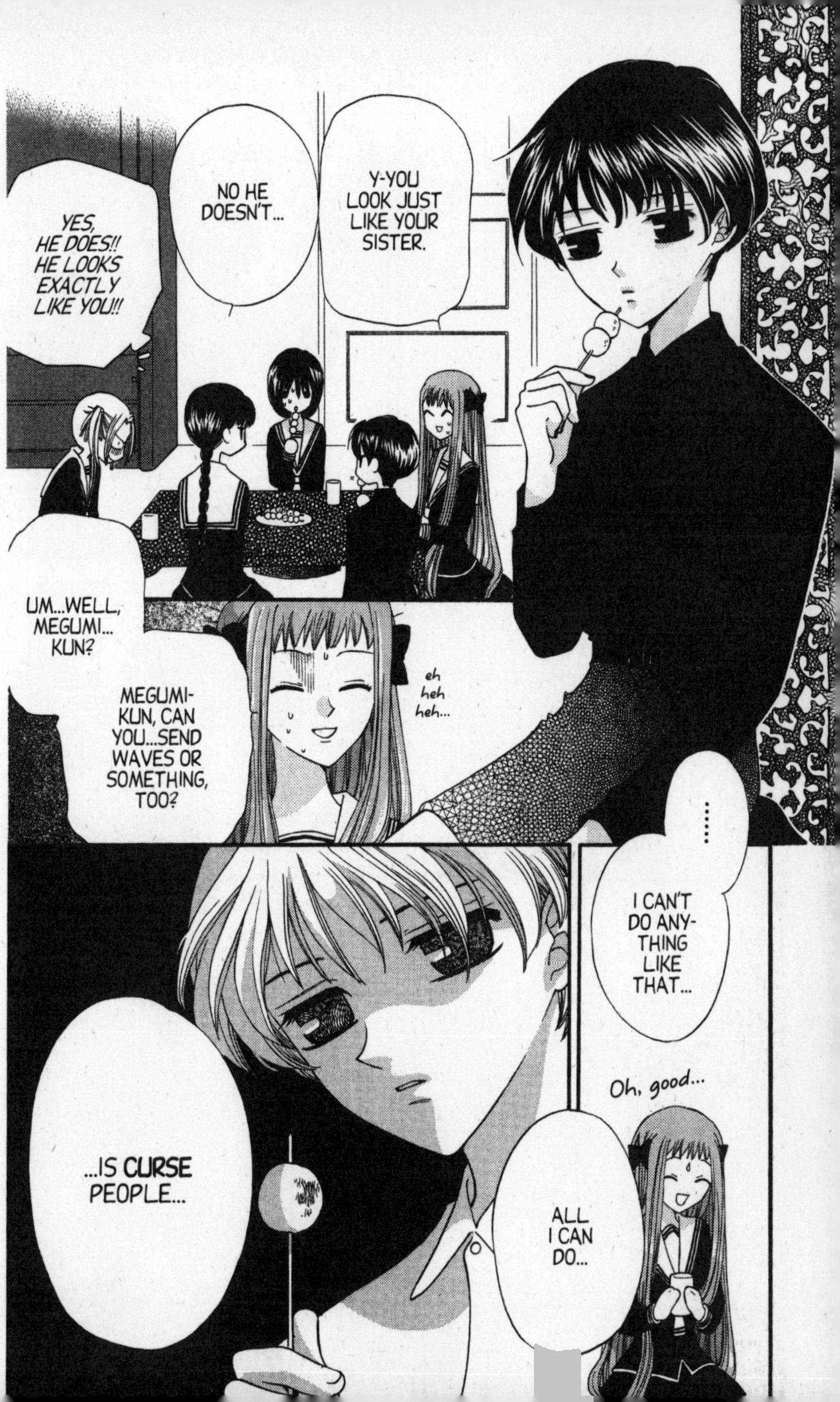
Y-YOU LOOK JUST LIKE YOUR SISTER.
NO HE DOESN'T...
YES, HE DOES!! HE LOOKS EXACTLY LIKE YOU!!
eh heh heh...
UM...WELL, MEGUMI... KUN?
MEGUMI-KUN, CAN YOU...SEND WAVES OR SOMETHING, TOO?
......
I CAN'T DO ANYTHING LIKE THAT...
Oh, good...
ALL I CAN DO...
...IS CURSE PEOPLE...

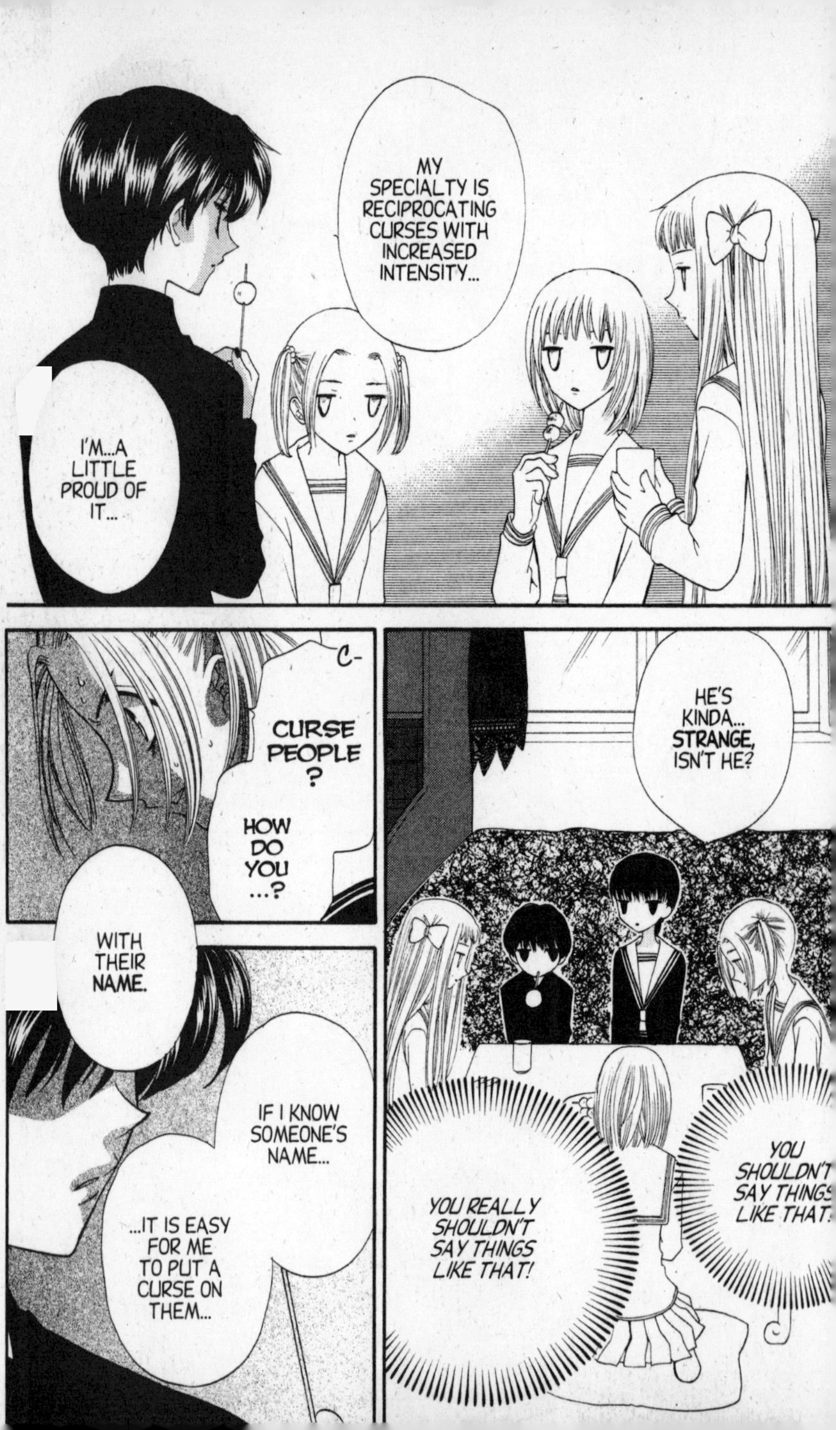
MY SPECIALTY IS RECIPROCATING CURSES WITH INCREASED INTENSITY...
I'M...A LITTLE PROUD OF IT...
HE'S KINDA... STRANGE, ISN'T HE?
YOU SHOULDN'T SAY THINGS LIKE THAT.
YOU REALLY SHOULDN'T SAY THINGS LIKE THAT!
C-
CURSE PEOPLE?
HOW DO YOU ...?
WITH THEIR NAME.
IF I KNOW SOMEONE'S NAME...
...IT IS EASY FOR ME TO PUT A CURSE ON THEM...

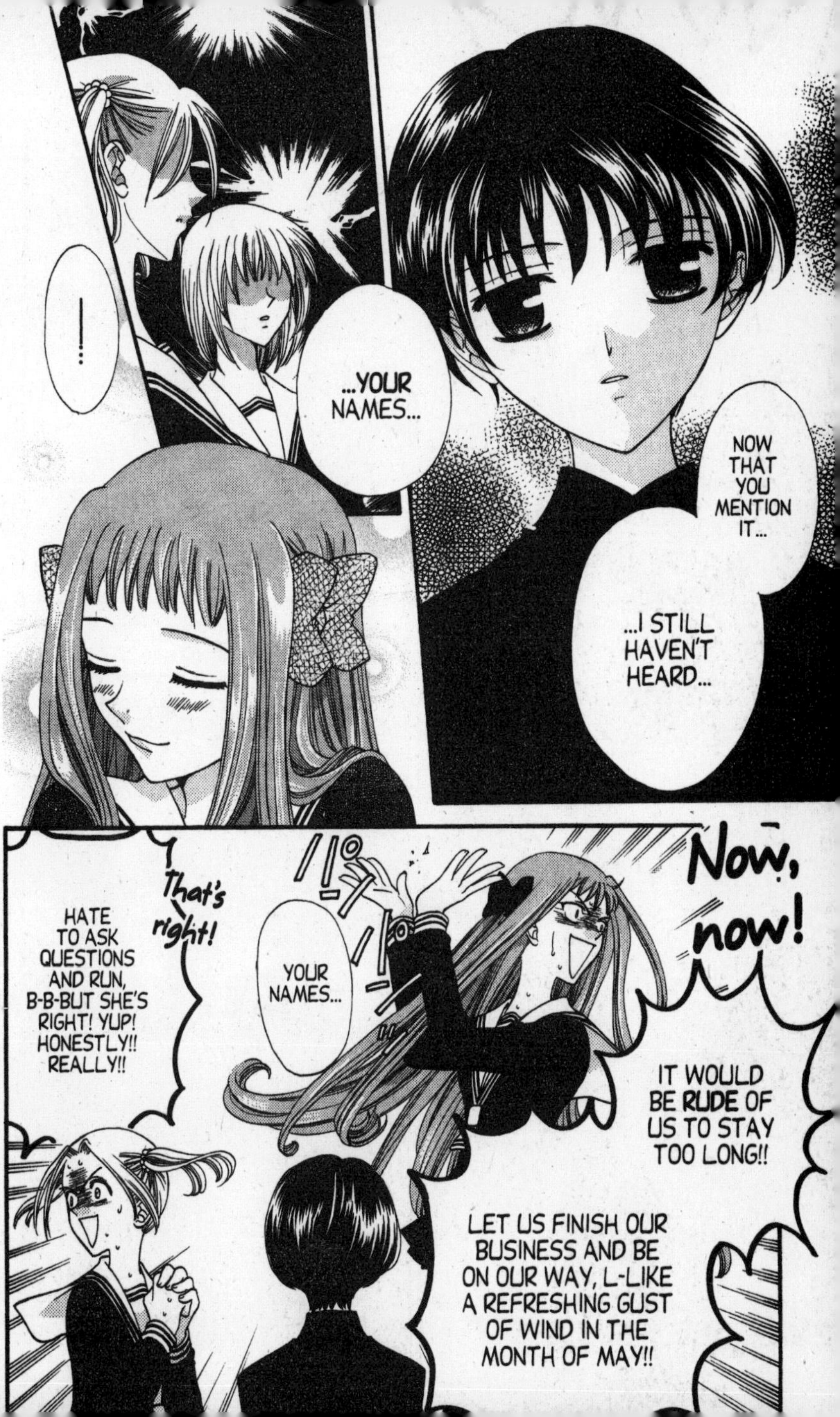
NOW THAT YOU MENTION IT...
...I STILL HAVEN'T HEARD...
...YOUR NAMES...
......!
Now, now!
IT WOULD BE **RUDE** OF US TO STAY TOO LONG!!
LET US FINISH OUR BUSINESS AND BE ON OUR WAY, L-LIKE A REFRESHING GUST OF WIND IN THE MONTH OF MAY!!
YOUR NAMES...
That's right!
HATE TO ASK QUESTIONS AND RUN, B-B-BUT SHE'S RIGHT! YUP! HONESTLY!! REALLY!!

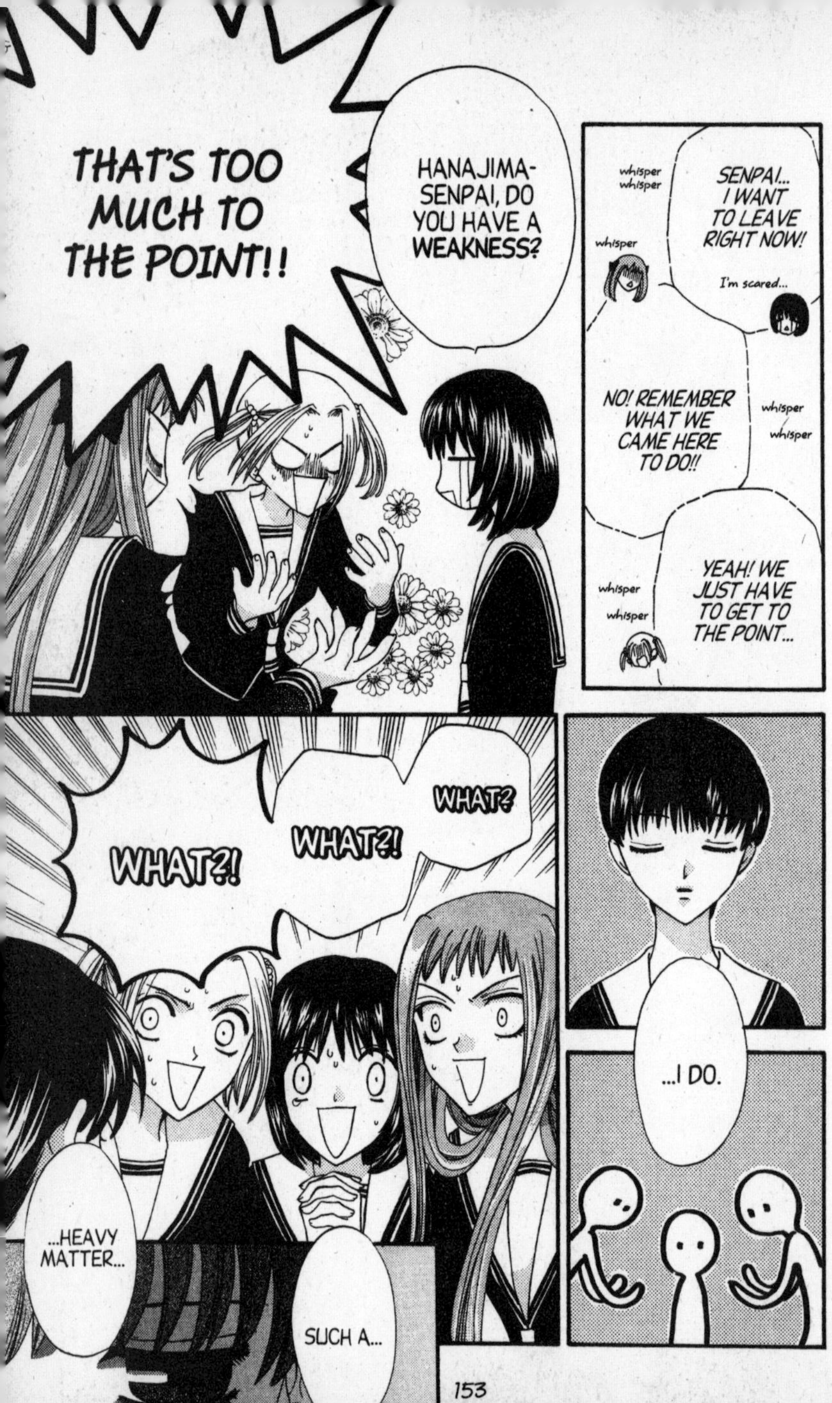
whisper
whisper
SENPAI... I WANT TO LEAVE RIGHT NOW!
whisper
I'm scared...
NO! REMEMBER WHAT WE CAME HERE TO DO!!
whisper
whisper
YEAH! WE JUST HAVE TO GET TO THE POINT...
whisper
whisper
HANAJIMA-SENPAI, DO YOU HAVE A WEAKNESS?
THAT'S TOO MUCH TO THE POINT!!
...I DO.
WHAT?
WHAT?!
WHAT?!
SUCH A...
...HEAVY MATTER...

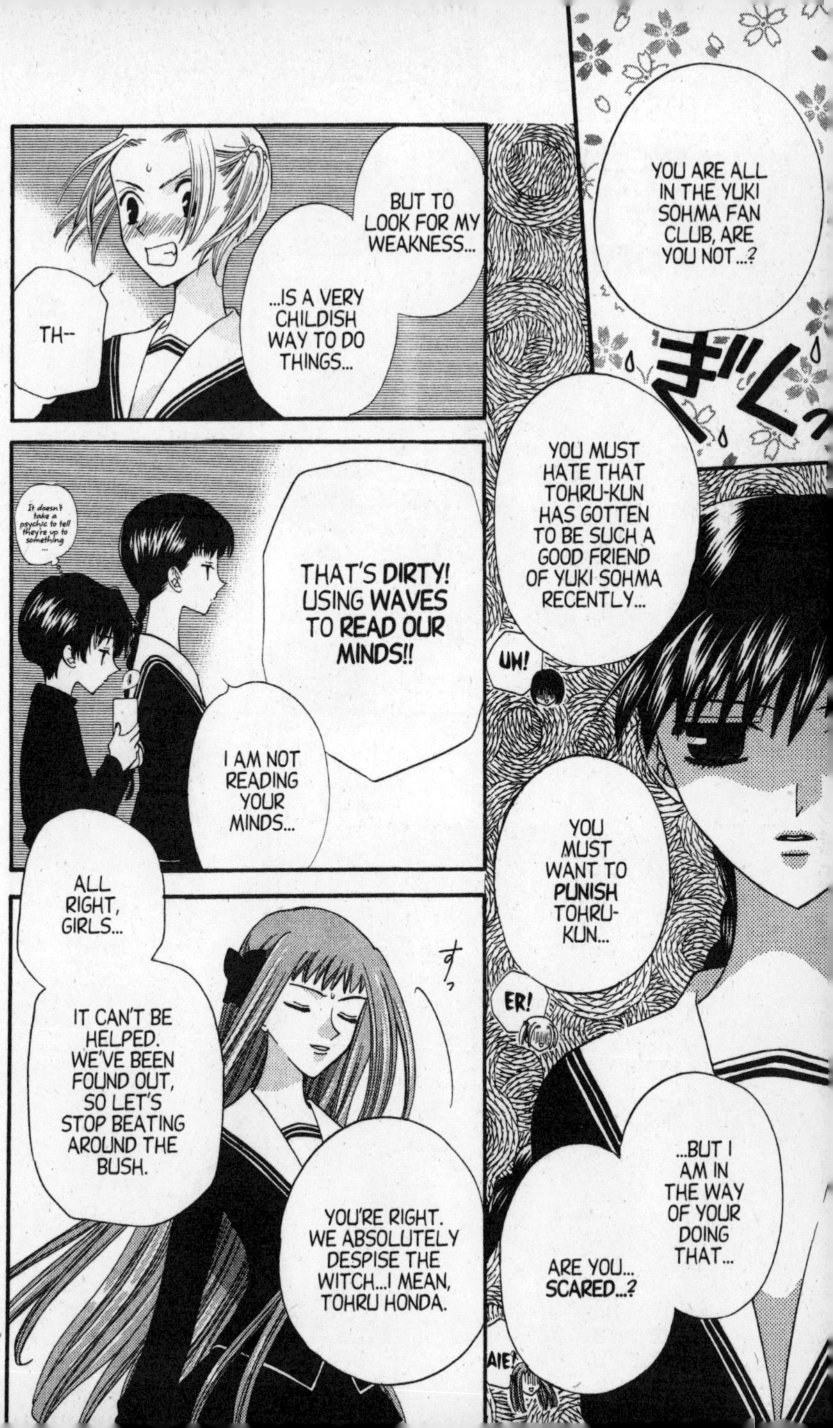
YOU ARE ALL IN THE YUKI SOHMA FAN CLUB, ARE YOU NOT...?
ぎくっ
YOU MUST HATE THAT TOHRU-KUN HAS GOTTEN TO BE SUCH A GOOD FRIEND OF YUKI SOHMA RECENTLY...
UH!
YOU MUST WANT TO PUNISH TOHRU-KUN...
ER!
...BUT I AM IN THE WAY OF YOUR DOING THAT...
ARE YOU... SCARED...?
AIE!
BUT TO LOOK FOR MY WEAKNESS...
...IS A VERY CHILDISH WAY TO DO THINGS...
TH--
THAT'S DIRTY! USING WAVES TO READ OUR MINDS!!
It doesn't take a psychic to tell they're up to something ...
I AM NOT READING YOUR MINDS...
すっ
ALL RIGHT, GIRLS...
IT CAN'T BE HELPED. WE'VE BEEN FOUND OUT, SO LET'S STOP BEATING AROUND THE BUSH.
YOU'RE RIGHT. WE ABSOLUTELY DESPISE THE WITCH...I MEAN, TOHRU HONDA.

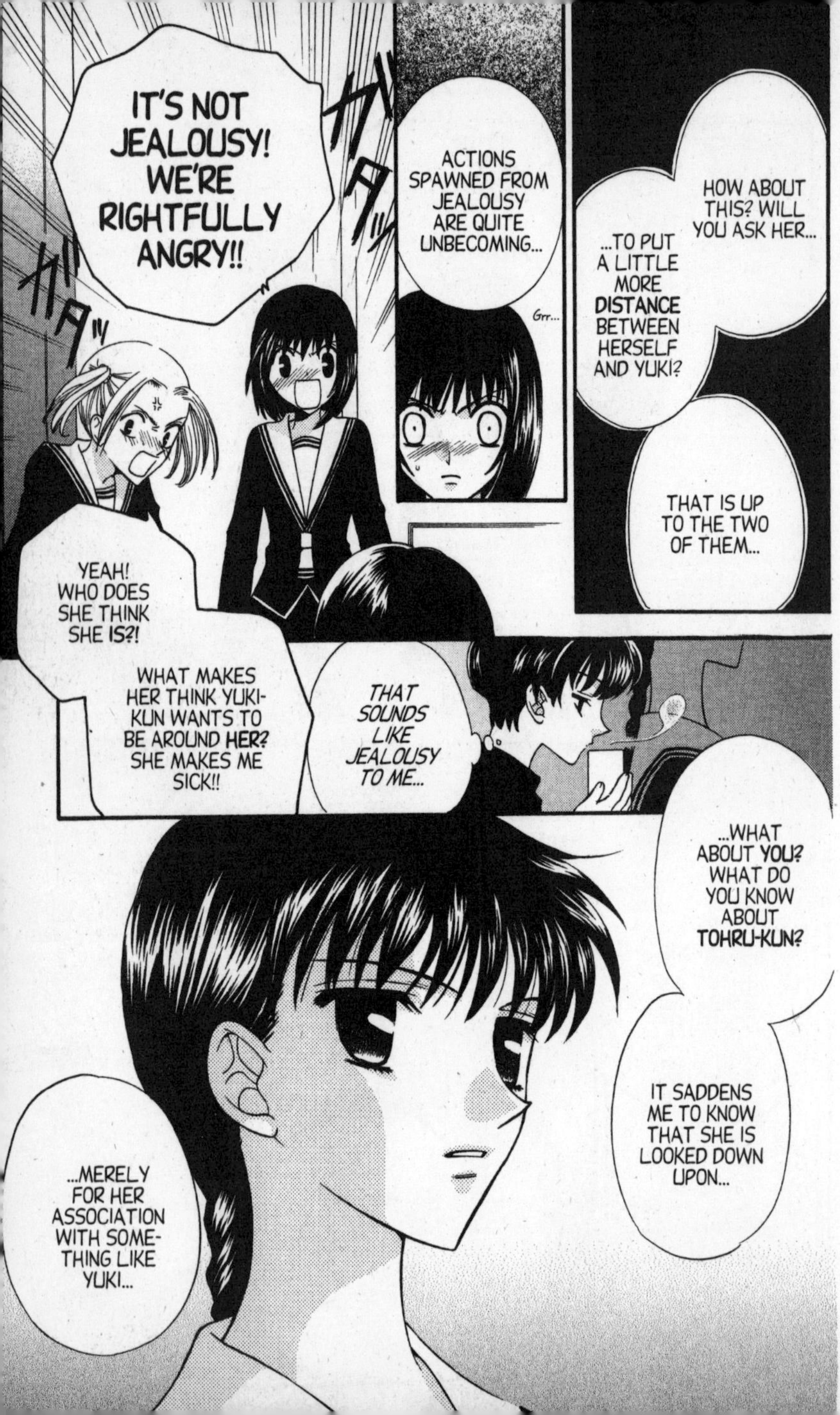
HOW ABOUT THIS? WILL YOU ASK HER...
...TO PUT A LITTLE MORE DISTANCE BETWEEN HERSELF AND YUKI?
THAT IS UP TO THE TWO OF THEM...
ACTIONS SPAWNED FROM JEALOUSY ARE QUITE UNBECOMING...
Grr...
IT'S NOT JEALOUSY! WE'RE RIGHTFULLY ANGRY!!
YEAH! WHO DOES SHE THINK SHE IS?!
WHAT MAKES HER THINK YUKI-KUN WANTS TO BE AROUND HER? SHE MAKES ME SICK!!
THAT SOUNDS LIKE JEALOUSY TO ME...
...WHAT ABOUT YOU? WHAT DO YOU KNOW ABOUT TOHRU-KUN?
IT SADDENS ME TO KNOW THAT SHE IS LOOKED DOWN UPON...
...MERELY FOR HER ASSOCIATION WITH SOME-THING LIKE YUKI...

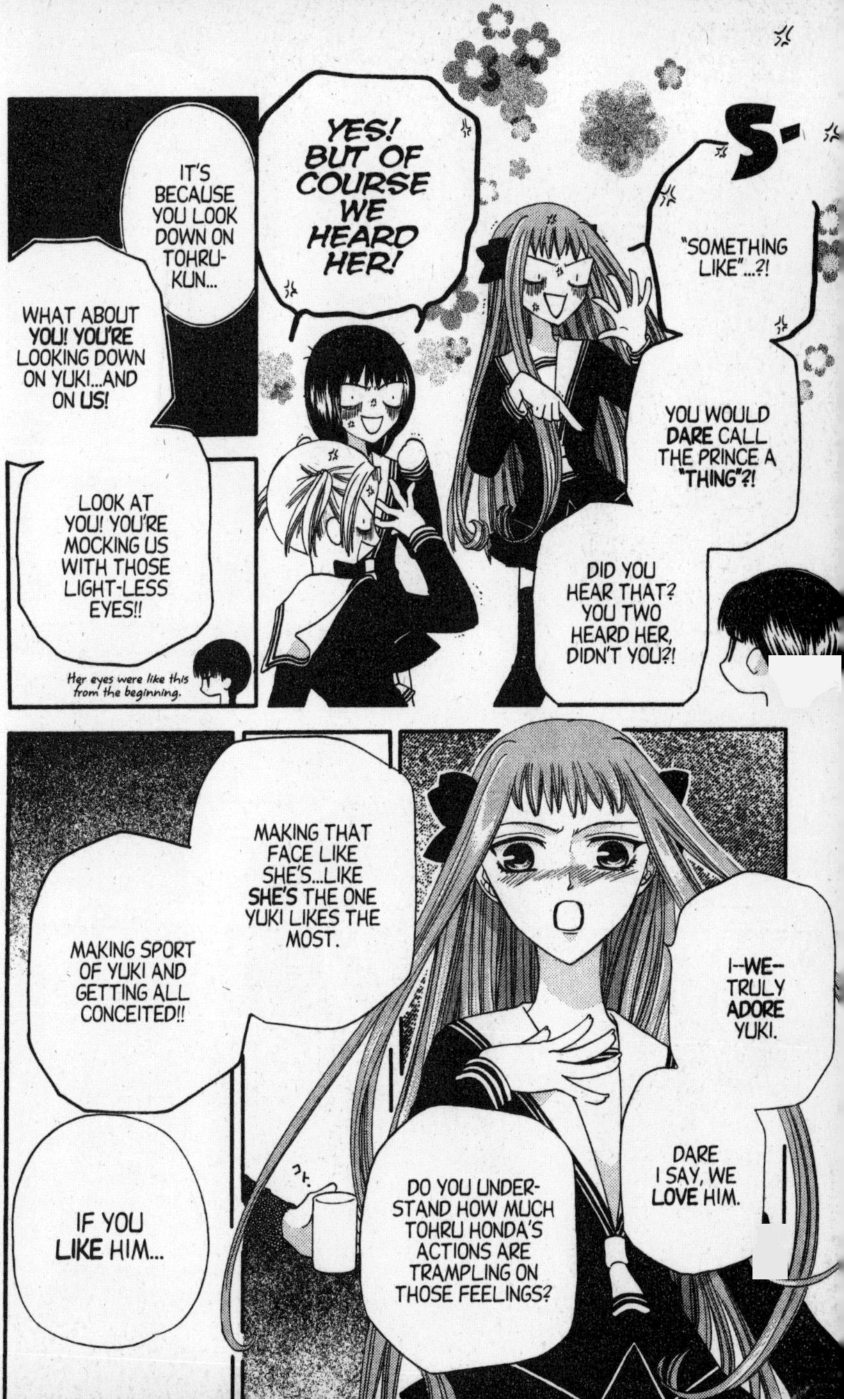
S-
"SOMETHING LIKE"...?!
YOU WOULD DARE CALL THE PRINCE A "THING"?!
DID YOU HEAR THAT? YOU TWO HEARD HER, DIDN'T YOU?!
YES! BUT OF COURSE WE HEARD HER!
IT'S BECAUSE YOU LOOK DOWN ON TOHRU-KUN...
WHAT ABOUT YOU! YOU'RE LOOKING DOWN ON YUKI...AND ON US!
LOOK AT YOU! YOU'RE MOCKING US WITH THOSE LIGHT-LESS EYES!!
Her eyes were like this from the beginning.
I--WE--TRULY ADORE YUKI.
DARE I SAY, WE LOVE HIM.
DO YOU UNDERSTAND HOW MUCH TOHRU HONDA'S ACTIONS ARE TRAMPLING ON THOSE FEELINGS?
MAKING THAT FACE LIKE SHE'S...LIKE SHE'S THE ONE YUKI LIKES THE MOST.
MAKING SPORT OF YUKI AND GETTING ALL CONCEITED!!
IF YOU LIKE HIM...

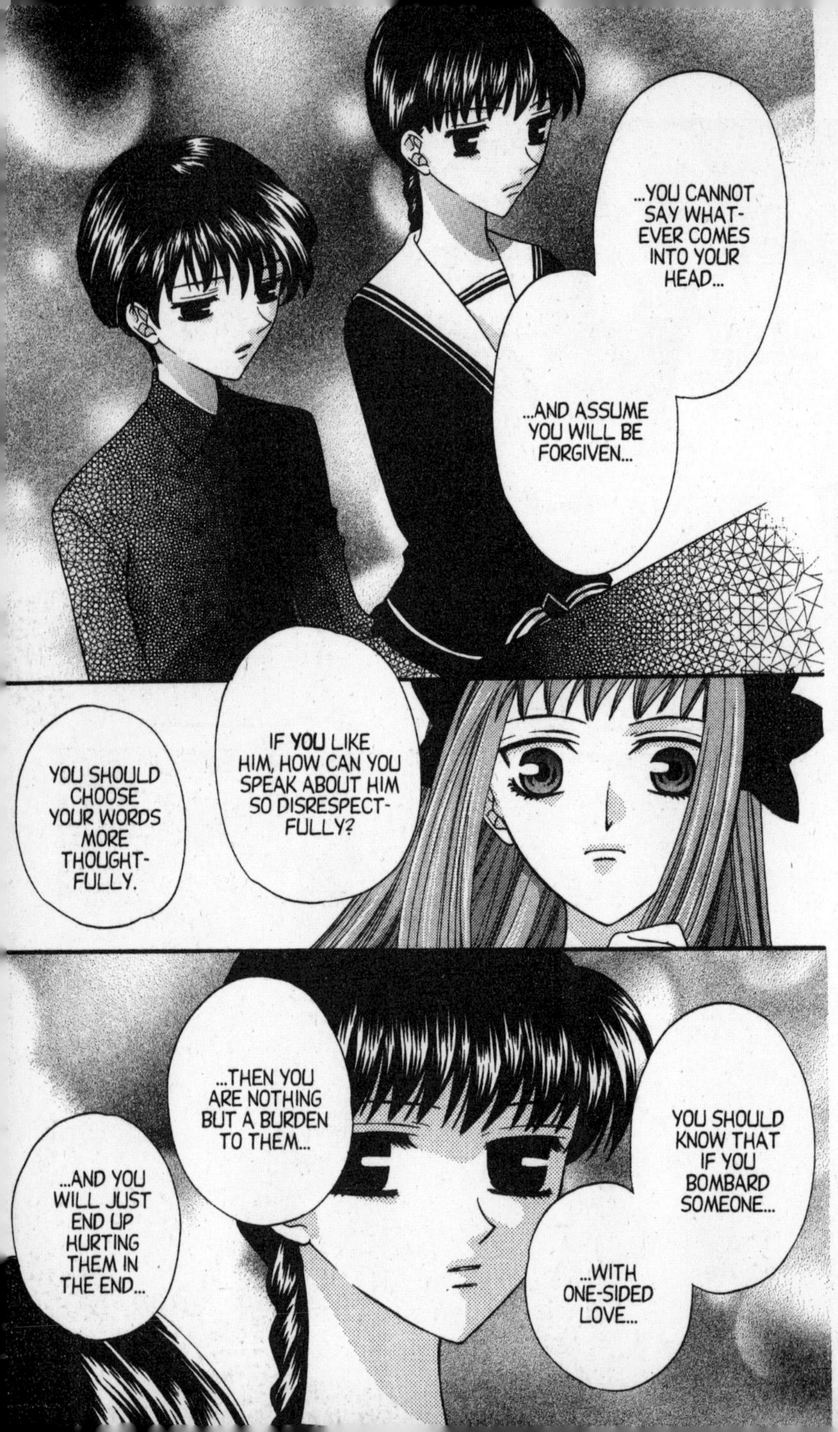
...YOU CANNOT SAY WHATEVER COMES INTO YOUR HEAD...
...AND ASSUME YOU WILL BE FORGIVEN...
IF YOU LIKE HIM, HOW CAN YOU SPEAK ABOUT HIM SO DISRESPECTFULLY?
YOU SHOULD CHOOSE YOUR WORDS MORE THOUGHTFULLY.
YOU SHOULD KNOW THAT IF YOU BOMBARD SOMEONE...
...WITH ONE-SIDED LOVE...
...THEN YOU ARE NOTHING BUT A BURDEN TO THEM...
...AND YOU WILL JUST END UP HURTING THEM IN THE END...

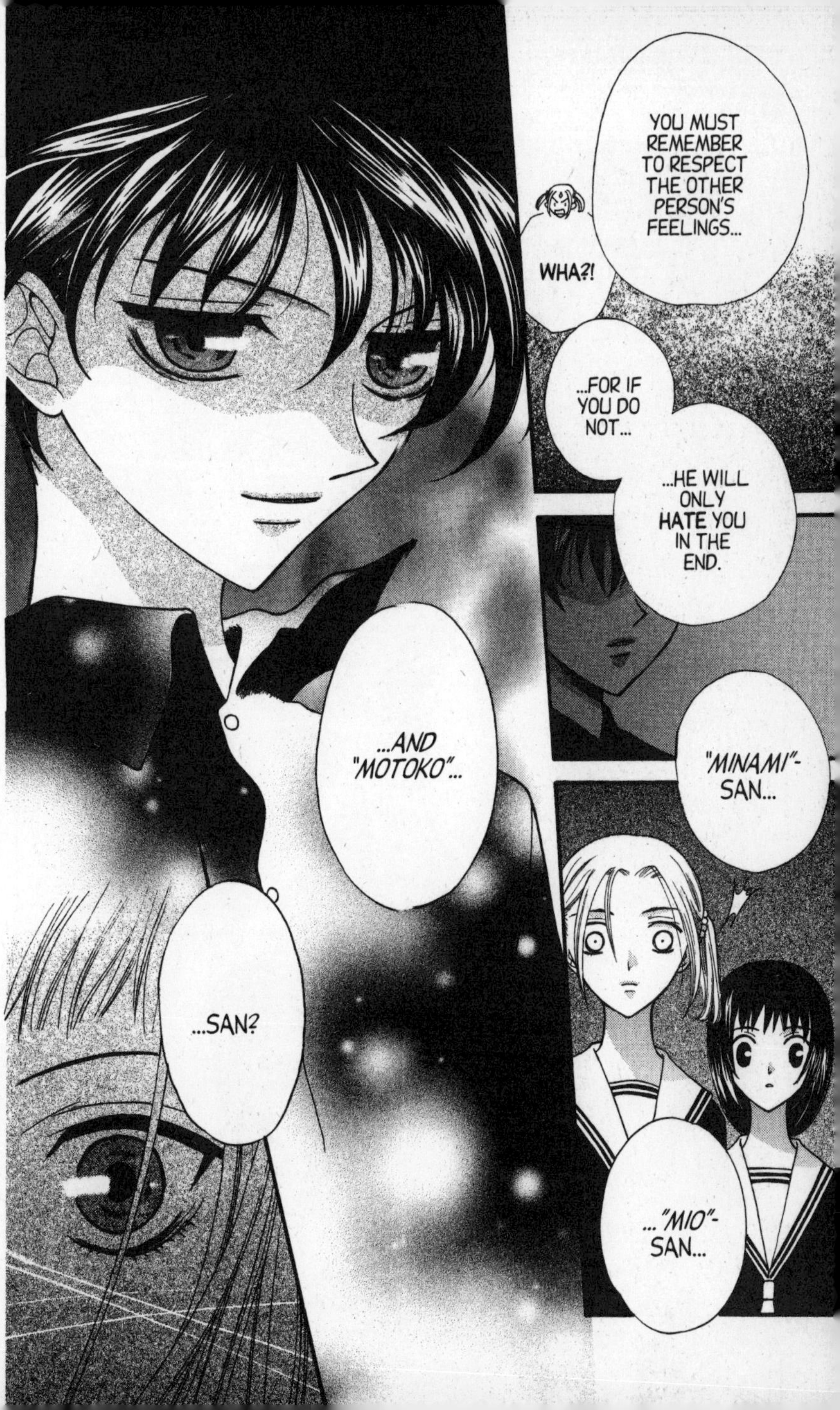
YOU MUST REMEMBER TO RESPECT THE OTHER PERSON'S FEELINGS...
WHA?!
...FOR IF YOU DO NOT...
...HE WILL ONLY HATE YOU IN THE END.
"MINAMI"-SAN...
..."MIO"-SAN...
...AND "MOTOKO"...
...SAN?

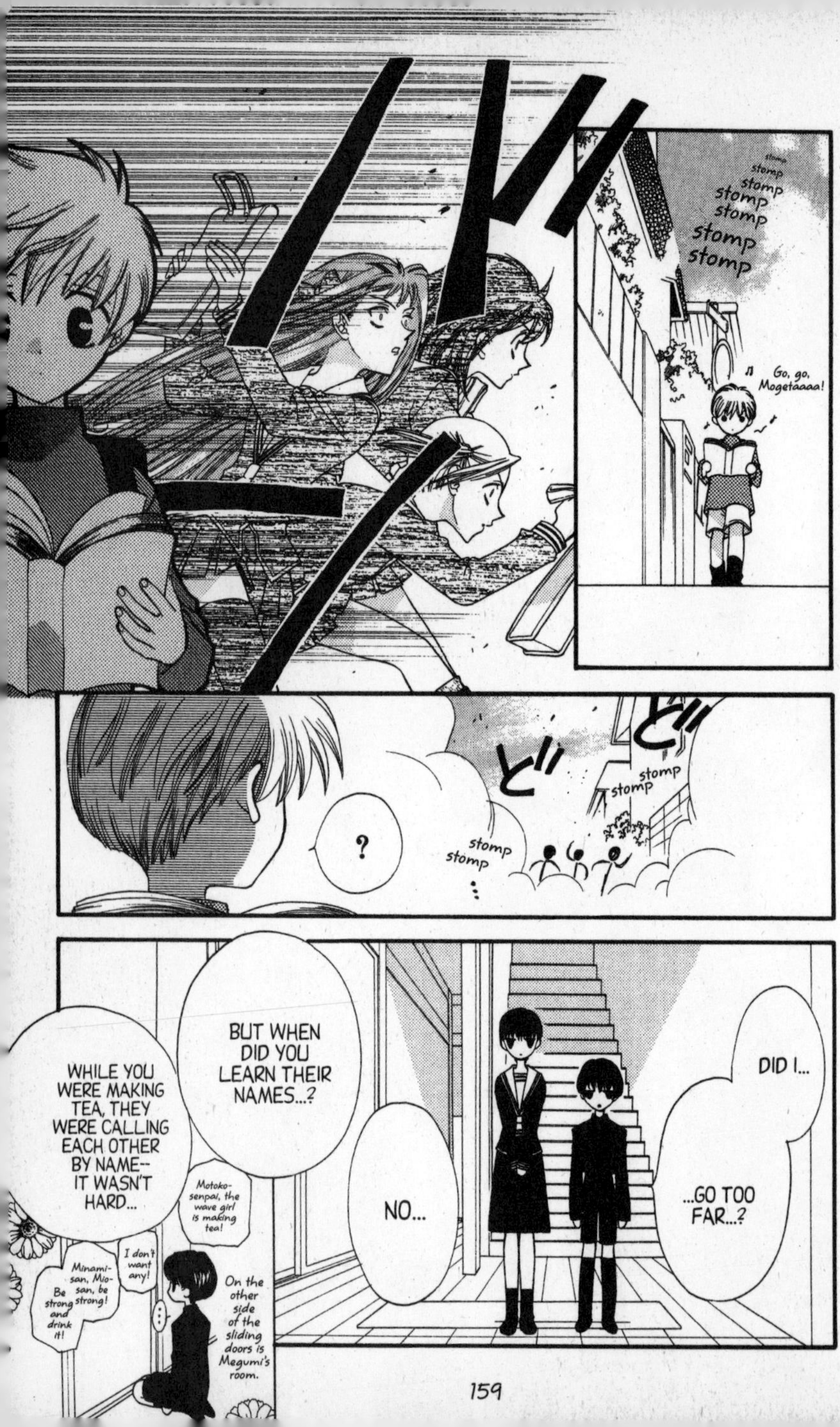

stomp stomp stomp stomp stomp stomp
Go, go, Mogetaaaa!
どど
stomp stomp
stomp stomp
?
...
DID I...
...GO TOO FAR...?
NO...
BUT WHEN DID YOU LEARN THEIR NAMES...?
WHILE YOU WERE MAKING TEA, THEY WERE CALLING EACH OTHER BY NAME-- IT WASN'T HARD...
Motoko-senpai, the wave girl is making tea!
I don't want any!
Minami-san, Mio-san, be strong!
Be strong and drink it!
...
On the other side of the sliding doors is Megumi's room.

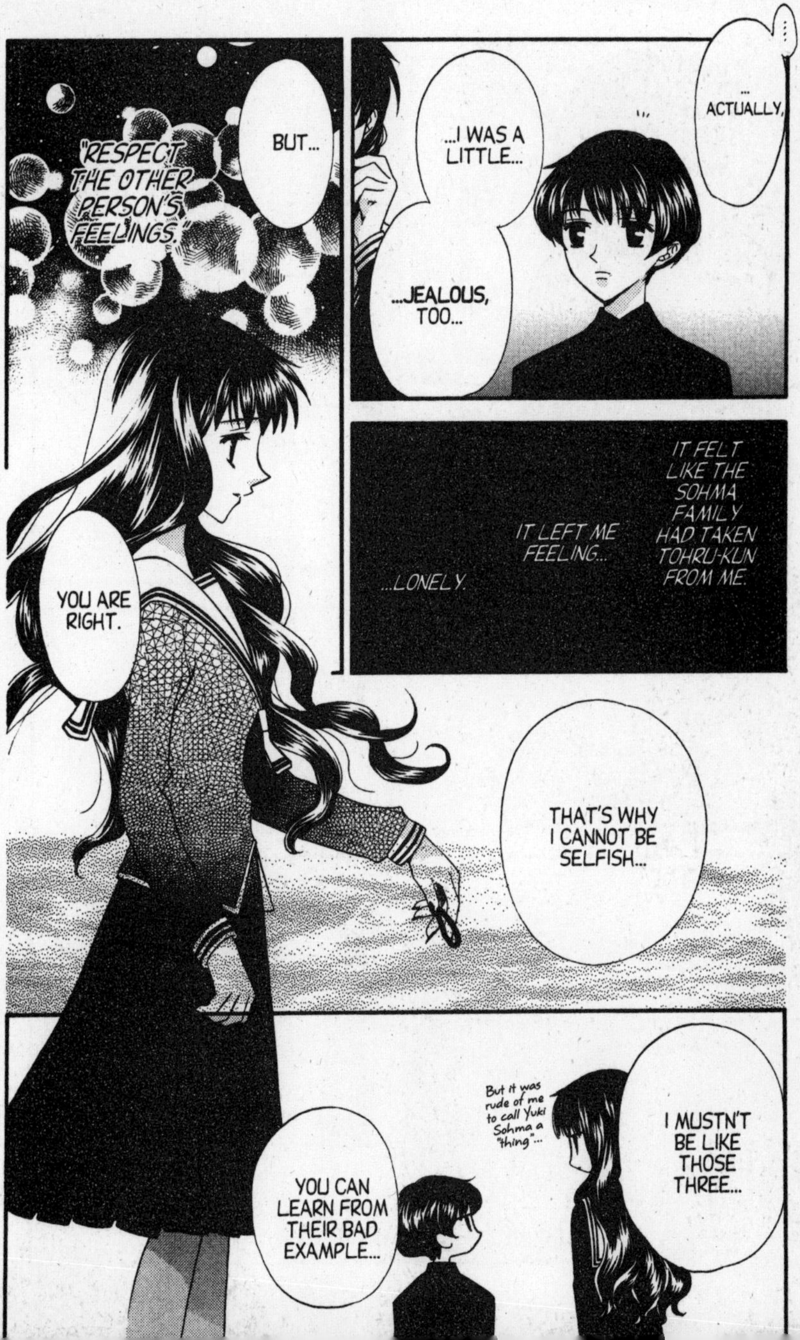
...
... ACTUALLY,
...I WAS A LITTLE...
...JEALOUS, TOO...
IT FELT LIKE THE SOHMA FAMILY HAD TAKEN TOHRU-KUN FROM ME.
IT LEFT ME FEELING...
...LONELY.
BUT...
"RESPECT THE OTHER PERSON'S FEELINGS."
YOU ARE RIGHT.
THAT'S WHY I CANNOT BE SELFISH...
I MUSTN'T BE LIKE THOSE THREE...
But it was rude of me to call Yuki Sohma a "thing"...
YOU CAN LEARN FROM THEIR BAD EXAMPLE...

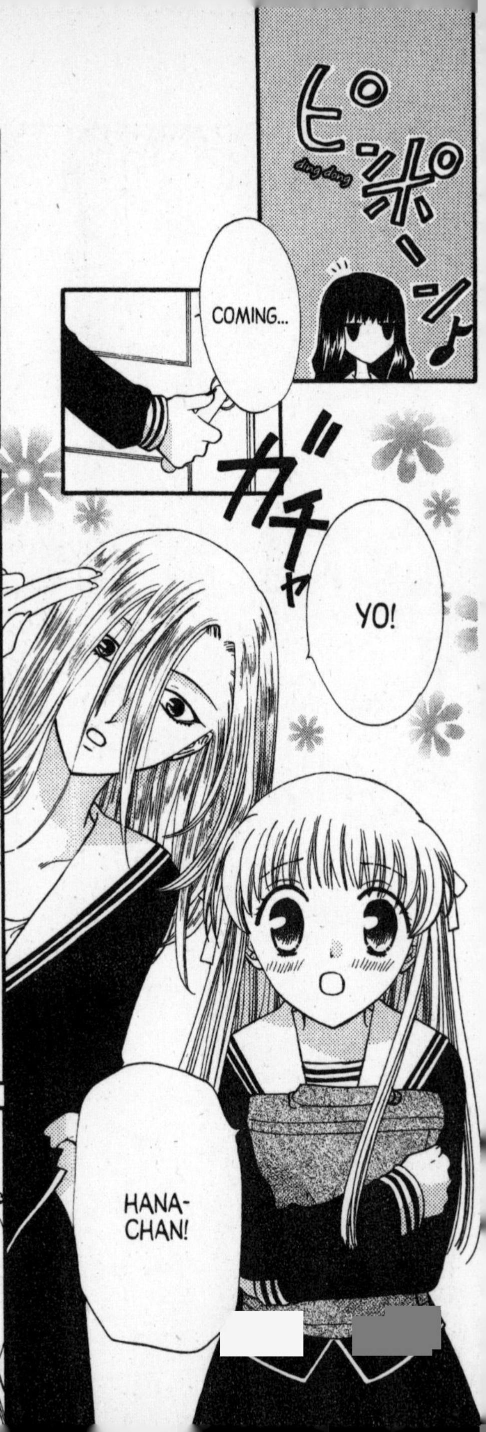
ピンポーン
ding dong
COMING...
ガチャ
YO!
HANA-CHAN!

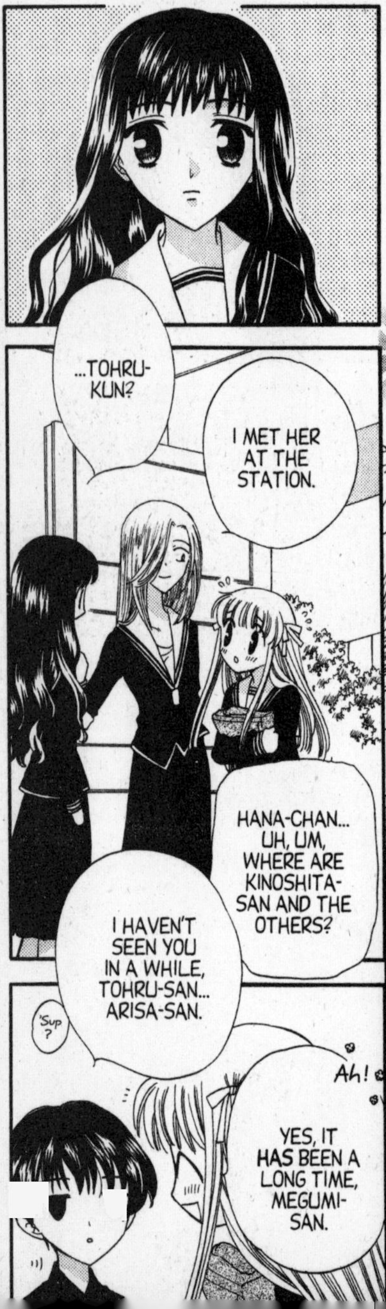
...TOHRU-KUN?
I MET HER AT THE STATION.
HANA-CHAN... UH, UM, WHERE ARE KINOSHITA-SAN AND THE OTHERS?
I HAVEN'T SEEN YOU IN A WHILE, TOHRU-SAN... ARISA-SAN.
'Sup?
Ah!
YES, IT HAS BEEN A LONG TIME, MEGUMI-SAN.

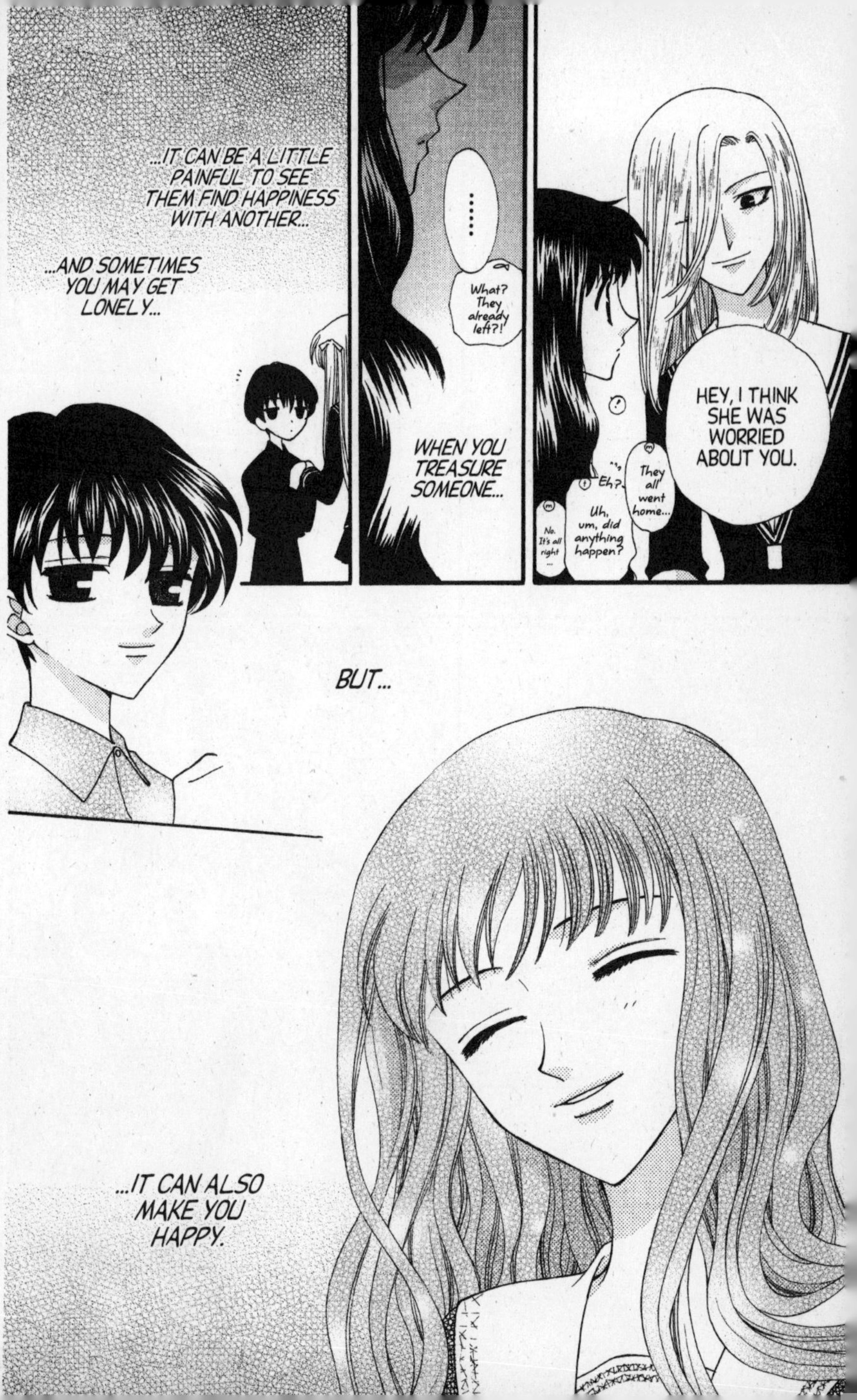
HEY, I THINK SHE WAS WORRIED ABOUT YOU.
They all went home...
Eh?
Uh, um, did anything happen?
No. It's all right...
......
What? They already left?!
WHEN YOU TREASURE SOMEONE...
...IT CAN BE A LITTLE PAINFUL TO SEE THEM FIND HAPPINESS WITH ANOTHER...
...AND SOMETIMES YOU MAY GET LONELY...
BUT...
...IT CAN ALSO MAKE YOU HAPPY.

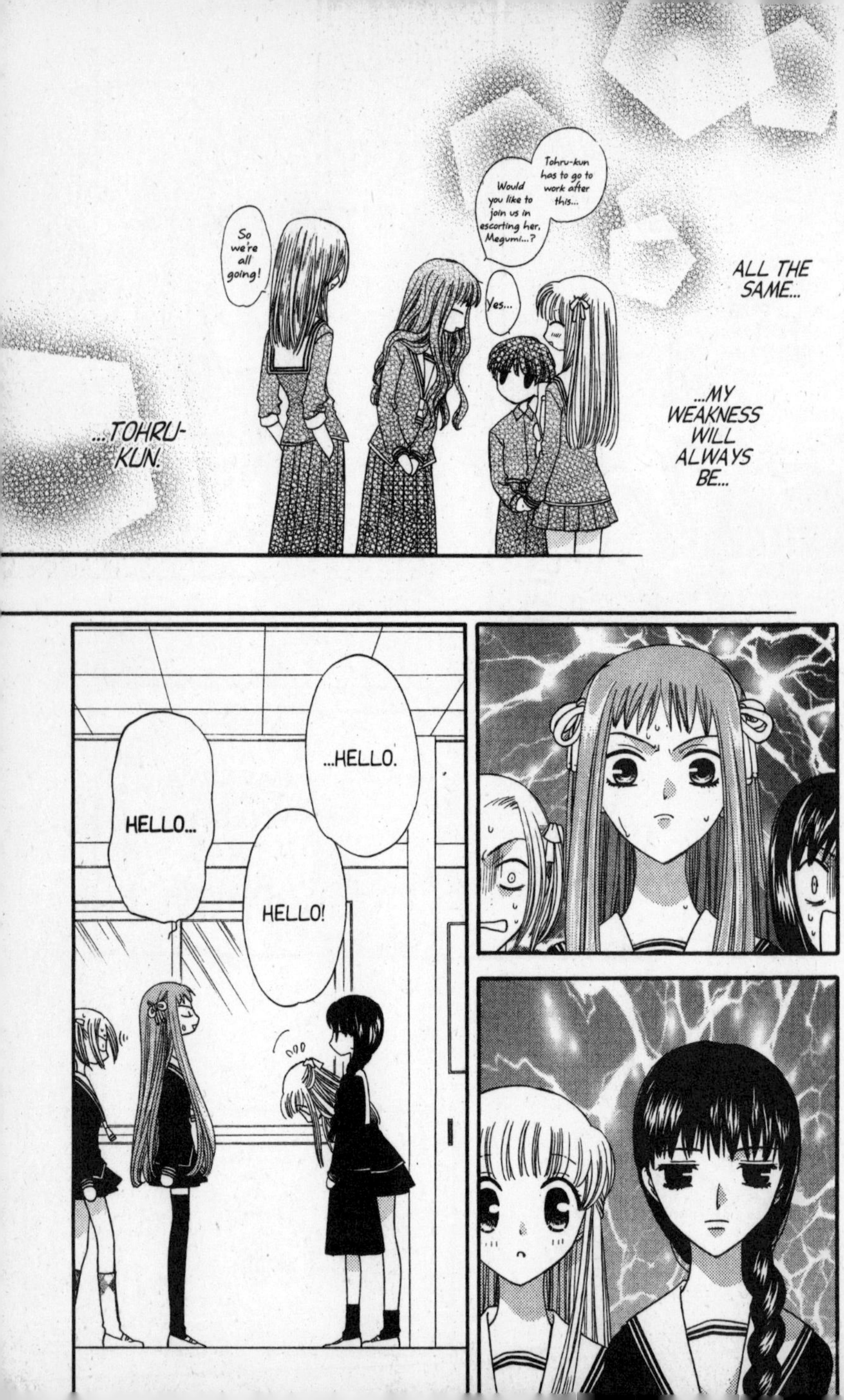
ALL THE SAME...
...MY WEAKNESS WILL ALWAYS BE...
Tohru-kun has to go to work after this...
Would you like to join us in escorting her, Megumi...?
Yes...
So we're all going!
...TOHRU-KUN.
...HELLO.
HELLO!
HELLO...

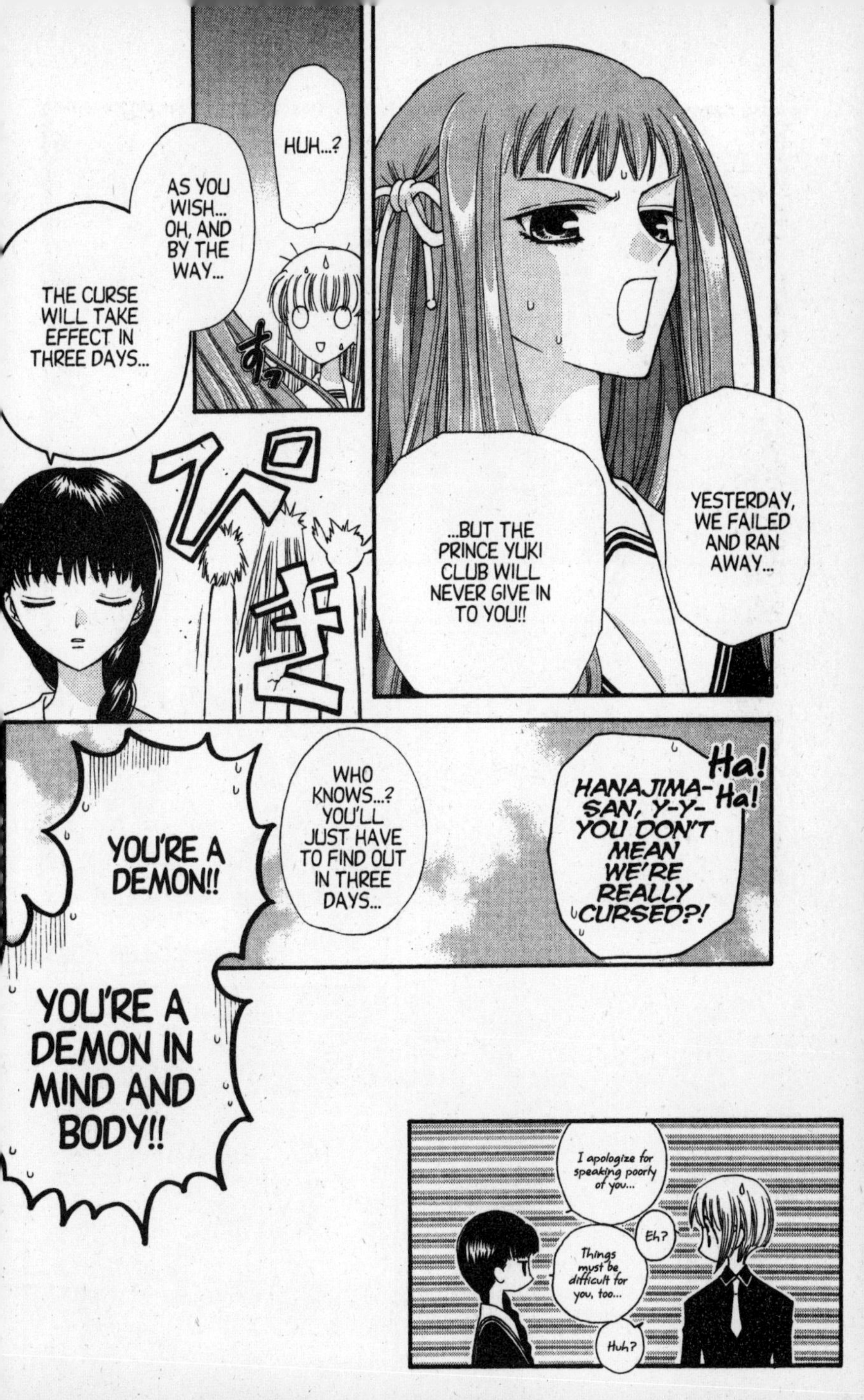
YESTERDAY, WE FAILED AND RAN AWAY...
...BUT THE PRINCE YUKI CLUB WILL NEVER GIVE IN TO YOU!!
HUH...?
AS YOU WISH... OH, AND BY THE WAY...
THE CURSE WILL TAKE EFFECT IN THREE DAYS...
Ha! Ha!
HANAJIMA-SAN, Y-Y-YOU DON'T MEAN WE'RE REALLY CURSED?!
WHO KNOWS...? YOU'LL JUST HAVE TO FIND OUT IN THREE DAYS...
YOU'RE A DEMON!!
YOU'RE A DEMON IN MIND AND BODY!!
I apologize for speaking poorly of you...
Eh?
Things must be difficult for you, too...
Huh?

**Chapter 30**

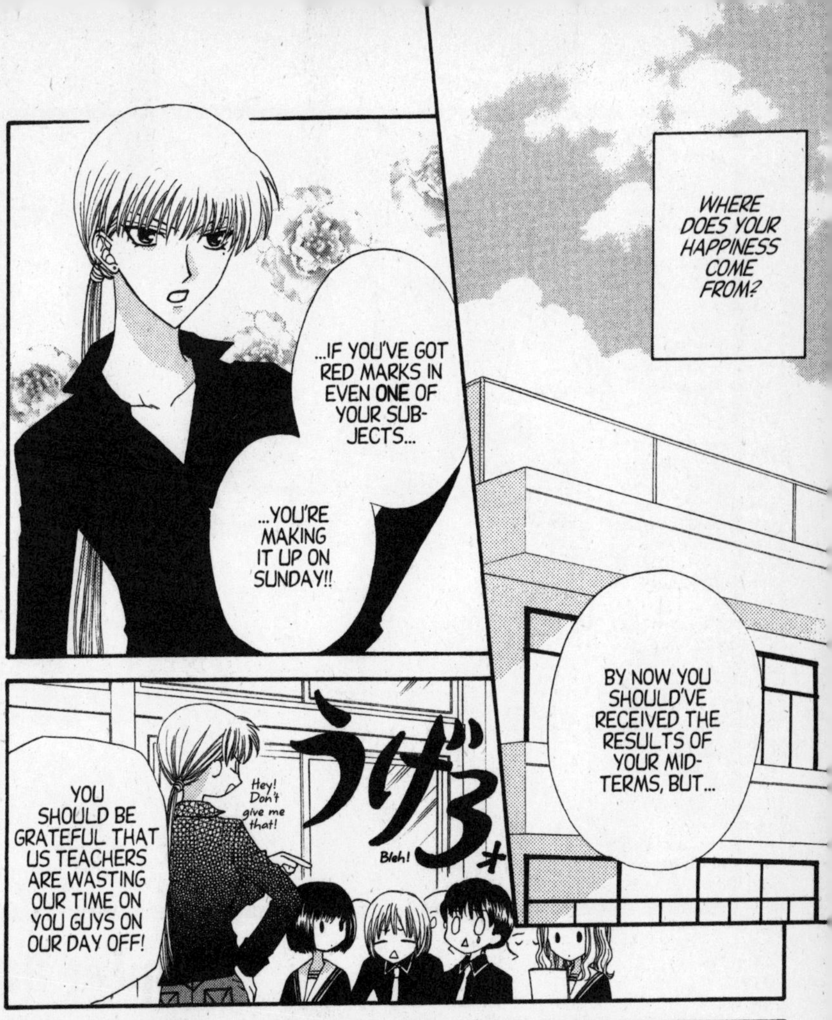
WHERE DOES YOUR HAPPINESS COME FROM?
BY NOW YOU SHOULD'VE RECEIVED THE RESULTS OF YOUR MID-TERMS, BUT...
...IF YOU'VE GOT RED MARKS IN EVEN ONE OF YOUR SUB-JECTS...
...YOU'RE MAKING IT UP ON SUNDAY!!
うげろォ
Bleh!
Hey! Don't give me that!
YOU SHOULD BE GRATEFUL THAT US TEACHERS ARE WASTING OUR TIME ON YOU GUYS ON OUR DAY OFF!

## ULTRA SPECIAL BLAH BLAH BLAH 6

What phrase were Shigure and Momiji using? Good question... (I just like to make them sing.) Oh, by the way, Tohru fell down once, but after that, she managed to walk home.

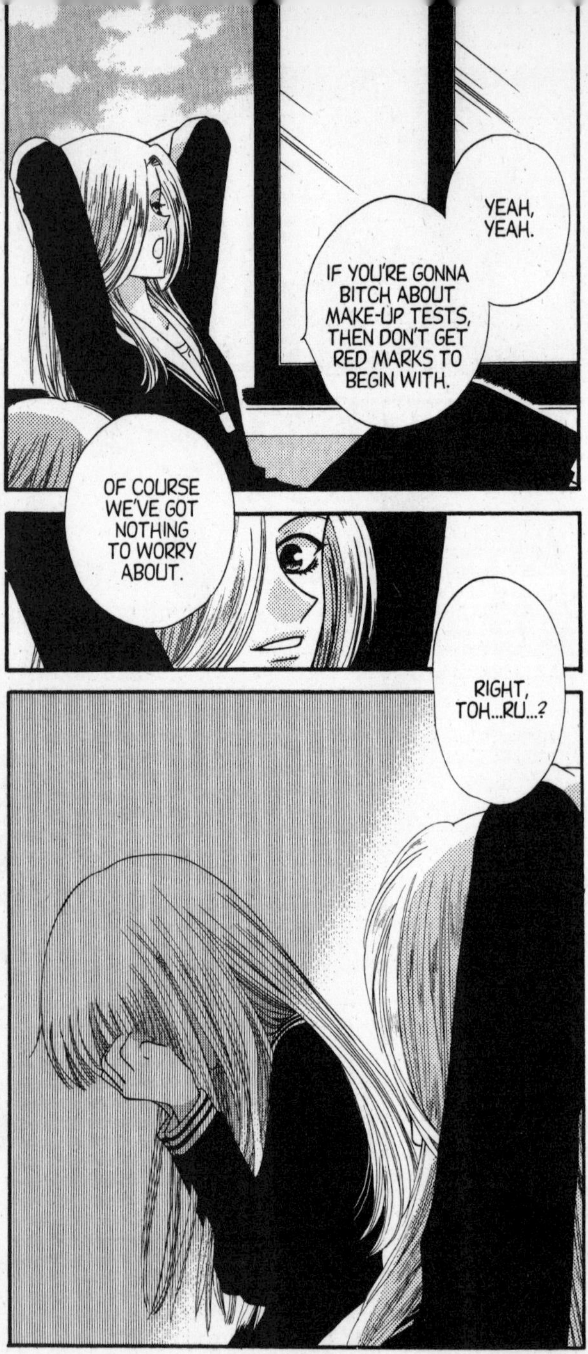
YEAH, YEAH.
IF YOU'RE GONNA BITCH ABOUT MAKE-UP TESTS, THEN DON'T GET RED MARKS TO BEGIN WITH.
OF COURSE WE'VE GOT NOTHING TO WORRY ABOUT.
RIGHT, TOH...RU...?

### Fruits Basket 5 Part 6:

Strangely, I'm really into candy lately. Cotton candy in particular. I like to keep some on hand to munch on. Only problem is, I've been making myself sick! (You're eating too much, duh.) Of course my brain tells me, "you've had enough!" But... (laugh) My favorite candy is gum. I'm always chewing it. As for Japanese sweets, I like things like dango*. But I don't like azuki beans*, so when I have a taiyaki* or something, I'll squeeze all the paste out and then eat it. (You're probably wondering why I even bother trying to eat it.) ♡ The only thing I can eat even with the bean-paste in it is kashiwa mochi.* When it comes to cake, I'm a cheesecake kind of girl. Yup. (Why am I talking about my favorite foods...?) As for rice, I like it with thick flavoring. So if it's too bland, I don't like it.

*dango: dumplings of mochi (a chewy dough made of rice flour)
*azuki beans: sweet red beans used in desserts throughout Asia
*taiyaki: fish-shaped pancakes filled with azuki bean paste
*Kashiwa mochi: mochi balls filled with azuki beans

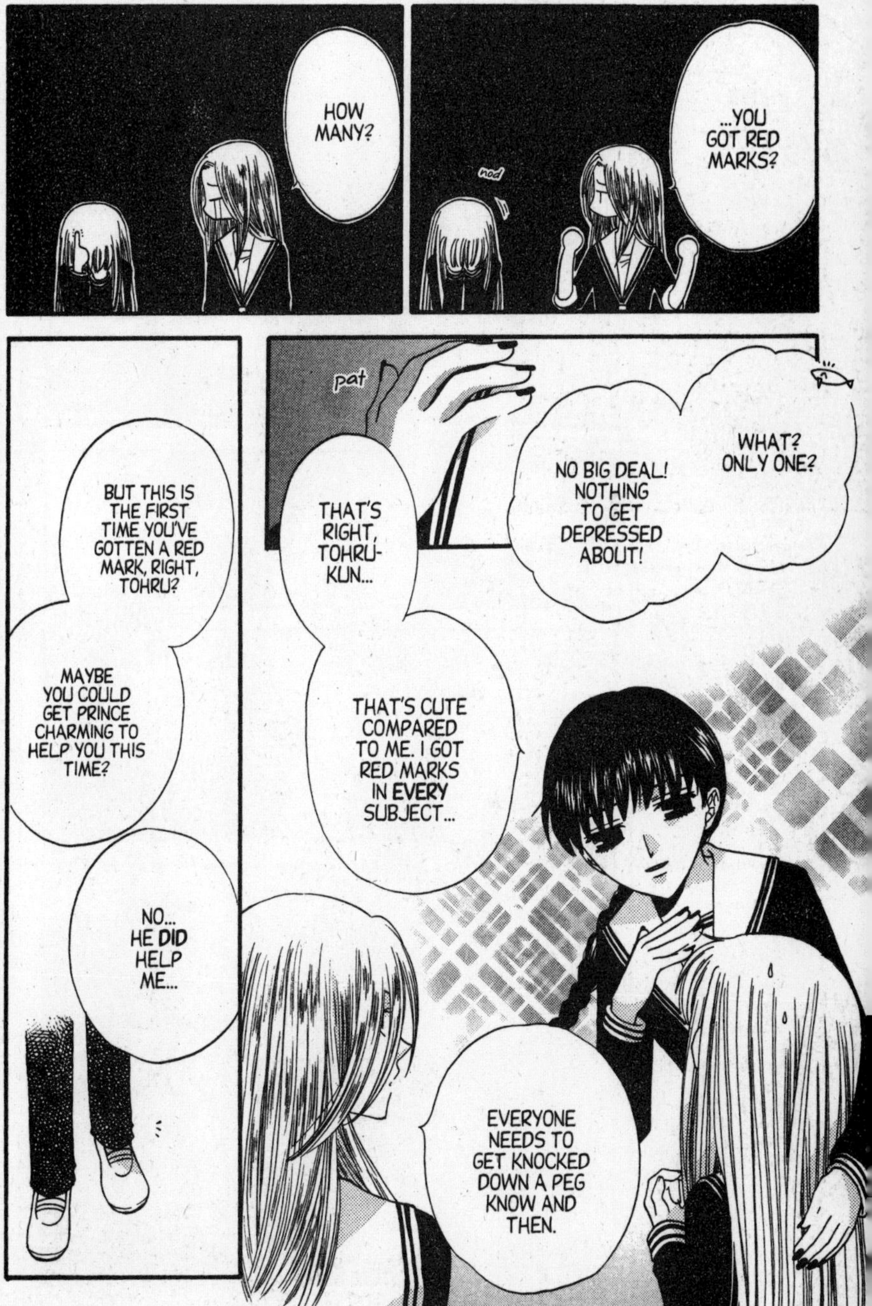
...YOU GOT RED MARKS?
nod
HOW MANY?
WHAT? ONLY ONE?
NO BIG DEAL! NOTHING TO GET DEPRESSED ABOUT!
pat
THAT'S RIGHT, TOHRU-KUN...
THAT'S CUTE COMPARED TO ME. I GOT RED MARKS IN EVERY SUBJECT...
EVERYONE NEEDS TO GET KNOCKED DOWN A PEG KNOW AND THEN.
BUT THIS IS THE FIRST TIME YOU'VE GOTTEN A RED MARK, RIGHT, TOHRU?
MAYBE YOU COULD GET PRINCE CHARMING TO HELP YOU THIS TIME?
NO... HE DID HELP ME...

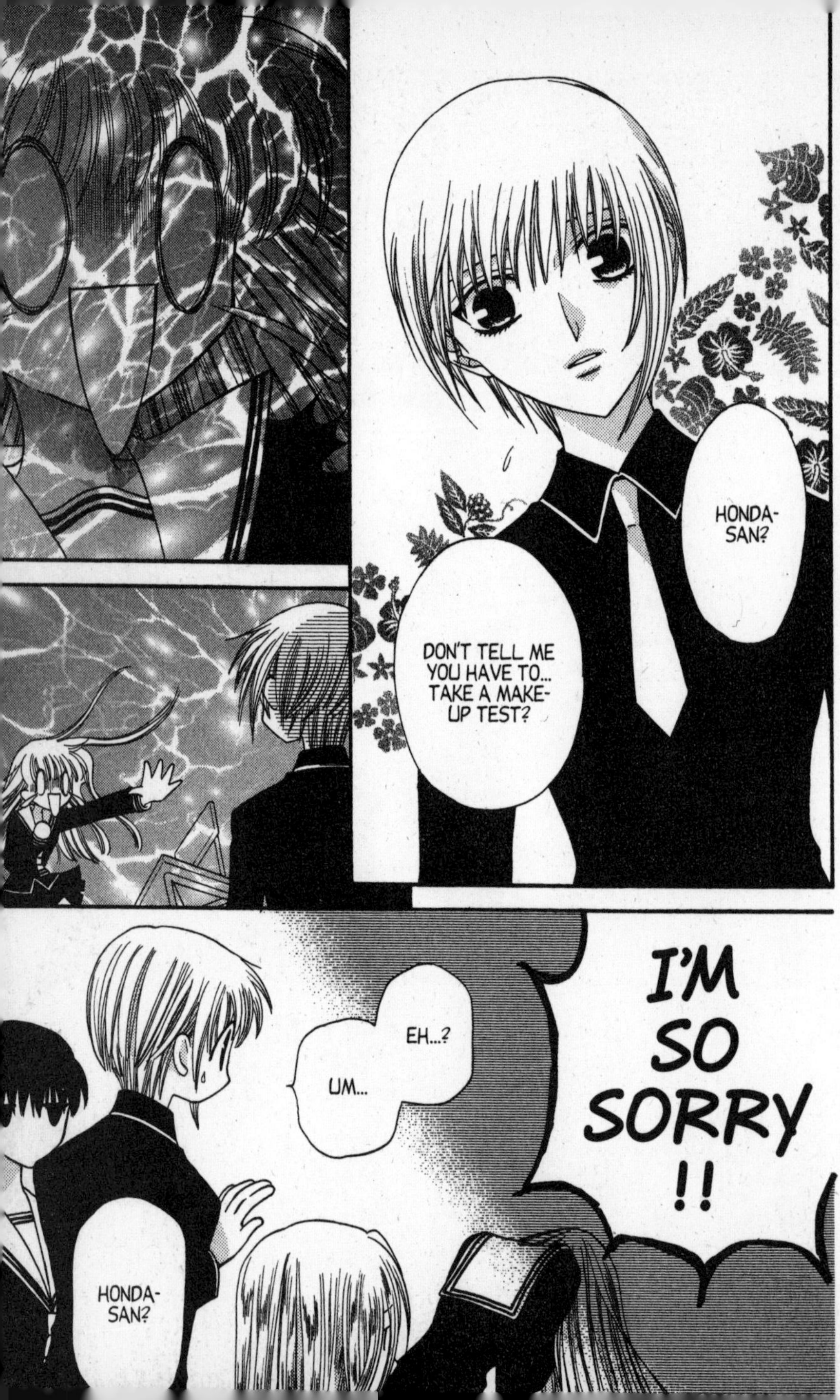
HONDA-SAN?
DON'T TELL ME YOU HAVE TO... TAKE A MAKE-UP TEST?
I'M SO SORRY!!
EH...?
UM...
HONDA-SAN?

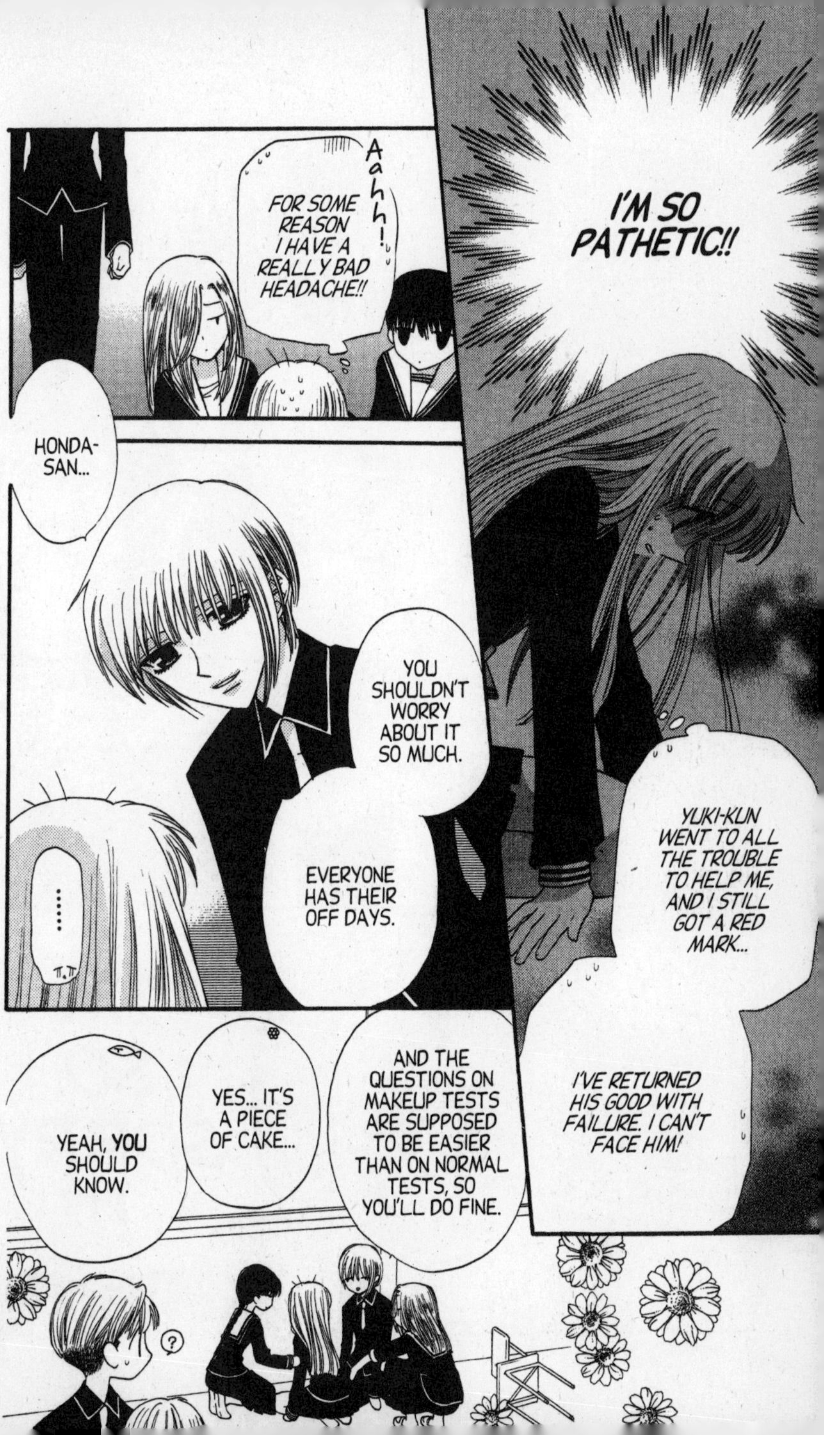
I'M SO PATHETIC!!
YUKI-KUN WENT TO ALL THE TROUBLE TO HELP ME, AND I STILL GOT A RED MARK...
I'VE RETURNED HIS GOOD WITH FAILURE. I CAN'T FACE HIM!
Aahh!
FOR SOME REASON I HAVE A REALLY BAD HEADACHE!!
HONDA-SAN...
YOU SHOULDN'T WORRY ABOUT IT SO MUCH.
EVERYONE HAS THEIR OFF DAYS.
......
AND THE QUESTIONS ON MAKEUP TESTS ARE SUPPOSED TO BE EASIER THAN ON NORMAL TESTS, SO YOU'LL DO FINE.
YES... IT'S A PIECE OF CAKE...
YEAH, YOU SHOULD KNOW.
?

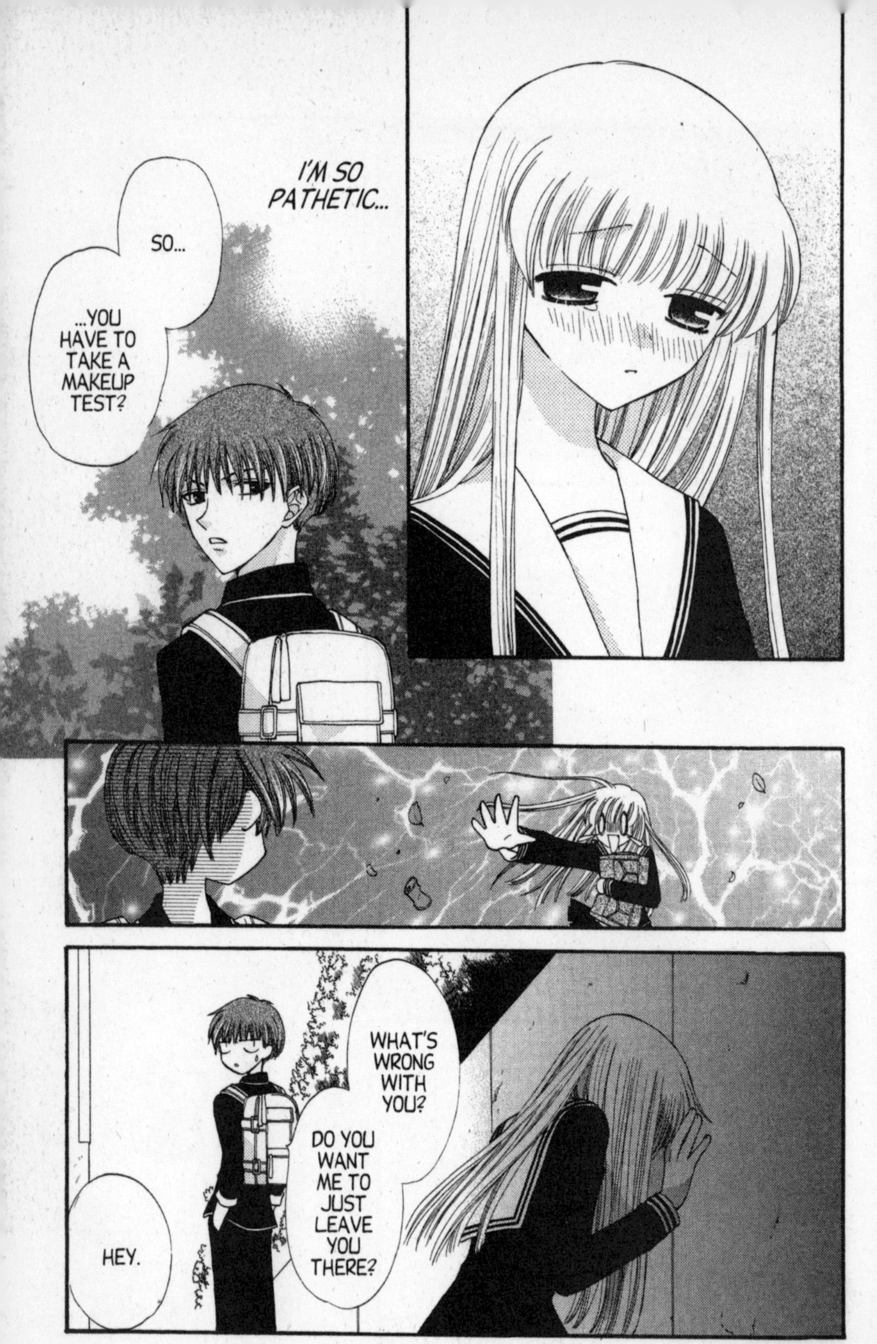
I'M SO PATHETIC...
SO...
...YOU HAVE TO TAKE A MAKEUP TEST?
WHAT'S WRONG WITH YOU?
DO YOU WANT ME TO JUST LEAVE YOU THERE?
HEY.

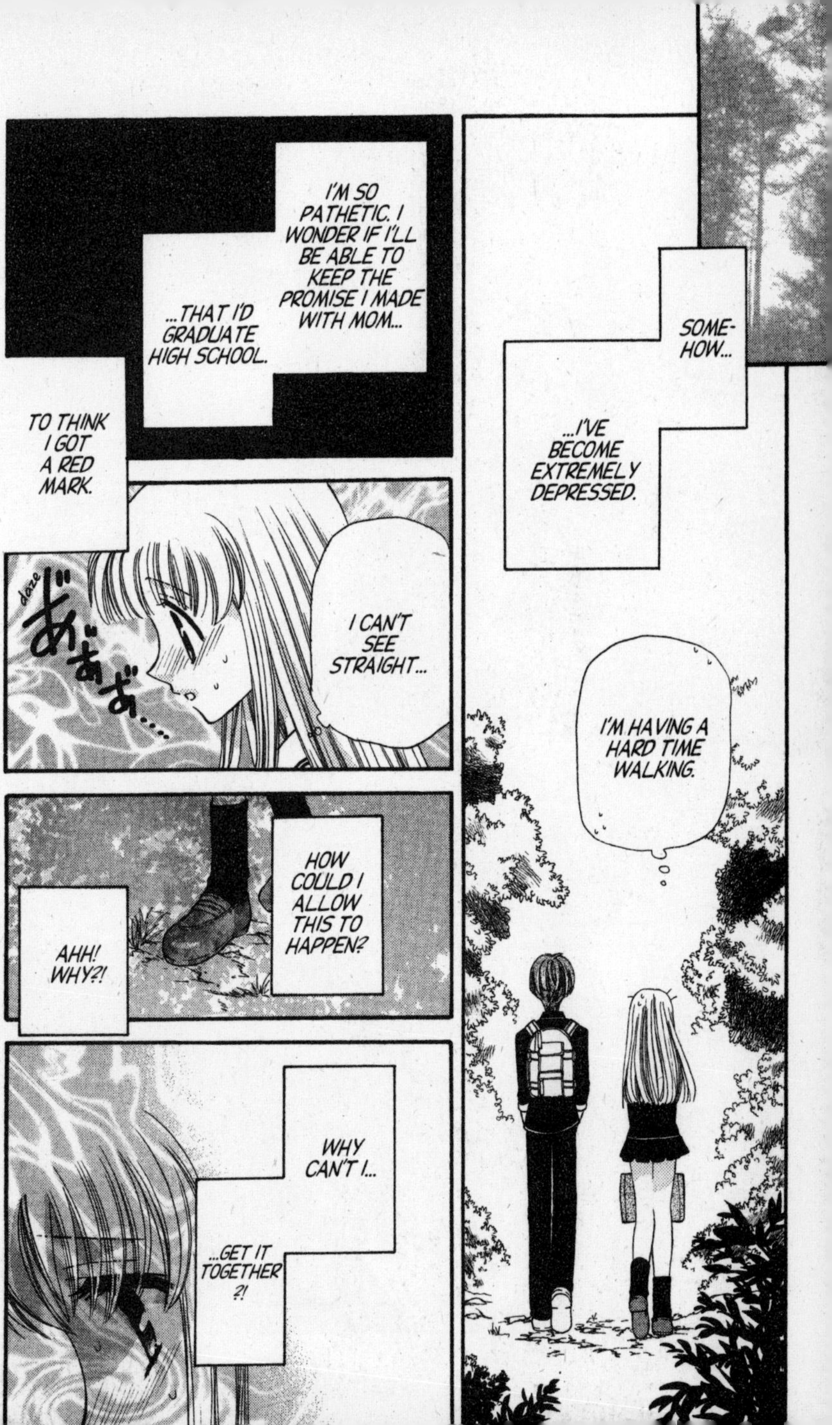
SOME-
HOW...
...I'VE BECOME EXTREMELY DEPRESSED.
I'M HAVING A HARD TIME WALKING.
I'M SO PATHETIC. I WONDER IF I'LL BE ABLE TO KEEP THE PROMISE I MADE WITH MOM...
...THAT I'D GRADUATE HIGH SCHOOL.
TO THINK I GOT A RED MARK.
I CAN'T SEE STRAIGHT...
daze
HOW COULD I ALLOW THIS TO HAPPEN?
AHH! WHY?!
WHY CAN'T I...
...GET IT TOGETHER?!

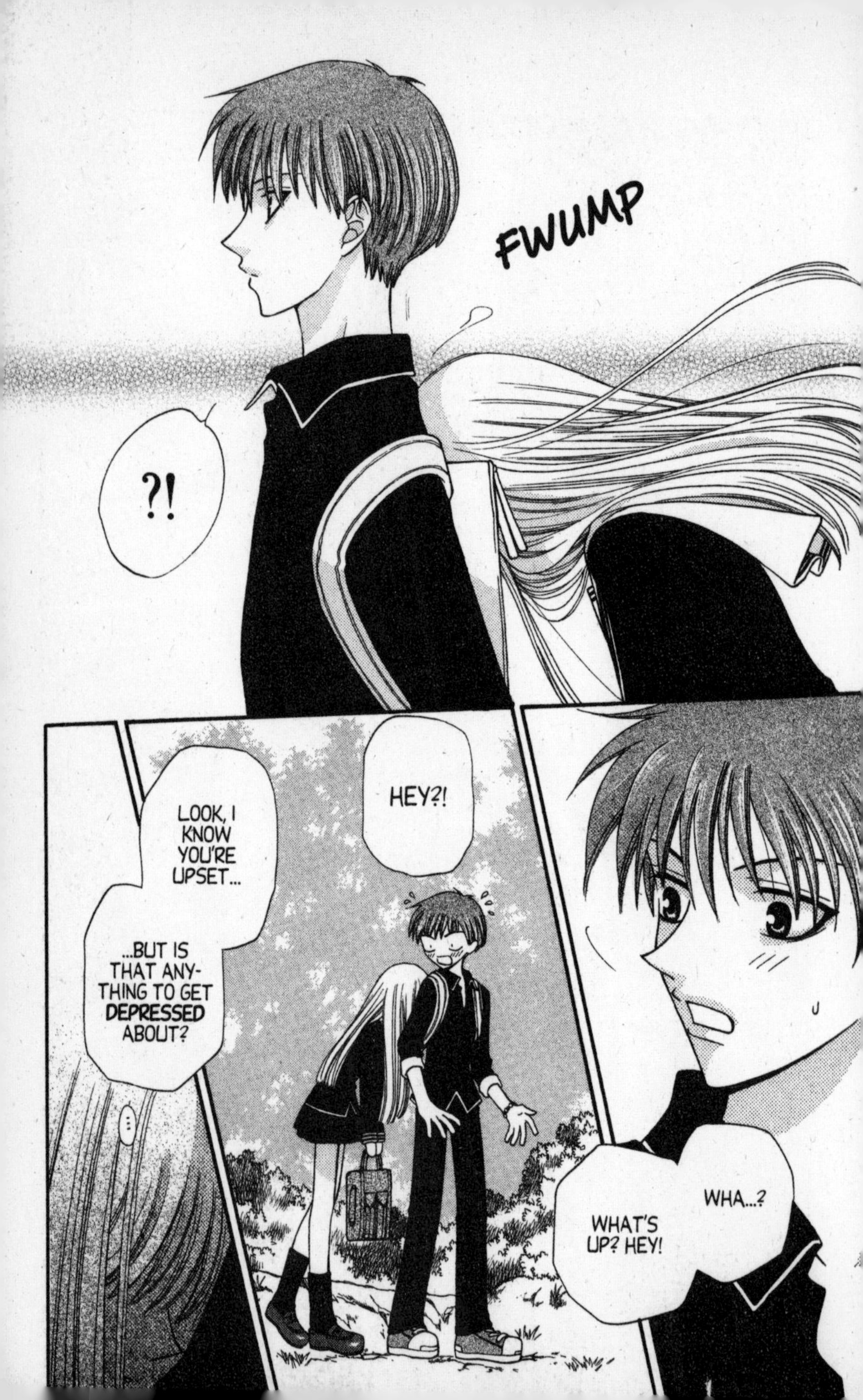
FWUMP
?!
WHA...?
WHAT'S UP? HEY!
HEY?!
LOOK, I KNOW YOU'RE UPSET...
...BUT IS THAT ANY-THING TO GET **DEPRESSED** ABOUT?
...

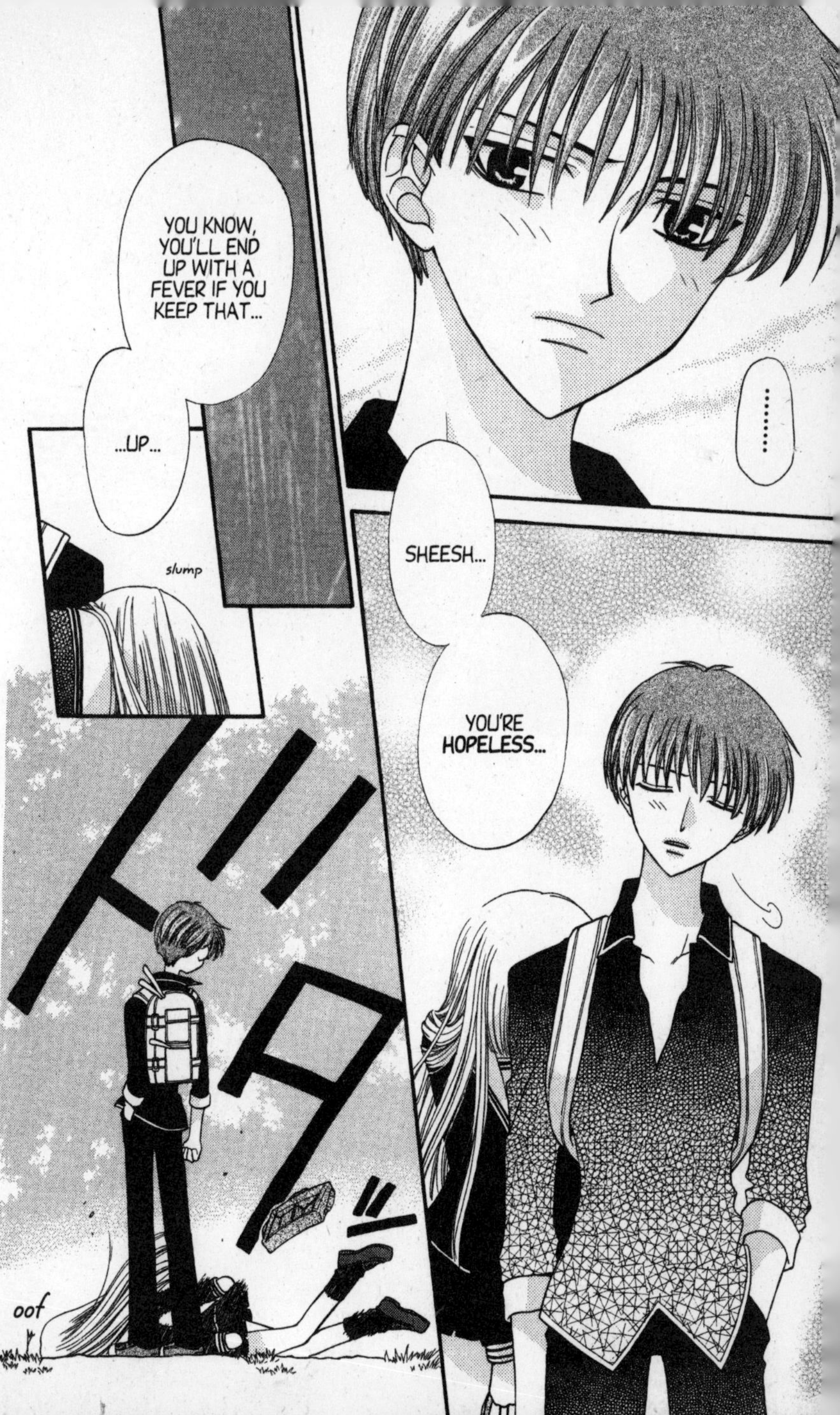
......
YOU KNOW, YOU'LL END UP WITH A FEVER IF YOU KEEP THAT...
...UP...
slump
SHEESH...
YOU'RE HOPELESS...
ドタ
oof

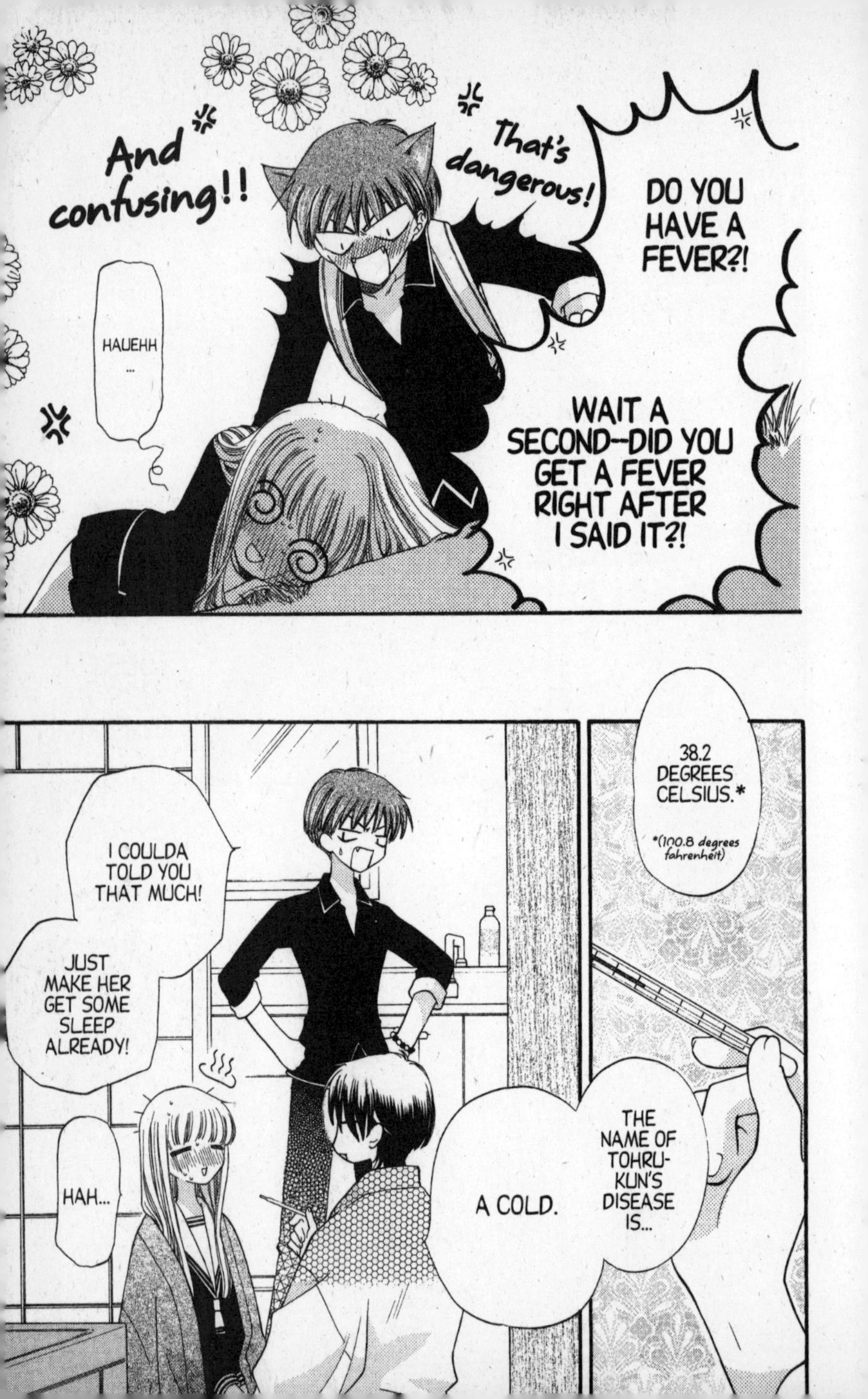
DO YOU HAVE A FEVER?!
That's dangerous!
And confusing!!
WAIT A SECOND--DID YOU GET A FEVER RIGHT AFTER I SAID IT?!
HAUEHH ...
38.2 DEGREES CELSIUS.*
*(100.8 degrees fahrenheit)
THE NAME OF TOHRU-KUN'S DISEASE IS...
A COLD.
I COULDA TOLD YOU THAT MUCH!
JUST MAKE HER GET SOME SLEEP ALREADY!
HAH...

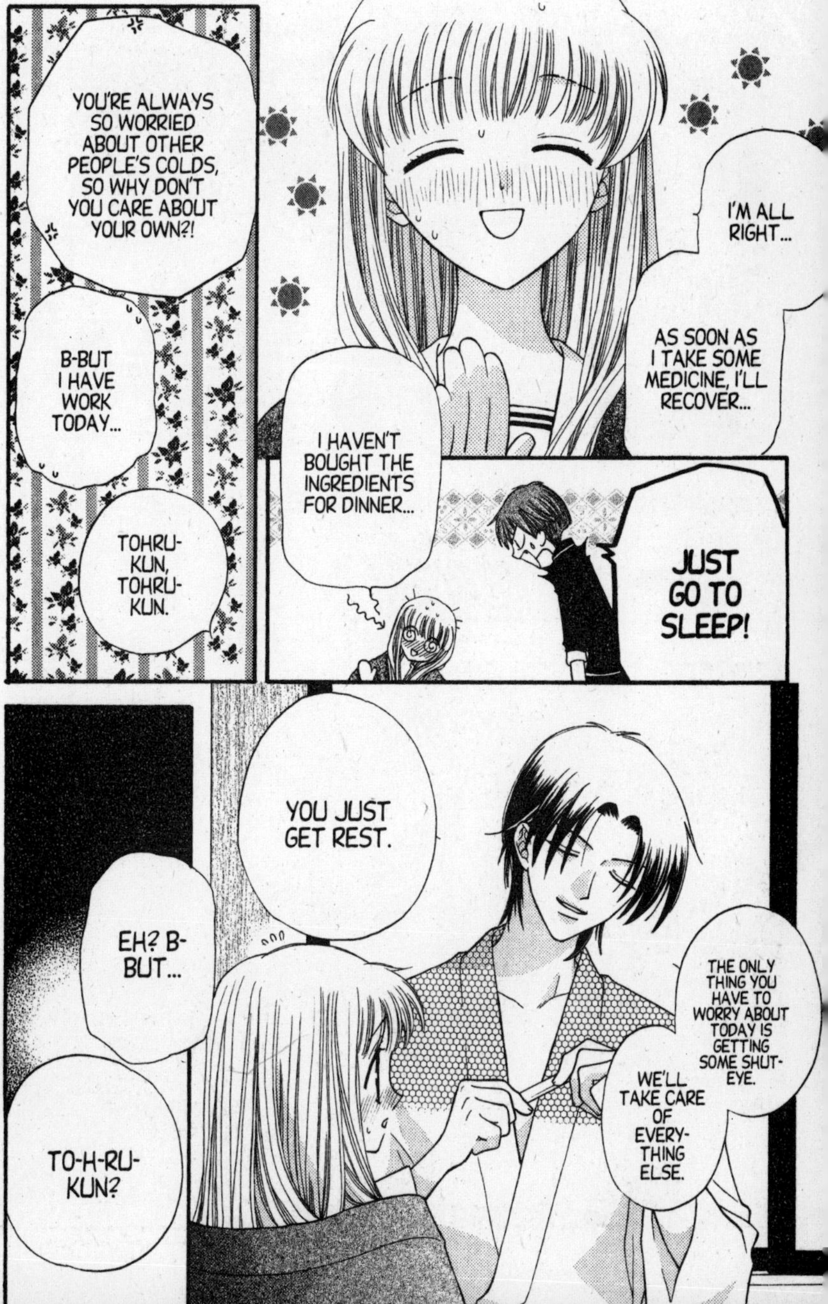
I'M ALL RIGHT...
AS SOON AS I TAKE SOME MEDICINE, I'LL RECOVER...
I HAVEN'T BOUGHT THE INGREDIENTS FOR DINNER...
JUST GO TO SLEEP!
YOU'RE ALWAYS SO WORRIED ABOUT OTHER PEOPLE'S COLDS, SO WHY DON'T YOU CARE ABOUT YOUR OWN?!
B-BUT I HAVE WORK TODAY...
TOHRU-KUN, TOHRU-KUN.
YOU JUST GET REST.
EH? B-BUT...
THE ONLY THING YOU HAVE TO WORRY ABOUT TODAY IS GETTING SOME SHUT-EYE.
WE'LL TAKE CARE OF EVERY-THING ELSE.
TO-H-RU-KUN?

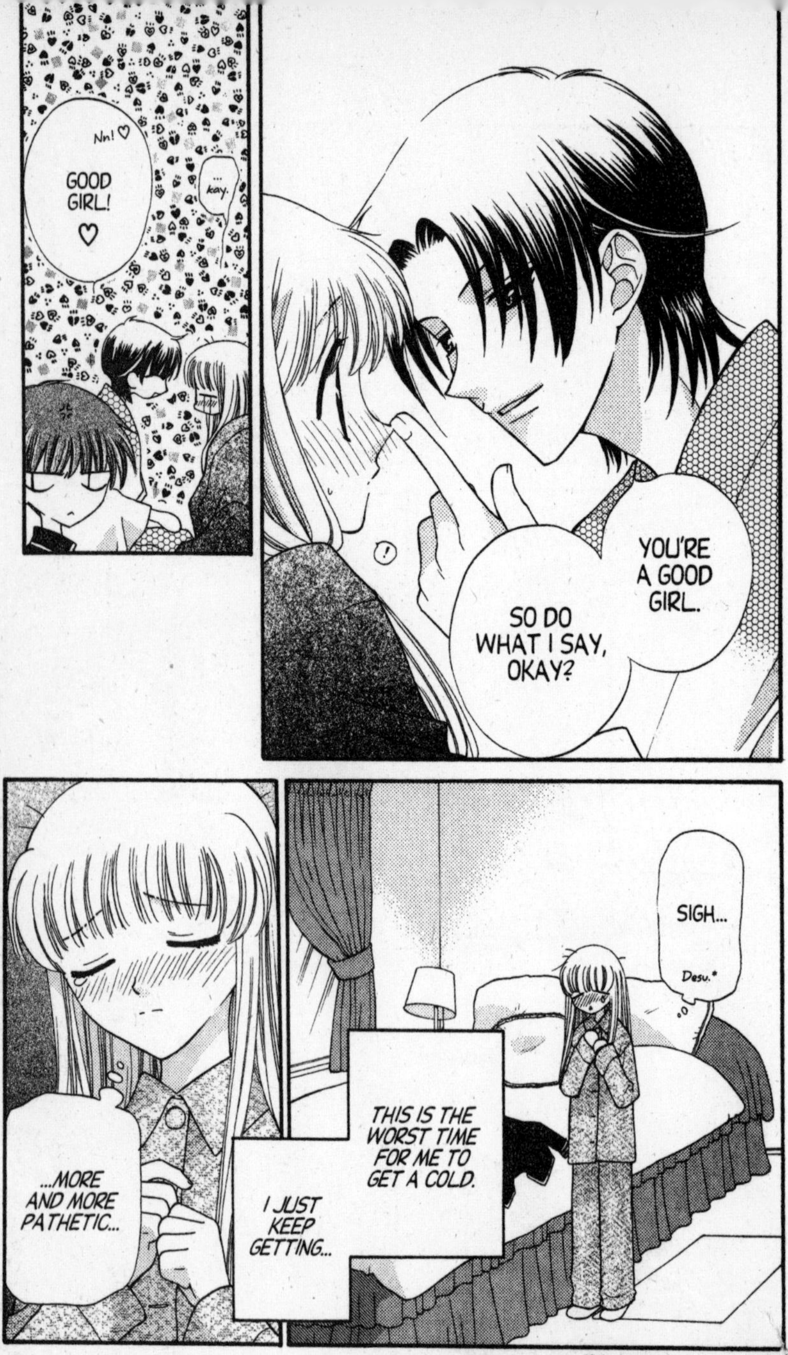
YOU'RE A GOOD GIRL.
SO DO WHAT I SAY, OKAY?
!
Nn! ♡ GOOD GIRL! ♡
... kay.
SIGH...
Desu.*
THIS IS THE WORST TIME FOR ME TO GET A COLD.
I JUST KEEP GETTING...
...MORE AND MORE PATHETIC...

*Tahru's polite, even when she sighs!

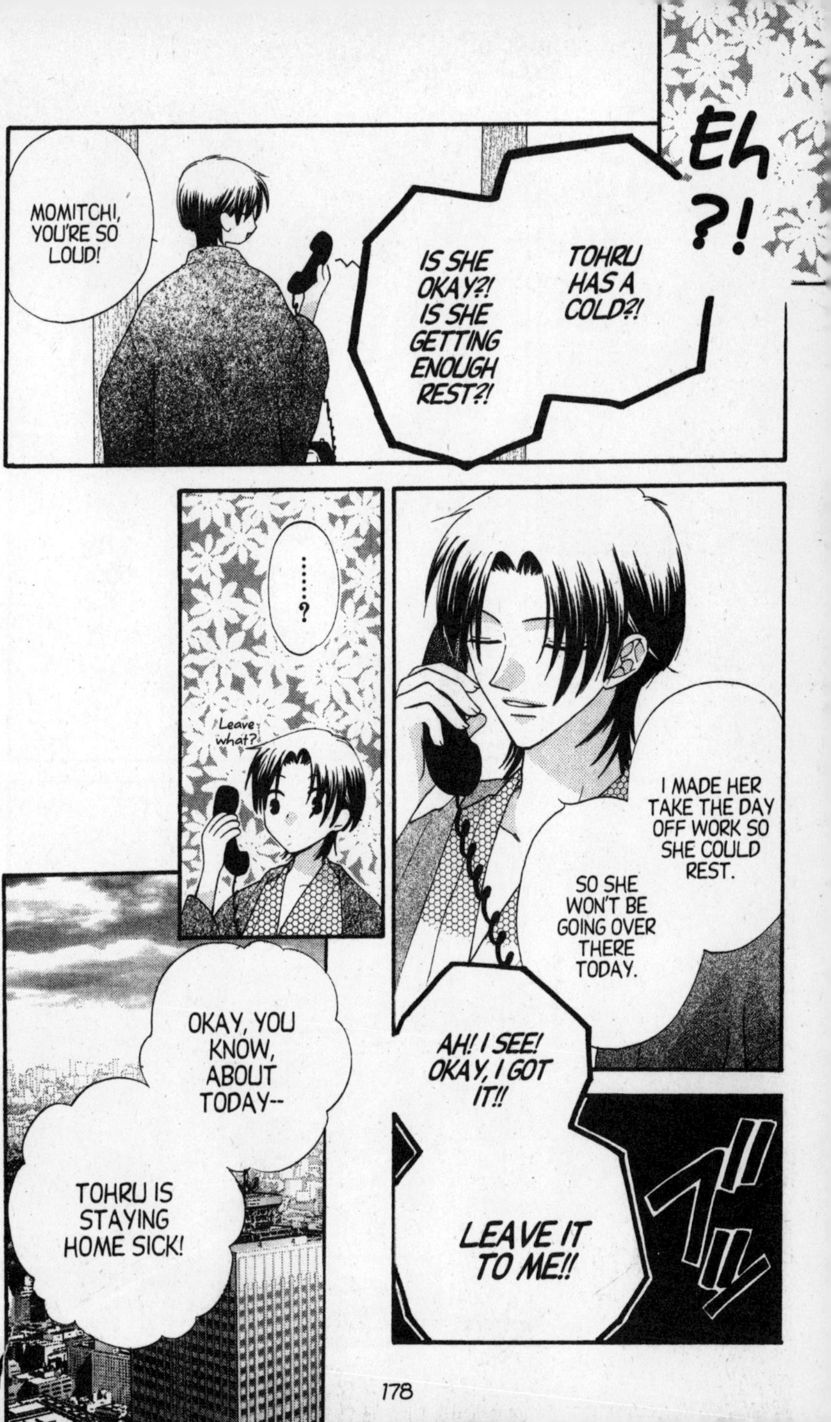

Eh ?!
TOHRU HAS A COLD?!
IS SHE OKAY?! IS SHE GETTING ENOUGH REST?!
MOMITCHI, YOU'RE SO LOUD!
I MADE HER TAKE THE DAY OFF WORK SO SHE COULD REST.
SO SHE WON'T BE GOING OVER THERE TODAY.
AH! I SEE! OKAY, I GOT IT!!
LEAVE IT TO ME!!
......?
Leave what?
OKAY, YOU KNOW, ABOUT TODAY--
TOHRU IS STAYING HOME SICK!

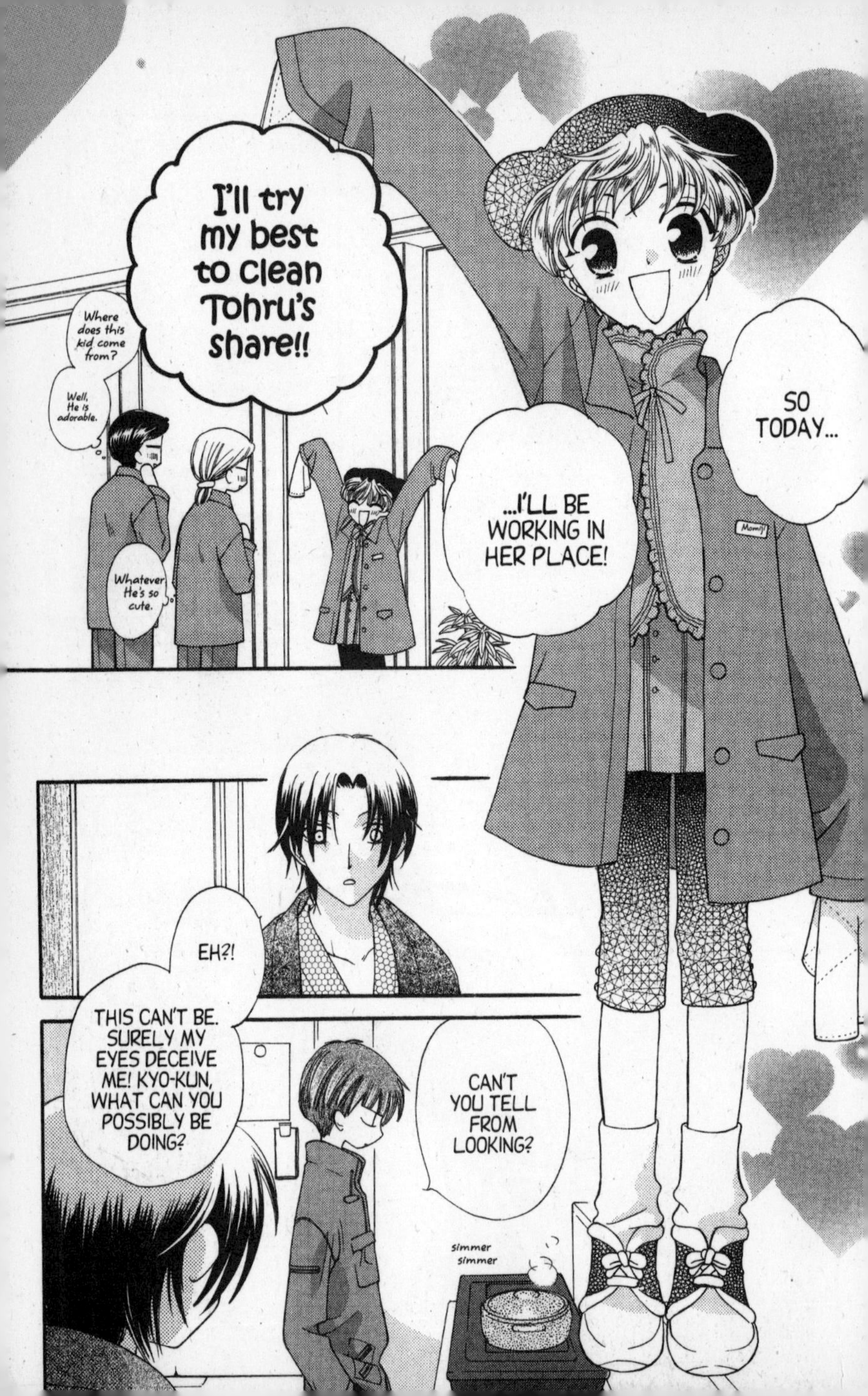
SO TODAY...
...I'LL BE WORKING IN HER PLACE!
I'll try my best to clean Tohru's share!!
Where does this kid come from?
Well, He is adorable.
Whatever He's so cute.
EH?!
THIS CAN'T BE. SURELY MY EYES DECEIVE ME! KYO-KUN, WHAT CAN YOU POSSIBLY BE DOING?
CAN'T YOU TELL FROM LOOKING?
simmer simmer

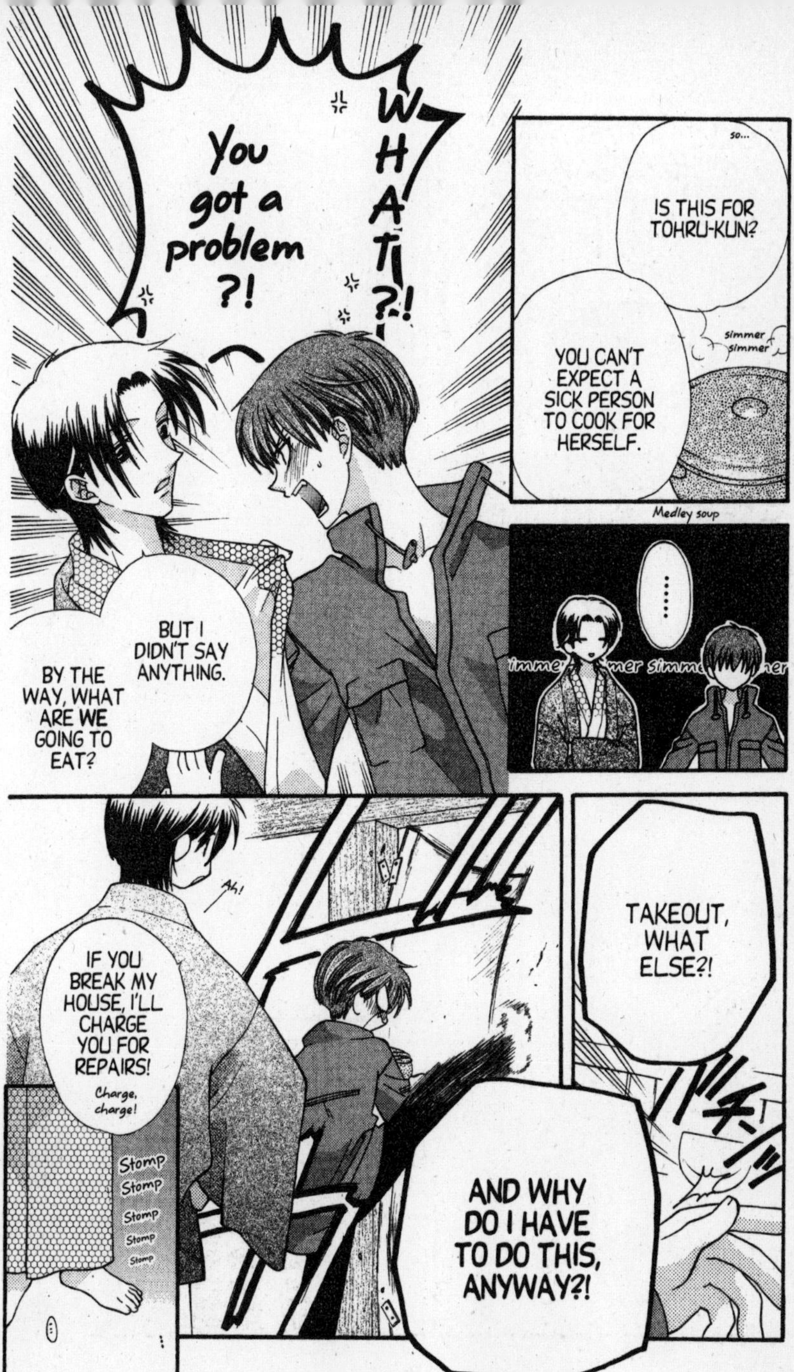
So...
IS THIS FOR TOHRU-KUN?
YOU CAN'T EXPECT A SICK PERSON TO COOK FOR HERSELF.
simmer simmer
Medley soup
......
WHAT?!
You got a problem?!
BUT I DIDN'T SAY ANYTHING.
BY THE WAY, WHAT ARE WE GOING TO EAT?
TAKEOUT, WHAT ELSE?!
AND WHY DO I HAVE TO DO THIS, ANYWAY?!
Ah!
IF YOU BREAK MY HOUSE, I'LL CHARGE YOU FOR REPAIRS!
Charge, charge!
Stomp Stomp Stomp Stomp Stomp

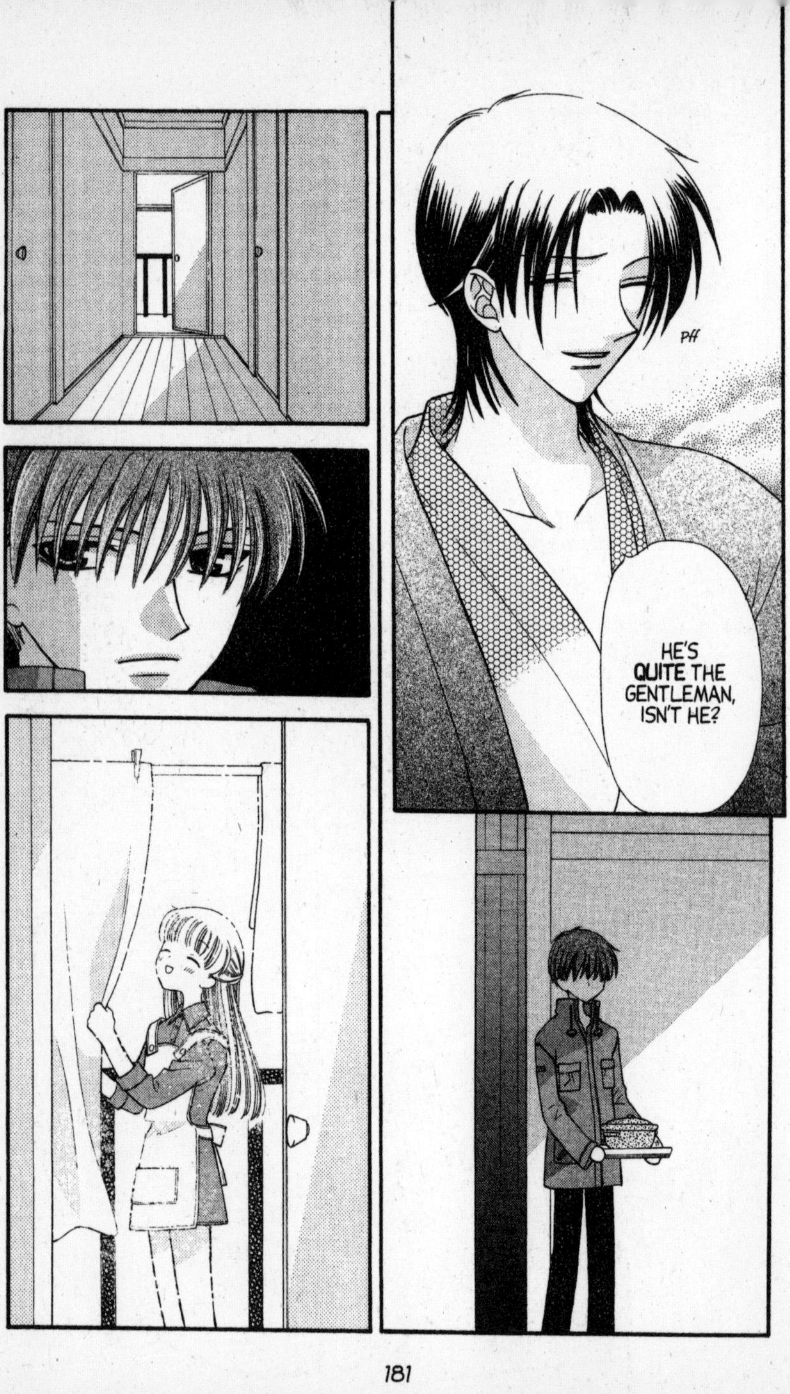
PFF
HE'S **QUITE** THE GENTLEMAN, ISN'T HE?

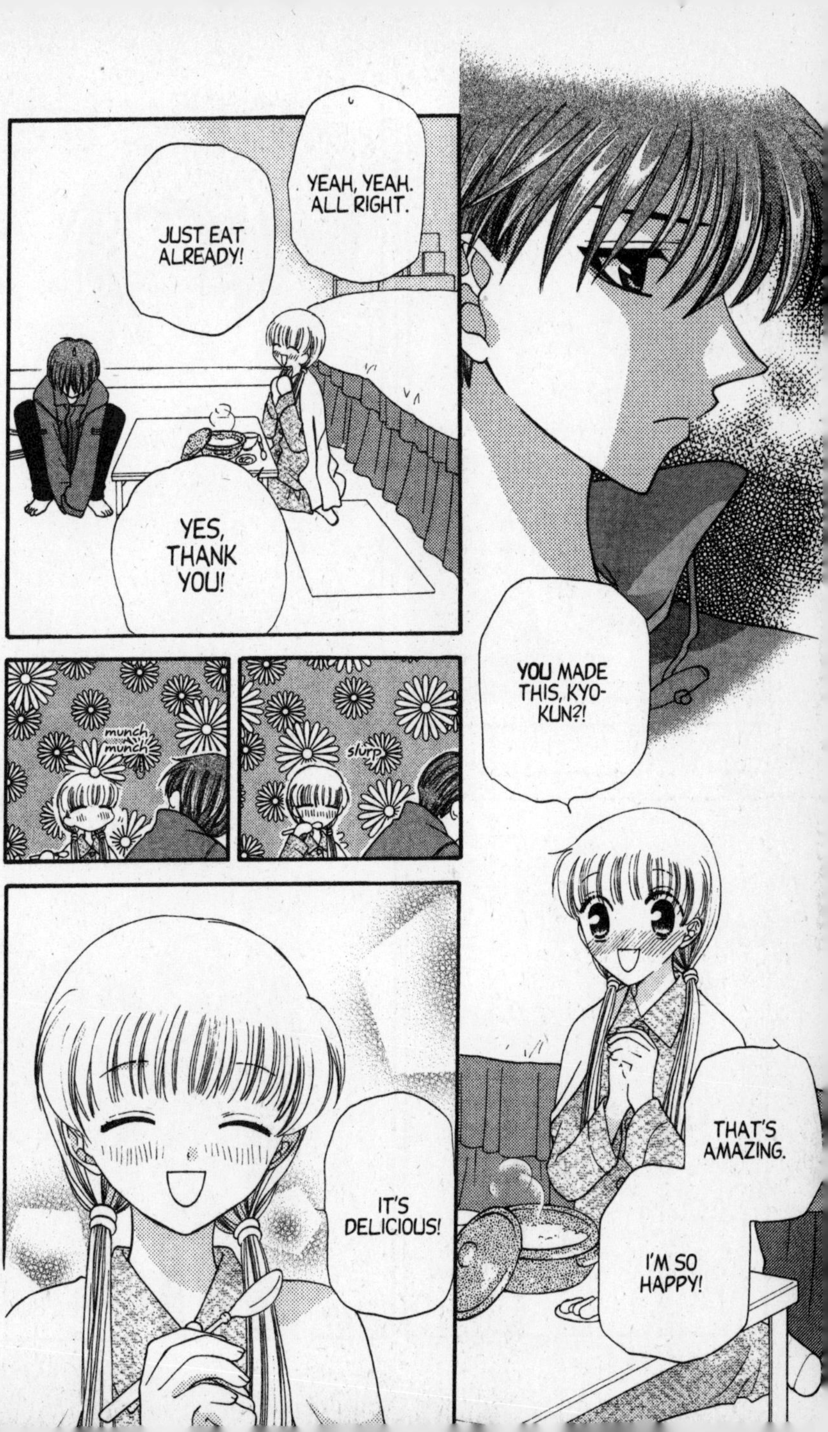
YOU MADE THIS, KYO-KUN?!
THAT'S AMAZING.
I'M SO HAPPY!
YEAH, YEAH. ALL RIGHT.
JUST EAT ALREADY!
YES, THANK YOU!
slurp
munch munch
IT'S DELICIOUS!

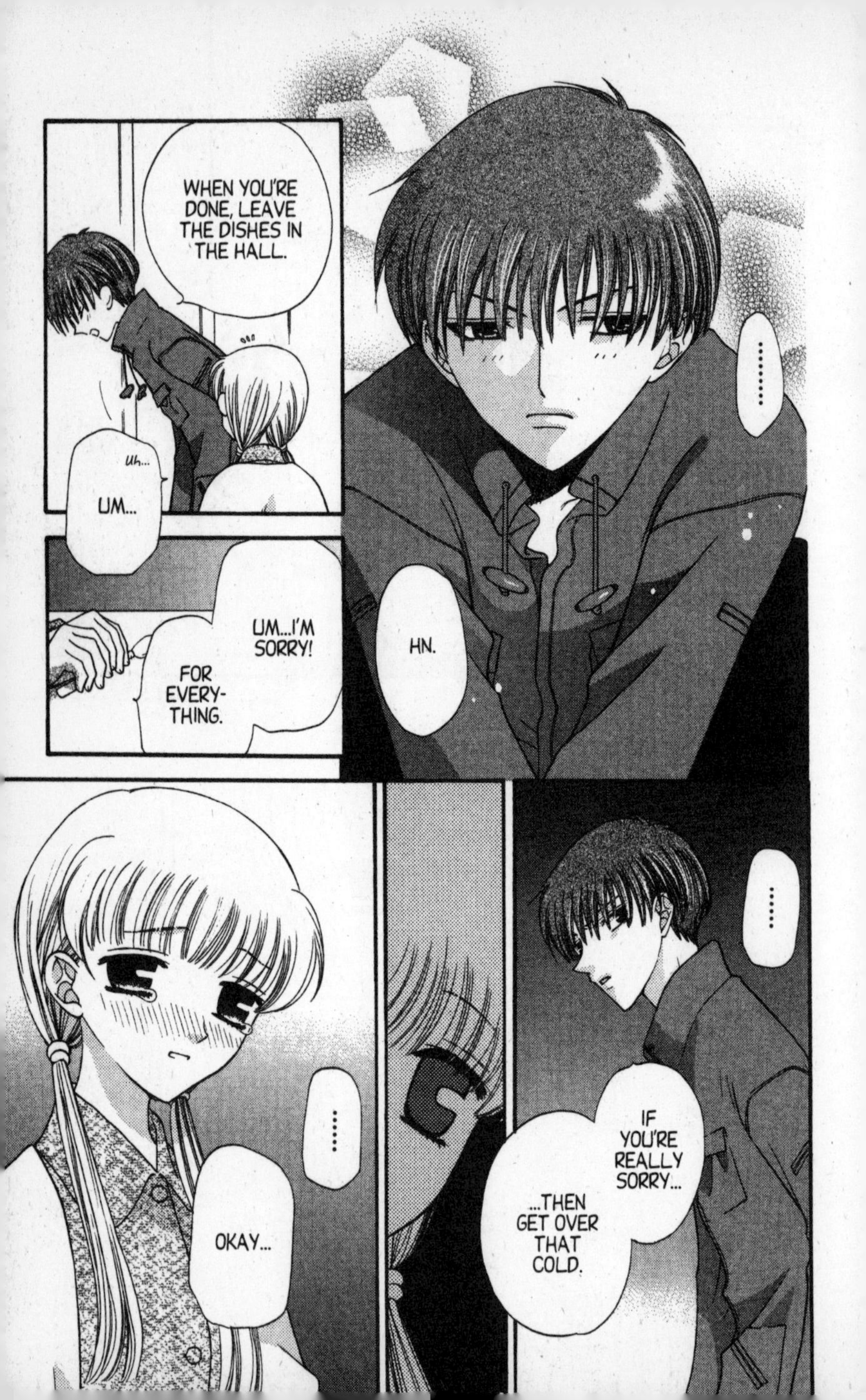
......
HN.
WHEN YOU'RE DONE, LEAVE THE DISHES IN THE HALL.
uh...
UM...
UM...I'M SORRY!
FOR EVERY-THING.
......
IF YOU'RE REALLY SORRY...
...THEN GET OVER THAT COLD.
......
OKAY...

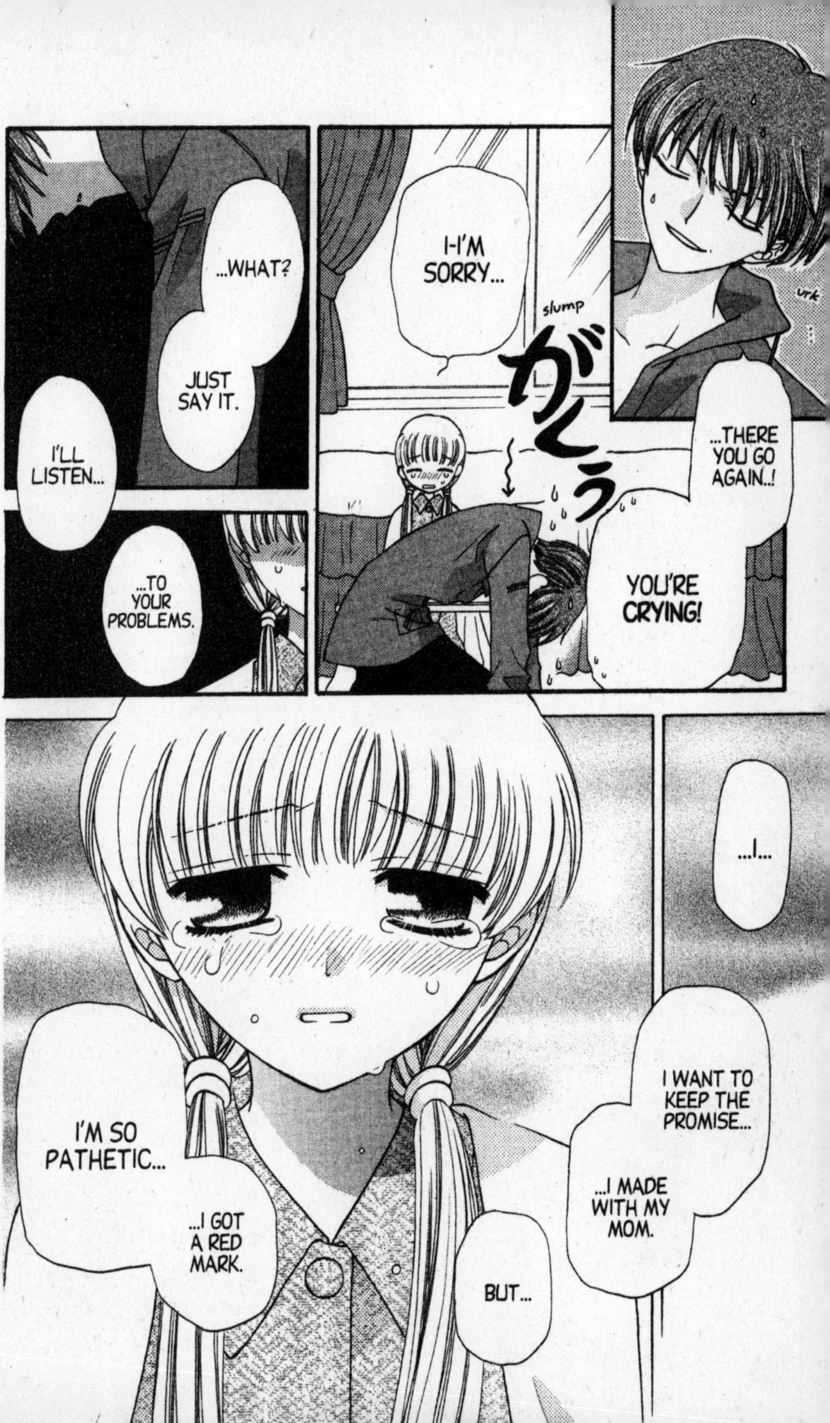

urk
I-I'M SORRY...
slump
がくぅ
...THERE YOU GO AGAIN..!
YOU'RE CRYING!
...WHAT?
JUST SAY IT.
I'LL LISTEN...
...TO YOUR PROBLEMS.
...I...
I WANT TO KEEP THE PROMISE...
...I MADE WITH MY MOM.
BUT...
I'M SO PATHETIC...
...I GOT A RED MARK.

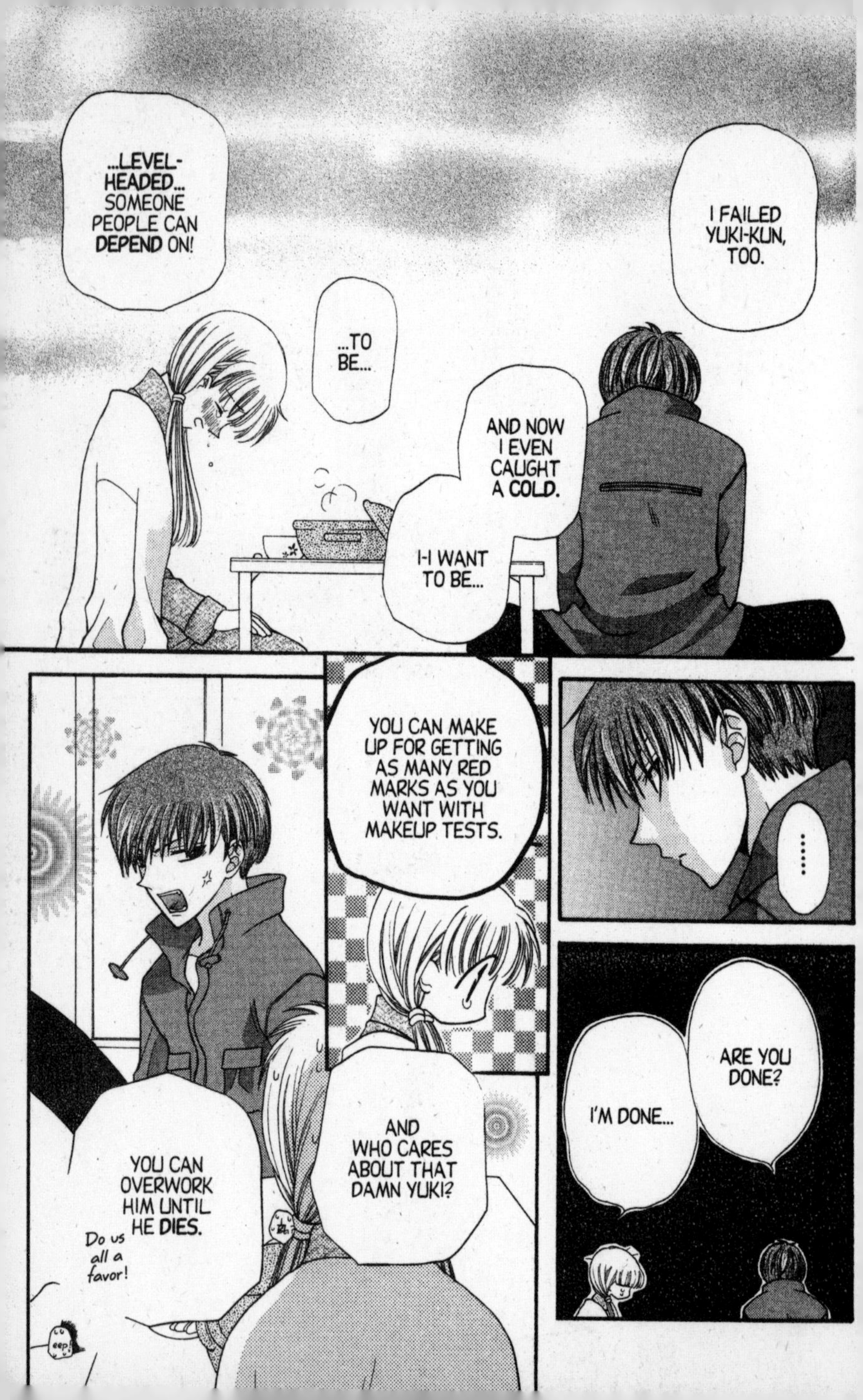
I FAILED YUKI-KUN, TOO.
AND NOW I EVEN CAUGHT A COLD.
I-I WANT TO BE...
...TO BE...
...LEVEL-HEADED... SOMEONE PEOPLE CAN DEPEND ON!
......
ARE YOU DONE?
I'M DONE...
YOU CAN MAKE UP FOR GETTING AS MANY RED MARKS AS YOU WANT WITH MAKEUP TESTS.
AND WHO CARES ABOUT THAT DAMN YUKI?
YOU CAN OVERWORK HIM UNTIL HE DIES.
Do us all a favor!
eep

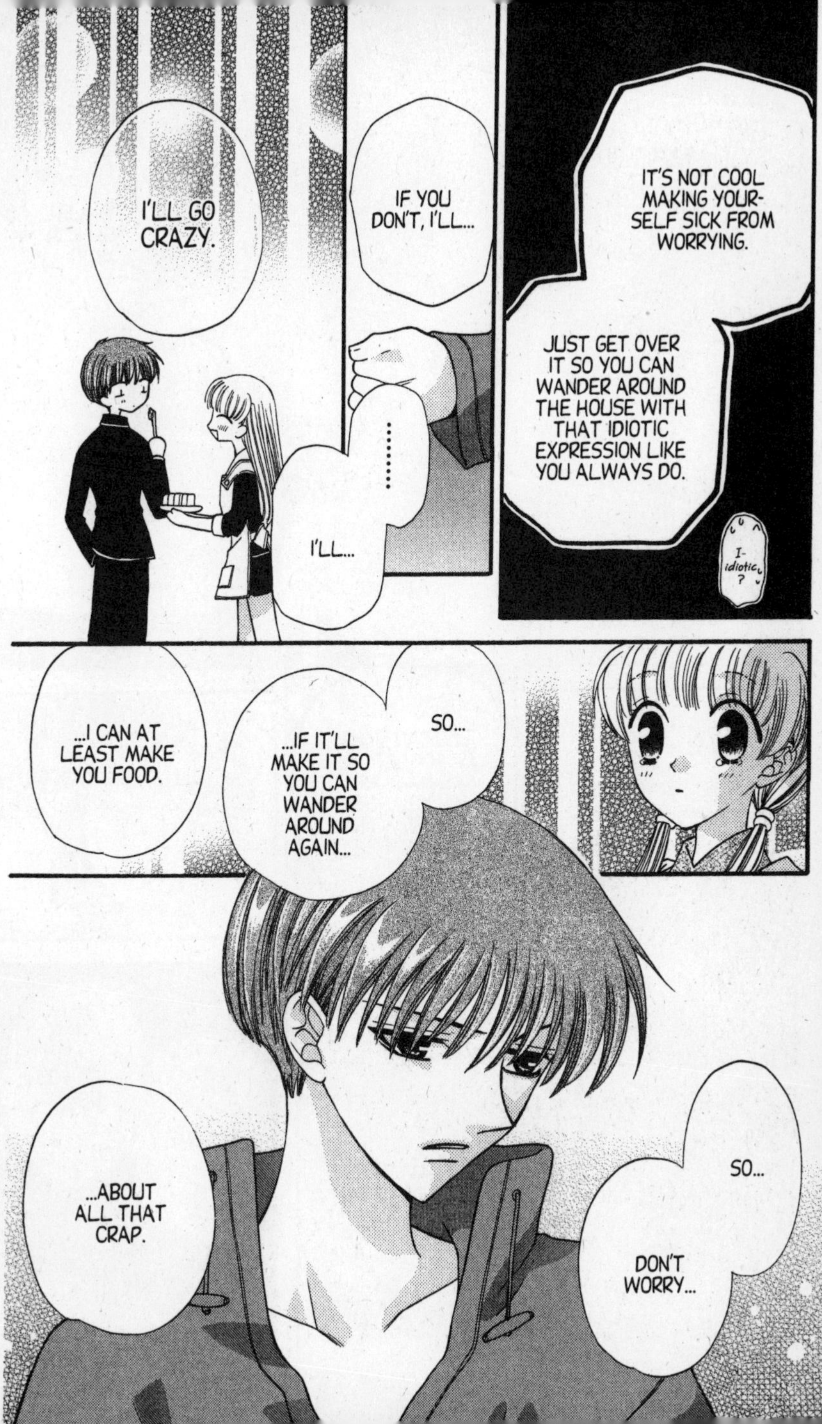
IT'S NOT COOL MAKING YOURSELF SICK FROM WORRYING.
JUST GET OVER IT SO YOU CAN WANDER AROUND THE HOUSE WITH THAT IDIOTIC EXPRESSION LIKE YOU ALWAYS DO.
I-idiotic?
IF YOU DON'T, I'LL...
......
I'LL...
I'LL GO CRAZY.
SO...
...IF IT'LL MAKE IT SO YOU CAN WANDER AROUND AGAIN...
...I CAN AT LEAST MAKE YOU FOOD.
SO...
DON'T WORRY...
...ABOUT ALL THAT CRAP.

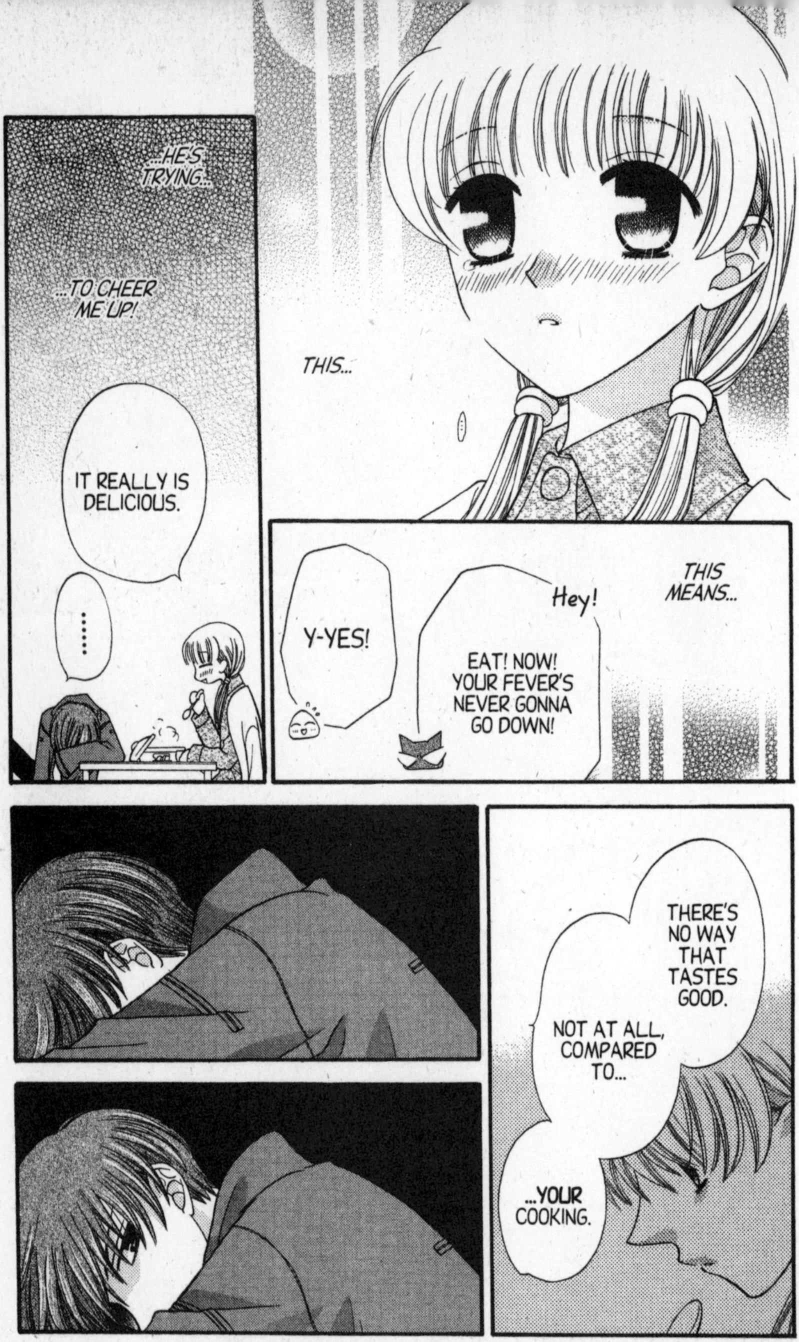
THIS...
THIS MEANS...
Hey!
EAT! NOW! YOUR FEVER'S NEVER GONNA GO DOWN!
Y-YES!
...HE'S TRYING...
...TO CHEER ME UP!
IT REALLY IS DELICIOUS.
......
THERE'S NO WAY THAT TASTES GOOD.
NOT AT ALL, COMPARED TO...
...YOUR COOKING.

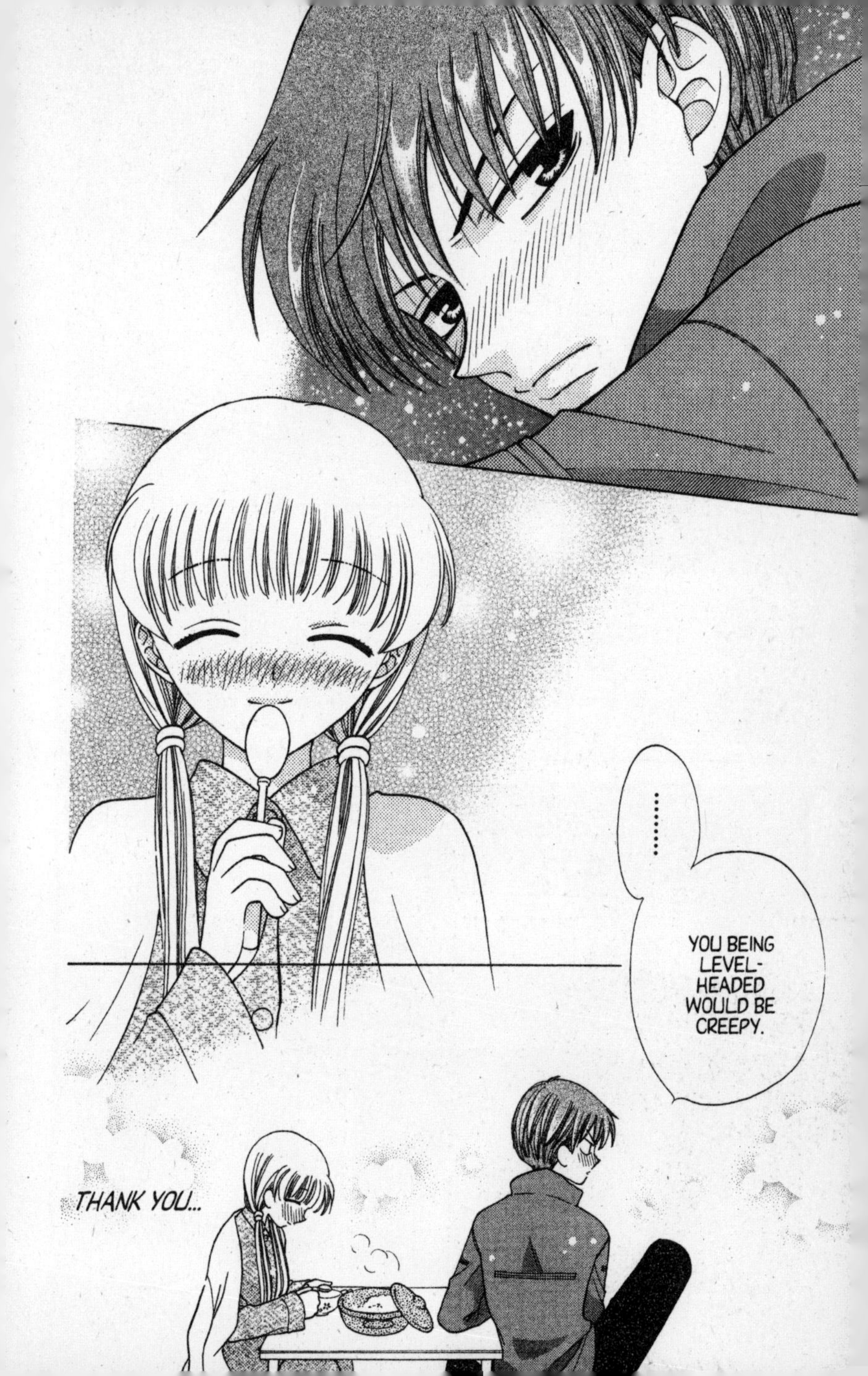
......
YOU BEING LEVEL-HEADED WOULD BE CREEPY.
THANK YOU...

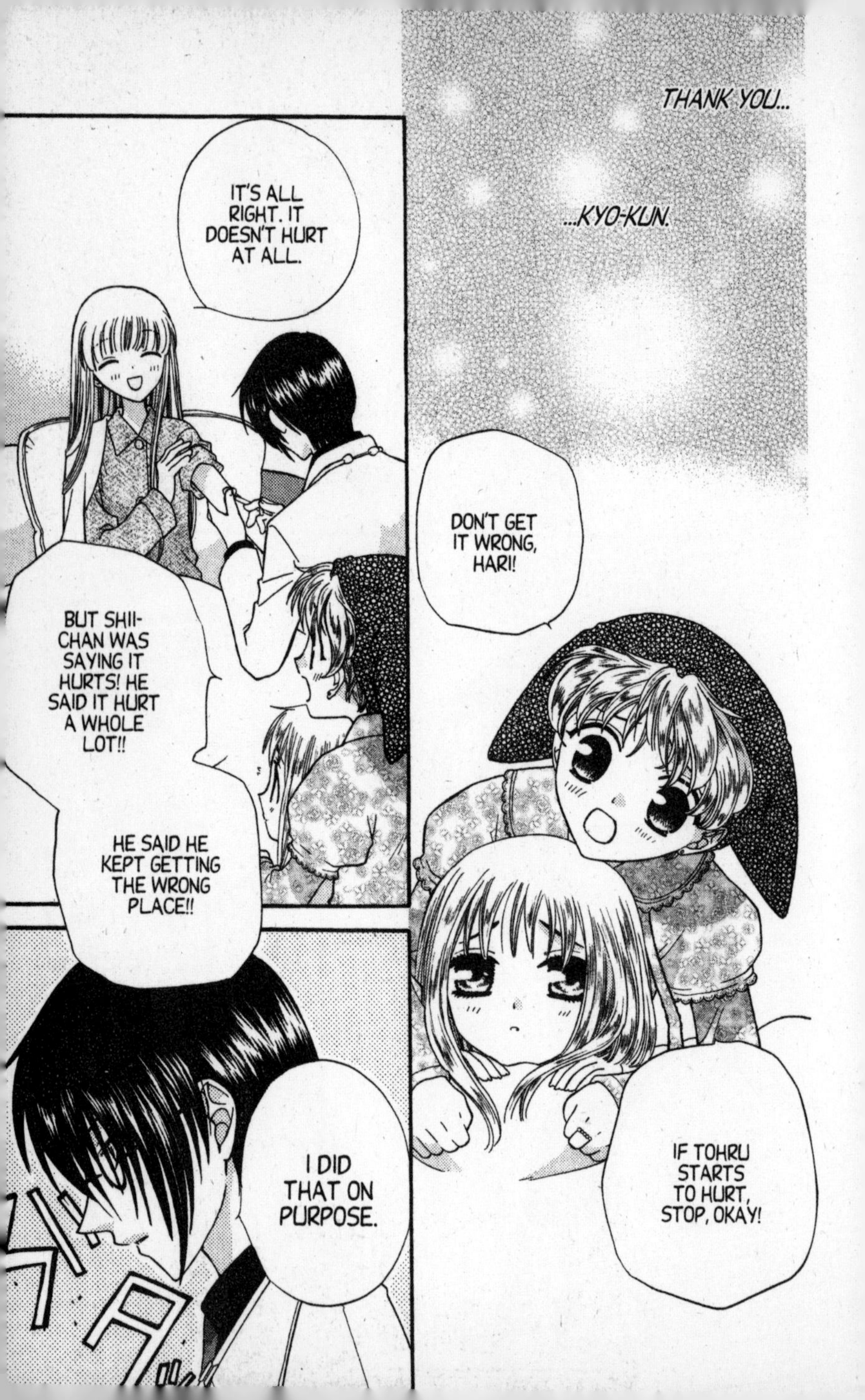
THANK YOU...
...KYO-KUN.
DON'T GET IT WRONG, HARI!
IF TOHRU STARTS TO HURT, STOP, OKAY!
IT'S ALL RIGHT. IT DOESN'T HURT AT ALL.
BUT SHII-CHAN WAS SAYING IT HURTS! HE SAID IT HURT A WHOLE LOT!!
HE SAID HE KEPT GETTING THE WRONG PLACE!!
I DID THAT ON PURPOSE.

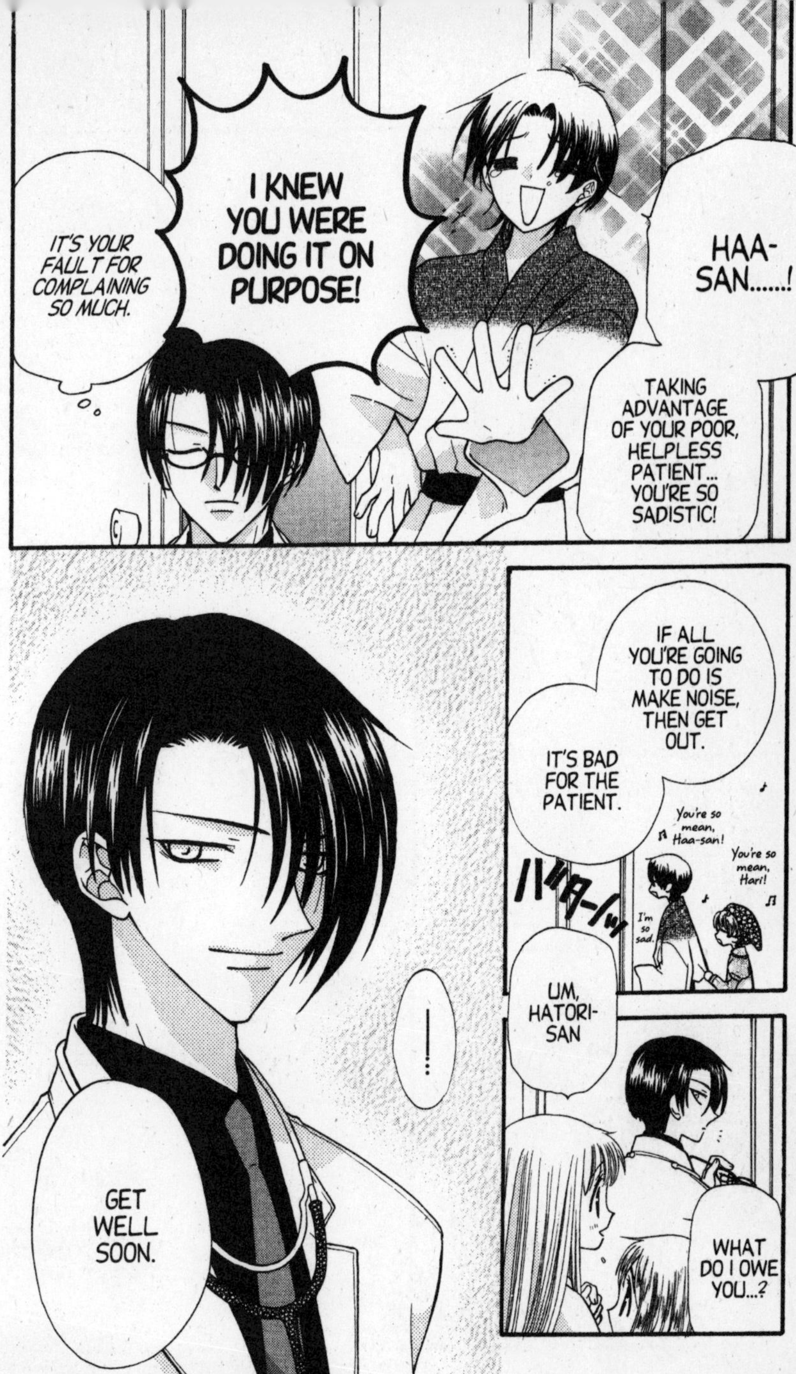
HAA-SAN......!
TAKING ADVANTAGE OF YOUR POOR, HELPLESS PATIENT... YOU'RE SO SADISTIC!
I KNEW YOU WERE DOING IT ON PURPOSE!
IT'S YOUR FAULT FOR COMPLAINING SO MUCH.
IF ALL YOU'RE GOING TO DO IS MAKE NOISE, THEN GET OUT.
IT'S BAD FOR THE PATIENT.
You're so mean, Hari!
You're so mean, Haa-san!
I'm so sad.
バターンッ
UM, HATORI-SAN
WHAT DO I OWE YOU...?
!...
GET WELL SOON.

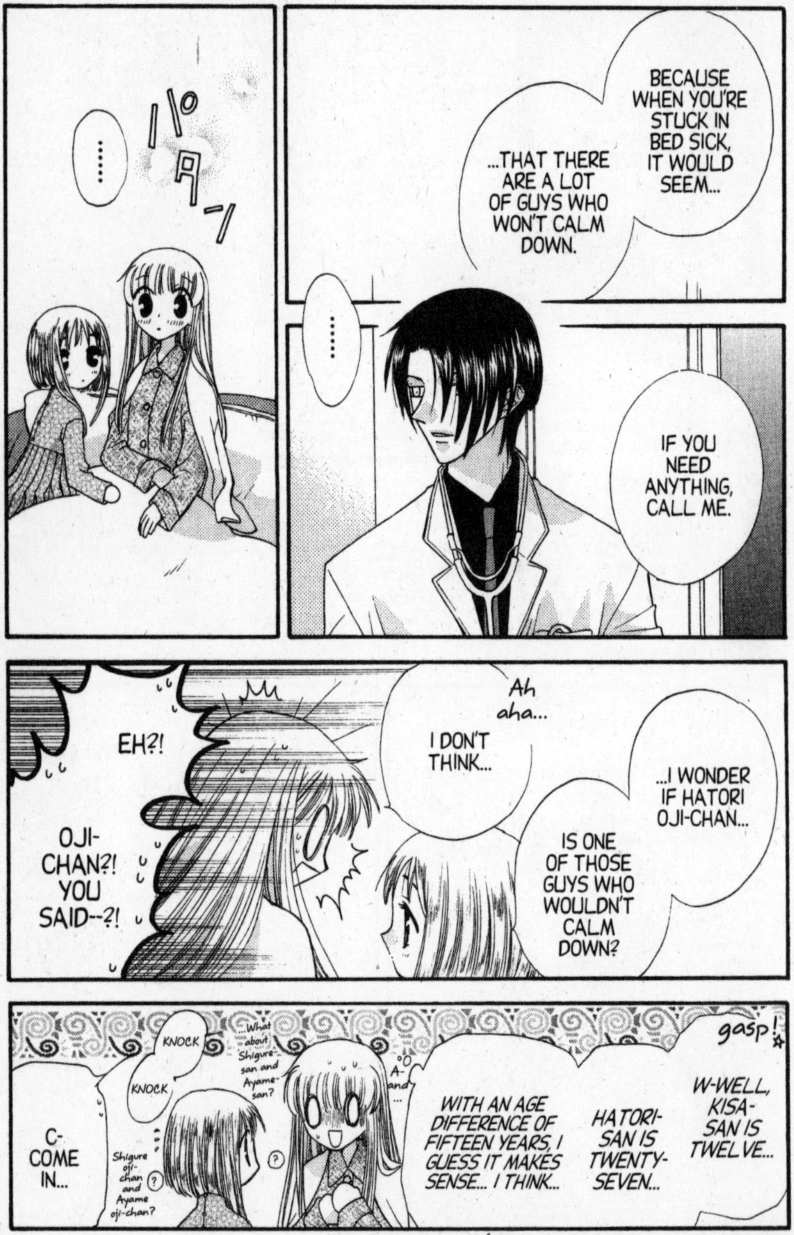
BECAUSE WHEN YOU'RE STUCK IN BED SICK, IT WOULD SEEM...
...THAT THERE ARE A LOT OF GUYS WHO WON'T CALM DOWN.
IF YOU NEED ANYTHING, CALL ME.
......
......
パターン
...I WONDER IF HATORI OJI-CHAN...
IS ONE OF THOSE GUYS WHO WOULDN'T CALM DOWN?
Ah aha...
I DON'T THINK...
EH?!
OJI-CHAN?! YOU SAID--?!
gasp!
W-WELL, KISA-SAN IS TWELVE...
HATORI-SAN IS TWENTY-SEVEN...
WITH AN AGE DIFFERENCE OF FIFTEEN YEARS, I GUESS IT MAKES SENSE... I THINK...
A-and...
...What about Shigure-san and Ayame-san?
KNOCK
KNOCK
Shigure oji-chan and Ayame oji-chan?
C-COME IN...

*oji= uncle. Usually reserved for middle-aged men and not someone in their twenties.

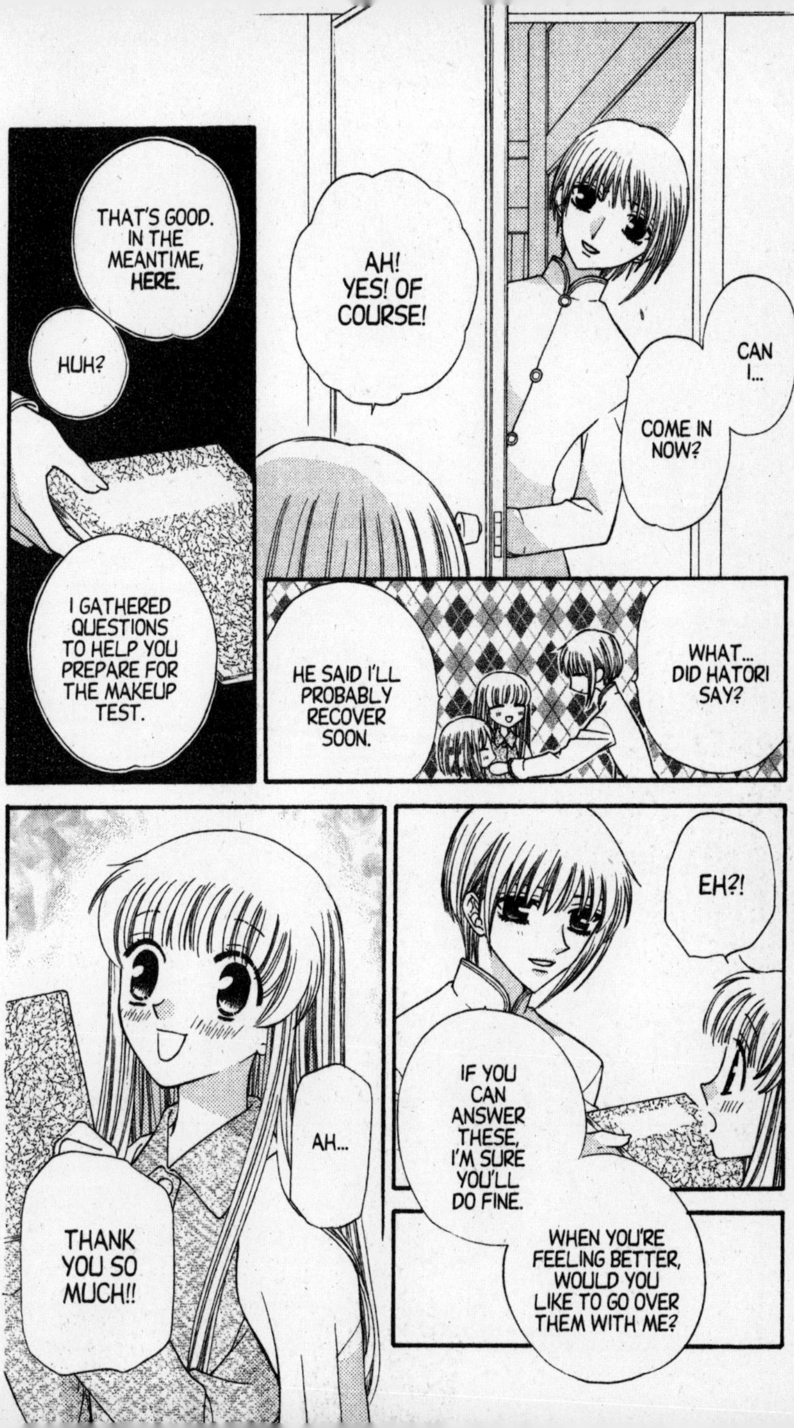
CAN I... COME IN NOW?
AH! YES! OF COURSE!
WHAT... DID HATORI SAY?
HE SAID I'LL PROBABLY RECOVER SOON.
THAT'S GOOD. IN THE MEANTIME, HERE.
HUH?
I GATHERED QUESTIONS TO HELP YOU PREPARE FOR THE MAKEUP TEST.
EH?!
IF YOU CAN ANSWER THESE, I'M SURE YOU'LL DO FINE.
WHEN YOU'RE FEELING BETTER, WOULD YOU LIKE TO GO OVER THEM WITH ME?
AH...
THANK YOU SO MUCH!!

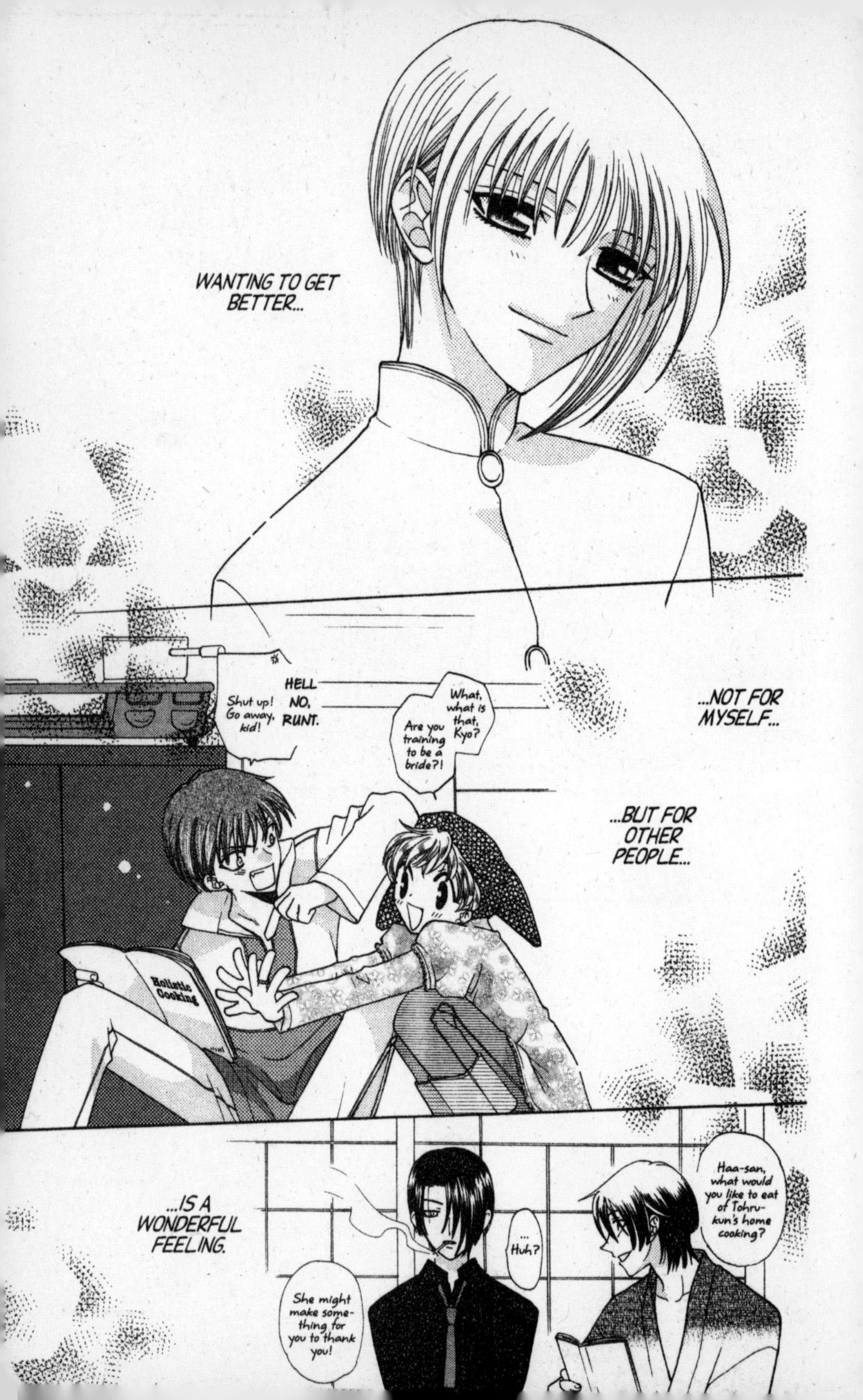
WANTING TO GET BETTER...
...NOT FOR MYSELF...
...BUT FOR OTHER PEOPLE...
What, what is that, Kyo?
Are you training to be a bride?!
HELL NO, RUNT.
Shut up! Go away, kid!
Holistic Cooking
Haa-san, what would you like to eat of Tohru-kun's home cooking?
She might make something for you to thank you!
... Huh?
...IS A WONDERFUL FEELING.

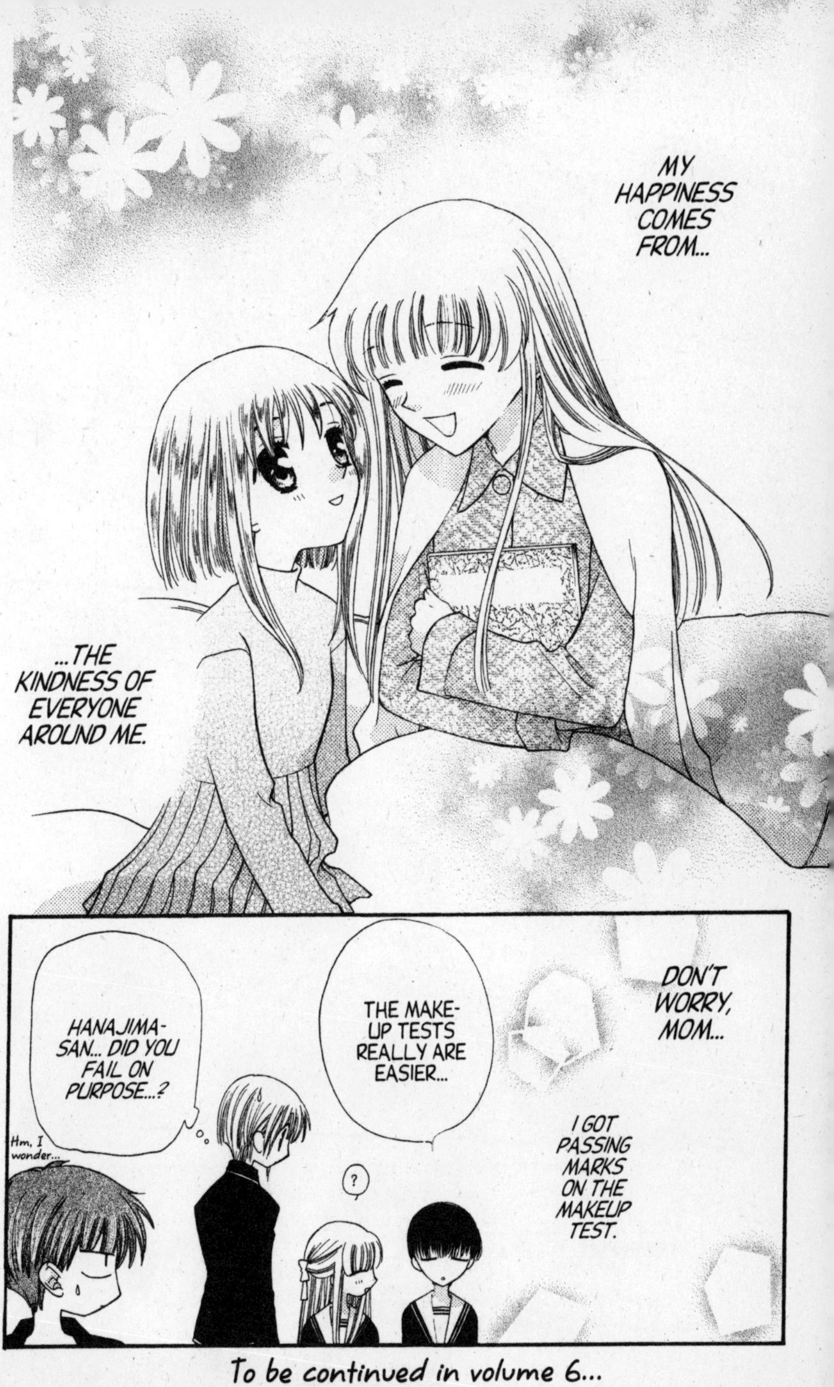
MY HAPPINESS COMES FROM...
...THE KINDNESS OF EVERYONE AROUND ME.
DON'T WORRY, MOM...
I GOT PASSING MARKS ON THE MAKEUP TEST.
THE MAKE-UP TESTS REALLY ARE EASIER...
HANAJIMA-SAN... DID YOU FAIL ON PURPOSE...?
?
Hm, I wonder...

To be continued in volume 6...

# Next time in...

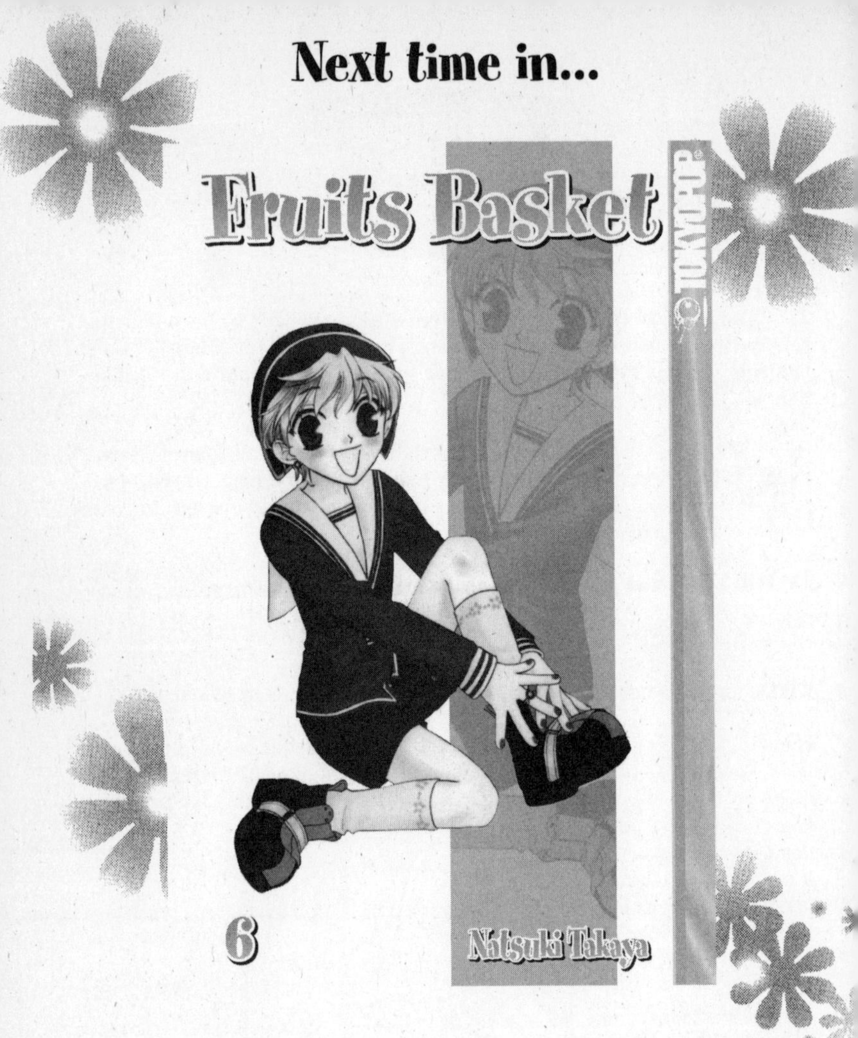
Fruits Basket
TOKYOPOP
6
Natsuki Takaya

## Secrets & Lies...

It's been raining for days on end and Tohru can't help worrying about Kyo's crankiness. On a particularly soggy day at the Sohma household, out of the rain steps Kyo's master! It is time for the Cat to learn the truth!! The drama is almost too much to bear in the 6th volume of the ever-popular Fruits Basket.

**Fruits Basket Volume 6**
**Available December 2004**

## Interview with Takaya-sensei
### Part 3

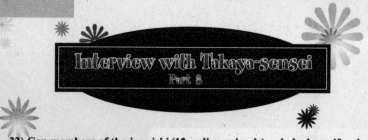

**22) Can members of the *juunishi* (12 zodiac animals) only be born if a close relative (parent/sibling/step-parent, etc…) is also one of the juunishi? Can "outside" Sohma members give birth to juunishi children, or only "inside" Sohmas?**

Being directly related to another juunishi and being "inside" or "outside" aren't factors in when a new juunishi is born. It's all a matter of timing. Basically, it's random. Right now all of the juunishi members are pretty close in age, but in the history of the Sohma family, this is unusual.

**23) Will Yuki's and Ayame's parents be making an appearance?**

At this time, they are scheduled to show up.

**24) Do any of the characters in *Fruits Basket* participate in school clubs?**

Hmm… Now that I think about it, I guess there isn't anyone who does club activities... I guess none of them have enough of an interest in such activities to get involved. Some of them do take extracurricular lessons, though. Like Kyo. Momiji takes lessons, too... But don't ask me to draw it! It's hard enough for me to tell the stories I'm already telling without getting into **that!**

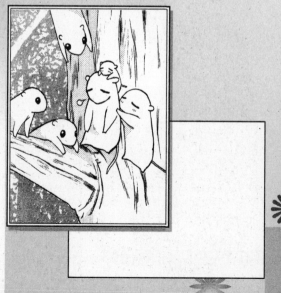

**25) It's been established that Kyo-kun hates onions, leeks and miso, but why these three things?**

He doesn't like the taste of onions. He hates the smell of leeks. And like many kids, he dislikes miso and other stinky bean curd products.

**26) Do Yuki-kun and other characters have likes and dislikes?**

Oh, they have their personal preferences, all right. I've been thinking how it'd be nice to write about such things. (But this is still pending...)

**27) How are the sales of Shigure's novels? Is he considered a fairly popular writer?**

At the moment, the books he wrote under the name "Karitani Noa" (Like *Summer-Colored Sigh*) seems to be the most popular. Incidentally, that's not the only pen name Shigure uses. Shigure will do whatever he can to not lose to Ayame. Seems like he's fairly popular.

### FRUITS BASKET– Original Drama CD

**28) The "Fruits Basket" CD has an original story, but why did you feature a crazy subject like nagashi soumen? (Note–see the omake comic in vol. 4!)**

Well, it's pretty much because I was thinking to myself how I'd never actually had any nagashi soumen. I certainly made things difficult for myself by making a story about that, huh?

**29) Did you also write the short, comedy story that's included in the interval of the main story?**

Yup. It was because I was practically itching to make the CD more fun and laughable. I feel that things that are fun make people happy.

**30) In that short story, what on earth was the thing that Kagura made?**

Obviously a cat backpack! She has such marvelous workmanship that she's a celebrity in her neighborhood... possibly. (laugh)

**31) Any last messages for your fans?**

Thank you so very much for reading! As the Fruits Basket characters keep grabbing for each other, laughing and crying, let's keep walking down the road of life. Please keep watching over me.

These three panels are early drafts for Takaya-sensei's previous work, *Tubasa O Motsu Mono (Those With Wings)*. You can see how much the designs influenced her newest work, the ever-popular *Fruits Basket*!

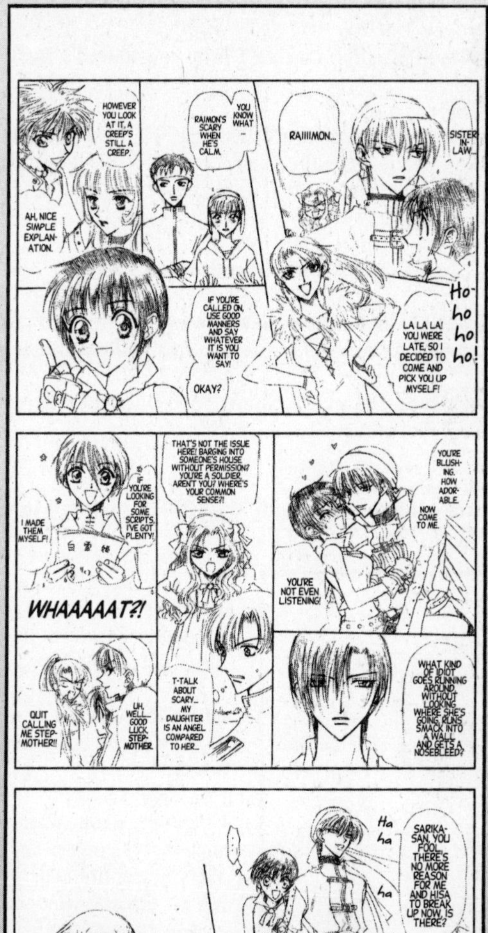
SISTER-IN-LAW...
RAIIIIMON...
Ho-ho ho ho!
LA LA LA! YOU WERE LATE, SO I DECIDED TO COME AND PICK YOU UP MYSELF!
YOU KNOW WHAT—
RAIMON'S SCARY WHEN HE'S CALM.
HOWEVER YOU LOOK AT IT, A CREEP'S STILL A CREEP.
AH, NICE SIMPLE EXPLANATION.
IF YOU'RE CALLED ON, USE GOOD MANNERS AND SAY WHATEVER IT IS YOU WANT TO SAY!
OKAY?
YOU'RE BLUSHING. HOW ADORABLE.
NOW COME TO ME.
YOU'RE NOT EVEN LISTENING!
WHAT KIND OF IDIOT GOES RUNNING AROUND WITHOUT LOOKING WHERE SHE'S GOING, RUNS SMACK INTO A WALL, AND GETS A NOSEBLEED?
THAT'S NOT THE ISSUE HERE! BARGING INTO SOMEONE'S HOUSE WITHOUT PERMISSION? YOU'RE A SOLDIER, AREN'T YOU? WHERE'S YOUR COMMON SENSE?!
T-TALK ABOUT SCARY... MY DAUGHTER IS AN ANGEL COMPARED TO HER...
IF YOU'RE LOOKING FOR SOME SCRIPTS, I'VE GOT PLENTY!
I MADE THEM MYSELF!
WHAAAAAT?!
UH, WELL... GOOD LUCK, STEP-MOTHER
QUIT CALLING ME STEP-MOTHER!!
Ha ha ha ha
SARIKA-SAN, YOU FOOL. THERE'S NO MORE REASON FOR ME AND HISA TO BREAK UP NOW, IS THERE?
ぎり ぎり
LIKE HELL I WILL.
OOOOKAY THEN. THAT'S WHAT I THOUGHT.

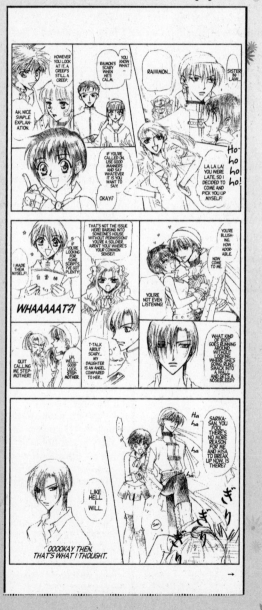

# Year of the Boar: Going Whole Hog

## Boar

**Years*:** 1947, 1959, 1971, 1983, 1995, 2007, 2019, 2031, 2043
**Positive Qualities:** reliable, sincere, tolerant, caring, industrious, persistent, brave
**Negative Qualities:** shy, one-track mind, short tempered, headstrong
**Suitable Jobs:** teacher, nurse, researcher
**Compatible With:** Rabbits, Sheep, Tiger (and Cats!)
**Must Avoid:** Snake, Monkey, other Boars
**Ruling Hours:** 9 PM to 11 PM
**Season:** Fall
**Ruling Month:** November
**Sign Direction:** North-Northwest
**Fixed Element:** Water
**Corresponding Western Sign:** Scorpio

The Boar is the last of the twelve great animals of the Zodiac. While it can generally be assumed that the Boar was off feeding its face for most of the great race, one lesser-known version of the fable centers on the animals being asked to tell why they deserved to reside at the top of the Zodiac. While the Bull said it helped the farmer plow the fields and the Snake talked about how smart it was, all the boar could come up with was that the meat on its bones tasted good to eat. Sure this might not sound like a very positive thing to say, but at least the Boar was being honest.

Boars are born with an inner strength that few others can match. Offsetting the Boar's bravery is their horribly short temper that makes it all to easy for a Boar to fly into a rage at the slightest provocation. Luckily, Boars generally dislike having arguments and seldom harbor any long-term grudges against anyone that has the unfortunate luck of crossing them. For anyone lucky enough to befriend a Boar though, they are often greatly rewarded as Boars are extremely loyal and prefer to have a smaller, more close knit group of friends that are with them a lifetime.

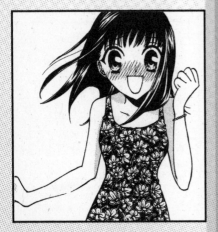

Another interesting point to bring up about Boars is that women born in this year tend to be neat freaks--especially where their home is concerned. You would be hard pressed to find a speck of dirt or dust anywhere in sight. Male Boars on the other hand will never be able to shake the troublesome stigma that all they would rather do is wallow in the mud all day.

Even so, Boars of both sexes have a genuine thirst for knowledge and are typically well-informed individuals. They are hard working and have almost too much energy at times. Boars are often taken advantage of because they can never say "no" when asked for help. Sadly, this tends to lead them into money problems at some point or another in their life. And while Boars do manage to find a way to crawl out of their rut, they can never quite seem to keep themselves out of it due to their inability to see the sky for the trees.

**Celebrity Boars:**
Christina Applegate
Tom Arnold
David Boreanaz
Val Kilmer
Stephen King
Winona Ryder
Miss Piggy

* Note: If you were born in January or early February, then chances are you are probably the animal of the preceding year. The only way to know for certain is to know on which day Chinese New Year's was held. Example: 1983 actually starts on February 13, so anyone born between January 1 and February 12 is still a Dog.

# Fans Basket

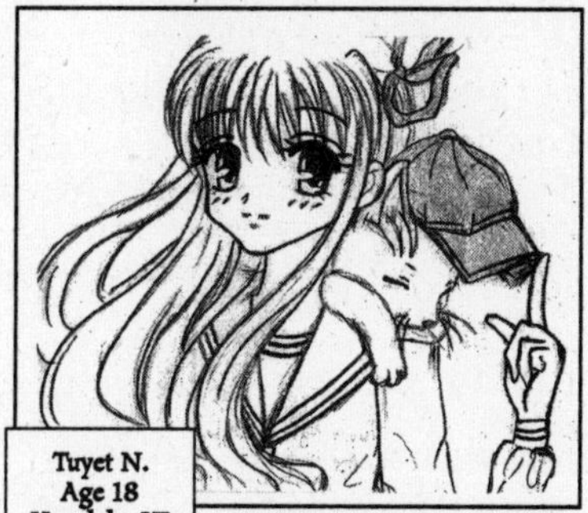

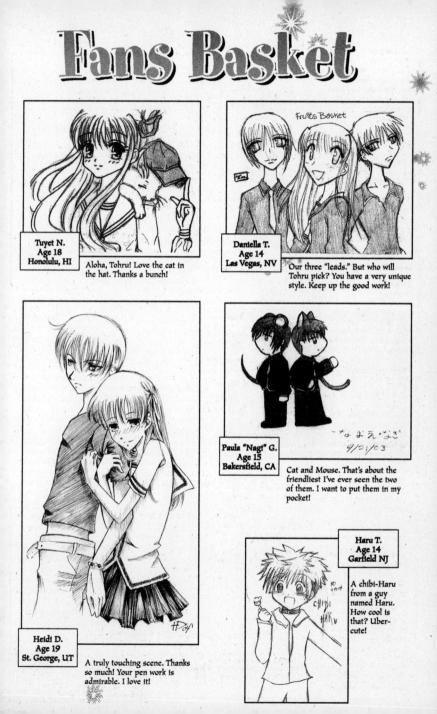

Tuyet N.
Age 18
Honolulu, HI

Aloha, Tohru! Love the cat in the hat. Thanks a bunch!

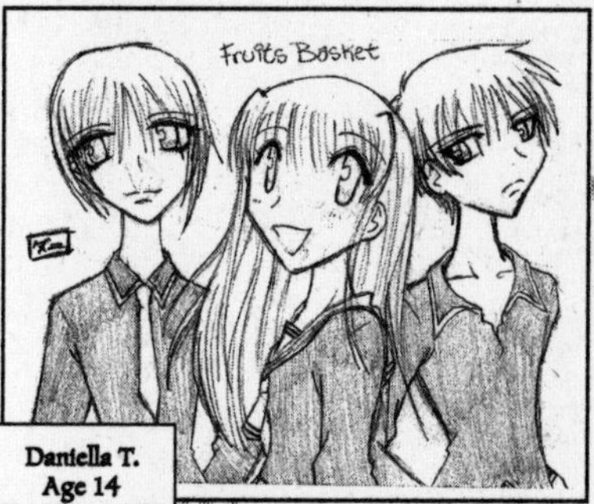
Fruits Basket

Daniella T.
Age 14
Las Vegas, NV

Our three "leads." But who will Tohru pick? You have a very unique style. Keep up the good work!

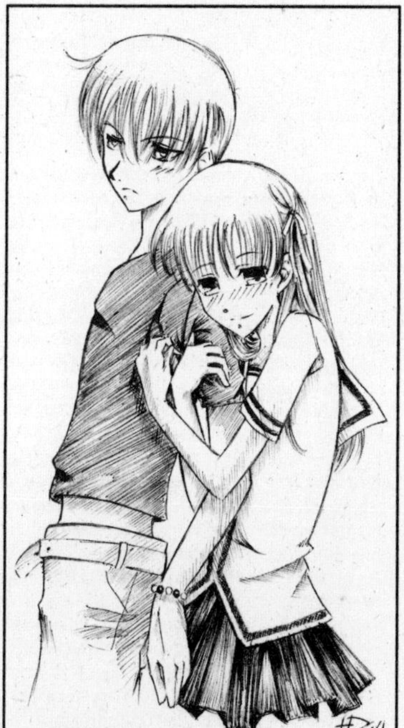

Heidi D.
Age 19
St. George, UT

A truly touching scene. Thanks so much! Your pen work is admirable. I love it!

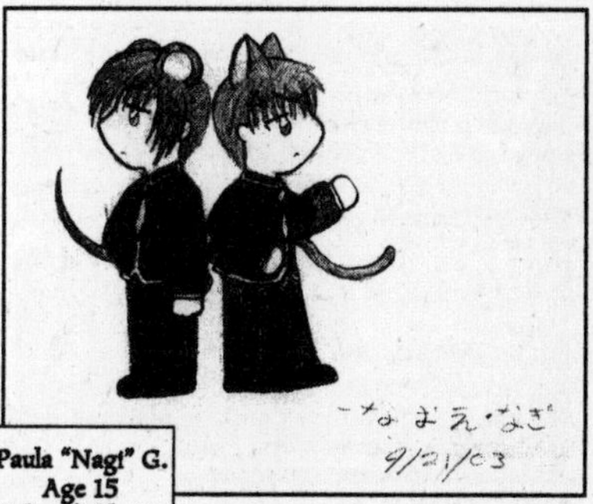
ーなおえ・なぎ
9/21/03

Paula "Nagi" G.
Age 15
Bakersfield, CA

Cat and Mouse. That's about the friendliest I've ever seen the two of them. I want to put them in my pocket!

Haru T.
Age 14
Garfield NJ

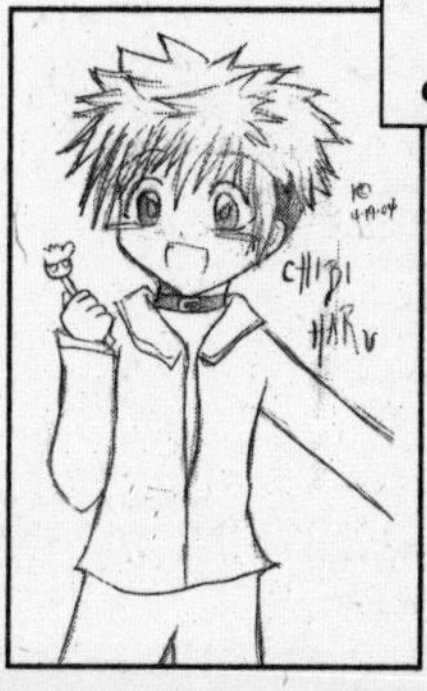
CHIBI
HARU

A chibi-Haru from a guy named Haru. How cool is that? Uber-cute!

Do you want to share your love for *Fruits Basket* with fans around the world? "Fans Basket" is taking submissions of fan art, poetry, cosplay photos, or any other Furuba fun you'd like to share!

How to submit:

1) Send your work via regular mail (NOT e-mail) to:

"Fans Basket"
c/o TOKYOPOP
5900 Wilshire Blvd.
Suite 2000
Los Angeles, CA 90036

2) All work should be in black-and-white and no larger than 8.5" x 11". (And try not to fold it too many times!)

3) Anything you send will not be returned. If you want to keep your original, it's fine to send us a copy.

4) Please include your full name, age, city and state for us to print with your work. If you'd rather us use a pen name, please include that, too.

5) IMPORTANT: If you're under the age of 18, you must have your parent's permission in order for us to print your work. Any submissions without a signed note of parental consent cannot be used.

6) For full details, please check out our website: http://www.tokyopop.com/aboutus/fanart.php

Disclaimer: Anything you send to us becomes the exclusive property of TOKYOPOP Inc. and, as we said before, will not be returned to you. We will have the right to print, reproduce, distribute, or modify the artwork for use in future volumes of Fruits Basket or on the web royalty-free.

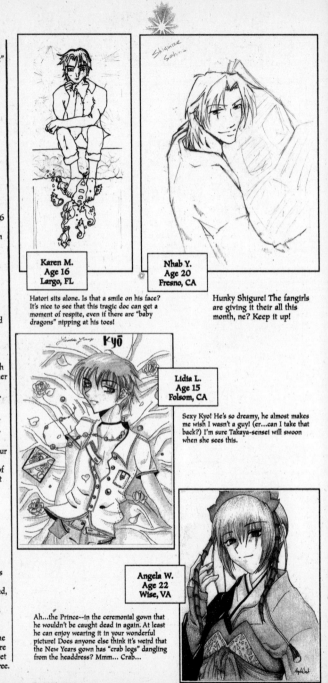

**Karen M.**
**Age 16**
**Largo, FL**

Hatori sits alone. Is that a smile on his face? It's nice to see that this tragic doc can get a moment of respite, even if there are "baby dragons" nipping at his toes!

**Nhab Y.**
**Age 20**
**Fresno, CA**

Hunky Shigure! The fangirls are giving it their all this month, ne? Keep it up!

**Lidia L.**
**Age 15**
**Folsom, CA**

Sexy Kyo! He's so dreamy, he almost makes me wish I wasn't a guy! (er...can I take that back?) I'm sure Takaya-sensei will swoon when she sees this.

**Angela W.**
**Age 22**
**Wise, VA**

Ah...the Prince--in the ceremonial gown that he wouldn't be caught dead in again. At least he can enjoy wearing it in your wonderful picture! Does anyone else think it's weird that the New Years gown has "crab legs" dangling from the headdress? Mmm... Crab...

# Special Intern Alley!

**Manga-ka have their assistants-- manga editors have the help of interns. These hard-working students volunteer their summer to see what it takes to make manga, helping out with everything from proofreading, to translating bonus content like the interview in this book, to sorting the fan mail you send. Some of our interns even go on to get jobs here making manga! So as summer comes to a close and everyone heads back to school, thank you interns, for all your hard work!**

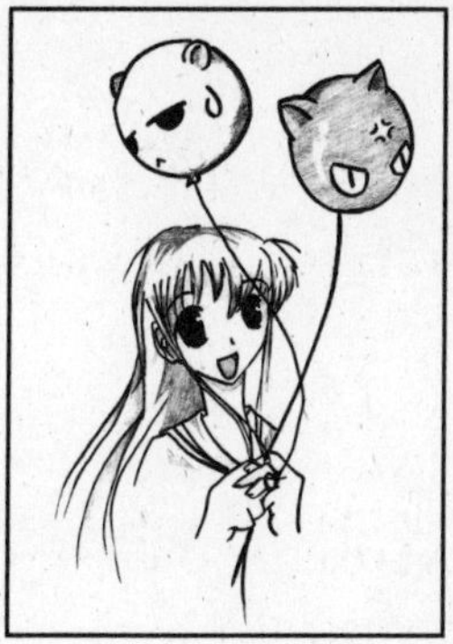

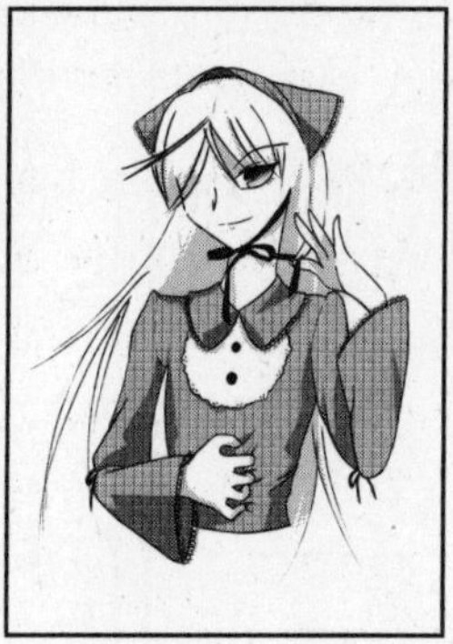

**The Schilling Sisters! Kathy and Chrissy: the wonder twins. These girls are great. Not only do they draw super-cute fan art, but they also do cosplay and translations! They also submitted the very first fan art for Furuba vol. 2. Thanks a lot, you two! Can you believe that TOKYOPOP has actually had four sets of identical twin interns? FOUR!! And all of them cosplay. What are the odds?**

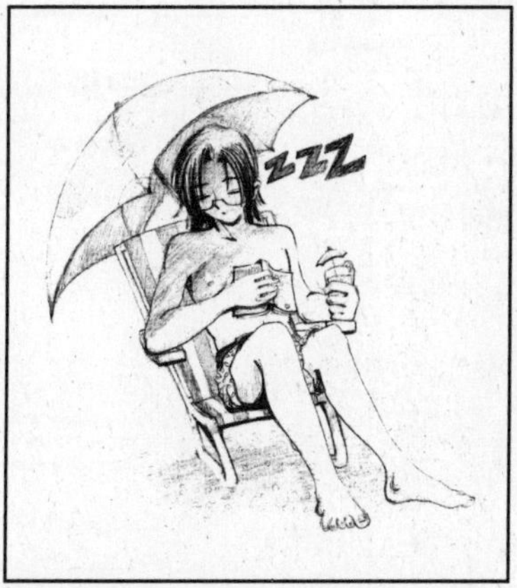

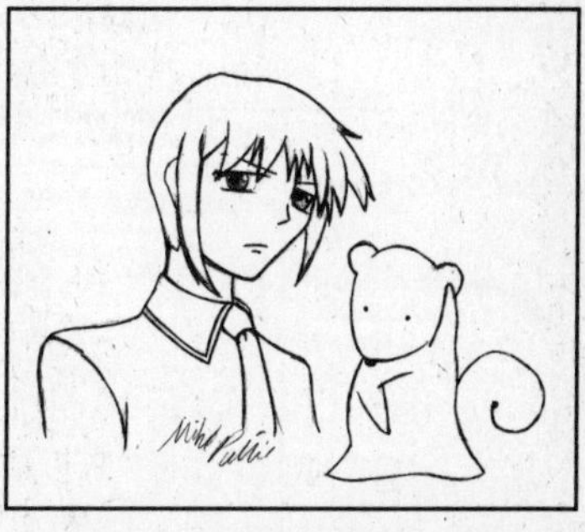

**Mike Paolilli has been helping out our art department. With all the covers TOKYOPOP has to design, his filing and sorting services has been invaluable. Hey, filing's fun, right? I'm sure you'll see his design work in the future. And thanks for the Yuki pics!**

**Hope Donnovan's a double major in Art and English, so working in manga's the perfect fit. Isn't her snoozing Shigure just the greatest? Today's her last day...we'll really miss you! On her first week here I took her to a Japanese restaurant and ordered bite-sized whole fish–Hope wasn't afraid to eat the whole things, eyeballs and all! We've lost all Hope... but someday, Hope will come again! Sorry...You're sick of bad puns on your name aren't you?**

**Michelle Nguyen is an anime character brought to life. Her fashions and hair color must be seen to be believed–she's so cute! At this year's Anime Expo, her Princess Ai cosplay was the hit of the TOKYOPOP booth. Michelle personally hand-delivers your Fans Basket mail to my cluttered desk on a daily basis, and she helps sort the fan art to make sure we get a good mix. She was a little embarrassed about submitting Furuba fan art, but it was definitely worth it, ne? Thanks so much for your help!**

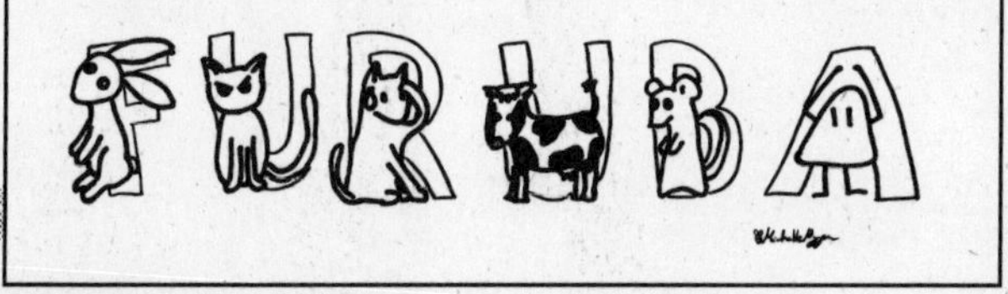
FURUBA

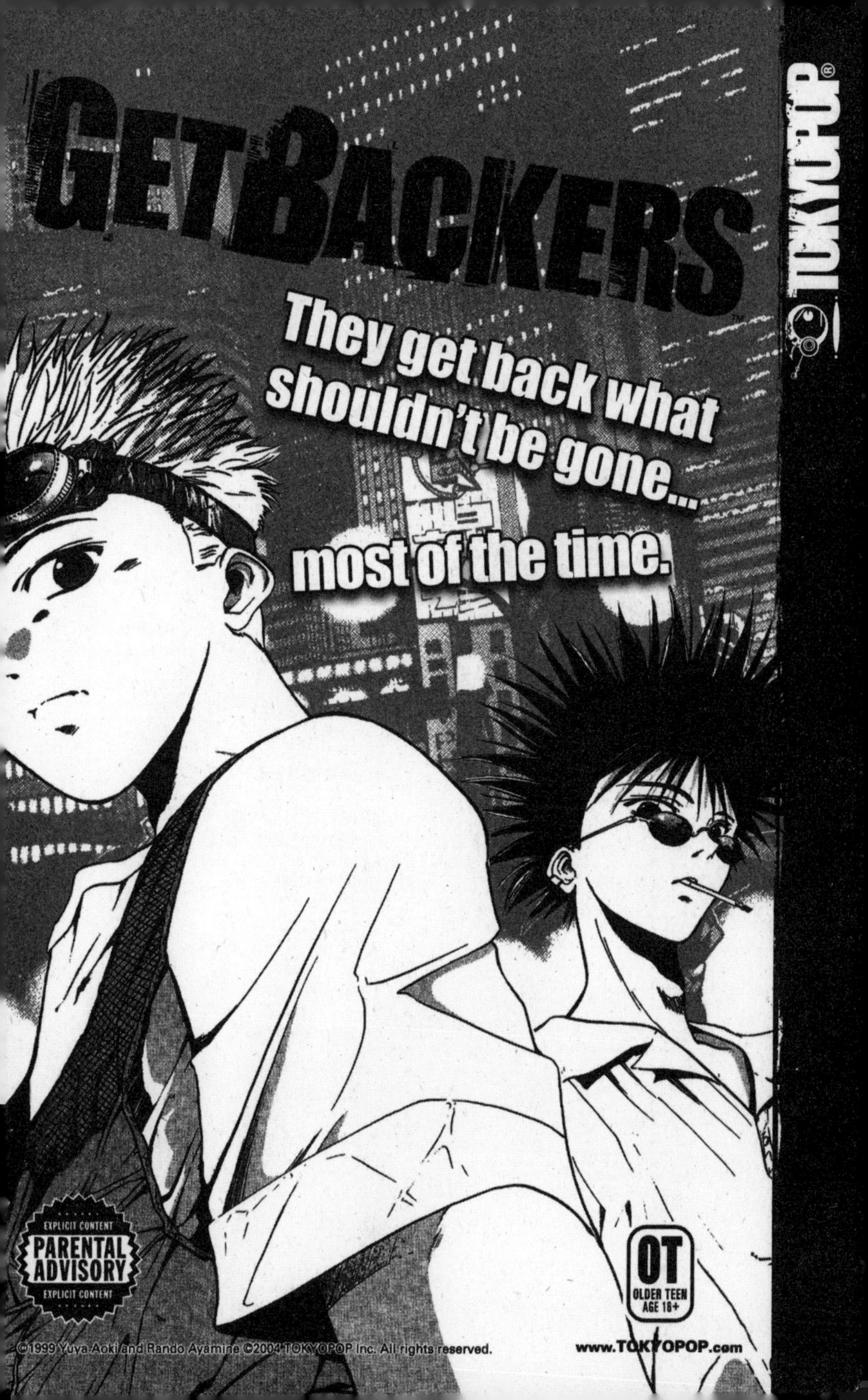
GETBACKERS™
They get back what shouldn't be gone...
most of the time.
TOKYOPOP®
EXPLICIT CONTENT
PARENTAL ADVISORY
EXPLICIT CONTENT
OT
OLDER TEEN AGE 16+
©1999 Yuya Aoki and Rando Ayamine ©2004 TOKYOPOP Inc. All rights reserved.
www.TOKYOPOP.com

# ALSO AVAILABLE FROM TOKYOPOP®

## MANGA

.HACK//LEGEND OF THE TWILIGHT
@LARGE
ABENOBASHI: MAGICAL SHOPPING ARCADE
A.I. LOVE YOU
AI YORI AOSHI
ANGELIC LAYER
ARM OF KANNON
BABY BIRTH
BATTLE ROYALE
BATTLE VIXENS
BOYS BE...
BRAIN POWERED
BRIGADOON
B'TX
CANDIDATE FOR GODDESS, THE
CARDCAPTOR SAKURA
CARDCAPTOR SAKURA - MASTER OF THE CLOW
CHOBITS
CHRONICLES OF THE CURSED SWORD
CLAMP SCHOOL DETECTIVES
CLOVER
COMIC PARTY
CONFIDENTIAL CONFESSIONS
CORRECTOR YUI
COWBOY BEBOP
COWBOY BEBOP: SHOOTING STAR
CRAZY LOVE STORY
CRESCENT MOON
CROSS
CULDCEPT
CYBORG 009
D•N•ANGEL
DEMON DIARY
DEMON ORORON, THE
DEUS VITAE
DIABOLO
DIGIMON
DIGIMON TAMERS
DIGIMON ZERO TWO
DOLL
DRAGON HUNTER
DRAGON KNIGHTS
DRAGON VOICE
DREAM SAGA
DUKLYON: CLAMP SCHOOL DEFENDERS
EERIE QUEERIE!
ERICA SAKURAZAWA: COLLECTED WORKS
ET CETERA
ETERNITY
EVIL'S RETURN
FAERIES' LANDING
FAKE
FLCL
FLOWER OF THE DEEP SLEEP, THE
FORBIDDEN DANCE
FRUITS BASKET

G GUNDAM
GATEKEEPERS
GETBACKERS
GIRL GOT GAME
GRAVITATION
GTO
GUNDAM SEED ASTRAY
GUNDAM WING
GUNDAM WING: BATTLEFIELD OF PACIFISTS
GUNDAM WING: ENDLESS WALTZ
GUNDAM WING: THE LAST OUTPOST (G-UNIT)
HANDS OFF!
HAPPY MANIA
HARLEM BEAT
HYPER RUNE
I.N.V.U.
IMMORTAL RAIN
INITIAL D
INSTANT TEEN: JUST ADD NUTS
ISLAND
JING: KING OF BANDITS
JING: KING OF BANDITS - TWILIGHT TALES
JULINE
KARE KANO
KILL ME, KISS ME
KINDAICHI CASE FILES, THE
KING OF HELL
KODOCHA: SANA'S STAGE
LAMENT OF THE LAMB
LEGAL DRUG
LEGEND OF CHUN HYANG, THE
LES BIJOUX
LOVE HINA
LOVE OR MONEY
LUPIN III
LUPIN III: WORLD'S MOST WANTED
MAGIC KNIGHT RAYEARTH I
MAGIC KNIGHT RAYEARTH II
MAHOROMATIC: AUTOMATIC MAIDEN
MAN OF MANY FACES
MARMALADE BOY
MARS
MARS: HORSE WITH NO NAME
MINK
MIRACLE GIRLS
MIYUKI-CHAN IN WONDERLAND
MODEL
MOURYOU KIDEN: LEGEND OF THE NYMPHS
NECK AND NECK
ONE
ONE I LOVE, THE
PARADISE KISS
PARASYTE
PASSION FRUIT
PEACH GIRL
PEACH GIRL: CHANGE OF HEART
PET SHOP OF HORRORS
PITA-TEN

07.15.04T

W9-AJT-423

# STOP!

## This is the back of the book.
## You wouldn't want to spoil a great ending!

This book is printed "manga-style," in the authentic Japanese right-to-left format. Since none of the artwork has been flipped or altered, readers get to experience the story just as the creator intended. You've been asking for it, so TOKYOPOP® delivered: authentic, hot-off-the-press, and far more fun!

# DIRECTIONS

If this is your first time reading manga-style, here's a quick guide to help you understand how it works.

It's easy... just start in the top right panel and follow the numbers. Have fun, and look for more 100% authentic manga from TOKYOPOP®!

100% AUTHENTIC MANGA